RESEARCH METHODS
ARE YOU EQUIPPED?

RESEARCH METHODS
ARE YOU EQUIPPED?

Jennifer Bonds-Raacke

Fort Hays State University

John Raacke

Fort Hays State University

Prentice Hall

Boston   Columbus   Indianapolis   New York   San Francisco   Upper Saddle River
Amsterdam   Cape Town   Dubai   London   Madrid   Milan   Munich   Paris   Montreal   Toronto
Delhi   Mexico City   Sao Paulo   Sydney   Hong Kong   Seoul   Singapore   Taipei   Tokyo

Executive Acquisitions Editor: Susan Hartman
Editorial Assistant: Courtney Elezovic
Marketing Manager: Nicole Kunzmann
Marketing Assistant: Shauna Fishweicher
Associate Production Project Manager: Maggie Brobeck
Editorial Production and Composition Service: Integra Software Services Pvt. Ltd.
Manufacturing Buyer: Debbie Rossi
Cover Designer: Joel Gendron

Credits appear on page 327, which constitutes an extension of the copyright page.

Many of the designations by manufacturers and sellers to distinguish their products are claimed as trademarks. Where those designations appear in this book, and the publisher was aware of a trademark claim, the designations have been printed in initial caps or all caps.

Library of Congress Cataloging-in-Publication Data
Bonds-Raacke, Jennifer.
 Research methods : are you equipped?/Jennifer Bonds-Raacke, John Raacke.
  p. cm.
 Includes bibliographical references and index.
 ISBN-13: 978-0-13-502268-9 (alk. paper)
 ISBN-10: 0-13-502268-1 (alk. paper)
 1. Psychology—Research—Methodology. I. Raacke, John. II. Title.
BF76.5.B66 2012
150.72—dc22

                                                                    2010040109

10 9 8 7 6 5 4 3 2 1 15 14 13 12 11

Prentice Hall
is an imprint of

www.pearsonhighered.com

ISBN-10: 0-13-502268-1
ISBN-13: 978-0-13-502268-9

Dedication

Our work is dedicated to our daughters, Callie and Brooke, and to the memory of Eugene C. Bonds.

BRIEF CONTENTS

CONTENTS

PREFACE

We are all consumers—each one of us, every day. Consider your role as a consumer in today's world. When you start your day by taking a shower and eating breakfast before classes, you consume energy in the form of heated water and nutrients. When you listen to the radio in your car on the way to work, you consume fossil fuel and information in the form of news reports, talk radio debate, or music. And, when you decide which college to attend and pay your tuition bill, you consume an educational experience. As consumers, we make very personal choices about what, where, and how we experience most things in our daily lives. Similarly, psychologists are consumers of research. Psychologists use the principles of research methods to study topics of interest to the field and society. For example, through the application of research methodology, psychologists have conducted studies which have helped us better understand allocation of resources while driving and talking on a cell phone, the role of subliminal advertising and buying behaviors, and potential benefits to children from viewing series such as *Baby Einstein*. As you can see, psychological research plays a vital role in our ability to make educated decisions about our lives. Students who are equipped with skills to understand research methodology and interpret research findings carry this knowledge with them always. Thus, the central goal of our text is to provide you with an understanding of research methods with a focus on helping you become a more educated consumer of research.

Toward that goal, this text offers several pedagogical tools to reinforce research methodology and its relevance in psychology and the world around us.

- **Are You Equipped? Boxes**   Featured at the beginning and end of each chapter, these boxes present examples from everyday life or from classic psychological research. You are introduced to new topics and asked to critically evaluate each to demonstrate mastery of previously covered concepts. Examples include, "Does the input of the *American Idol* judges influence how viewers vote?" and "How much can you trust the feedback about your professors posted online?"
- **You Try It! Exercises**   You get hands-on practice in testing various research methodologies and conducting research. For example, you will obtain practice at differentiating between positive and negative correlations, identifying variables used in a research design, and generating hypotheses. These exercises will help prepare you to conduct your own research.
- **Student-Centered Writing Style and Organization**   Each chapter is written with a goal of optimizing your experience for greater understanding and class success. A direct, concise, and engaging writing style supported by relevant examples works to help you tackle concepts more easily. In addition, key terms are bolded within the narrative, with full definitions provided on page in the running glossary. A chapter summary highlights key points for you to aid in the review and study process.

- **APA Learning Outcomes** To better provide you a way to assess your knowledge of the chapter concepts, each chapter opens with a list of relevant learning outcomes as outlined by the American Psychological Association (APA) and ends with an overview of examples from the chapter showing how those outcomes were covered. For nonpsychology majors, this feature provides another way to gauge understanding of the chapter material as well as provides a guideline for review. For psychology majors, this feature allows you to track which APA outcomes you have mastered as you work through the course. In addition, the outcomes and review use APA language to correspond to courses employing these outcomes across the discipline. The APA Guidelines for Undergraduate Psychology are:

  Goal 1. Knowledge Base of of Psychology Students will demonstrate familiarity with the major concepts, theoretical perspectives, empirical findings, and historical trends in psychology.
  Goal 2. Research Methods in Psychology Students will understand and apply basic research methods in psychology, including research design, data analysis, and interpretation.
  Goal 3. Critical Thinking Skills in Psychology Students will respect and use critical and creative thinking, skeptical inquiry, and, when possible, the scientific approach to solve problems related to behavior and mental processes.
  Goal 4. Application of Psychology Students will understand and apply psychological principles to personal, social, and organizational issues.
  Goal 5. Values in Psychology Students will be able to weigh evidence, tolerate ambiguity, act ethically, and reflect other values that are the underpinnings of psychology as a science.
  Goal 6. Information and Technological Literacy Students will demonstrate information competence and the ability to use computers and other technology for many purposes.
  Goal 7. Communication Skills Students will be able to communicate effectively in a variety of formats.
  Goal 8. Sociocultural and International Awareness Students will recognize, understand, and respect the complexity of sociocultural and international diversity.
  Goal 9. Personal Development Students will develop insight into their own and others' behavior and mental processes and apply effective strategies for self-management and self-improvement.
  Goal 10. Career Planning and Development Students will emerge from the major with realistic ideas about how to implement their psychological knowledge, skills, and values in occupational pursuits in a variety of settings.

We hope that you find these pedagogical techniques useful and that you actually enjoy reading your textbook. Research methods relates not only to the field of psychology but to many facets of everyday life. It is our hope that through the variety of examples used in the textbook, you will see the importance of the material for you. If you ever have any ideas or suggestions, please let us know. We would love to hear from you!

SUPPLEMENTS FOR THE INSTRUCTOR

The following supplements are available to qualified instructors who have adopted this textbook.

- **Instructor's Resource Manual (ISBN: 0135022711).** Written by the authors of this book, the Instructor's Resource Manual includes learning objectives, key terms and concepts, self-contained lecture suggestions and class activities for each chapter with handouts, supplemental reading suggestions, and an annotated list of additional multimedia resources.

  The Instructor's Resource Manual will be available for download via the Pearson Instructor's Resource Center (www.pearsonhighered.com) or on the MyPsychologyLab platform (www.mypsychlab.com).

  This Instructor Supplement also includes:

  - **Chapter-at-a-glance** tables to summarize all of the resources available to the instructor for each chapter
  - **Learning Objectives** for each chapter
  - **Chapter Summaries** to provide a quick overview of each chapter
  - **Lecture Outlines**, which provide a detailed overview of each chapter to help instructors plan their lectures
  - **Lecture Launchers and/or Discussion Topics**, which are ideas to introduce topics or get students involved in discussing issues
  - **Key Terms**
  - **Website Resources**
  - **Bibliography**

- **PowerPoint® Lecture Slides (ISBN: 0135022738).** The lecture slides have been authored by the textbook's authors Jennifer Bonds-Raacke and John Raacke, and feature prominent figures and tables from the text. The PowerPoint Lecture Slides are available for download via the Pearson Instructor's Resource Center (www.pearsonhighered.com) or on the MyPsychologyLab platform (www.mypsychlab.com).

- **MyTest (ISBN: 013502272X).** The test item file has been written by the textbook authors and comes with the NEW Pearson MyTest, a powerful assessment generation program the helps instructors easily create and print quizzes and exams. Questions and tests can be authored online, allowing instructors ultimate flexibility and the ability to efficiently manage assessments anytime, anywhere. For more information, go to www.PearsonMyTest.com.

- **MyPsychLab (ISBN: 9780205179213).** MyPsychLab offers students useful and engaging self-assessment tools, and instructors flexibility in assessing and tracking student progress. To instructors, MyPsychLab is a powerful tool for assessing student performance and adapting course content to students' changing needs—without investing additional time or resources. Students benefit from an easy-to-use site on which they can test themselves on key content, track their progress, and utilize individually tailored study plan. MyPsychLab includes multimedia tutorials, audio, video, simulations, animations, and controlled assessments to completely engage students and reinforce learning.

MyPsychLab is designed with instructor flexibility in mind—you decide the extent of integration into your course—from independent self-assessment for students tracked in a gradebook to total instructor-driven course management. Instructors are provided with the results of student diagnostic tests in a gradebook and can view performance of individual students or an aggregate report of their class. Instructors can access the remediation activities students receive within their customized study plans, and can also link to extra lecture notes, video clips, and activities that reflect the content areas their class is struggling with. Instructors can bring these resources to class, or easily post them on-line for students to access.

SUPPLEMENTS FOR THE STUDENT

- **CourseSmart eTextbook (ISBN: 0135022703).** This new Pearson Choice offers students an online subscription to *Research Methods: Are You Equipped? 1/e*, at 60% savings. With the CourseSmart eTextbook, students can search the text, make notes online, print our reading assignments that incorporate lecture notes, and bookmark important passages. Ask your Pearson sales representative for details or visit www. coursesmart.com.

- **MyPsychLab (ISBN: 9780205179213).** With this exciting new interactive and instructive multimedia resource, students are able to self-assess using embedded diagnostic tests and instantly view results along with a customized study plan. The customized study plan will focus on the student's strengths and weaknesses, based on the results of the diagnostic testing, and present a list of activities and resources for review and remediation, organized by chapter and section. Some study resources intended for use with portable electronic devices are made available exclusively through MyPsychLab, such as key terms, flashcards, and video clips. Students will be able to quickly and clearly analyze their own comprehension level of the course material and study more efficiently, leading to exceptional exam results!

ACKNOWLEDGMENTS

A project of this scope would not have been possible without the valuable assistance of numerous people. We would like to take a moment to thank all of our reviewers who provided helpful insights and comments on earlier drafts of the chapters.

Alison Thomas-Cottingham, *Rider University*
Constance Jones, *California State University, Fresno*
Heidi Burross, *University of Arizona*
Jay Gould, *University of West Florida*
Jonathan Amburgey, *University of Utah*
Katia Shkurkin, *St. Martin*
Keiko Taga, *California State University, Fullerton (former)*
Maria Dittrich, *George Washington University*
Marianne Lloyd, *Seton Hall University*
Marvin Lee, *Tennessee State University*
Merry Sleigh-Ritzer, *Winthrop University*
Michael Dudley, *Southern Illinois University Edwardsville*
Pamela Costa, *Tacoma Community College*
Roger Chadwick, *New Mexico State University*
Shelley Kilpatrick, *Southwest Baptist University*
Stephen Burgess, *Southwestern Oklahoma State University*

We would also like to thank the team at Pearson, in particular Jeff Marshall and Susan Hartman, for their support and assistance on the project. Last but not least, thanks to all of our students over the years (Chris Barlett, Rebecca Schlegel, Natalie (Nygaard) Ieorger, Kendra Homan, Fantasy Lozada, Nicole Gillenwater, J. Emilio Piocuda, Kelly Niccum) who have challenged us to think critically about the way we teach.

RESEARCH METHODS:
ARE YOU EQUIPPED?

Introduction to Research Methods

Psychology as a Science

Are You Equipped?

When your textbook author, Jenn, was eight years old, she fell off the monkey bars at school and scratched her cornea. It was a very painful experience. In order to protect the eye while it healed, the doctor covered the eye with a patch. Jenn wore the patch for a little over a week. It was during this time that Jenn realized she was not like everyone else—she had the ability to "see" colors by touch. Jenn became a psychology major as an undergraduate student and read reports from the American Psychological Association (APA), she learned her ability was known as dermo-optical perception. In fact, through APA, she was able to purchase a device that demonstrated her powers. Jenn uses this device today when she teaches General Psychology to illustrate dermo-optical perception to her students.

We wish that you could be in Jenn's class for the demonstration. After she gives it, she has to leave the room for a brief amount of time to recover from the physical demands of using this ability. When she returns, she shares another secret with the class—the demonstration was rigged. Jenn does not have the ability to see colors by touch. In fact, there is no such ability as dermo-optical perception. Therefore, APA has never written reports on the topic nor is there a device available for purchase. In reality, Jenn's demonstration was a complete fabrication.

You might want to know what would possess Jenn to lie to her students. It does not make sense on the surface to trick students who trust and respect her. The reason is that she wants to teach her students a very valuable life lesson: Do not confuse pseudoscience with science. As you will learn in this chapter, there are some fields that masquerade as a real science. However, when empirically and systematically tested, a pseudoscience will not measure up to its claims. Furthermore, Jenn's demonstration illustrates the point that we should not blindly obey or believe authority figures. Pseudoscience relies on so-called experts and authority figures to convince people of the message. Sometimes people with limited knowledge of the field of psychology will assume it is a pseudoscience. Yet, psychology is a true science. In the following chapters, we will discuss how psychology uses the scientific method to arrive at conclusions. It is understandable that some students in Jenn's class believed in her abilities after witnessing the demonstration. However, by the end of this chapter, you should be skeptical of anyone claiming such amazing powers of mental ability.

As you go through this chapter, we also want you to keep in mind how the material relates to the APA goals for psychology majors. Specifically, this chapter will address the following goals:

- **Goal 1. Knowledge Base of Psychology**
  Students will demonstrate familiarity with the major concepts, theoretical perspectives, empirical findings, and historical trends in psychology.
- **Goal 2. Research Methods in Psychology**
  Students will understand and apply basic research methods in psychology, including research design, data analysis, and interpretation.
- **Goal 3. Critical Thinking Skills in Psychology**
  Students will respect and use critical and creative thinking, skeptical inquiry, and, when possible, the scientific approach to solve problems related to behavior and mental processes.
- **Goal 4. Application of Psychology**
  Students will understand and apply psychological principles to personal, social, and organizational issues.
- **Goal 5. Values in Psychology**
  Students will be able to weigh evidence, tolerate ambiguity, act ethically, and reflect other values that are the underpinnings of psychology as a discipline.
- **Goal 9. Personal Development**
  Students will develop insight into their own and others' behavior and mental processes, and apply effective strategies for self-management and self-improvement.
- **Goal 10. Career Planning and Development**
  Students will emerge from the major with realistic ideas about how to implement their psychological knowledge, skills, and values in occupational pursuits in a variety of settings.

We will relook at these goals again at the end of the chapter.

RESEARCH METHODS AND YOU

Psychologists use a variety of research methods to investigate topics of interest. This textbook will equip you to use these methods to conduct your own research. In addition, the information contained in this textbook will prepare you to be an educated consumer of research. This means that you will be able to read, understand, and draw conclusions based on the published work of other social scientists. This is important because when you graduate from your college or university you will no longer have professors to teach you about current developments within the field of psychology. It will become your responsibility to know what is going on. Therefore, no matter whether you are interested in becoming a clinical psychologist, an industrial/organizational psychologist, or any other kind of professional, you will need to stay current within your area.

Sources of Information

One way to know about recent developments is through scholarly resources. You can attend national conferences held by psychological organizations such as the **American Psychological Association (APA)** and the **Association for Psychological Science (APS).** This is an opportunity to hear about new theories, trends, and practices from colleagues across the country. Both APA and APS allow students taking psychology courses to join their organizations as student affiliates. The cost is under $40 per year and benefits include reduced conference rates, magazines, journals, and newsletters to name a few. If you are interested in learning more about the organizations or joining, visit the respective websites at the following addresses: *www.apa.org* and *www.psychologicalscience.org*.

APA

American Psychological Association.

APS

Association for Psychological Science.

Another way to learn of new developments in psychology is to read published research findings. While some journals are broad in scope and publish articles that span all areas of psychology, others are specific to subareas of psychology. You can subscribe to journals as an individual or, if you are affiliated with a university, you can access the journals through the library. In addition, as we mentioned above, membership in psychological organizations provides access to some journals.

You can also conduct your own research. Many psychologists have a research line or research agenda whereby they add to the existing body of knowledge within their area of expertise. By being actively engaged in research, psychologists remain current and have the latest information on a topic. At this point, the idea of conducting your own research might sound like a daunting task. But, by the end of this textbook, you will have the basic skills and foundations needed to investigate areas of psychology that are of interest to you. We think it is important for you to know that conducting research is not restricted to individuals with PhDs. The field of psychology has a strong tradition of involving undergraduate students in research. There are organizations (e.g., Psi Chi) and conferences (e.g., Great Plains Students' Psychology Convention) devoted to promoting and supporting student research. Be sure to ask your professor about what opportunities are available in your location.

A final source of information about developments within the field is media outlets. Journalists and editors are particularly interested in social science research findings, and it is not uncommon to see or read about psychological research in particular. However, as you will see in this chapter, media outlets do not always do such a great job of accurately conveying findings from social science research. In addition, entertainment media regularly contribute to popular myths about psychology through inaccurate portrayals. Therefore, it is important that you have a healthy skepticism when you are a consumer of research information from the media.

Importance of Being an Educated Consumer

Many times we obtain information about psychological topics from the media. We may purposively seek out information on psychological topics by conducting searches on the Web or we may form ideas about psychological topics through media that we consume for entertainment purposes. Yet, the information we obtain is not always accurate. Lilienfeld, Lynn, Ruscio, and Beyerstein (2010) recently published a book that examines myths in popular psychology. Take a look at some of the chapter titles below:

- "Most People Use Only 10% of Their Brain Power"
- "Extrasensory Perception Is a Well-Established Scientific Phenomenon"
- "Subliminal Messages Can Persuade People to Purchase Products"
- "Playing Mozart's Music to Infants Boosts Their Intelligence"
- "Most People Experience a Midlife Crisis in Their 40s or Early 50s"
- "Intelligence Tests Are Biased Against Certain Groups of People"
- "The Defining Feature of Dyslexia Is Reversing Letters"
- "Researchers Have Demonstrated That Dreams Possess Symbolic Meaning"
- "Opposites Attract: We Are Romantically Attracted to People Who Differ from Us"
- "People's Responses to Inkblots Tell Us a Great Deal about Their Personalities"
- "People with Schizophrenia Have Multiple Personalities"
- "Most Mentally Ill People Are Violent"

We can't help but think of how media portrayals have helped to reinforce these popular myths. For example, *Ghost Busters* (1984) was about "parapsychology" professors and included scenes with the professors testing extrasensory perception of participants. This could have contributed to the myth stating that extrasensory perception is a well-established phenomenon. In *Father of the Bride Part II* (1995), George Banks (played by Steve Martin) goes through a midlife crisis as his wife and daughter are pregnant at the same time. It is possible that such a depiction gives the impression that a midlife crisis is typical or expected. Even the movie *Me, Myself, and Irene* (2000) confuses multiple personalities with schizophrenia. Certainly, media sources are not entirely to blame for the existence of these myths. Nevertheless, media channels do contribute to the popularization of the myths through inaccurate depictions. The examples we just presented were depictions from entertainment media. However, media outlets can also misinterpret research findings. For example, Larson (2003) notes that in the 2000 general election, 47% of the news stories did not accurately report the margin of error. Bushman and Anderson (2001) also note that while the scientific community is reaching a consensus on the negative effects of exposure to violent media, news reports paint the picture that there is only a weak link between media violence and aggression.

Disconnect between Media and Psychological Research

While there is not one reason in particular why a disconnect exists between media and psychological research findings, scholars have proposed a few possible explanations. For example, Harris (2004) points out that journalists and psychologists use very different languages. Psychologists are very careful not to imply cause and effect from correlational results and prefer to stay away from sweeping generalizations. Yet, this approach does not always make for interesting reading. Psychologists do not receive any formal training in how to bridge this gap, and thus the two groups have difficulty communicating on a topic. Harris also mentions that when journalists present both sides of an issue, they may be lending credit to positions not supported in the scientific community. Journalists may feel that presenting both sides of an issue is balanced reporting. But, balanced reporting, in cases where one side is supported by extensive research findings and the other side is conjecture, is not always accurate reporting. Even introductory textbooks on mass communication provide examples of how balanced reports can lead to inaccurate coverage (Vivian, 2008).

Recommendations

Throughout this textbook, we provide you with specific information to help you interpret research findings presented in the media. The specific information will be related to the information covered in the chapter and examples from the media will be provided. At this point, we would like to share with you some general guidelines you should consider. You will be able to understand more about each guideline later in the semester but it is a good idea to begin thinking about each of them now.

General Guidelines for Interpreting Research in the Media

1. **Locate original sources:** To begin, it is always a good idea to locate the original source of the story. Typically, the researchers' names and affiliations are provided. With a simple Internet search, you can find the scholarly reference. Then, you can use your university library to locate the reference. Although this sounds time consuming, we have found that you can locate original sources pretty quickly. Moreover, having the original source will give you access to all of the research findings and you can draw your own conclusions.

2. **Look for correlational findings:** Many times psychological research examines how factors in life are related to one another. Later in this textbook we will discuss how this type of research, known as correlational research, does much to advance our knowledge on psychological issues. However, correlational research does not establish cause and effect. It is not uncommon for media sources to imply that correlational research findings do more than establish a link between variables of interest. Having the original sources (as mentioned in the previous point) will allow you to know what conclusions can be drawn.

3. **Watch for balanced reporting, misinterpretation of numbers, and generalizations:** We hope that after reading this textbook you will have developed a keen eye for issues to be aware of when consuming research. For example, balanced reporting can be a less preferred approach because it can give the impression that the psychological community is divided on an issue when the reality is very different. Similarly, interpreting numbers requires an understanding of statistics and it is not unheard of for media reports to inaccurately explain results or margins of error. Finally, you should watch for sweeping generalizations. Psychological research is conducted in such a way that findings can be applied to specific groups of people. If research findings are presented in a manner that implies that *all* people think or behave in a certain way, this is probably not accurate.

Now that we have discussed how research methods relate to you in terms of your career in psychology and in terms of being an educated consumer of research findings in everyday life, we want to talk about psychology as a science. To do so, we will begin by differentiating between science and pseudoscience.

Section Summary

- There are many sources from which someone can obtain information in the field of psychology. Information can be obtained (p. 5)
  - from conferences conducted by organizations such as APA and APS;
  - by reading journal articles, books, or book chapters on the field of psychology;
  - by conducting your own research on a topic within psychology; and
  - through the media (p. 5).
- However, there are some caveats when obtaining information through the media (pp. 6–7).
  - Media outlets do not always present information accurately (p. 6).
  - This can occur because of the disconnect in the use of language by psychologists and the media (p. 7).
  - Also, the media typically presents both sides of an issue in a way that lends credibility to nonscientific viewpoints (p. 7).
- In order to be confident in information reported in the media, make sure to:
  - Locate the original sources (p. 7).
  - Look for correlational findings (p. 7).
  - Watch for balanced reporting, misinterpretation of numbers, and generalizations (p. 7).

SCIENCE VERSUS PSEUDOSCIENCE

Have you ever read your horoscope? If so, you are not alone. Newspapers around the world print a daily horoscope for anyone who wishes to have a foreshadowing of the coming day. Reportedly, a horoscope uses the placement of the Sun on the day of a person's birth in conjunction with celestial events to make predictions about the daily dealings for that individual. Horoscopes were developed by those who study astrology. Astrology, the study of the position of celestial bodies and their influence over human behavior, has been studied and followed for thousands of years. By utilizing the placement of celestial bodies in relation to the Earth, astrologers claim to explain past behavior and use it to predict future events.

We started off with this example to help explain the difference between a science and a pseudoscience. Astrology, including its aspects such as horoscopes, is classified as a pseudoscience. A pseudoscience is any theory, method, or belief that appears to be based in science but in reality is not. Even though the description of astrology provided above sounded very scientific, it is not a science. This is because when subjected to scientific evaluation, astrology fails to produce any substantial results. Let's explore the differences between a science and pseudoscience further.

Pseudoscience

As mentioned earlier, a **pseudoscience** is any theory, method, or belief that appears to be based in science but is not. The word itself, *pseudoscience*, means "false science." A pseudoscience gives the appearance of being a science without the technical rigor or empirical evidence to back it up. Rather a pseudoscience benefits from gathering information via (a) intuition, (b) tenacity, or (c) authority to maintain its scientific appearance. The key is that a pseudoscience acquires its knowledge in ways that do not lend themselves to open criticisms or challenges. Let's take a look at the three ways a pseudoscience typically operates.

When evaluating arguments, we rely on our **intuition** every day. Intuition can be defined as understanding through the use of common sense based on observation. This means a person uses common sense in forming a judgment about the believability of an observed event. When using intuition, a person assumes that if something sounds plausible and looks to be plausible, then it must be true. For example, on the surface, some people would believe the following statements to be true:

- Cholesterol is bad.
- The country of Iceland is covered in ice.
- The country of Greenland has very little ice.
- The number-one killer of women is breast cancer.

However, are these examples true? The answer is no. Although it seems plausible that cholesterol is bad for you, there are types of cholesterol that are good for you and aid in neuronal development. Likewise, the countries of Iceland and Greenland are nothing like their names imply. In fact, each is the exact opposite. Iceland consists of a mostly green environment and Greenland consists of a mostly frozen environment. Lastly, although there has been much publicity about breast cancer and its effects on women, the number-one killer of women is heart disease. Heart disease leads to about 10 times as many deaths as compared with breast cancer. Hence, relying solely on your intuition will not always lead to the truth.

Tenacity is defined as the persistence to maintain over time. For a pseudoscience, tenacity is seen in the persistent ability of a belief, theory, or method to last over a significant amount of time. In particular, tenacity occurs when something is repeated over and over again to the point where people believe it to be true because (a) of the sheer number of times they have heard it or (b) they have heard it for a long amount of time. However, just because a belief, method, or theory has stayed around without anyone providing counter information does not make it a valid or true argument. In other words, just repeatedly saying something is true does not make it true. For instance, it is a commonly held belief among college students that those who are single engage in and enjoy more sexual activity as compared with people who are married. This belief has been portrayed in movies and on television shows for years. Each year college students come to campus believing this to be a scientific fact. However, General Psychology students learn that the opposite is the case. Research has shown that those who are married or cohabiting not only engage in greater amounts of sexual activity but also report higher levels of satisfaction with their sexual lives. Yet, because of the tenacity of this belief about single people, students next year will no doubt come to campus thinking this to be a proven fact.

PSEUDOSCIENCE

Any theory, method, or belief that appears to be based in science but is not.

INTUITION

Understanding through the use of common sense based on observation.

TENACITY

The persistence to maintain.

AUTHORITY

The appearance of expertise in a field of study.

Lastly, a pseudoscience benefits from **authority.** A pseudoscience gains traction when there is an authoritative figure who conveys the message. This figure can be real but is often times imagined. People who are believers of pseudoscience will use terms such as "they said" or "they have shown" without actually being able to identify who "they" are. You probably have seen television commercials where an actor or a real person is promoting a product. Oftentimes, this is a doctor who is supporting a new drug or weight loss remedy, or the fifth dentist who approves a certain brand of toothpaste. Typically, these advertisers will use terms such as "the experts" or "those researchers" to provide authority to back up the claims in the advertisement. People believe these claims by making the mental jump that the expert must be the person talking on the television or someone at the product's home company. After all, the advertising company would never insinuate a falsehood just to sell a product; they have "experts." Within a pseudoscience, this lack of clarity in authority is purposeful. It is this anonymity in the authoritative figure that allows the pseudoscience to go unchallenged. Specifically, a pseudoscience chooses an attitude of blind obedience to authority without challenging any of the held beliefs. This is unlike a science which continually challenges the held beliefs of authority. The problem with relying on intuition, tenacity, or authority to form opinions is that it is done without any reliance on critical objectivity or logical reasoning. It is for this reason that a pseudoscience is called a false science. Therefore, let's take a look at what makes a science a science and distinguishes a science from a pseudoscience.

Science

SCIENCE

The accumulation of knowledge via systematic observation or experimentation using the scientific method.

Science is defined as the accumulation of knowledge via systematic observation or experimentation using the scientific method. The scientific method is a step-by-step process by which hypotheses are tested and retested. We will discuss the scientific method further in Chapter 2. Right now, we focus on how a science distinguishes itself from a pseudoscience. The biggest differences between a science and a pseudoscience are how information is obtained and the extent to which science is challenged. Unlike a pseudoscience, a science relies on three stable ideals to acquire and distribute knowledge.

EMPIRICAL

Acquisition of knowledge via objective and systematic collection of data.

First, science is **empirical.** The word "empirical" means that knowledge is gained via observation, experience, or experimentation. However, we have already shown that mere observation and experience is not enough. Therefore, the use of the word "empirical" in science means that knowledge is obtained via objective and systematic collection of data. After data collection, scientists draw conclusions and make inferences about the topic of study. This is in direct contrast to a pseudoscience, which uses subjective evaluations.

SELF-CORRECTING

A system of challenges by which scientific claims can be verified.

Second, science is **self-correcting.** Unlike a pseudoscience that avoids challenges to its claims, science encourages challenges. In fact, researchers provide other researchers with the information needed to conduct the work again. It is through this process that information is verified. This provides science with a system by which claims can be verified as being true or false. In other words, science allows for a system of checks and balances to ensure that any information put forth is accurate. Again, this is not a claim that can be made by pseudoscience.

CONTROL

Direct manipulation of a desired variable or the management or removal of unwanted factors that can influence observations or experiments.

Finally, science applies measures of **control.** In scientific research, control is determined by either (a) direct manipulation of a desired variable or (b) management or removal of unwanted factors that can influence observations or experiments. Thus, control allows science to determine which factors are important in research and which are not. Control also allows science to make direct comparisons and in many cases demonstrate cause and effect. Without the use of scientific control, researchers would be unable to determine which factors influence which behaviors. For example, psychics (who would come under the category of pseudoscience) most often fail to demonstrate special powers when tested by researchers in controlled environments. Specifically, when a psychic is placed in a situation where a researcher removes the ability of reading body language or facial expression, the psychic's abilities are greatly diminished. It is this management or removal of unwanted factors that allows the researcher to demonstrate the psychic's mental abilities as false.

In this section, we have investigated the differences between science and pseudoscience. In the next chapter, we will begin to explore the idea that psychology falls under the category of science. In particular, we will be discussing the use of the scientific method to illustrate how findings of psychologists are scientific.

Section Summary

- ◆ A distinction must be made between pseudoscience and science (pp. 8–10).
  - ◆ Pseudoscience is any theory, method, or belief that appears to be based in science but is not (p. 9).
  - ◆ Pseudoscience is aided by three principles: intuition, tenacity, and authority (p. 9).
  - ◆ Intuition is the understanding through the use of common sense based on observation (p. 9).
  - ◆ Tenacity is the persistence to maintain (p. 9).
  - ◆ Authority is the appearance of expertise in a field of study (p. 10).
- ◆ Science is the accumulation of knowledge via systematic observation or experimentation using the scientific method (pp. 10–11).
  - ◆ Science is empirical. Empiricism is the acquisition of knowledge via objective and systematic collection of data (p. 10).
  - ◆ Science is self-correcting. Specifically, science allows for a system of challenges by which scientific claims can be verified (p. 10).
  - ◆ Science exerts measures of control. Control is the direct manipulation of a desired variable or the management or removal of unwanted factors that can influence observations or experiments (pp. 10–11).

WHAT YOU CAN EXPECT

Just as at the beginning of a semester you wonder what your professors will be like, you might want to know what you can expect from us as the authors of your textbook. To begin, Experimental Psychology (research methods) is one of our favorite courses to teach. The reason is that most students come to the class with a preconceived notion that they will not like the material. This gives us the unique opportunity to show students how the material can be exciting and relate to the real world. Second, our approach in this textbook is to communicate the material to you as if you were one of our own students. To help you succeed in the course, we have incorporated many student-friendly features in this textbook, which are presented in the list below.

RELEVANT AND INTERESTING EXAMPLES.   We provide you with many examples to help you understand key concepts. We use examples that relate to your life and examples that are well known within the field of psychology. We also offer examples that appeal to students with a broad range of backgrounds and interests. This includes traditional and nontraditional students, as well as those pertaining to the many different areas of interest in psychology. It is our hope that by giving such examples you will find it easier to remember and apply the information.

SECTION AND CHAPTER SUMMARIES.   We provide you with summaries at the end of each section within a chapter and at the end of each chapter. The summaries draw your attention to important concepts and terms. Included in the summaries are pages numbers, allowing you to easily locate concepts and terms within the chapter. The summaries are also a great way to check your comprehension of the material presented.

EASY-TO-UNDERSTAND DEFINITIONS.   When introducing new terms, we avoid using technical or jargon-filled language. Rather, we explain the concept in easy-to-understand language. After you are comfortable with the new information, we illustrate how the term is used within the field. You will find that new terms and concepts are presented in bold font within the paragraphs and new terms are also defined in the margins. This will help you to easily spot new information as you are reading the textbook.

CONVERSATIONAL, ENGAGING TONE.   Our tone in the textbook is very friendly and approachable. This is reflective of our teaching styles. Our goal is that you will want to read the textbook! We also believe it is important to talk to you about the material rather than at you in a lecture style.

OPPORTUNITIES FOR PRACTICE.   Finally, you will find that this textbook is packed full of opportunities for you to practice. We find that students appreciate the opportunity to practice what they have learned and this helps to prepare you for quizzes and exams. We would like to call your attention to two types of practice opportunities: "You Try It!" and "Are You Equipped?"

"You Try It!" and "Are You Equipped?" Exercises

Two ways that we give you the opportunity to practice the material is through "You Try It!" and "Are You Equipped?" exercises. The "You Try It!" exercises are found throughout the chapters after a new topic is presented. It is not uncommon to have more than one such exercise in a given chapter (except for this chapter). Typically, we walk you through an example and then give you the chance to try it on your own. After you try the material for yourself, we talk about the answers. "Are You Equipped" exercises are found at the beginning and at the end of chapters. These exercises at the beginning of the chapters are designed to introduce you to a new topic. For example, the "Are You Equipped" at the beginning of this chapter introduced us to the topic of pseudoscience. You are not expected to know the answers. It is a fun way to get you thinking about the upcoming topics in the chapter. The "Are You Equipped Now" exercises at the end of the chapters are designed to ensure you understand the material before moving on to the next chapter. This is an opportunity for you to test your knowledge of the material before you take an exam. We provide you with the answers to these exercises so that you can see how you are doing. To get you familiar with the "Are You Equipped Now?" exercises, take a look at the one below.

Are You Equipped Now?

On October 24, 2009, the *New York Times* printed an article titled, "No Einstein in Your Crib? Get a Refund." The article discusses the recent move by the Walt Disney Company to offer refunds to those individuals who purchased videos from the Baby Einstein series. The article outlines how advocacy groups such as the Campaign for a Commercial-Free Childhood believe that some companies including Disney and Brainy Baby market videos as having an educational benefit, when they believe research is lacking to back up the claims. The Campaign for a Commercial-Free Childhood has approached the Federal Trade Commission about the issue. Since that time, the word "educational" has been removed from the marketing of the videos, but the advocacy group believes that the wording of the marketing still implies educational benefits.

We find the issue discussed in this article to be interesting for two reasons. First, it relates to the idea of being an educated consumer of media, in particular advertising. The second reason is that we are parents of young children. As we mentioned at the beginning of this chapter, it is wise to be hesitant at believing everything you hear and read through media. In fact, some of the guidelines that we have discussed in this chapter would have been helpful to parents when deciding whether to purchase the videos for what they believed to be educational benefits. What are two of the guidelines and how might these guidelines have helped the parents?

Answers

We think that the guidelines regarding locating original sources and watching for generalizations would be very helpful for parents. For example, it is not uncommon for the back of DVDs and videos to contain information on the product. Parents can compare the information on the back of the video to research findings in the field. This will help parents to draw their own conclusions about the benefits of the content. Advertisers routinely use generalizations, so it is helpful to be aware of the language used in advertising. You might have listed some of the other guidelines as being helpful to parents, which are also correct responses. The next time you watch a commercial on TV, see if you can use these general guidelines to become a responsible consumer of media.

This textbook has five main parts. Part one of the textbook contains the first three chapters. The next two chapters that you will read about are goals and methods of psychology and ethics. These chapters taken together provide a foundation for the remainder of the course. As we proceed through the material, information will become more challenging. However, our approach of presenting the material in a way you can understand and relate to will remain the same.

Chapter Summary

- There are many sources from which someone can obtain information in the field of psychology. Information can be obtained (p. 5)
    - from conferences conducted by organizations such as APA and APS;
    - by reading journal articles, books, or book chapters on the field of psychology;
    - by conducting your own research on a topic within psychology; and
    - through the media (p. 5).
- However, there are some caveats when obtaining information through the media (pp. 6–7).
    - Media outlets do not always present information accurately (p. 6).
    - This can occur because of the disconnect in the use of language by psychologists and the media (p. 7).
    - Also, the media typically presents both sides of an issue in a way that lends credibility to nonscientific viewpoints (p. 7).
- In order to be confident in information reported in the media, make sure to:
    - Locate the original sources (p. 7).
    - Look for correlational findings (p. 7).
    - Watch for balanced reporting, misinterpretation of numbers, and generalizations (p. 7).
- A distinction must be made between pseudoscience and science (pp. 8–10).
    - Pseudoscience is any theory, method, or belief that appears to be based in science but is not (p. 9).
    - Pseudoscience is aided by three principles: intuition, tenacity, and authority (p. 9).
    - Intuition is the understanding through the use of common sense based on observation (p. 9).
    - Tenacity is the persistence to maintain (p. 9).
    - Authority is the appearance of expertise in a field of study (p. 10).
- Science is the accumulation of knowledge via systematic observation or experimentation using the scientific method (pp. 10–11).
    - Science is empirical. Empiricism is the acquisition of knowledge via objective and systematic collection of data (p. 10).
    - Science is self-correcting. Specifically, science allows for a system of challenges by which scientific claims can be verified (p. 10).
    - Science exerts measures of control. Control is the direct manipulation of a desired variable or the management or removal of unwanted factors that can influence observations or experiments (pp. 10–11).

APA Learning Goals Linkage

- **Goal 1.** *Knowledge Base of Psychology*
  Students will demonstrate familiarity with the major concepts, theoretical perspectives, empirical findings, and historical trends in psychology.
  Sections Covered: Science versus Pseudoscience

(Continued)

Explanation of the Goal: It is important to understand the nature of psychology as a discipline. To begin, psychology is a science. Therefore, we have examined the characteristics of psychology that make it a science. This included the use of (a) empirical data, (b) a system to challenge scientific claims, and (c) controls in observations and experiments.

- **Goal 2.** *Research Methods in Psychology*
  Students will understand and apply basic research methods in psychology, including research design, data analysis, and interpretation.

  Sections Covered: Recommendations, Science versus Pseudoscience

  Explanation of the Goal: This chapter has focused on the nature of psychology as a science. This is a starting point for research methods in psychology. We have also focused on the interpretation and use of psychological research findings. As we have seen, interpreting psychological claims correctly has important personal and societal ramifications.

- **Goal 3.** *Critical Thinking Skills in Psychology*
  Students will respect and use critical and creative thinking, skeptical inquiry, and, when possible, the scientific approach to solve problems related to behavior and mental processes.

  Sections Covered: Are You Equipped?, Importance of Being an Educated Consumer, Recommendations, Science versus Pseudoscience

  Explanation of the Goal: Many of the sections in this chapter involved Goal 3. This is because critical thinking is commonly used by psychologists in daily activities. Thus, we have introduced you to topics and situations where you would use critical and creative thinking, in addition to skeptical inquiry. The popular myths of psychology and blind obedience to authority by those in pseudoscience are two examples. As we have illustrated with these examples, it is by using critical thinking skills that we can recognize common fallacies in thinking and avoid being swayed by appeals to authority. Critical thinking also involves approaching topics with a skeptical inquiry. One way that skepticism can be demonstrated is by following the recommendations outlined when interpreting research in the media.

- **Goal 4.** *Application of Psychology*
  Students will understand and apply psychological principles to personal, social, and organizational issues.

  Sections Covered: Are You Equipped?, Importance of Being an Educated Consumer, Disconnect between Media and Psychological Research, Recommendations, Science versus Pseudoscience, Are You Equipped Now?

  Explanation of the Goal: It is important that you are able to explain how psychological principles can be used in society. Therefore, we have given many examples in this chapter where concepts, theories, and research findings can be applied to your everyday life. This includes

(*Continued*)

applying psychology principles to everyday activities like buying children's videos and being aware of how psychological research findings are often misunderstood by the public, such as the belief that a midlife crisis is typical and expected.

- **Goal 5. *Values in Psychology***
Students will be able to weigh evidence, tolerate ambiguity, act ethically, and reflect other values that are the underpinnings of psychology as a discipline.

  Sections Covered: Are You Equipped?, Importance of Being an Educated Consumer, Disconnect between Media and Psychological Research, Recommendations, Science versus Pseudoscience, Are You Equipped Now?

  Explanation of the Goal: As a psychology major, you want to understand the causes of behaviors and cognitions. In understanding these factors, you will want to look for scientific research findings to evaluate claims and weigh evidence. This becomes particularly important when differentiating between science and pseudoscience. On the other hand, sometimes you need to be willing to tolerate ambiguity. For example, even though we know there is a disconnect between media reports and psychological research, there is not always a clear answer or immediate solution to the situation.

- **Goal 9. *Personal Development***
Students will develop insight into their own and others' behavior and mental processes, and apply effective strategies for self-management and self-improvement.

  Sections Covered: Recommendations

  Explanation of the Goal: In the recommendations section, we have provided general guidelines that you can use when interpreting research findings presented in the media. Following these guidelines will help you to apply psychological principles to promote personal development. In addition, you are engaging in metacognition. This will enable you to evaluate the quality of your own thinking.

- **Goal 10. *Career Planning and Development***
Students will emerge from the major with realistic ideas about how to implement their psychological knowledge, skills, and values in occupational pursuits in a variety of settings.

  Sections Covered: Sources of Information

  Explanation of the Goal: While completing your major, it is important to learn how your knowledge and skills in psychology will be used after graduation. At the beginning of this chapter, we devoted time to explaining how you will obtain information on the recent developments within the field later in your career. We also encouraged you to join APA and APS as student affiliates and to become involved in undergraduate research. Becoming familiar with these national psychological organizations will provide you with information on the academic experiences needed to achieve your career goals.

2

Goals and Methods of Psychology

CHAPTER OUTLINE

Are You Equipped?

Have you ever sat in a movie theater and wondered why snack foods are always advertised before the start of the movie? Or, furthermore, does anyone actually go out and buy the snack foods because of the advertisements? The advertisement of snack foods before a movie starts can be traced back to an early research study. In the mid-1950s, research came out that claimed if a movie theater used subliminal advertising, snack sales could be increased. Specifically, an owner, and in this case also the researcher, of a movie theater decided to flash a subliminal message during the screening of a show. The owner flashed "Eat Popcorn" and "Drink Coca-Cola" at an exposure rate of 1/3,000 per second on the screen during the presentation of a movie. The messages flashed on the screen were far below a person's threshold for conscious experience (i.e., subliminal). The owner conducted this experiment over a six-week period and his results indicated a 50%

increase in Coca-Cola sales and an 18% increase in popcorn sales (McConnell, Cutler, & McNeil, 1958).

This experiment was hailed as a breakthrough in advertising. So popular were these results that the researcher of this experiment opened his own subliminal advertising firm and charged clients for his new technique. This one event also sparked a plethora of research on the topic of subliminal messages. In fact, subliminal messages and subliminal advertising became part of the global culture after the reporting of these findings. The interesting part of this story was that a few years later, the results were discredited and consequently the researcher admitted to falsifying his results. You might wonder how it came to pass that the results were called into question.

The answer is a result of a simple method that psychologists adopted years before: the scientific method. The scientific method provides a framework from which psychologists are able to systematically study behavior and mental processes. As we will discuss, part of the scientific method involves the reporting of research methodologies and findings. In this case, when the research on subliminal advertising was first publicized, other researchers could not reproduce the claimed results, even when using the exact methodology as the theater owner. It was through this process of reporting (commonly referred to as dissemination) and replication that the researcher was shown to be fabricating his results. In this chapter, we will discuss the steps of the scientific method, as well as the goals of psychological research, hypothesis generation, and theory development.

As you go through this chapter, we also want you to keep in mind how the material relates to the APA goals for psychology majors. Specifically, this chapter will address the following goals:

- **Goal 1. Knowledge Base of Psychology**
  Students will demonstrate familiarity with the major concepts, theoretical perspectives, empirical findings, and historical trends in psychology.
- **Goal 2. Research Methods in Psychology**
  Students will understand and apply basic research methods in psychology, including research design, data analysis, and interpretation.
- **Goal 3. Critical Thinking Skills in Psychology**
  Students will respect and use critical and creative thinking, skeptical inquiry, and, when possible, the scientific approach to solve problems related to behavior and mental processes.
- **Goal 4. Application of Psychology**
  Students will understand and apply psychological principles to personal, social, and organizational issues.

INTRODUCTION

This chapter will introduce you to the goals of psychological research and the method that psychologists use to achieve these goals, which is known as the scientific method. The scientific method is used by many disciplines and allows psychologists, in particular, to investigate areas of interest regarding human thought and behavior. Finally, this chapter will begin to show you how to utilize those student-friendly features that we discussed in Chapter 1. Let's get started!

GOALS OF PSYCHOLOGICAL RESEARCH

Psychologists carry out research with four goals in mind (Figure 2.1). These four goals build upon one another, creating a pyramid for researchers. The four goals are to (a) describe, (b) explain, (c) predict, and (d) influence behavior and mental processes.

The underlying goal that lays the groundwork for all research is to **describe** an event or process. This need to describe events is inherent in our nature as curious human beings. For instance, how often do you walk between classes and something catches your attention? You might wonder when you see something in the hallway, "What is going on here?" This is exactly what a researcher does too. A researcher sees a behavior or process and wants to describe it. For example, a researcher walking down the hallway might see five students using text messaging and wonder, "What is this?" As the researcher attempts to describe the behavior, he or she is using the first goal of psychological research. In fact, researchers have studied text messaging behaviors and published findings describing the behavior. For example, text messages are limited to around 160 characters and have become a very popular low-cost means of communication for today's youth (Grinter & Palen, 2002). As can be seen, this is a description of the event.

Once a description of a behavior or process has been adequately provided, researchers move on to **explain** the behavior or process. Now, the question changes from, "What is going on?" to "Why is this happening?" The process moves from describing the behavior or event to attempting to explain why this behavior or process is occurring. Let's go back to the text messaging example. Previously, we described what text messaging is, a low-cost means of communication between cellular phones. The next goal is to explain why people engage in this form of communication. There are many approaches that a researcher can take when attempting to explain this behavior. Research can attempt to explain the socio-emotional aspects of text messaging, the linguistic advantages of text messaging, or the prevalence of texting messaging in different social situations. The key is that the research goal has moved beyond documentation to generating explanations.

The third goal of psychological research is to **predict** the occurrence of a behavior or process. Knowing what the event is and also why it happens allows researchers to begin to predict where it will, or will not, occur. The question for this goal is, "Where will this behavior or event be exhibited?" Researchers

DESCRIBE

The first goal is to *describe* behavior or mental processes.

EXPLAIN

The second goal is to *explain* behavior or mental processes.

PREDICT

The third goal is to *predict* behavior or mental processes.

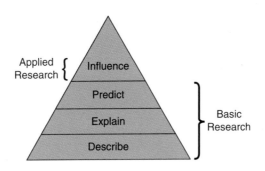

FIGURE 2.1 Four Goals of Psychological Research.

working on this goal will look to predict events in specific situations. Therefore, a researcher who knows what text messaging is (describe) and knows why people use text messaging (explain) will now try to predict text messaging occurrences. For example, if a researcher knows that text messaging is a means of communication (describe) used by those who prefer to avoid confrontation or unpleasant interactions (explain), the researcher might predict that text messaging will become a popular tool for people wanting to end a romantic relationship. To confirm the prediction, he or she might investigate current ways of ending relationships with significant others and ask specifically about the role of text messaging.

Up until this point, the goals of psychological research have fallen into a category known as **basic research.** Basic research is conducted to further the collective knowledge about a topic within a field of study. In this particular case of text messaging, the field is psychology but basic research can be conducted in any field. With the last goal of psychological research, we move into a category known as **applied research.** Applied research occurs when research is conducted to solve a practical problem within a field of study.

The last goal of psychological research is to **influence** the studied behavior or process. The question for this goal becomes, "How can I enhance or reduce the exhibited behavior or process?" When a researcher attempts to influence a behavior or process, he or she is essentially looking to solve a problem (applied research). A researcher investigating text messaging with this goal in mind would look to take from all previous research and try to enhance or reduce text messaging in people. Therefore, a researcher at a national cellular phone company might create several advertisements which illustrate the practice of using text messaging to end a romantic relationship with a significant other. These advertisements could then be used in future campaigns to increase texting use (an enhancement) by suggesting that text messaging helps to avoid unpleasant interactions. On the other hand, a floral company might want to create the opposite effect and develop an advertisement showing how impersonal text messaging is as opposed to sending flowers, thereby attempting to lessen the impact of text messaging (a reduction).

BASIC RESEARCH

Research conducted to further the collective knowledge about a topic within a field of study.

APPLIED RESEARCH

Research conducted to solve a practical problem within a field of study.

INFLUENCE

The fourth goal is to *influence* behavior or mental processes.

YOU TRY IT!

In Chapter 1, we mentioned two ways in which we wanted to help you practice the material that is covered. One of the ways was through exercises called "You Try It!" Here is our first one. Don't worry if you struggle at first; you will get the feel for how to work through these exercises the more you do them.

Questions

We have just gone over the four goals of psychological research and presented them with a running example about text messaging. We would like you to try and apply each of these goals to a topic area in psychology. In this exercise, we will use the topic area of depression. Think about how researchers would investigate the topic of depression using the four goals of psychology, and answer the following questions.

(Continued)

1. For the first goal, what would be the research question? Explain what the researcher would hope to accomplish in terms of information gained on the topic of depression.

2. For the second goal, what would be the research question? Explain what the researcher would hope to accomplish in terms of information gained on the topic of depression.

3. For the third goal, what would be the research question? Explain what the researcher would hope to accomplish in terms of information gained on the topic of depression.

4. For the fourth goal, what would be the research question? Explain what the researcher would hope to accomplish in terms of information gained on the topic of depression.

Answers

Psychologists have been interested in clinical topics such as depression for many years. The information we know about depression has come via research using each of these four goals.

1. A researcher using the first goal would focus on the question, "What is depression?" The researcher would attempt to describe depression. This would include a definition and the ways to identify depression (i.e., symptoms). In psychology, this has been done by researchers and can be found in the *Diagnostic and Statistical Manual of Mental Disorder (DSM-IV-TR)*. Most college libraries have a copy of this manual and you might find it interesting to read about various disorders as they are described. The next revision to the manual (*DSM-V*) is scheduled to be published in 2012.

2. Researchers using the second goal would focus on the question, "Why do people get depressed?" Here, researchers would attempt to identify those situations that lead to depression, such as environmental/social situations (e.g., being homesick, being lonely), biological factors (e.g., a chemical imbalance in the brain), or other plausible explanations.

3. When looking at the third goal, researchers ask the question, "Where or when will people get depressed?" A researcher might predict that freshman college students are susceptible to depression because they have left home for the first time and may feel isolated. Understanding specific situations in which depression occurs will help researchers with goal four.

4. Researchers who engage in the last goal of influence ask the question, "How can I reduce depression?" In this area, therapies and drug treatments have been developed to alleviate or reduce the symptoms of depression. Again, you might find the manual to be informative as it provides information on common treatments for each disorder described.

As you were completing the You Try It exercise, your answers might have been similar to ours or a little different. As long as your answers addressed the correct question for each goal (e.g., what is going on? why is this happening? where will it happen? and how can I influence it?), you are on the right track.

Be sure to ask your professor if you have any concerns. As can be seen, the goals of research determine the direction your studies will take.

Now that we have practiced applying the goals of psychological research, let's return to the issue of basic and applied research. Although the distinction between the two types of research appears clear in the definitions provided earlier, distinguishing between the two can sometimes be problematic. In part, this is due to the fact that some research studies are both basic and applied in nature. Listed below are abstracts from recent issues of the journal *Psychological Science*. We would like for you to read each abstract. As you are reading the abstract, do not get overwhelmed with the details of the study. Rather, look for information that helps you determine if the nature of the study was basic (i.e., furthering collective knowledge on a topic), applied (i.e., solving practical problems), or both. After reading each abstract, we will discuss the appropriate categorization.

- Biederman, I., Yue, X., & Davidoff, J. (2009). Representation of shape in individuals from a culture with minimal exposure to regular, simple artifacts: Sensitivity to nonaccidental versus metric properties. *Psychological Science, 20*, 1437–1442.

  Many of the phenomena underlying shape recognition can be derived from the greater sensitivity to nonaccidental properties of an image (e.g., whether a contour is straight or curved), which are invariant to orientation in depth, than to the metric properties of an image (e.g., a contour's degree of curvature), which can vary with orientation. What enables this sensitivity? One explanation is that it derives from people's immersion in a manufactured world in which simple, regular shapes distinguished by nonaccidental properties abound (e.g., a can, a brick), and toddlers are encouraged to play with toy shape sorters. This report provides evidence against this explanation. The Himba, a seminomadic people living in a remote region of northwestern Namibia where there is little exposure to regular, simple artifacts, were virtually identical to Western observers in their greater sensitivity to nonaccidental properties than to metric properties of simple shapes.

  Category: Based on the information available in this abstract, you could argue that this research is basic in nature. This is because the goal of the research is to further our understanding of how individuals recognize shapes. In particular, the article focuses on how individuals from a culture with minimal exposure to simple artifacts compare to Western individuals in identifying shapes.

- Cowan, N. (2010). The magical mystery four: How is working memory capacity limited, and why? *Current Directions in Psychological Science, 19*, 51–57.

  Working memory storage capacity is important because cognitive tasks can be completed only with sufficient ability to hold information as it is processed. The ability to repeat information depends on task demands but can be distinguished from a more constant, underlying mechanism: a central memory store limited to 3 to 5 meaningful items for young adults. I discuss why this central limit is important, how it can be observed, how it differs among individuals, and why it may exist.

Category: This abstract would be categorized as basic research. The author discusses how the manuscript will describe and explain how working memory functions. In doing so, the manuscript meets the goals of basic research.

- Dye, M. W. G., Green, C. S., & Bavelier, D. (2009). Increasing speed of processing with action video games. *Current Directions in Psychological Science, 18,* 321–326.

In many everyday situations, speed is of the essence. However, fast decisions typically mean more mistakes. To this day, it remains unknown whether reaction times can be reduced with appropriate training, within one individual, across a range of tasks, and without compromising accuracy. Here we review evidence that the very act of playing action video games significantly reduces reaction times without sacrificing accuracy. Critically, this increase in speed is observed across various tasks beyond game situations. Video gaming may therefore provide an efficient training regimen to induce a general speeding of perceptual reaction times without decreases in accuracy of performance.

Category: This abstract might have been difficult to place into a category. That is because it is both basic and applied in nature. On the one hand, the research is basic in nature as it advances our understanding of speed of processing in many situations. On the other hand, it also addresses a practical problem. Specifically, is it possible to reduce your reaction time in a video game and not increase the number of mistakes? Thus, it is also applied in nature.

- Weis, R., & Cerankosky, B. C. (2010). Effects of video-game ownership on young boys' academic and behavioral functioning: A randomized, controlled study. *Psychological Science, 21,* 463–470.

Young boys who did not own video games were promised a video-game system and child-appropriate games in exchange for participating in an "ongoing study of child development." After baseline assessment of boys' academic achievement and parent and teacher-reported behavior, boys were randomly assigned to receive the video-game system immediately or to receive the video-game system after follow-up assessment, 4 months later. Boys who received the system immediately spent more time playing video games and less time engaged in after-school academic activities than comparison children. Boys who received the system immediately also had lower reading and writing scores and greater teacher-reported academic problems at follow-up than comparison children. Amount of video-game play mediated the relationship between video-game ownership and academic outcomes. Results provide experimental evidence that video games may displace after-school activities that have educational value and may interfere with the development of reading and writing skills in some children.

Category: This research addresses a current problem in society. The problem is the influence of video-game ownership on young adults. This is an example of applied research as it illustrates how video-game ownership influences academic and behavioral functioning in young boys.

- Zarkadi, T., Wade, K. A., & Stewart, N. (2009). Creating fair lineups for suspects with distinctive features. *Psychological Science, 20,* 1448–1453.

    In their descriptions, eyewitnesses often refer to a culprit's distinctive facial features. However, in a police lineup, selecting the only member with the described distinctive feature is unfair to the suspect and provides the police with little further information. For fair and informative lineups, the distinctive feature should be either replicated across foils or concealed on the target. In the present experiments, replication produced more correct identifications in target-present lineups—without increasing the incorrect identification of foils in target-absent lineups— than did concealment. This pattern, and only this pattern, is predicted by the hybrid-similarity model of recognition.

    Category: In this final abstract, we see another example of applied research. In this article, researchers are trying to understand the influence of lineups on eyewitnesses' abilities to identify suspects with distinctive features. By providing police offers with information on how to improve lineups, this research is solving a practical problem in our society.

We shared these examples with you to illustrate how current research can be conducted to further collective knowledge, solve practical problems, or, in some cases, accomplish both goals. This is the first time in the textbook that we have presented you with excerpts from published manuscripts. If you have little previous experience with reading published manuscripts in the field, this may have been challenging for you. However, we will practice this skill throughout the chapters so that your comfort level in reading journal articles will increase.

Section Summary

- There are four goals that psychologists have when conducting research (pp. 19–20).
    - The first goal is to *describe* behavior or mental processes. The question researchers ask is, "What is this?" (p. 19).
    - The second goal is to *explain* behavior or mental processes. The question researchers ask is, "What is going on?" (p. 19).

- ◆ The third goal is to *predict* behavior or mental processes. The question researchers ask is, "Where will this take place?" (p. 19).
  - ◆ The fourth goal is to *influence* behavior or mental processes. The questions researchers ask is, "How can I impact this?" (p. 20).
- ◆ The first three goals fall under *basic research*. Basic research is conducted to further the collective knowledge about a topic within a field of study (p. 20).
- ◆ The last goal falls under *applied research*. Applied research is conducted to solve a practical problem within a field of study (p. 20).

USE OF THE SCIENTIFIC METHOD—STEPS AND IMPORTANCE

In order to accomplish the goals of psychological research, psychologists have borrowed the scientific method from other fields. The scientific method provides a framework for the systematic study of behavior and mental processes. There are six steps in the scientific method that psychologists use when conducting research. The steps are: (a) problem identification, (b) hypothesis formation, (c) collection of data, (d) analysis of data, (e) conclusion, and (f) reporting of findings (Figure 2.2).

The first step in the scientific method is known as problem identification. Sometimes this is known as question identification. No matter what the title, this step involves identifying a topic to research, as well as doing an initial review of the literature to determine what previous research has been conducted on the topic. We will discuss further how to identify a topic of interest and conduct a literature review later on in Chapter 6. The second step in the scientific method is to formulate a hypothesis. A popular definition of a hypothesis is an educated guess. However, for the purposes of conducting research, that definition is not sufficient.

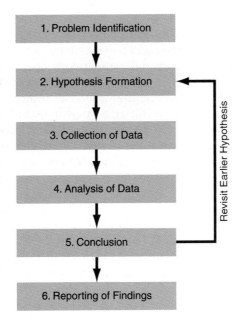

FIGURE 2.2   Steps of the Scientific Method.

HYPOTHESIS

A statement about the relationship between variables.

A more useful definition is that a **hypothesis** is a statement about the relationship between variables. When going through the scientific method, a researcher must develop a hypothesis. Typically, the hypothesis is derived from the first step after which a thorough review of information regarding the topic of interest has been completed. The hypothesis is also used to guide the next step in the scientific method, designing a study or experiment.

The third step is to collect data on your topic to test your hypothesis. To do this, researchers typically design an experiment or develop a study in which the variables of interest can be tested. One of the purposes of this textbook is to explain the types of research designs that can be used. The fourth step is to take the data collected and conduct data analysis. Data analysis involves the use of statistics. The results that the statistical analyses yield are used to guide the fifth step, conclusion. The fifth step is very important in the research process. This is the step where a researcher revisits the hypothesis. At this point, the researcher, using the results from the analysis of the data, will make a judgment about the hypothesis. Based on the results of the study, a researcher will then decide to either support or reject the earlier hypothesis. Interestingly, it is at this step that many researchers will reevaluate the hypothesis and research design. This reevaluation can lead the researcher to make changes to the study. If a change does occur, the steps in the scientific method are carried out again starting with Step 2. In essence, the fifth step allows for a feedback loop in the scientific method, giving researchers the opportunity to correct any problems discovered along the way.

The final step, although crucial, is often overlooked. This step is reporting your findings. To conduct the research is not enough. As a researcher, you must make sure the information you have learned from your experiment or study is disseminated. Keeping the information to yourself only hinders the advancement of the field. The manner in which you disseminate your research is also important. In particular, research must be shared in such a way that the experiment or study can be replicated. **Replication** occurs when a research experiment or study is reproduced using the exact methodology and procedure. Thus, when reporting findings, the procedure and methodology need to be clearly communicated, with no ambiguity. Failure to do so could result in conflicting information on a topic. However, if a study is communicated accurately and the researchers replicating the study find similar results, the original researchers can have greater confidence that the results are indeed true. It should be noted that, for the most part, research studies that find new results are typically published, while studies failing to add to the body of knowledge are not. Researchers prefer to publish their findings in what is known as peer-reviewed sources. This means that other scholars have reviewed the content of the manuscript and judged it to be worthy of publication and free from error.

REPLICATION

A research experiment or study that is reproduced using the exact methodology and procedure.

To further illustrate these steps applied to psychological research, let's look at an example. Recently, there has been a push for young females to receive the human papillomarivus (HPV) vaccine. This vaccine can prevent some types of cervical cancer and genital warts. This topic has received a lot of attention from the media, health-care providers, and parents alike regarding the risk of contracting HPV, which can lead to cervical cancer in females.

Cox, Cox, Sturm, and Zimet (2010) decided this was a worthy topic to research. In other words, they identified a problem (Step 1). After researching the topic further, Cox et al. developed several hypotheses (Step 2). For the purpose of this example, we will focus on their first hypothesis. This hypothesis stated that the graphic representation of risk statistics regarding HPV and cervical cancer in young women would increase mothers' intention to have their daughters vaccinated.

In order to test their hypothesis, Cox et al. (2010) developed an experiment in which they presented information on the risks of developing cervical cancer as a result of contracting HPV with and without graphical statistics to mothers of female children (Step 4). Upon the completion of the study, the researchers analyzed their results using several different statistical techniques. Interestingly, the researchers found that mothers who viewed the graphical message had significantly higher levels of intention to have their daughters vaccinated than those who did not view a graphical message. From these results, the researchers concluded that a graphical message used by health-care providers could lead to higher levels of HPV vaccination (Step 5). The last step is to report the findings (Step 6). This occurred given that we are sharing with you the published findings. In the future, another researcher will more than likely replicate this study to verify that the results obtained by Cox et al. are accurate.

When followed, the scientific method allows a researcher to systematically study a topic. It is this approach that psychologists follow when conducting research. Although this approach was borrowed over a hundred years ago, it still has an impact on science. The remainder of this textbook will provide you with the necessary tools to engage in the first three steps of the scientific method in psychology.

YOU TRY IT!

Questions

Using the information about the scientific method we have just discussed, answer the following questions about the research processes in the field of psychology.

1. A researcher is interested in determining if the racial makeup of an audience influences perceptions of humor. The researcher has conducted a review of previous research and has developed the hypothesis that audience racial makeup will influence perceptions of humor. Using the scientific method, what is the next step that needs to be taken by the researcher?

2. A group of undergraduate students are investigating whether the skills acquired when playing a real-world game are helpful when a simulated version of it is played as a video game. The students have hypothesized that taking a class in bowling will improve a person's skill and confidence level when playing bowling on the Nintendo Wii. The undergraduate researchers have designed a study and collected their data. However, they are now unsure of what to do. What is the next step that these undergraduates must take in the scientific method?

(Continued)

(Continued)

Answers

1. Once a researcher has decided on a topic, reviewed the relevant work on that topic, and developed a hypothesis, the researcher is ready to pursue the third step of the scientific method. In particular, this is the point where the researcher must develop a research design (i.e., an experiment or a study) and collect data to test the hypothesis.

2. In this example, the researchers have gone through the first three steps in the scientific method. This puts the researchers halfway through the steps in the scientific method. The next steps would be to analyze the data, draw conclusions, and report the findings.

Section Summary

- There are six steps in the scientific method that psychologists use when conducting research (pp. 25–26).
  - The steps are: (a) problem identification, (b) hypothesis formation, (c) collection of data, (d) analysis of data, (e) conclusion, and (f) reporting of findings.
    - The step of problem identification involves indentifying a topic of study and conducting an initial review of the work already done on the topic (p. 25).
    - The step of hypothesis formation involves the development of a hypothesis. A hypothesis is a statement about the relationship between variables (p. 26).
    - The third step involves data collection. Data collection occurs through the design of an experiment or development of a study in which the variables of interest can be tested (p. 26).
    - The fourth step of data analysis involves using statistics to analyze the data collected in the previous step (p. 26).
    - The fifth step involves drawing conclusions about the data that were collected and analyzed. It is in this step that many will revisit their original hypothesis to make any changes that are necessary (p. 26).
    - The final step involves the dissemination of the findings. This allows others to confirm or disprove the findings of the study (p. 26).

THE RESEARCH PROCESS

Before concluding this chapter, we have two more things that we would like to discuss. Earlier, we mentioned the term "hypothesis" when explaining the scientific method. We defined a hypothesis as a statement about the relationship between two or more variables. However, the tricky part to a hypothesis is developing one. A hypothesis has to be worded in such a way that it can be tested.

For example, a researcher would never have a hypothesis such as, "Religious groups are moral." This hypothesis is not testable. In this case, the question is of morality and how that is defined is determined by the individual.

However, a researcher could have a hypothesis such as, "Members of religious groups consider themselves to be moral." Now, the question is not whether religious groups are moral. Rather, the question is whether those in religious groups believe they are moral. This can be tested. We will discuss hypothesis generation in detail in Chapter 6.

The other concept that we want to mention before closing the chapter is that of a **theory.** A theory is an overarching principle that explains separate research findings in an area. After researchers have produced consistent findings on a topic, psychologists need to propose a theory that will account for those findings. Specifically, a theory uses a set of interrelated concepts to explain a large body of findings on a topic which will then be used to make future predictions about the topic.

THEORY

An overarching principle that explains separate research findings in an area.

For example, in the area of media research, researchers have consistently shown that (a) people who watch a lot of TV think that the world is more crime-ridden than it really is and (b) the more TV you watch, the more your political views reflect the mainstream. A theory known as the "cultivation theory" was proposed to account for these separate findings (Gerbner & Gross, 1976). Cultivation theory states that after repeated exposure to media, one's worldviews are shaped and changed. This would account for each of the aforementioned separate findings about media exposure and can be tested with future research.

As researchers, we look not only to create theories but also to disprove them. Attempts to disprove theories typically yield two outcomes, both of which are positive for researchers. First, if a theory is disproven, then the scientific community will discard it and work to create a new and improved theory that will benefit all researchers. Second, when researchers attempt to disprove a theory and fail, they are strengthening the likelihood that the theory is good. This is beneficial in that when a theory stands up to scrutiny, the validity of the theory becomes stronger.

Section Summary

- A hypothesis must be worded in such a way that it can be tested. Hypotheses are not worded using ambiguous language (p. 28).
- A theory is an overarching principle that explains separate research findings in an area (p. 29).
- A theory is more difficult to develop than a hypothesis (p. 29).

Are You Equipped Now?

Recently, a study was conducted at the Scripps Research Institute to evaluate compulsive eating behaviors that can lead to obesity. Researchers Johnson and Kenny (2010) conducted an experiment with two goals in mind. The first goal was to describe how the processes of obesity and drug addiction are similar, and the second goal was to explain how the process occurred. In order to achieve these goals, Kenny and Johnson fed one group of rats a high-calorie, high-fat diet consisting mainly of human junk food, whereas the other group of rats was given healthier diets. Once the junk food was removed, the rats receiving the high-calorie, high-fat diets simply refused the healthier diet. In fact, those rats would choose to eat junk food over healthy food even if they anticipated receiving an electrical shock. For the researchers, the willingness to receive shock indicated the levels of desirability in the rats to consume an unhealthy diet.

The researchers explained that the mechanism in the brain for pleasure becomes overstimulated with the junk food to the point that the pleasure activity is decreased. This decrease is due to the junk food acting as a substitute. However, with this decrease in brain pleasure activity, the rats begin to eat more junk food to compensate, leading to the rats gradually becoming obese. Kenny and Johnson showed that this is similar to the way that drug addiction occurs in humans, with the decrease in brain pleasure activity being supplemented by the increase in drug consumption. The researchers reported that like drugs, high-calorie, high-fat food diets may lead to increased levels of addiction and obesity.

Questions

1. Can you identify the psychological goal(s) that the researchers are investigating in their study?
2. What step are the researchers currently taking in the scientific method? And, what steps in the scientific method should come next?

Answers

1. For this particular study, there are two goals that are being addressed. The first is the goal of *describe*. Specifically, the researchers are describing the effects of a high-calorie, high-fat diet and the impacts of overeating and obesity. This is done by observing the rats that consumed the healthy and unhealthy food options. Second, the goal of *explain* is being addressed. Once the researchers have described the behavior they witnessed in their experiment, they sought to explain it. Specifically, the researchers were able to show that the same brain areas that are impacted by drug addiction are also affected with a high-calorie, high-fat diet. Therefore, the researchers explained that unhealthy (i.e., junk food) diets can lead to addiction problems similar to those in drug addicts.

2. The researchers are currently on the last step of the scientific method. They have conducted all the other steps including problem identification, hypothesis formation, collection of data, analysis of data, and conclusion. The researchers have now reported their findings. Therefore, other researchers can replicate the experiment to see if similar results are achieved.

Chapter Summary

- There are four goals that psychologists have when conducting research (pp. 19–20).
    - The first goal is to *describe* behavior or mental processes. The question researchers ask is, "What is this?" (p. 19).
    - The second goal is to *explain* behavior or mental processes. The question researchers ask is, "What is going on?" (p. 19).
    - The third goal is to *predict* behavior or mental processes. The question researchers ask is, "Where will this take place?" (p. 19).
    - The fourth goal is to *influence* behavior or mental processes. The question researchers ask is, "How can I impact this?" (p. 20).

- The first three goals fall under *basic research*. Basic research is conducted to further the collective knowledge about a topic within a field of study (p. 20).
- The last goal falls under *applied research*. Applied research is conducted to solve a practical problem within a field of study (p. 20).
- There are six steps in the scientific method that psychologists use when conducting research. They are: (a) problem identification, (b) hypothesis formation, (c) collection of data, (d) analysis of data, (e) conclusion, and (f) reporting of findings (pp. 25–26).
    - The first step of problem identification involves indentifying a topic of study and conducting an initial review of the work already done on the topic (p. 25).
    - The second step of hypothesis formation involves the development of a hypothesis. A *hypothesis* is a statement about the relationship between variables (p. 26).
    - The third step involves data collection. Data collection occurs through the design of an experiment or development of a study in which the variables of interest can be tested (p. 26).
    - The fourth step of data analysis involves using statistics to analyze the data collected in the previous step (p. 26).
    - The fifth step involves drawing conclusions about the data that were collected and analyzed. It is in this step that many will revisit their original hypothesis to make any changes that are necessary (p. 26).
    - The final step involves the dissemination of the findings. This allows others to confirm or disprove the findings of the study (p. 26).
- A hypothesis must be worded in such a way that it can be tested. Hypotheses are not worded using ambiguous language (p. 28).
- A theory is an overarching principle that explains separate research findings in an area (p. 29).
- A theory is more difficult to develop than a hypothesis (p. 29).

APA Learning Goals Linkage

- **Goal 1. *Knowledge Base of Psychology***
  Students will demonstrate familiarity with the major concepts, theoretical perspectives, empirical findings, and historical trends in psychology.

    Sections Covered: Goals of Psychological Research, Use of the Scientific Method, The Research Process

    Explanation of the Goal: In this chapter, we have identified and explained the primary goals of psychology, which are to describe, explain, predict, and influence behavior and mental processes. We have also discussed major concepts in the field such as basic research, applied research, and theory. Finally, we continued our discussion from Chapter 1 regarding why psychology is a science through learning the steps of the scientific method.

(Continued)

(Continued)

- **Goal 2.** *Research Methods in Psychology*
  Students will understand and apply basic research methods in psychology, including research design, data analysis, and interpretation.

  Sections Covered: Goals of Psychological Research, The Research Process

  Explanation of the Goal: It is important to be able to describe how various research methods address different types of questions. We began to develop this skill through examining how the goals of the research influence the type of research question formed. While learning the steps of the scientific method, we introduced the idea of replication. As psychologists, we must be cautious in predicting behavior from a single study. However, as findings are replicated, we can become more confident in our predictions.

- **Goal 3.** *Critical Thinking Skills in Psychology*
  Students will respect and use critical and creative thinking, skeptical inquiry, and, when possible, the scientific approach to solve problems related to behavior and mental processes.

  Sections Covered: Goals of Psychological Research, Use of the Scientific Method

  Explanation of the Goal: We expanded our critical thinking skills by learning to apply the scientific approach to solve problems related to behavior and mental processes. You also completed numerous exercises that required you to think critically. These included forming research questions for each goal in psychological research, identifying basic and applied research, and determining what step is needed next to complete the scientific method.

- **Goal 4.** *Application of Psychology*
  Students will understand and apply psychological principles to personal, social, and organizational issues.

  Sections Covered: Are You Equipped, Goals of Psychological Research, Use of the Scientific Method, Are You Equipped Now?

  Explanation of the Goal: We have applied topics from psychology to numerous personal and social issues in this chapter. These topics include subliminal advertising, the effects of video-game ownership, creating fair police lineups, decisions to receive the HPV vaccine, and addictions.

Ethics

CHAPTER OUTLINE

Are You Equipped?

Back in the 1950s, researchers wanted to better understand how members of a jury reached a verdict. In particular, the researchers wanted to know if the behavior of the attorneys influenced how jury members thought about the case. The researchers needed to be able to listen to a jury deliberate but without the members of the jury knowing their conversations were being heard. This was an important aspect to control because jury members might change what they were saying if they knew other individuals were listening.

The researchers set about conducting the study by obtaining permission from the judge and both attorneys to record the deliberations. However, the jury members were not informed that the discussions were being recorded. After the trial had ended, information regarding the research became known to the public through presentation of the research at a professional conference. The news that the researchers had recorded conversations without obtaining permission (consent) from the jury members caused many people to become upset. Although the researchers had good intentions, people were concerned that this event might influence the integrity of the system in future cases. More specifically, future jury members might be reserved and less willing to speak their minds, knowing that their conversation might be on tape. Shortly thereafter, a law was passed by U.S. Congress preventing jury deliberations from being recorded. If you would like to know more about this study, known as the Wichita Jury Study, please refer to Amdur (2003) and the website of the Drug Institute (*www.drugstudy.md/resource3.html*).

This study helped shape the way we conduct research today. The researchers were interested in a very valid research question and the results had the potential to advance our knowledge within the field. However, does this potential knowledge give researchers the right to not inform individuals of their participation in an experiment? In this chapter, we will discuss ethical questions just like this one. Although there are now federal guidelines to help protect research participants, psychologists and social scientists still face situations where the answer is not always clear. For example, is it acceptable to use deception if there is no other feasible way to conduct a study? By the end of this chapter, we want you to be informed of your rights as a participant in research and as a consumer of research. In addition, we want you to know how to conduct experiments that meet ethical guidelines. Let's begin!

As you go through this chapter, we also want you to keep in mind how the material relates to the APA goals for psychology majors. Specifically, this chapter will address the following goals:

- **Goal 1. Knowledge Base of Psychology**
  Students will demonstrate familiarity with the major concepts, theoretical perspectives, empirical findings, and historical trends in psychology.
- **Goal 2. Research Methods in Psychology**
  Students will understand and apply basic research methods in psychology, including research design, data analysis, and interpretation.
- **Goal 3. Critical Thinking Skills in Psychology**
  Students will respect and use critical and creative thinking, skeptical inquiry, and, when possible, the scientific approach to solve problems related to behavior and mental processes.
- **Goal 4. Application of Psychology**
  Students will understand and apply psychological principles to personal, social, and organizational issues.
- **Goal 5. Values in Psychology**
  Students will be able to weigh evidence, tolerate ambiguity, act ethically, and reflect other values that are the underpinnings of psychology as a discipline.
- **Goal 8. Sociocultural and International Awareness**
  Students will recognize, understand, and respect the complexity of sociocultural and international diversity.

CONSUMERS OF RESEARCH

When our oldest daughter was in first grade, we went to her elementary school for a parent–teacher conference. In addition to discussing our daughter's progress, we were given a survey to complete. Our daughter's teacher did a great job of conveying to us that a teacher at another school in our school district was currently working on his or her master's degree and the survey was part of the work. Our daughter's teacher also emphasized that completing the survey was voluntary. We nodded our heads to indicate we understood and took the survey home. That evening we sat down to complete the survey. Having gone through the process of conducting research for our degrees, we wanted to be as helpful as possible. The survey was on the topic of students wearing uniforms and the resulting behavior in the school. The questionnaire required us to share our current feelings about the elementary school and how uniforms might help improve behavior. This placed us in a difficult situation. We had candid opinions to share. However, the way the surveys were to be returned was not anonymous. In fact, the surveys were to be returned in our daughter's homeroom folder so our responses could be easily identified. Furthermore, the survey was not accompanied by a consent form. This meant that we had no way of knowing how the confidentially of our responses would be maintained. We have both served on Institutional Review Boards (IRBs), which we will discuss in this chapter, so we found it strange that a survey requiring us to divulge such opinions would not have guidelines to protect our rights. Although we completed the survey, Jenn placed a note on the back indicating that a consent form or debriefing statement explaining how the responses would be shared with the school administrators and how our responses would be protected should have been included.

You might think that we overreacted to this situation. However, research participants should not fear that their responses can be identified or used against them by a governing body. As a consumer of research, you should be aware of the federal guidelines that protect you. In this chapter, we will tell you about these federal guidelines and also guidelines developed especially for psychologists by the APA.

Institutional Review Board

An Institutional Review Board (IRB) is a committee that reviews proposals of intended research and evaluates if the research is ethical and if the rights of the participants are being protected. Although colleges and universities have IRBs which review all research conducted on campus, IRBs are not relegated to only the academic world. They can also be found in hospitals and the corporate world. IRBs are a relatively new entity and have been developed, in part, because of past research that could be considered unethical. The Wichita Jury Study from the beginning of this chapter was one research study that led the government to intervene in how research is conducted. However, the Wichita Jury Study was not the only study that prompted the formation of IRBs. Amdur (2003) provides a listing of other questionable research that played a role. Some examples include the research conducted by Nazi leaders in concentration camps, the administration of a drug called thalidomide to pregnant women without informing the women the drug was in an experimental testing stage, and injecting hepatitis into mentally impaired children who were residents of a state school.

You probably noticed that the previous examples of questionable research are not just from the social sciences. Rather, the examples are from many areas of inquiry. This chain of events prompted the government in 1974 to pass the National Research Act, which established the IRB system and formed a commission to protect participants of research. This commission developed a report known as the Belmont Report in the late 1970s, which outlined three principles that should be used by the IRB. The three principles are respect, beneficence, and justice. These three principles are used by committee members to evaluate the research that is being proposed in terms of informed consent, assessment of risk/benefit, and selection of participants. If you plan to conduct research at your college or university, you will be required to go through IRB. This means that you will outline your research and present it to the IRB committee. The committee will evaluate your proposed research on the principles above. Most universities have a standard form that you will need to use. If your university does not provide a standard format for you, ask the faculty member you are working with to provide you a sample from his or her previous research. Once you have practiced completing the forms, it is a rather simple task.

It is not uncommon for IRBs to take special precautions with certain groups of participants. If you plan to conduct research with minors (under the age of 18), prisoners, the mentally impaired, or pregnant women, you can expect the IRB to require you to describe how you will protect the rights of your participants. Using these populations might also involve additional steps in the research process. For example, several of our colleagues have investigated gender roles and career development in preschool children from a local church day care. Even before data collection, the researchers had to secure permission from the child-care advisory board of the church, teachers, and parents.

Now that we have given you some background information on the establishment of today's IRB system, we would like to switch gears and discuss the topic of ethics and research with respect to the standards provided by the APA. If you have questions right now about informed consent, assessment of risk/benefit, and selection of participants, they will be answered in the next section.

YOU TRY IT!

Questions

1. Think about the Wichita Jury Study. In your opinion, what were some of the potential benefits to society from conducting the study?

2. In addition to the one mentioned, what were some of the risks to participants who were involved with the study?

3. Do you think that the benefits to society outweighed the individual risks to participants?

Answers

1. For this You Try It section there are really no right or wrong answers. We just wanted you to get practice thinking about research projects in terms that the IRB uses. One benefit to the Wichita Study would be to see how a lawyer can influence jury members and thus the verdict on a case. Understanding how juries make decisions (and the role the lawyer plays in that decision) is very important information.

2. We had already mentioned that this study might prevent future jury members from speaking freely. However, there could have been potential risks for individuals in the study as well. It is possible that the individuals could have been identified by their voices and confronted by others regarding the content of the deliberations. In a worst case scenario, a convicted criminal might try and seek revenge on jury

(Continued)

members or their families. A researcher must consider all foreseeable risks and describe these to the IRB.

3. This is a tough question. It is not easy to decide if the benefits gained from a study are greater than the possible risks to participants. However, this is the job of the members of the IRB. The Belmont Report acknowledges this difficult situation and stresses that a study should be designed to minimize such risks. Researchers can aid the IRB committee by explicitly stating how risks are minimized and the importance of the findings to the scientific community.

Section Summary

- The Institutional Review Board (IRB) is a committee which reviews proposals of intended research to determine if the research is ethical and that the rights of the participants are being protected (p. 35).
- IRBs can be found on university campuses, hospitals, and in many corporations where research on human participants is conducted (p. 35).
- IRBs are a result of government intervention in 1974 via the National Research Act (p. 35).
    - This commission developed the Belmont Report, which outlined three guiding principles for human participant research: respect, benefits, and justice (pp. 35–36).

APA'S ETHICS CODE

APA developed an ethics code (most recently revised in 2010) to guide psychologists in their professional work. For our purposes, we will focus on the ethical standard related to research and publication. The ethical standard related to research is 8.0 and it contains 15 guidelines. As we discuss each of these guidelines, please see the accompanying table for a summary.

- **8.01 *Institutional Approval.*** The first guideline for psychologists conducting research is that they secure permission from the institution (usually a college or university) before conducting their research. This institutional approval is typically given after going through the IRB process we just described. It is very important that psychologists obtain permission from their university before conducting any research and not after the fact. It should also be noted that APA expects psychologists to conduct the research as outlined in the proposal to the university. If, for some reason, the research procedure needs to be modified during the experiment, the psychologist needs to contact the university and go through the proper steps to have the modified procedure approved.

- **8.02 *Informed Consent.*** Before participating in a research study, participants are given an informed consent (commonly referred to as a consent form). APA requires that the consent form address specific topics.

- To begin, your consent form should tell participants information about the research being conducted. It should also give the participants an estimate of how long it will take them to participate and a brief overview of what they will be required to do.

- The consent form should clearly inform participants that they do not have to participate in the study. This means that participation in the research is voluntary. Participants should also be told that they may stop, withdraw, from the study at any point. This includes withdrawing participation even after the study has started.

- If there are consequences to not participating or withdrawing from the study, these should be explained to the participant.

- Any potential risks of participating (if there are any) and research benefits should be stated.

- It should be made clear to participants if their responses are anonymous or confidential. Oftentimes, researchers and participants confuse these two concepts. When a study is anonymous, the researcher has ensured that no identifying information is gathered and participants cannot be identified once the study is concluded. If a study is confidential, the participants can be identified by information that is gathered. However, this information is kept in a manner that participant responses are not shared with others and the participants cannot be identified. Finally, if there are limits to the confidentiality, the limits should be addressed.

- When incentives are offered for participation such as a monetary compensation, the incentives should be explained.

- Finally, the consent form should close with information on how participants can contact the researcher(s) if they have questions.

Jenn is currently collaborating with a colleague on Facebook usage and unwanted pursuit. Her colleague, Dr. Amy Lyndon, used the consent form below when gathering data at her institution. You will notice that Dr. Lyndon's consent form addresses the specific topics required by APA. In addition, her consent form is written in simple language that college freshmen will most likely understand.

Sample Consent Form

Psychologists at the university study problems in society, health problems, environmental problems, behavior problems, and the human condition. Our goal is to try to find ways to improve the lives of you and others. To do this, we need the help of people who are willing to take part in research. The person who is in charge of this research is called the Principal Investigator. The Principal Investigator may have other research staff members who will perform some of the procedures. You may have questions that this form does not answer. If you do, feel free to contact the person explaining the study. You may have questions later and you should ask those questions. There is no time limit for asking questions about this research. You do not have to take part in this research. Take your time and think about the information that

(Continued)

is provided. If you want, have a friend or family member go over this form with you before you decide. It is up to you. If you choose to be in the study, then you participate when you are comfortable that you understand the information provided. If you do not want to take part in the study, you should not. That decision is yours and it is okay to decide not to volunteer.

- Why is this research being done?

  The purpose of this research is to learn more about how people use Facebook in romantic relationships, and to learn what relationship characteristics predict that and the behavior of unwanted pursuit. The decision to take part in this research is yours to make. By doing this research, we hope to learn more about these relationships.

- Why am I being invited to take part in this research?

  If you volunteer to take part in this research, you will be one of about 300 people to do so.

- Are there reasons I should not take part in this research?

  Participants should be those people who have either been in a committed romantic relationship in the past or are currently in one. If you have never been in a committed romantic relationship, then you should not take this survey. There are no other restrictions.

- What other choices do I have if I do not take part in this research?

  You have the choice of not taking part in this research study. You may earn your research credits through answering questions about research articles as described in your Psychology class. You may talk about this alternative with other people.

- Where is the research going to take place and how long will it last?

  The research procedures will be conducted online. The total amount of time you will be asked to volunteer for this study is 30 minutes.

- What will I be asked to do?

  You will be asked to do the following: Answer questions about your usage of Facebook, questions about your personality and relationship types, and questions about unwanted pursuit in an online survey.

- What possible harms or discomforts might I experience if I take part in the research?

  There are always risks (the chance of harm) when taking part in research. It has been determined that the risks associated with this research are no more than what you would experience in a normal life. However, some people react to things differently so it is important for you to tell us as quickly as possible if you experience any negative feelings. You can contact Dr. Amy Lyndon by calling XXX-XXXX or e-mailing at xxx@xxx.edu.

- Are there any reasons you might take me out of the research?

  During the study, information about this research may become available that would be important to you. This includes information that, once learned, might cause you to change your mind about wanting to be in the study. If this occurs, you may stop participating by not answering any more questions and closing your Internet browser.

- What are the possible benefits I may experience from taking part in this research?

  We do not know if you will get any benefits by taking part in this study. This research might help us learn more about how people are using Facebook in their romantic relationships and whether that is related to personality characteristics

(Continued)

(Continued)

and relationship pursuit. There may be no personal benefit from your participation but the information gained by doing this research may help others in the future.

- Who will know that I took part in this research and learn personal information about me?

  No one will be able to connect your responses to your name. Your responses will be saved on a secure and password-protected server and computers of the researchers. Scientific reports will be based on group data and will not identify you or any individual as being in this project.

  With your permission, the following people may use your private—but anonymous—information to do this research:

  The University & Medical Center Institutional Review Board (UMCIRB) and its staff, who have responsibility for overseeing your welfare during this research, and other staff at the university who oversee this research. Dr. Amy Lyndon, Psychology Department and trained research assistants.

- How will you keep the information you collect about me secure? How long will you keep it?

  Your responses will be downloaded onto a secure server and saved onto password-protected computers. This information will be kept for five years after they have been used anonymously in publication of research reports.

- What if I decide I do not want to continue in this research?

  If you decide you no longer want to be in this research after it has already started, you may stop at any time. You will not be penalized or criticized for stopping. You will not lose any benefits that you should normally receive.

- Who should I contact if I have questions?

  The people conducting this study will be available to answer any questions concerning this research, now or in the future. You may contact the Principal Investigator (Dr. Amy Lyndon) at this email address xxx@xxx.edu or at XXX-XXXX. If you have questions about your rights as someone taking part in research, you may call the UMCIRB Office at phone number XXX-XXX-XXXX (days, 8:00 am–5:00 pm). If you would like to report a complaint or concern about this research study, you may call the Director of UMCIRB Office, at XXX-XXX-XXXX.

- Is there anything else I should know?

  You may wish to take note of your surroundings to insure privacy as you take this online survey. When you finish the survey, you should close the browser (e.g., Internet Explorer).

- I have decided I want to take part in this research. What should I do now?

  Read the statements below and if you agree to participate in this research, click the button below to proceed to the survey. This indicates that you have given your consent.

  - I have read (or had read to me) all of the above information.
  - I have had an opportunity to ask questions about things in this research I did not understand and have received satisfactory answers.
  - I understand that I can stop taking part in this study at any time.
  - By clicking "proceed," which indicates consent, I know that I am not giving up any of my rights.
  - I may print out a copy of this consent document, which is mine to keep.

Source: Lyndon and Dutton, 2010.

Guideline 8.02 of the ethics code also provides guidelines for research that involves an experimental and control group. This section is primarily written for research involving drug or therapeutic treatments and therefore is not usually needed by undergraduates conducting research.

- **8.03 *Informed Consent for Recording Voices and Images in Research.*** This guideline explains to psychologists that participants' permission to be recorded must be obtained prior to data collection. The only exceptions to this guideline are if the recordings take place in a naturalistic observation or psychologists are using deception and permission will be obtained at the conclusion of the study.

- **8.04 *Client/Patient, Student, and Subordinate Research Participants.*** Sometimes it occurs that a client, student, or research assistant is recruited to participate in a research study. If this situation occurs, it is the psychologist's responsibility to protect the participant from negative consequences should the participant decide not to participate or terminate participation once the study has started. Also, psychologists must offer alternative activities to research participation if it is required for a class or offered as extra credit in a class.

YOU TRY IT!

Tiffany is a new faculty member at a state college. She has designed a research study and is ready to collect data. Furthermore, she would like to provide students who are enrolled in her class the opportunity to participate in the study for extra credit. Based on what you know thus far about APA's ethical guidelines for research, answer the following questions:

1. What should Tiffany do before she collects any data?

2. What information can you tell Tiffany about allowing her students to participate in the study for extra credit?

Answers

1. Before Tiffany begins the data collection process, it is important that she check to see if her state college requires institutional approval. If it does (and it more than likely will), Tiffany will need to complete the IRB process.

2. You could tell Tiffany that the APA ethics code does permit her to allow students in her classes to participate for extra credit. However, because the potential participants are currently enrolled in her class, Tiffany will need to protect the students from negative consequences if they decide not to participate or to withdraw. In addition, Tiffany must provide students in her class an alternative to the research study should they decide not to participate.

- **8.05 *Dispensing with Informed Consent for Research.*** There are some situations in which APA does not require informed consent. Please note that even if APA does not require informed consent in specific situations, an institution still may, and thus you will need to follow your institution's guidelines. See the table containing the ethical standards to learn more about specific situations when informed consent can be dispensed with.

- **8.06** *Offering Inducements for Research Participation.*   It is not uncommon for psychologists to offer inducements for research participation. The most common inducement is financial. But, it is important that the inducement or financial compensation is equivalent to the amount of effort put forth by the participant. For example, if researchers offer an excessive amount of cash to participate in a study, the participants might feel coerced to participate and this situation should be avoided. This ethical guideline also provides information on how to use psychological services as inducement. Since undergraduates typically do not do so in their studies, we will not go into more detail on this caveat.

- **8.07** *Deception in Research.*   Deception in research can occur in two ways, either as active deception or as passive deception. Active deception is deception by commission. In particular, this is deception that occurs when a researcher deliberately misleads the participant. This can happen when a researcher gives participants false information or when a researcher embeds a confederate into a study. A **confederate** is a participant in the study but is also part of the research team. Confederates' participation is meant to influence other participants who are not members of the research team. In the famous study on conformity conducted by Asch (1951), he used confederates alongside participants to influence behavior. Specifically, Asch had confederates respond incorrectly to questions to see if "real" participants would conform to the incorrect answers. Here, Asch actively deceived the participants to gain results for his study.

  The other type of deception is passive deception. Passive deception is deception by omission. This type of deception occurs when a researcher withholds information about the nature of a study from the participants. For example, sometimes psychologists are prevented from explaining fully the purpose of their research design at the onset of a study. Doing so might change the way participants respond in the study. This occurs many times when researchers attempt to study concepts where participants are less likely to disclose their true behavior (e.g., cheating instances).

  The topic of deception is continually debated to this day. Specifically, researchers and others have debated whether deception is helpful or harmful in research. APA states that psychologists may use deception in research if it is needed to study a particular topic and if its use is justified by the knowledge gained. When deception is used, participants should be told about the deception as soon as possible and it should be clearly explained why this method was used and the anticipated benefits should be clearly explained. Participants are given the opportunity to withdraw their data if desired. Although deception is permitted in special cases, APA has made it clear that psychologists are not allowed to deceive participants with regard to physical or emotional pain.

- **8.08** *Debriefing.*   We will never forget the first time Jenn told an undergraduate assistant that he or she needed to "debrief" the participants, and the assistant thought she meant to take their underwear off. Fortunately, the assistant asked for clarification before following instructions! In general, you want to provide participants with information about the study

CONFEDERATE

A participant in a study but is also part of the research team. The participation of confederates is meant to influence other participants.

immediately after the data are collected. If the results are not yet available, you can provide participants with the contact information of the researcher so the participants can learn of the findings when they are prepared. Sometimes it is necessary to withhold a debriefing until all participants have completed the study. If this situation occurs, psychologists must be sure to reduce the risk of harm to the participants. It is also important that if psychologists know that a participant has been harmed during the study (either physically or emotionally) that they immediately try to minimize the harm.

• **8.09 *Humane Care and Use of Animals in Research.*** Psychologists who conduct research with animals have additional government policies to be aware of than those we discussed for humans earlier in this chapter. The purpose of this section is not to provide a detailed account of policies with animals. However, you should be aware that in addition to the APA guidelines, animal researchers also must follow local, state, and federal guidelines. If you are interested in learning more about research with animals, you can visit the website for the Institutional Animal Care and Use Committee (IACUC): *www.unmc.edu/iacuc*.

The APA requires that psychologists first meet all government laws and standards with animal research. Furthermore, APA states that psychologists trained in research methods and with experience working with lab animals are responsible for caring for the animals and training assistants to care for the animals. In addition, animal pain should be minimized and procedures involving pain to animals are only used when other methods are not feasible. If pain is to occur, the result should greatly advance scientific knowledge and the study should be conducted with the use of anesthesia and postsurgery care. If an animal's life needs to be terminated, psychologists are required to again minimize pain and follow current government policies.

Research using animals has been controversial for many years. People can fall into one of two categories when discussing animals in research. The first group are the animal rights activists. These individuals assert that animals are no different from humans and should be given the same rights. Typically, these individuals do not support animal research in any form. The second group are the animal welfare activists. The animal welfare activists believe that animal research is necessary but should be conducted in the most humane manner as possible. It is more common that researchers who work with animals subscribe to the animal welfare activist point of view.

YOU TRY IT!

A former student once conducted a study to examine the relationship between ethnicity, faculty mentorship, and co-curricular activities. The student was interested in determining if students of different ethnicities were equally likely to have a faculty mentor and be involved in campus activities. The debriefing statement that the student used is given below. Why did the student provide information about when the results would be complete?

Thank you for participating in this experiment. The purpose of this experiment was to see whether a difference existed among ethnicities when it comes to commitment to

(Continued)

(Continued)

ethnicity, faculty mentorship, and co-curricular activities. Specifically, we were interested in how individuals among various ethnicities experienced on-campus activities, and if they had a faculty advisor.

If you would like to know the results from this experiment, we would be happy to provide you with a copy of them. No names or identifying information would be on the results. Rather, it will provide you only with information as to the differences among ethnicities and their involvement with campus activities and faculty mentorship. Results are typically ready to share with the public in about 10 to 12 months. Please let me know if this is something you would like to have.

If any questions or concerns arise about the experiment you participated in, please feel free to contact me Student A at XXX-XXX-XXXX or Dr. Smith at XXX-XXX-XXXX. Once again thank you for participating.

Answer

The student was following the APA ethical standard regarding debriefing. After explaining to participants the purpose of her study, she gave participants the opportunity to learn of the results. This is important because some participants may be interested in the topics covered in a research study and appreciate the chance to hear the findings.

- **8.10 Reporting Research Results.**   The ethical guidelines that we have discussed up to this point (8.01–8.09) were provided for psychologists conducting research. The remaining ethical guidelines (8.10–8.15) are provided to guide psychologists during the publication process. To begin, psychologists do not make up data. This is known as fabricating data. In addition, once results have been published, psychologists correct any errors that are found later through reasonable means.

- **8.11 Plagiarism.**   We will talk more extensively about plagiarism in the chapter on writing in APA style. For now, we want to mention that this ethical guideline tells psychologists to not plagiarize. This means not presenting the work of others as your own work.

- **8.12 Publication Credit.**   It is important that authorship is given to individuals based on their contributions to the study. This means that rank, position, or status does not equal authorship. When faculty members and students work together on projects, authorship should be discussed as soon as possible and reevaluated when needed.

- **8.13 Duplicate Publication of Data.**   Typically, psychologists publish data only one time. However, sometimes data can be republished or cross-published. This process is acceptable as long as it is clearly documented. For example, a colleague was invited to submit an expert commentary to an edited book and was later asked by the same publishers to cross-publish the commentary in one of their journals. This colleague denotes on her resume (known as a vita) that the journal publication is a cross-publication from the edited book.

- **8.14 Sharing Research Data for Verification.**   When psychologists publish data, they should share the data with other professionals if such a request is made for verification purposes. Psychologists can request published data only for the purpose of reanalysis and are responsible for any cost associated with the process.

- *8.15 Reviewers.*   When psychologists complete their research, they typically submit the research for publication. During the publication process, professionals in the field (reviewers) will review the work to ensure it is ready for publication. Those serving as reviewers are expected to respect confidentiality. In addition, reviewers are not to steal the work of others.

We hope that you have seen in this chapter how the IRB process and APA's ethical guidelines work together. It is important to remember that as psychologists we must be aware of and consult APA's ethical guidelines. However, this does not mean that we have the right to ignore any additional information or steps required by the IRB. Conversely, if APA requires steps that the IRB does not, we still need to follow them. For example, at our previous institution, the IRB does not require a debriefing statement. However, the APA does. In this situation, we are required to go above the basic requirements of the IRB and also prepare a debriefing statement. If a situation arises where the IRB and APA's ethical guidelines are in conflict (what we described above is not a conflict), you should make known your commitment to the ethics code but in the end obey any state and federal laws. Both the IRB process and the APA ethical guidelines are designed with you in mind. Your rights as a participant and your rights as a researcher are better protected with these regulations in place.

Section Summary

- The APA began developing an ethics code in 1949. The most recent version of the code was published in 2010 (p. 37).
- Within the APA ethics code there is a section for ethics in research. This is section 8.0 of the ethics code. This section contains 15 guidelines for ethical research (p. 37).
    - 8.01 Institutional Approval (p. 37).
    - 8.02 Informed Consent (pp. 37–41).
    - 8.03 Informed Consent for Recording Voices and Images in Research (p. 41).
    - 8.04 Client/Patient, Student, and Subordinate Research Participants (p. 41).
    - 8.05 Dispensing with Informed Consent for Research (p. 41).
    - 8.06 Offering Inducements for Research Participation (p. 42).
    - 8.07 Deception in Research (p. 42).
    - 8.08 Debriefing (pp. 43–44).
    - 8.09 Humane Care and Use of Animals in Research (p. 44).
    - 8.10 Reporting Research Results (p. 44).
    - 8.11 Plagiarism (p. 44).
    - 8.12 Publication Credit (p. 44).
    - 8.13 Duplicate Publication of Data (p. 44).
    - 8.14 Sharing Research Data for Verification (pp. 44–45).
    - 8.15 Reviewers (p. 45).

Ethical Standard 8. Research and Publication

8.01 Institutional Approval

When institutional approval is required, psychologists provide accurate information about their research proposals and obtain approval prior to conducting the research. They conduct the research in accordance with the approved research protocol.

8.02 Informed Consent to Research

(a) When obtaining informed consent as required in Standard 3.10, Informed Consent, psychologists inform participants about (1) the purpose of the research, expected duration, and procedures; (2) their right to decline to participate and to withdraw from the research once participation has begun; (3) the foreseeable consequences of declining or withdrawing; (4) reasonably foreseeable factors that may be expected to influence their willingness to participate such as potential risks, discomfort, or adverse effects; (5) any prospective research benefits; (6) limits of confidentiality; (7) incentives for participation; and (8) whom to contact for questions about the research and research participants' rights. They provide opportunity for the prospective participants to ask questions and receive answers. (See also Standards 8.03, Informed Consent for Recording Voices and Images in Research; 8.05, Dispensing With Informed Consent for Research; and 8.07, Deception in Research.)

(b) Psychologists conducting intervention research involving the use of experimental treatments clarify to participants at the outset of the research (1) the experimental nature of the treatment; (2) the services that will or will not be available to the control group(s) if appropriate; (3) the means by which assignment to treatment and control groups will be made; (4) available treatment alternatives if an individual does not wish to participate in the research or wishes to withdraw once a study has begun; and (5) compensation for or monetary costs of participating including, if appropriate, whether reimbursement from the participant or a third-party payor will be sought. (See also Standard 8.02a, Informed Consent to Research.)

8.03 Informed Consent for Recording Voices and Images in Research

Psychologists obtain informed consent from research participants prior to recording their voices or images for data collection unless (1) the research consists solely of naturalistic observations in public places, and it is not anticipated that the recording will be used in a manner that could cause personal identification or harm, or (2) the research design includes deception, and consent for the use of the recording is obtained during debriefing. (See also Standard 8.07, Deception in Research.)

8.04 Client/Patient, Student, and Subordinate Research Participants

(a) When psychologists conduct research with clients/patients, students, or subordinates as participants, psychologists take steps to protect the prospective participants from adverse consequences of declining or withdrawing from participation.

(b) When research participation is a course requirement or an opportunity for extra credit, the prospective participant is given the choice of equitable alternative activities.

8.05 Dispensing with Informed Consent for Research

Psychologists may dispense with informed consent only (1) where research would not reasonably be assumed to create distress or harm and involves (a) the study of normal educational practices, curricula, or classroom management methods conducted in educational settings; (b) only anonymous questionnaires, naturalistic observations, or archival research for which disclosure of responses would not place participants at risk of criminal or civil liability or damage their financial standing, employability, or reputation, and confidentiality is protected; or (c) the study of factors related to job or organization effectiveness conducted in organizational settings for which there is no risk to participants' employability, and confidentiality is protected or (2) where otherwise permitted by law or federal or institutional regulations.

8.06 Offering Inducements for Research Participation

(a) Psychologists make reasonable efforts to avoid offering excessive or inappropriate financial or other inducements for research participation when such inducements are likely to coerce participation.

(Continued)

(b) When offering professional services as an inducement for research participation, psychologists clarify the nature of the services, as well as the risks, obligations, and limitations. (See also Standard 6.05, Barter With Clients/Patients.)

8.07 Deception in Research

(a) Psychologists do not conduct a study involving deception unless they have determined that the use of deceptive techniques is justified by the study's significant prospective scientific, educational, or applied value and that effective nondeceptive alternative procedures are not feasible.

(b) Psychologists do not deceive prospective participants about research that is reasonably expected to cause physical pain or severe emotional distress. APA Ethics Code 2002 Page 12

(c) Psychologists explain any deception that is an integral feature of the design and conduct of an experiment to participants as early as is feasible, preferably at the conclusion of their participation, but no later than at the conclusion of the data collection, and permit participants to withdraw their data. (See also Standard 8.08, Debriefing.)

8.08 Debriefing

(a) Psychologists provide a prompt opportunity for participants to obtain appropriate information about the nature, results, and conclusions of the research, and they take reasonable steps to correct any misconceptions that participants may have of which the psychologists are aware.

(b) If scientific or humane values justify delaying or withholding this information, psychologists take reasonable measures to reduce the risk of harm.

(c) When psychologists become aware that research procedures have harmed a participant, they take reasonable steps to minimize the harm.

8.09 Humane Care and Use of Animals in Research

(a) Psychologists acquire, care for, use, and dispose of animals in compliance with current federal, state, and local laws and regulations, and with professional standards.

(b) Psychologists trained in research methods and experienced in the care of laboratory animals supervise all procedures involving animals and are responsible for ensuring appropriate consideration of their comfort, health, and humane treatment.

(c) Psychologists ensure that all individuals under their supervision who are using animals have received instruction in research methods and in the care, maintenance, and handling of the species being used, to the extent appropriate to their role. (See also Standard 2.05, Delegation of Work to Others.)

(d) Psychologists make reasonable efforts to minimize the discomfort, infection, illness, and pain of animal subjects.

(e) Psychologists use a procedure subjecting animals to pain, stress, or privation only when an alternative procedure is unavailable and the goal is justified by its prospective scientific, educational, or applied value.

(f) Psychologists perform surgical procedures under appropriate anesthesia and follow techniques to avoid infection and minimize pain during and after surgery.

(g) When it is appropriate that an animal's life be terminated, psychologists proceed rapidly, with an effort to minimize pain and in accordance with accepted procedures.

8.10 Reporting Research Results

(a) Psychologists do not fabricate data. (See also Standard 5.01a, Avoidance of False or Deceptive Statements.)

(b) If psychologists discover significant errors in their published data, they take reasonable steps to correct such errors in a correction, retraction, erratum, or other appropriate publication means.

(Continued)

(Continued)

8.11 Plagiarism

Psychologists do not present portions of another's work or data as their own, even if the other work or data source is cited occasionally.

8.12 Publication Credit

(a) Psychologists take responsibility and credit, including authorship credit, only for work they have actually performed or to which they have substantially contributed. (See also Standard 8.12b, Publication Credit.)

(b) Principal authorship and other publication credits accurately reflect the relative scientific or professional contributions of the individuals involved, regardless of their relative status. Mere possession of an institutional position, such as department chair, does not justify authorship credit. Minor contributions to the research or to the writing for publications are acknowledged appropriately, such as in footnotes or in an introductory statement.

(c) Except under exceptional circumstances, a student is listed as principal author on any multiple-authored article that is substantially based on the student's doctoral dissertation. Faculty advisors discuss publication credit with students as early as feasible and throughout the research and publication process as appropriate. (See also Standard 8.12b, Publication Credit.)

8.13 Duplicate Publication of Data

Psychologists do not publish, as original data, data that have been previously published. This does not preclude republishing data when they are accompanied by proper acknowledgment. APA Ethics Code 2002 Page 13

8.14 Sharing Research Data for Verification

(a) After research results are published, psychologists do not withhold the data on which their conclusions are based from other competent professionals who seek to verify the substantive claims through reanalysis and who intend to use such data only for that purpose, provided that the confidentiality of the participants can be protected and unless legal rights concerning proprietary data preclude their release. This does not preclude psychologists from requiring that such individuals or groups be responsible for costs associated with the provision of such information.

(b) Psychologists who request data from other psychologists to verify the substantive claims through reanalysis may use shared data only for the declared purpose. Requesting psychologists obtain prior written agreement for all other uses of the data.

8.15 Reviewers

Psychologists who review material submitted for presentation, publication, grant, or research proposal review respect the confidentiality of and the proprietary rights in such information of those who submitted it.

Are You Equipped Now?

In 1924, Landis conducted a study with the purpose of determining what facial expressions, if any, are expressed for given emotions. When participants arrived to the experiment, burnt cork was used to draw lines on participants' facial muscles and a picture was taken. Next, participants were exposed to a total of 16 conditions, including: smelling ammonia, imagining self being exposed to skin diseases as depicted in pictures, examining a set of French pornographic photographs, placing a hand in a pail filled with frogs, and being told to cut off the head of a rat. Pictures were taken as participants were exposed to each of the conditions. Landis then compared the facial expression from the picture taken at the beginning of the experiment to the pictures taken after being exposed to each of the conditions. He compared the pictures by noting the amount of change in the muscles. Examples of the pictures taken can be found in the appendix of the research article. Landis found that while individuals have variations in their emotional responses, there was not a typical expression for any of the conditions examined. However, he did note the differences between how men and women responded. Landis found that men were more expressive in the conditions than women. Furthermore, men were more likely to express anger while women were more likely to cry.

As you were reading over this experiment, the last condition of cutting off a rat's head probably got your attention the most. It is hard to believe but participants were instructed to hold the rat with one hand and cut off the head with the other hand. If the participants refused to do so, the researcher cut off the rat's head while the participant watched. We also found it interesting that one of the participants in the experiment was a 13-year-old boy who had been admitted to a hospital for high blood pressure that was likely caused by "emotional instability." The hospital referred the boy to the Psychology Department and Landis included the boy in the experiment, noting that the boy's reactions did not differ significantly from the reactions of the other participants.

In this chapter, we have discussed the IRB process and APA's guidelines for ethical research. However, Landis' research was conducted prior to the establishment of these bodies. After reading this chapter on ethics, answer the questions below regarding Landis' work.

Questions:

1. If Landis were to conduct his experiment today, he would need a regular informed consent and an addition that addresses the recording of images. Why would Landis need an informed consent for the recording of images?

2. Psychologists must inform participants if their participation might cause severe emotional distress. Do you believe that Landis' participants should have been informed that their participation might cause distress?

3. The IRB committee pays special attention to research involving minors as participants. What additional steps might the IRB require of Landis?

4. With the current regulations for animal care, do you think Landis would be allowed to behead a rat if he wanted to replicate the experiment?

Answers:

1. Landis would need to address the recording of images in his informed consent because pictures of the participants were taken at the beginning of the experiment and during the experiment. Participants would need to further grant their permission for Landis to publish the pictures in the appendix of his research article.

2. We believe that participants in this situation should have been forewarned. Participants could have been informed that the purpose of the experiment was to elicit emotional responses and thus some stimuli might cause strong reactions such as anger. Landis might have argued that telling participants in advance about the nature of the stimuli might have reduced the initial response to the conditions. However, we would respond by stating that participants have the right to know in advance if they will be exposed to more than minimal risk and make an informed decision about whether they would like to participate. Beheading an animal is certainly above the events of a typical day for most people.

3. Today, the IRB would require that the boy's parents or legal guardians give their permission and that the boy give his assent. The IRB might also require that the boy's medical doctor review the experimental procedure and decide if the procedure posed a risk to the boy's physical health.

4. We do not think that the current policies would allow Landis to replicate his experiment and behead a rat. APA explicitly states that only those individuals trained in the care of lab animals are allowed to handle the animals and that the termination of an animal's life should involve minimal pain. The procedure described in Landis' research does not fit with either requirement. In fact, Landis describes in his article that because the participants had many false starts and were unsure of how to cut off the head, the process was "prolonged." Furthermore, there are other feasible procedures to induce emotions besides beheading animals.

Chapter Summary

- The Institutional Review Board (IRB) is a committee which reviews proposals of intended research to determine if the research is ethical and that the rights of the participants are being protected (p. 35).
- IRBs can be found on university campuses, hospitals, and in many corporations where research on human participants is conducted (p. 35).
- IRBs are a result of government intervention in 1974 via the National Research Act (p. 35).
  - This commission developed the Belmont Report, which outlined three guiding principles for human participant research: respect, benefits, and justice (pp. 35–36).
- The APA began developing an ethics code in 1949. The most recent version of the code was published in 2010 (p. 37).
- Within the APA ethics code there is a section for ethics in research. This is section 8.0 of the ethics code. This section contains 15 guidelines for ethical research (p. 37).
  - 8.01 Institutional Approval (p. 37).
  - 8.02 Informed Consent (pp. 37–41).
  - 8.03 Informed Consent for Recording Voices and Images in Research (p. 41).
  - 8.04 Client/Patient, Student, and Subordinate Research Participants (p. 41).
  - 8.05 Dispensing with Informed Consent for Research (p. 41).
  - 8.06 Offering Inducements for Research Participation (p. 42).
  - 8.07 Deception in Research (p. 42).
  - 8.08 Debriefing (pp. 43–44).
  - 8.09 Humane Care and Use of Animals in Research (p. 44).
  - 8.10 Reporting Research Results (p. 44).
  - 8.11 Plagiarism (p. 44).
  - 8.12 Publication Credit (p. 44).
  - 8.13 Duplicate Publication of Data (p. 44).
  - 8.14 Sharing Research Data for Verification (pp. 44–45).
  - 8.15 Reviewers (p. 45).

APA Learning Goals Linkage

• **Goal 1.** *Knowledge Base of Psychology*
  Students will demonstrate familiarity with the major concepts, theoretical perspectives, empirical findings, and historical trends in psychology.

  Sections Covered: Are You Equipped?, Consumers of Research, APA's Ethics Code, Are You Equipped Now?

  Explanation of the Goal: Many historical aspects of the field of psychology were examined in this chapter on ethics. For example, we discussed key studies outside of the field (e.g., Wichita Jury Study) and within the field (e.g., Landis' research) that led to the development of the Belmont Report and today's IRBs. For each study presented, we discussed relevant ethical issues and provided a general understanding of the APA's Code of Ethics. We also took an in-depth look at ethical standard 8.0 and the corresponding 15 guidelines, which relate to conducting research.

• **Goal 2.** *Research Methods in Psychology*
  Students will understand and apply basic research methods in psychology, including research design, data analysis, and interpretation.

  Sections Covered: APA's Ethics Code, Are You Equipped Now?

  Explanation of the Goal: As psychologists, we are expected to follow APA's Code of Ethics in the treatment of human and nonhuman participants when conducting research. This includes designing a study, data collection, data interpretation, and reporting of psychological research. In the APA's Ethics Code section of the chapter, we examined these issues. For example, we discussed institutional approval, informed consent, debriefing, deception, and use of animals, to name a few. In the review at the end of the chapter, we assessed how these ethical issues were related to a historical psychological research experiment.

• **Goal 3.** *Critical Thinking Skills in Psychology*
  Students will respect and use critical and creative thinking, skeptical inquiry, and, when possible, the scientific approach to solve problems related to behavior and mental processes.

  Sections Covered: Are You Equipped?, Consumers of Research, APA's Ethics Code, Are You Equipped Now?

  Explanation of the Goal: It could be argued that there is no single topic in which psychologists use critical thinking more than the topic of ethics. Although the APA provides ethical standards and corresponding guidelines for many topic areas, implementing the standards is not always easy and requires the use of effective critical thinking. To help prepare you for this task, we examined several research scenarios and asked you to solve problems consistent with ethical standards. In completing the scenarios, you engaged in critical thinking. In some scenarios such as

(Continued)

(Continued)

evaluating the benefits and risks of the Wichita Jury Study, the answers were not always simple.

• **Goal 4.** *Application of Psychology*
Students will understand and apply psychological principles to personal, social, and organizational issues.

Sections Covered: Are You Equipped?, Consumers of Research, APA's Ethics Code, Are You Equipped Now?

Explanation of the Goal: Social science research, such as in psychology, is often conducted to improve the quality of life and solve everyday problems. Thus, psychological principles can easily be applied to personal, social, and organizational issues. This was illustrated in this chapter on ethics through controversial examples such as administering experimental drugs to pregnant women without their knowledge and injecting mentally impaired children with hepatitis. We also saw how psychological principles are applied to everyday situations with the example of research being conducted at our daughter's school. Another important facet that we examined was how ethically complex situations can develop when psychological principles are applied. This includes the controversial examples mentioned above as well as other issues including (a) inducement for research participation, (b) deception, and (c) the use of animals in research.

• **Goal 5.** *Values in Psychology*
Students will be able to weigh evidence, tolerate ambiguity, act ethically, and reflect other values that are the underpinnings of psychology as a discipline.

Sections Covered: APA's Ethics Code, Are You Equipped Now?

Explanation of the Goal: It is important to recognize the necessity for ethical behavior in all aspects of the science and practice of psychology. Our coverage of standard 8.0 was an introduction to engaging in ethical behavior in carrying out the science of psychology through research.

• **Goal 8.** *Sociocultural and International Awareness*
Students will recognize, understand, and respect the complexity of sociocultural and international diversity.

Sections Covered: Consumers of Research, APA's Ethics Code, Are You Equipped Now?

Explanation of the Goal: IRBs and the APA's ethics code specifically address how psychologists should engage in research to protect special populations (e.g., minors, pregnant women, and the mentally impaired) and respect animal and human rights as research participants. This is an important task, as privilege and power may affect inequities in research.

Nonexperimental Research Methods and Variables

Nonexperimental Research Methods

CHAPTER OUTLINE

Are You Equipped?

How do you pick what classes you will take each semester? Many students at our university visit a website called *ratemyprofessors.com*. At this website, students can literally rate their professor on many different attributes including clarity, ease, helpfulness, and even hotness (i.e., attractiveness). Other students can then see the professor's average score for each of these attributes to help decide if they want to have that professor for a particular class. Recently, websites like Facebook have started to offer similar systems where students can rate professors. These websites bring up an interesting question. Specifically, is attractiveness of professor related to student satisfaction with the course? How could we answer this question? Take a minute and think about how you could gather information to address this question. What would you do?

There are numerous ways to gather information to find out if a professor's attractiveness is related to student satisfaction with the course. The fact that there is more than one way to gather information on this topic illustrates that social scientists have a plethora of research methods at their disposal. In this chapter, we are going to focus on nonexperimental research methods. We could use nonexperimental research methods to examine the relationship between attractiveness of professors and student satisfaction in several ways. First, we could use the existing records provided by the websites mentioned above. This would allow us to see if the two variables were related to one another. Using existing records such as those from *ratemyprofessors.com* is known as archival research. Another way to see if the two variables were related to one another would be to ask students. You could have students complete a questionnaire asking about their opinions. This is known as survey research. Archival and survey research are just two examples of nonexperimental research which seeks to examine relationships among variables. We will talk in more detail about these methods and others throughout the chapter. Before we begin, you might want to know that research has been conducted on this topic and a relationship does exist between a professor's attractiveness and overall quality. In general, the more attractive a professor is, the higher students rate his or her overall quality as a teacher (Bonds-Raacke & Raacke, 2007).

As you go through this chapter, we also want you to keep in mind how the material relates to the American Psychological Association goals for psychology majors. Specifically, this chapter will address the following goals:

- **Goal 2. Research Methods in Psychology**
  Students will understand and apply basic research methods in psychology, including research design, data analysis, and interpretation.
- **Goal 3. Critical Thinking Skills in Psychology**
  Students will respect and use critical and creative thinking, skeptical inquiry, and, when possible, the scientific approach to solve problems related to behavior and mental processes.
- **Goal 4. Application of Psychology**
  Students will understand and apply psychological principles to personal, social, and organizational issues.
- **Goal 5. Values in Psychology**
  Students will be able to weigh evidence, tolerate ambiguity, act ethically, and reflect other values that are the underpinnings of psychology as a discipline.
- **Goal 7. Communication Skills**
  Students will be able to communicate effectively in a variety of formats.

QUALITATIVE

Research methodologies where researchers seek subjectivity through in-depth collection of information and emerging hypotheses.

DIFFERENTIATING AMONG METHODS

Psychology is the scientific study of thoughts and behaviors. Therefore, psychologists, and social scientists in general, use a variety of research methods to study what people think and do. There are two main ways to differentiate among types of research. First, you can describe a research method as being either qualitative or quantitative. **Qualitative** research is inductive by nature. Researchers using this methodology seek subjectivity through in-depth collection of information and emerging hypotheses. Researchers gather the data and draw conclusions based on their observations. On the other hand, **quantitative** research is deductive by nature. Researchers using this methodology seek objectivity through testable hypotheses and carefully designed studies. Researchers gather data that can be reported in numbers and statistics. Conclusions are drawn from statistics and generalized to populations of interest. It is interesting that most researchers are trained in either the qualitative or quantitative approach. Very few researchers routinely use both approaches. However, the two approaches need not be viewed in opposition, as both can shed light on understanding variables of interest. A second way to differentiate among types of research is by describing if the research is experimental or nonexperimental. **Experimental research** involves the manipulation of a variable of interest and assignment of participants to treatment conditions. We will spend more time in later chapters talking about how to design and interpret experimental research. **Nonexperimental research** does not rely on manipulating variables. Rather, it makes observations about how variables are related to one another and describes the findings.

Introduction to Correlational Methods

As mentioned above, nonexperimental research does not manipulate variables of interest. However, even without direct manipulation, you can still explore relationships between variables using **correlational research methods**. Correlational research methods are very important to the field. This methodology provides us with information on the initial link between variables of interest. Correlational research methods are also frequently reported in the media. We want to tell you about two correlational studies recently reported in the media examining issues related to weight and obesity. The first study was conducted by Kopycka-Kedzierawski, Auinger, Billings, and Weitzman (2008) at the Eastman Dental Center, which is part of the University of Rochester Medical Center. Kopycka-Kedzierawski and colleagues found that for children between the ages of 6 and 18 there was a relationship between weight and tooth decay. Surprisingly, as weight increased, the risk of tooth decay decreased. We will talk a little later on about why these results might have been obtained. For now, we want to focus your attention on how this study shows that two variables (i.e., weight and tooth decay) are related to one another. Our second news story reported that Gazdzinski, Kornak, Weiner, Meyerhoff, and Nat (2008) found that weight was related to biochemical deficiencies. Specifically as weight increased for individuals, researchers found lower-than-normal levels of markers for neuronal health and cell membrane synthesis. We will return to understanding these results in just a minute when we discuss the advantages and disadvantages of this method.

When you have a correlational research method, your results will tell you if the two variables are related. Variables can be either positively or negatively related. Do not be confused by the labels of positive correlation and negative correlation. This does not mean that positive correlations are good and negative correlations are bad. Rather, **positive correlations** have variables that vary in the same direction and **negative correlations** have variables that vary in opposite directions. To make this clear, we want to tell you about some examples of positive and negative correlations. We have also provided you with the figure below to visually represent each type of correlation. Two variables that are positively

QUANTITATIVE

Research methodologies that seek objectivity through testable hypotheses and carefully designed studies.

EXPERIMENTAL RESEARCH

A class of research methodologies that involve manipulation of a variable.

NONEXPERIMENT-AL RESEARCH

A class of research methodologies that involve the study of how variables are related.

CORRELATIONAL RESEARCH METHODS

Research methodologies that evaluate the relationship between variables.

POSITIVE CORRELATION

Two or more variables vary in the same direction.

NEGATIVE CORRELATION

Two or more variables vary in opposite directions.

correlated are years of education and salary. This is a positive correlation because as scores on one variable increase so too do scores on the second variable. Similarly, as scores on one variable decrease so too do scores on the second variable. In this situation, the more number of years of education a person has, the higher the salary. Conversely, the fewer number of years of education a person has, the lower the salary. In both instances, the two variables either increased or decreased together, making this a positive correlation. Another example of a positive correlation is time spent studying for a test and performance on the test. In general, the more you study for a test, the higher your grade on the test, and the less you study for a test, the lower your grade on the test. Again, this is a positive correlation because both variables are increasing or decreasing together. A final example of a positive correlation is the amount of food consumed and weight. The more food that you consume, the higher your weight and the less food that you that consume, the lower your weight.

With negative correlations, the two variables of interest are related to one another as well. However, as one variable increases, the other variable decreases, or as one variable decreases, the other variable increases. An example of a negative correlation is marital satisfaction and likelihood of divorce. As marital satisfaction increases, the likelihood of divorce decreases, and as marital satisfaction decreases, the likelihood of divorce increases. The two examples that we presented earlier from news reports were also examples of negative correlations. Remember that as weight of children increased, the risk for tooth decay decreased. The reverse can also be stated. As the risk of tooth decay increased, the weight of children decreased. Thus, these two variables were related to one another but in opposite directions. Similarly, in the second report, as weight of individuals increased, normal levels of brain functioning decreased, or as normal functioning increased, weight of individuals decreased. We find it helpful to draw arrows for each of the variables that we are reading about. If the variable is increasing, we draw an up arrow. If the variable is decreasing, we draw a down arrow (Figure 4.1). We can then look at the arrows to see if they are both pointing in the same direction (positive correlation) or in different directions (negative correlation).

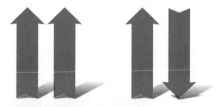

FIGURE 4.1   Arrows for Positive and Negative Correlations.

YOU TRY IT!

We want you to get some practice in determining if correlational results are positive or negative. Take a look at the findings below and state whether each of them is a positive or negative correlation.

Research findings:

1. As ice-cream sales increase, murder rates increase.
2. As the speed of a vehicle increases, the time to reach a destination decreases.

(*Continued*)

3. As people's happiness levels increase, people's helpfulness levels increase.
4. The more a baby is held, the less a baby cries.

Answers

1. It is hard to believe but this first example is a true one. Research on this topic has found that as ice-cream sales increase, rates of murder also increase. We will talk about what is going on in this situation in a minute. For right now, we want to draw your attention to the fact that this example is a positive correlation. It is a positive correlation because as one variable goes up (ice-cream sales) so too does the second variable (murder rates). It would be visually represented as:

2. This is an example of a negative correlation because the two variables are pointing in opposite directions. As one variable increases (speed), the other variable decreases (time to destination). Again, you could draw arrows to help determine the type of correlation. For this, the arrows would be:

3. This is also an example of a positive correlation because both variables (happiness level and helpfulness level) are increasing together. Also, note that the reverse statement is true. As happiness levels decrease, helpfulness levels decrease.

4. Finally, there is a negative relationship between how often a baby is held and how often a baby cries. As one variable increases (how often a baby is held), the other variable decreases (how often a baby cries). This brings us to an interesting point to consider. Specifically, how do you interpret these correlational research findings? Should you hold your baby all the time so he or she does not cry? Not necessarily. We will discuss three questions to ask yourself when interpreting correlational research findings in just a moment.

(*Continued*)

(Continued)

How did you do with these four examples? We should mention that sometimes the direction of a variable is not as clearly stated in the media or in a research article as we did in our examples. However, if you stop and think about the results, you will be able to determine if the scores are increasing or decreasing for the variable.

As with any research method, there are advantages and disadvantages to examining correlations between variables. One major advantage of correlational research is that it allows us to make predictions. For example, if we know marital satisfaction and likelihood of divorce are negatively correlated, it can help us in counseling couples who are experiencing low marital satisfaction. Many times, examining correlations between variables is a great starting point to researching a topic. Plus, it is a useful method when conducting a true experiment would not be ethical. This brings us to a limitation of the method, determining cause and effect. Using a previous example, should we stop buying ice cream so that we can reduce the number of murders committed? This even sounds like a strange question to ask. When you have a correlation, you must think about the directionality of the correlation and ask yourself the following questions:

• Is X causing Y?
• Is Y causing X?
• Is there a third variable causing both X and Y to be related?

In the example of ice-cream sales and murder rates, you would ask yourself the following questions:

• Does eating ice cream (X) cause you to commit murder (Y)?
• Does committing murder (Y) cause you to eat ice cream (X)?
• Is there a third variable that is causing ice-cream sales (X) and murder rates (Y) to be related?

It really does not make sense that eating ice cream would cause you to commit murder or that murdering people would cause you to eat ice cream. However, it does make sense that a third variable (like heat) is related to both. Specifically, as it gets hotter, ice-cream sales increase. Also, as it gets hotter, murder rates increase. Therefore, in this example, it is likely that a third variable was influencing both variables. We cannot emphasize enough on how important it is to not infer cause and effect from correlational research. Remember that this method provides very useful information as to how variables are related but other factors could be causing the finding.

Section Summary

- *Qualitative* research methodologies seek subjectivity through in-depth collection of information and emerging hypotheses (pp. 56–57).
- *Quantitative* research methodologies seek objectivity through testable hypotheses and carefully designed studies (pp. 56–57).
- *Experimental research* is a class of research methodologies that involves direct manipulation of a variable (p. 57).
- *Nonexperimental research* is a class of research methodologies that does not rely on manipulating variables (p. 57).
- *Correlational research methods* evaluate the relationship between variables (pp. 57–60).
  - *Positive correlations* have variables that vary in the same direction. (pp. 57–58)
  - *Negative correlations* have variables that vary in opposite directions. (pp. 57–58)

NONEXPERIMENTAL METHODS

So far, we have provided you with introductory information that will be helpful as you learn about nonexperimental designs. In this chapter, we will discuss the following nonexperimental designs: ethnography, naturalistic observation, case studies, archival research, content analysis, and survey. It is important to note that all these nonexperimental designs can examine relationships among variables as mentioned previously under correlational methodologies. We will begin with **ethnography**. Typically, ethnographies are associated with the field of anthropology and are used to describe new cultures. The purpose of this method is to describe a culture in detail. In doing so, the researcher records and transcribes events that he or she witnesses and shares these findings with others. Many times ethnographic questions concern the relationship between culture and behavior, and thus other social scientists are interested in the method. For example, Durán (2009) used ethnographic techniques to learn more about inner-city Mexican American experiences with police gang enforcement. One advantage to this methodology is that you can get "rich" or detailed information from an insider's perspective. Disadvantages include the lack of a testable hypothesis, the inability to infer cause and effect, and little ability to generalize the results to other groups (to be discussed further in Chapter 5).

ETHNOGRAPHY

Used to describe a culture in detail by recoding and transcribing events that are witnessed.

    Naturalistic observation is where you observe people or animals in their natural settings. These observations can occur in the field (sometimes called field studies) or in the laboratory (referred to as laboratory observations). Studying people in their natural setting means many things. One of the most famous naturalistic observations was conducted by Jane Goodall. In the summer of 1960, Goodall went to East Africa to live among the chimpanzee population. There were many aspects about chimpanzees that Goodall wanted to learn such as if chimps used tools. She believed the best way to understand the chimp behavior was to observe them in their natural environment. Goodall's work has lead to numerous publications on the life of chimps.

NATURALISTIC OBSERVATION

A research methodology where a researcher observes people or animals in their natural setting.

We want to follow up this classic example of naturalistic observation with more everyday examples to illustrate that natural settings are diverse and you are not required to travel to far-off destinations. First, Middlemist, Knowles, and Matter (1976) wanted to know how the presence of another man in the bathroom influenced men's selection of a urinal and urinating behaviors. To do so, the researcher hung out in front of the bathroom mirror. The researcher gathered information on which urinals men used and their urinating behaviors (i.e., length of time to begin urinating and duration of urination). Results indicated that men prefer not to use a urinal next to another man. In addition, the closer a man is to another man in terms of urinal distance, the longer it takes for them to begin urinating and the shorter the duration of urination. It would be interesting to see if gender differences occur in this behavior. Another example of a naturalistic observation comes from developmental psychologists who routinely use laboratory observations to study children. Important developmental information has been gained by bringing children into the lab and observing their interactions with their mom and dad. Examples include information on attachment style and stages of development such as object permanence. Finally, we use naturalistic observations in the world of teaching. It is not uncommon for fellow professors to observe one another in the classroom. These observations are used early on in a faculty member's teaching career to provide them with constructive criticism and later on in a career to support decisions regarding promotion and tenure.

The three examples of naturalistic observation that I have shared with you are varied in topic and scope. However, there are some commonalities in these observations. To begin, the researcher had to decide on a topic of behavior to observe and whether his or her presence would be known or hidden to the participants. In Goodall's situation it was almost unavoidable that the chimps were aware of her presence. Similarly, when a professor has their teaching observed by a colleague, the professor and the students in the class are aware of the observation. In fact, students will quickly recognize a new face in the crowd. However, it was possible for the researcher in the urinal research example to hide his true purpose and pretend to be using the restroom too. Developmental psychologists often hide their presence by videotaping children's interactions with parents and responses to new stimuli from another room. Another commonality in our examples was that the researcher engaged in a systematic observation of specified activities. Sometimes a coding system is used to describe the observed behaviors and researchers must be trained prior to their observations. Finally, to carry out their observations, researchers will need equipment to note their observations and may use a video camera.

There are many advantages to this methodology. To begin, the behavior being observed is natural and spontaneous. For the most part, participants being observed in naturalistic observations are just doing what they normally do in life. This is an advantage over research procedures that require people to participate in a lab setting or participate in tasks that are unfamiliar to them. It would be very difficult to answer questions about male bathroom behavior in a more realistic way. However, this method also has several disadvantages that you must consider. One main disadvantage is how the observer changes people's behavior by his or her presence. For instance, we can talk about this limitation with the example of teaching observations. Every time a peer has observed our classes, the students act differently. They become shy and well behaved compared to a typical day.

This could be due to the fact that the students are trying to behave and make us look good to the observer or we are acting differently and the students are picking up on our changed behavior. Either way, the observation itself changed the natural setting. If a researcher decided to avoid this disadvantage by hiding his or her presence, he or she must consider the participant's right to privacy as well. Another disadvantage is that the researcher has to wait for events to occur. It might have taken a few hours before a man came to use the restroom; and Goodall waited months before seeing chimps use tools. Researchers also need to be careful not to introduce bias in their observations. For example, researchers might be looking for a particular behavior and report "seeing it" when others would not. A well-known example of this has occurred with observation research of chimps using sign language. Some researchers reported seeing animals use sign language, while other researchers reported the animals were not signing. Finally, cause and effect cannot be determined from naturalistic observations.

YOU TRY IT!

We have just covered information on naturalistic observations. If you wanted to examine how children play with one another and how frequently aggressive behaviors occurred, how could you use a naturalistic observation to investigate these topics? Discuss in your answer how you could conduct the study when your presence was known and unknown to the children.

Answer

You could investigate how children play with one another and their aggressive acts during play by going to a place where children naturally play together, like a playground. This could be at a community park or at a school. You could hide your presence if you are worried that children will play differently knowing you are watching. For example, you could watch children on a school playground from a classroom window or you could take your own child to the park and be just another parent. On the other hand, you might decide that children knowing you are around will not terribly influence their behavior so you could just sit and watch. In making your observations, you would probably have devised a coding system in advance. This way you would know what was considered violent behavior. If possible, another person could watch with you and make observations, allowing for you to compare observations.

The next nonexperimental research method that we want to discuss is a case study. A **case study** is an in-depth observation of an individual, animal, event, or treatment method. Typically, an intensive observation is done and detailed account is taken because the event is extremely rare and unusual. Case studies in the field are not just limited to Freud's psychiatric applications. There are other classic examples of case studies in the field. These include Phineas Gage and cases of feral children. Phineas Gage provided us with information on the link between personality and parts of the brain. Specifically, in 1848, an explosion sent a tamping iron through Gage's skull. Surprisingly, Gage survived the explosion but his behavior changed greatly due to the damage in the frontal lobes of his brain. Researchers have long been interested in providing a detailed account of what took place and how Gage's behavior changed as a result. Cases of feral children have provided the field with information on the importance of early exposure to

CASE STUDY

A research methodology that is an in-depth observation of an individual, animal, event, or treatment method.

language. For example, a child who is referred to as Genie was found around the age of 13. Until she was found, Genie had been kept in isolation and deprived of any exposure to language. This case study was an opportunity to see how language deprivation would influence Genie's ability to later acquire a language. Genie was able to learn some level of English. However, her fluency was impaired and the actual level of her fluency is debated among experts (Curtiss, 1977).

When telling students about case studies, we always mention the two classics above. In addition to these, we have two more case studies that we heard about during our studies and have not forgotten. The first case study is from the area of human sexuality (Linnau & Mann, 2003). A male patient was admitted to the hospital for severe abdominal pain. When questioned, the patient admitted to swallowing Barbie doll heads (including hair) for sexual gratification. Researchers were interested in understanding how this provided the patient with sexual gratification and how such a behavior develops. A final case study is that of Clive Wearing. Clive Wearing was a brilliant musician. However, due to a case of viral encephalitis, Clive lost the ability to form new memories. This is known as anterograde amnesia. *The Mind*, a series by BBC, documents the events leading up to and after Clive's memory loss. Researchers are particularly interested in the parts of the brain damaged and the result on Clive's memories and behaviors.

The major advantage to case studies is that we can study rare events that would be unethical to study otherwise. It would be extremely unethical to deprive a child of language, make people swallow objects, or damage parts of the brain to see how the event influenced an individual's behavior. Therefore, case studies provide us with unique opportunities to better understand situations that we could not study experimentally. Despite this advantage, there are limitations to this method. First, we do not always know the cause of the behavior. In trying to understand the male patient admitted to the hospital, researchers attempted to reconstruct events from his past to explain his current situation. Yet, this procedure introduces bias because the researchers are selecting what information from his past they think is important. There could be other variables that the patient and the researchers were unaware of that influenced him. Second, these unusual events might not influence everybody in the same manner. For example, Gage was extremely fortunate to have survived the explosion. Not all people would have survived. Furthermore, not all people would have experienced the same resulting behavior. Thus, when using case studies, it is important to keep in mind the limitations of the findings.

ARCHIVAL RESEARCH

A nonexperimental method where the researcher uses existing records and selects portions of the records to examine.

Archival research is a nonexperimental method where you use existing records and select portions of the records to examine. These existing records were collected by other people as a form of public records. Some examples include census information, marriage applications, police arrests, and reports prepared by your university. One of Jenn's first studies as an undergraduate student was an archival study. Jenn was examining sex and age differences in couples applying for marriage. To do so, she obtained the local newspaper's listing of couples applying for marriage licenses in Shelby County, Tennessee, for one month. This provided 783 couples. For each listing, the newspaper provided the name and age of the applicants with the male's name listed first. Jenn found that in 63% of the couples the male was older than the female. She discussed these findings in relation to sociobiological theories (Bonds & Nicks, 1999). Jenn has continued to use archival studies in her career. For example, she has used existing records to: (a) compare the number of women to men journal editors in psychology, (b) determine the level of engagement in the classroom of Native American students compared to other ethnic groups at an east coast university, and (c) examine rates of graduation for honors students compared to nonhonors students. Within the field, archival research is used to investigate a variety of topics. For example, O'Neil, Steele, Huisingh, and Smith (2008) used data from the U.S. Consumer Product Safety Commission to determine how often individuals were injured on escalators, and Gentile (2007) used data from the 2007 Harris Poll to examine pathology among video-game players.

YOU TRY IT!

Many universities have a research day at the end of the academic year. This is one day out of the year where students showcase to the university community the products of their scholarly endeavors. Typically a program is provided for the event which lists the following information: student's name, student's major, title of work, and faculty advisor. The information in the program is collected by the program director. However, you could use the existing data in the program to conduct an archival study. How would you examine rates of student participation across majors using the program?

Answer

The program provides the readers with a record of the events that took place. By examining the program, you could compare the number of students across majors to examine rates of participation. You might find that 50% of the student presenters at the research day were from majors in the natural sciences, and fewer numbers were from students in the arts and humanities. This information could be helpful in numerous ways. First, the people who sponsor the research day might want to consider actively advertising the event to professors and students in the arts and humanities. Second, they may also need to reconsider how work is displayed so that artists can display physical pieces of work and theater/music majors can perform their work.

There are many positive points to using an archival method. For example, you do not have to spend time collecting data yourself. In addition, you might find that more information on the topic was gathered for public records than you would have gathered on your own. Jenn found this to be the case with her archival study on Native Americans at an east coast university. She used existing records collected by the university and was able to examine variables that she had not originally considered because the information was available. On the other hand, sometimes the records that you need have not been collected or are incomplete. Another disadvantage is that you cannot infer cause and effect. For example, you could not claim that a student's major causes him or her to be more involved with the research day. It could be additional factors (as mentioned above) leading to varying rates of participation across majors.

Before we move on to survey research, we want to briefly discuss content analysis. **Content analysis** is very similar to archival research in that you are examining existing documents. In this research method, you basically count the

CONTENT ANALYSIS

A research methodology where a researcher counts the number of times a particular piece of content occurs.

number of times a particular content of interest occurs. This is a common method used to examine media. For example, researchers will count the number of characters of different racial, gender, or ethnic groups on television. Researchers using content analysis need to utilize similar definitions of content to obtain the same results. We will talk about this issue of similar definitions in Chapter 7. Typically, content analysis is conducted before an experiment in media research. Here is an example. First, researchers might use a content analysis to examine the frequency of racists' portrayals of a minority group in the media. If such portrayals of the minority group do exist, researchers could then conduct an experiment to see if these racists' portrayals influenced viewers' attitudes and behaviors toward that minority group.

*SURVEY
RESEARCH*
_____

A research methodology where one designs a questionnaire to obtain information regarding behaviors, attitudes, or opinions.

The last type of nonexperimental research that we will cover in this chapter is survey research. **Survey research** is where you design a questionnaire to obtain information regarding individuals' behaviors, attitudes, or opinions. This questionnaire can be administered in a variety of formats. Maybe the most common format is the written format. Questions are typed up and can be administered to participants in person by having them answer on paper or computer, through a mailed survey, and even over the Internet. Another format of administering the questionnaire is via telephone. You can ask people questions verbally in person, which is known as a face-to-face interview, or gather a small group of people together to discuss the questions, which is known as a focus group. Each of these formats has its own advantages and disadvantages. A lengthy discussion of each is out of the scope of this book. However, pros and cons regarding the use of surveys in general will be discussed later in the chapter.

In April 2008, the National Sleep Foundation (NSF) released findings from a survey they conducted. The NSF collected information regarding participants' behavior and sleep patterns. Among the results reported, 36% of respondents fell asleep while driving, 29% reported becoming very tired at work within the last month, and 20% reported having sex less often due to a lack of sleep. Survey research has also examined sleep patterns in children. Specifically, survey research found a link between sleep, television viewing, and weight in children. Taveras and colleagues (2008) found that children are more likely to be overweight by age three if: (a) the child sleeps less than 12 hours per day and (b) the child watches more than two hours of television per day. Thus, survey research provides us with a wealth of information in terms of what people are doing and thinking on a given topic.

In order to obtain this information from participants, researchers must carefully construct surveys. Survey construction is a skill that takes practice to learn. For those thinking of graduate school, learning how to ask other people questions in a systematic manner will be an extremely valuable skill. Even if you are not planning on attending graduate school, we believe knowledge of survey construction to be of value to you. We have put together a few general suggestions on survey construction. Refer to Table 4.1 as we will talk you through these suggestions with an example.

The first step to survey construction is to determine what information you want to gather from participants. In other words, you want to think about the purpose of your survey. Although this may sound simple, it is an important step. It is easy to get carried away and ask too many questions, which may be off topic

TABLE 4.1   Survey Suggestions.
Suggestions for Survey Construction
1. Determine purpose of questionnaire
2. Determine type of questions
3. Ask about one issue per question
4. Make alternatives clear
5. Write questions in an unbiased manner
6. Avoid negative wording
7. Avoid leading questions
8. Most importantly, obey the law of parsimony

from your original purpose. For our example, the purpose of the questionnaire will be to measure a faculty member's teaching ability.

In the second step, you will want to determine the type of question to ask. This includes deciding whether you will use open-ended questions or closed-ended questions. **Open-ended questions** are written to elicit detailed and thoughtful answers from respondents. With open-ended questions, the respondents do not have a set way to answer. For example, you might want to ask students how prepared a faculty member was for class. You could ask, "How prepared was the faculty member for class?" and leave the response section open so students could write in an answer to the question. This would be an open-ended question. On the other hand, you could ask, "How prepared was the faculty member for class?" and have students select from a predetermined list of options (e.g., 1 = never prepared, 2 = somewhat prepared, 3 = always prepared). This would be a **closed-ended question**. There are pros and cons to both types of questions. Open-ended questions allow you to gather responses that you might not have thought of, whereas closed-ended responses limit you to only the responses provided by the researcher. However, closed-ended responses are typically easier to score, whereas open-ended responses take time to quantify. Remember that not all of your questions have to be of the same type. It is possible to have a combination of both.

Third, be sure when you are asking questions that you only ask about one item or factor per question. For example, you would not want to ask about a faculty member's preparedness for class and promptness in returning assignments in the same question.

To what degree do you agree with this statement?

> I find the professor to be prepared for class and prompt at returning graded work.
>
> Not at all   1   2   3   4   5   6   7   Very Much

This is because the student may have different ratings of each. The student might want to rate the faculty member highly on preparedness and poorly on promptness. However, if both factors are asked about in one question, you will not be able to see the difference between the two factors in students' responses.

OPEN-ENDED QUESTIONS

Questions in which a response is elicited and there is not a predetermined list of responses.

CLOSED-ENDED QUESTIONS

Questions in which the answers must be selected from a predetermined list of responses.

The fourth suggestion that we have for you when constructing a survey is to make the alternatives clear. Below is an example of a closed-ended question with alternatives that are not clear.

How often did you seek help from the faculty member outside of class? (Check only one alternative)

____ 1–2 times during the semester
____ 2–3 times during the semester
____ 3–4 times during the semester
____ 4 or more times during the semester

The alternatives in this example are very ambiguous. If you had sought help from the faculty member three times during the semester, what option would you check? There are two options (i.e., 2–3 and 3–4) that include the number 3. It is much easier for a participant to answer questions when the alternatives are clearly presented and only one option is possible.

Number five on our list of suggestions is to write questions in an unbiased manner. For example, you would not want to refer to the faculty member as a "he" throughout the survey. This is because the faculty member could be a man or a woman. Sixth, it can also be helpful to avoid negative wording or wording that is complicated. Take a look at the example below.

The faculty member was not fair in his or her grading procedures.

Not at all true   1   2   3   4   5   6   7   Very True

To begin, the student completing the survey might not even notice that the word "not" is in the sentence. This could result in the faculty member receiving more negative evaluations on this item. You can help this situation by offsetting the word "not" (see below).

The faculty member was *not* fair in his or her grading procedures.

Not at all true   1   2   3   4   5   6   7   Very True

However, even with measures to draw students' attention to the negative word, some students still might find the question confusing. You do not want to give participants a headache trying to determine if higher scores on the scale are a good or a bad thing.

Seventh, you should avoid the use of leading questions. If you want to ask students about how professional a faculty member was in class, it would be unwise to do so in the following manner:

Directions: Sometimes faculty members fail to act in a professional manner.

To what extent did the faculty member act in a professional member?

Not at all professional   1 2 3 4 5 6 7   Very professional

Beginning the directions by stating that sometimes faculty members will fail to act professionally will prime students to think about times in which this did occur. You want to be sure that you ask questions in such a way that participants are not primed or led to think of events in a particular frame of mind. The eighth, and the most important, step is to obey law of parsimony. In other words, you want to keep the survey as simple as possible to complete. When participants become confused or frustrated, they are more likely to give up or provide responses that are less accurate.

Before moving on to the last You Try It! section, we want to mention that survey research is not always nonexperimental in nature. Sometimes surveys are used to gather data after participants have been exposed to the variable of interest, which the researcher manipulated. However, if no manipulation occurred prior to completing the survey, the survey would be nonexperimental in nature. Jenn and colleagues (2007) primed participants to recall either a positive or negative portrayal of a homosexual in the media. After being either positively primed or negatively primed, participants completed a survey on their attitudes toward gay men and lesbians. This is an example of how a survey can be used in an experimental research design.

YOU TRY IT!

We are going to tell you about a survey that a group of students working for Jenn constructed. Take a look at one question below from their survey. Which of the eight suggestions regarding survey construction did they fail to use?

Please indicate your current religion? (check only one)

_____ Catholic
_____ Lutheran
_____ Protestant
_____ Methodist
_____ Baptist
_____ Presbyterian
_____ Jewish
_____ Other

Answer

Probably the biggest suggestion that this group of students failed to use was the fourth suggestion—make the alternatives clear. The alternatives listed are just not clear. For example, Lutheran, Methodist, Baptist, and Presbyterian are all examples of Protestant religions. This would make looking at the data very confusing. One would be unsure if those who checked "Protestant" were from one of the Protestant faiths listed or a different Protestant faith not included in the list. So it is always important to be sure the alternatives are clear and that only one alternative is possible. As we mentioned, learning how to write questions is not a skill that comes easy to most people. It takes time and lots of practice. In Chapter 7, we will return to the issue of survey construction and wording questions to obtain specific types of data.

As with the other methods discussed in this chapter, there are advantages and disadvantages to using surveys. Surveys are convenient to use as they are easy to administer and you can obtain responses from numerous participants. Another big advantage is that you can gather information on a variety of issues and with regard to behaviors, attitudes, and opinions. However, surveys can be costly to administer. Copies need to be made and possibly an assistant hired to administer the survey. Depending of the format of the survey (such as with a telephone or a mail survey), there are typically a low number of participants who respond. Also, those participants who do respond could be different from those participants who do not respond. For all surveys, you must consider the fact that participants might lie or that the wording of the question could influence a participant's response. In face-to-face interviews, the characteristics of the researcher (e.g., ethnicity and sex) could influence how people respond to particular questions. Finally, participants may answer questions in such a way to be viewed positively by the researchers. This is known as social desirability.

Section Summary

- *Ethnography* is used to describe a culture in detail by recoding and transcribing events that are witnessed (p. 61).
- *Naturalistic observation* occurs when a researcher observes people or animals in their natural setting (pp. 61–63).
- *A case study* is an in-depth observation of an individual, animal, event, or treatment method (pp. 63–64).
- *Archival research* occurs when a researcher uses existing records and selects portions of the records to examine (pp. 64–65).
- *Content analysis* is a research methodology similar to archival research. However, in a content analysis the researcher counts the number of times a particular piece of content occurs (p. 65).
- *Survey research* involves designing a questionnaire to obtain information regarding behaviors, attitudes, or opinions (pp. 66–70).

FACTORS TO CONSIDER WITH NONEXPERIMENTAL DESIGNS

We have discussed many types of nonexperimental research methods: ethnography, naturalistic observation, case studies, archival research, content analysis, and survey. For each method, we discussed the benefits and limitations. However, as a collective group, nonexperimental designs have a benefit of providing researchers with information that would many times be unethical or practically impossible to obtain otherwise. The primary limitation for these methods is the inability to determine cause and effect. Nevertheless, nonexperimental designs are extremely important to advancing the field.

CONVERGING RESEARCH METHODS

We have introduced and discussed nonexperimental designs thus far as an independent group in research methodologies. We have done this to highlight the uses and benefits of nonexperimental designs, as well as to separate nonexperimental designs from experimental designs. However, many researchers use both types of research methods when conducting a study. This is known as converging research methodologies. Converging research methodologies occur when a researcher uses more than one research methodology to study a single problem. By doing so, the researcher is able to use the strengths of one methodology to make up for the weaknesses of the other and vice versa.

For example, a researcher studying cheating has decided to use both a survey and an experimental methodology. Specifically, the researcher develops a survey to question participants on their history of cheating in the classroom. The researcher collects data on participants' self-reports of cheating behavior. After collecting data through the survey, the researcher develops an experiment in which the participants have the opportunity to earn money. However, unbeknownst to the participants, the only way they can earn the money is to cheat. The researcher then compares the participant's reported behaviors (through the survey) with their actual behaviors (through the experiment). Interestingly, this was an actual study conducted by Ong and Weiss (2000). By using both methodologies (experimental and nonexperimental), the researchers were better able to understand cheating while avoiding the disadvantages of both survey and experimental research.

Are You Equipped Now?

College campuses can be diverse in many ways. The U.S. News ranks the most racially diverse campuses in different regions of the country (i.e., North, South, Midwest, etc.) as well as the most economically diverse campuses in these same regions every year. The selected universities view their racial and economic diversity in a positive light, believing that it enriches the college experience. If a university wanted to investigate students' behaviors and opinions regarding how this diversity related to the overall college experience, how could a university do so using the nonexperimental research methods of case study, archival data, naturalistic observation, and survey?

Answer

Case Study

In order to conduct a case study, a university could select a student and follow that student during his or her college career. Throughout the study, the university could assess the student's behaviors as well as his or her opinions in regard to the diversity on campus and the college experience. The key here is that the study is an in-depth investigation of a single individual.

Archival Data

Most universities have an Office of Institutional Research or Institutional Effectiveness, where large amounts of data are collected and housed. If a researcher wanted to conduct an archival study, this office would be a great place to start.

First, the researcher would need to determine if the office had data related to the research question. If so, the researcher would not need to collect new data, but examine data previously collected by the university. It is even possible that such data could be available dating back multiple years.

Naturalistic Observation

To conduct a naturalistic observation, researchers would want to observe students' behaviors in a diverse environment. Specifically, researchers could sit in a university cafeteria and systematically observe interactions that students have with other students of different racial and economic backgrounds. The researchers could assess who students eat with, how conversations occur, and how the similarities and differences impact students' behaviors.

Survey

The easiest way for a researcher to evaluate the impact of diversity on a student's college experience is to administer a survey. In particular, a researcher could develop a survey to assess students' behaviors and opinions on diversity. Then, the researcher could obtain a sample of students from the larger university population that is representative of the university as a whole (we will discuss sampling procedures in Chapter 8). Finally, the researcher would administer the survey to the students and collect data on the impact that diversity has on their college experience.

Chapter Summary

- Research methodologies can be broken down into two types: qualitative and quantitative (pp. 56–57).
  - Qualitative research methodologies seek subjectivity through in-depth collection of information and emerging hypotheses (pp. 56–57).
  - Quantitative research methodologies seek objectivity through testable hypotheses and carefully designed studies (p. 57).
- Oftentimes, researchers prefer to distinguish research as either nonexperimental or experimental research methods (p. 57).
  - Experimental research is a class of research methodologies that involves direct manipulation of a variable (p. 57).
  - Nonexperimental research is a class of research methodologies that examines relationships among variables (p. 57).
- Correlational research establishes relationships between variables. Correlations can be either positive or negative (pp. 57–60).
  - Positive correlations have variables that vary in the same direction (pp. 57–58).
  - Negative correlations have variables that vary in opposite directions (pp. 57–58).
- There are six main types of nonexperimental research methods: ethnography, naturalistic observations, case study, archival research, and survey research (p. 61).
  - Ethnography is used to describe a culture in detail by recoding and transcribing events that are witnessed (p. 61).
  - Naturalistic observation occurs when a researcher observes people or animals in their natural setting (pp. 61–63).
  - A case study is an in-depth observation of an individual, animal, event, or treatment method (pp. 63–64).
  - Archival research occurs when a researcher uses existing records and selects portions of the records to examine (pp. 64–65).
  - A similar type of research methodology to archival research is a content analysis. However, in a content analysis the researcher counts the number of times a particular piece of content occurs (p. 65).
- Survey research involves designing a questionnaire to obtain information regarding behaviors, attitudes, or opinions (pp. 66–70).

♦ When conducting survey research, the construction of the questionnaire is vital to gathering data. To construct a strong questionnaire, there are eight steps you need to follow (pp. 66–69):

- ♦ Determine purpose of questionnaire (p. 66).
- ♦ Determine type of questions (p. 67).
- ♦ Ask about one issue per question (p. 67).
- ♦ Make alternatives clear (p. 68).
- ♦ Write questions in an unbiased manner (p. 68).
- ♦ Avoid negative wording (p. 68).
- ♦ Avoid leading questions (p. 68).
- ♦ Most importantly, obey law of parsimony (pp. 68–69).

APA Learning Goals Linkage

- **Goal 2.** *Research Methods in Psychology*
Students will understand and apply basic research methods in psychology, including research design, data analysis, and interpretation.

    Sections Covered: Differentiating among Methods, Introduction to Correlational Methods, Nonexperimental Methods

    Explanation of the Goal: Throughout this chapter, we have explored basic research methods in psychology such as the difference between qualitative and quantitative research designs. In addition, we have worked on distinguishing the nature of designs that permit causal inference from those that do not. The designs that do not permit causal inferences would include those that fall into the category of nonexperimental methods. Furthermore, we have described how various designs (i.e., correlational research, ethnography, naturalistic observations, survey, content analysis, etc.) address different types of questions and hypotheses, while also articulating the strengths and limitations for each of these methods.

- **Goal 3.** *Critical Thinking Skills in Psychology*
Students will respect and use critical and creative thinking, skeptical inquiry, and, when possible, the scientific approach to solve problems related to behavior and mental processes.

    Sections Covered: You Try It! in Introduction to Correlational Methods, Nonexperimental Methods, You Try It! in Surveys

    Explanation of the Goal: In many places in this chapter, we have worked on critical thinking skills. In order to complete the You Try It! section on identifying positive and negative correlations, you had to make linkages between diverse observations such as increases in ice-cream sales and murder rates. In addition, you worked on developing sound arguments based on reasoning while solving the You Try It! section using

(Continued)

(Continued)

archival methods to understand student participation in the research day. Finally, we spent time approaching problems effectively and evaluating the quality of a solution in the You Try It! section on survey construction.

- **Goal 4.** *Application of Psychology*
Students will understand and apply psychological principles to personal, social, and organizational issues.

    Sections Covered: Are You Equipped?, Introduction to Correlational Methods, Nonexperimental Methods

    Explanation of the Goal: There are multiple examples in this chapter where we applied psychology to solving problems, investigating behaviors of interest, explaining social issues, and informing public policy. First, we devoted time to indentifying appropriate applications of psychology to solve problems such as picking college courses. Second, time was spent investigating behaviors of interest like bathroom behaviors of males when another male is present. Finally, we articulated how psychological principles can be used to explain social issues and inform public policy when discussing marital satisfaction and counseling, as well as police interactions with Mexican American gangs.

- **Goal 5.** *Values in Psychology*
Students will be able to weigh evidence, tolerate ambiguity, act ethically, and reflect other values that are the underpinnings of psychology as a discipline.

    Sections Covered: Nonexperimental Methods

    Explanation of the Goal: As psychologists, we want to study behaviors and mental processes. However, oftentimes it is not ethical to conduct a true experiment with experimental manipulations. Therefore, this chapter covered alternative methodologies under the topic of nonexperimental designs that allow us to understand behaviors that ethically we cannot manipulate.

- **Goal 7.** *Communication Skills*
Students will be able to communicate effectively in a variety of formats.

    Sections Covered: Nonexperimental Methods

    Explanation of the Goal: In Chapter 4, we have discussed the importance of communicating effectively. This is especially true during survey construction. Specifically, we have shown that by articulating questions thoughtfully and purposefully when constructing a survey instrument, we can strengthen research results and limit spurious outcomes.

C H A P T E R

5

Variables, Reliability, and Validity

CHAPTER OUTLINE

Are You Equipped?

The debate between Apple and Microsoft has taken on new meaning as of late. Historically, these two companies have competed on an uneven playing field in the home/personal computer (PC) market, with Microsoft dominating. Recently, the two companies have hit the television airwaves putting out new advertisements aimed at getting people to buy either a PC or a Mac. Each company has gone about doing this in vastly different ways. Mac advertisements generally focus on the fact that Mac users are young and cool, while PC users are older and behind the times. In addition, Mac advertisements focus on the problems that accompany the use of a PC. On the other hand, PC advertisements have focused on the cost of each product. In their advertisements, Microsoft touts that Macs are affordable for only the elite, whereas PCs are priced for everyone. However, the goal for both companies is the same. The advertisements are developed to influence your choice when buying a computer.

These are commercials that you see regularly on television. Can you think of how using the commercials (to influence buyers' decisions) involve basic research elements? These commercials use basic research elements because of the use of variables. For example, the two competing commercials can serve as an independent variable. An independent variable is a variable that you think will produce a change or will influence the results. The two companies are producing commercials because they believe the commercials will influence buyers' decisions. The decisions of the buyers would be the dependent variable. A dependent variable is the variable that you observe and measure to see if the independent variable had an influence. You can bet that both companies are watching sales each month to see if the current commercials are working. In this chapter, we will provide more examples of independent and dependent variables. This will allow you to spot research design elements in everyday life.

As you go through this chapter, we also want you to keep in mind how the material relates to the APA goals for psychology majors. Specifically, this chapter will address the following goals:

- **Goal 1. Knowledge Base of Psychology**
  Students will demonstrate familiarity with the major concepts, theoretical perspectives, empirical findings, and historical trends in psychology.
- **Goal 2. Research Methods in Psychology**
  Students will understand and apply basic research methods in psychology, including research design, data analysis, and interpretation.
- **Goal 3. Critical Thinking Skills in Psychology**
  Students will respect and use critical and creative thinking, skeptical inquiry, and, when possible, the scientific approach to solve problems related to behavior and mental processes.
- **Goal 4. Application of Psychology**
  Students will understand and apply psychological principles to personal, social, and organizational issues.
- **Goal 5. Values in Psychology**
  Students will be able to weigh evidence, tolerate ambiguity, act ethically, and reflect other values that are the underpinnings of psychology as a discipline.

AN INTRODUCTION

In order to discuss different types of methodologies in research, we must first start with the basics. In this chapter we will focus on some of the elementary concepts of research. To begin, the chapter will introduce you to types of variables that are common in research. This will be followed by an overview of the importance of reliability in research designs. Finally, we will conclude with a discussion on validity and its role in maintaining sound research.

Variables—Independent and Dependent

VARIABLE

An event or characteristic that has at least two possible values.

INDEPENDENT VARIABLE

The variable in a study that is being manipulated.

A **variable** is an event or characteristic that has at least two possible values. For example, what would be the variable if we were to ask you, "How stressed are you about taking research methods?" In this example, the condition that can have an assigned or attached value is your level of stress. Furthermore, the amount of stress you indicate in your answer is the value that is associated with the variable. There are two variables that are essential to research. These two variables are the independent variable and the dependent variable.

The **independent variable** is the variable in a study that is being manipulated by the researcher. It is being manipulated because it is the variable that the researcher believes will produce a change in his or her study. The other variable of interest is the dependent variable. A **dependent variable** is the variable within a study that is observed or measured. Specifically, the dependent variable is the variable that a researcher believes will change or will be influenced in the study. Usually, any change that is seen within the dependent variable is a result of the independent variable. In other words, any measureable change from the independent variable's influence will be seen in the dependent variable. The way in which a dependent variable is measured is very important to the success of a research study. To help understand these two new terms, we will go through the example below.

DEPENDENT VARIABLE

The variable in a study that is observed or measured.

A marketing researcher has developed advertisements for television and radio for a new type of toothpaste. The researcher is looking to conduct a study to determine which advertisement is better at getting people interested in the toothpaste. The research question is, "Does the type of advertisement influence the level of interest in the toothpaste?" In order to test this research question, the researcher has participants listen to the radio advertisement or watch the television advertisement about the toothpaste. After listening to or viewing the advertisement, the researcher asks the participants how interested they would be in using the toothpaste in the advertisement by responding on a 7-point scale, with 1 indicating "not at all interested" and 7 indicating "very interested."

For this research study, the independent variable is the type of advertisement that was used (i.e., television or radio). Remember, the independent variable is the variable that the researcher believes will produce a change. In this case, the researcher wanted to know if a difference would be seen in the types of advertisements (i.e., television or radio). The dependent variable is the level of interest in the toothpaste expressed by the participants. Keep in mind, the dependent variable is the measurable variable in a study. Thus, it is the variable where a change can be observed. In this study, the level of interest can be measured for each participant using the 7-point scale. This measurement can be used to see if there was a difference between participants who listened to a radio advertisement and participants who viewed a television advertisement.

YOU TRY IT!

The Mozart effect is a psychological topic that has received much publicity over the past few decades. The Mozart effect is the theorized temporary increase in spatial reasoning abilities following listening to Mozart. The general public is very interested in this idea. In fact, when our oldest daughter was born, the hospital sent us home with a CD of classical music, instructing us to play the music to increase our daughter's intelligence. The scientific community has continuously studied the topic to determine if support for the effect can be found.

Recently, the Mozart effect was again studied by two researchers, Jones and Estell (2007). Part of the study was to assess whether listening to Mozart's music improves spatial reasoning skills in certain high-school populations. In order to make this determination, the researchers conducted a simple study. High-school students were divided into two groups of participants. The first group listened to Mozart's music for 7.5 minutes and the second group did not. Following the 7.5 minutes of either listening to music or not, both groups completed a series of spatial problems tasks. Results showed that the group of participants who listened to Mozart's music had higher scores on the spatial problems tasks compared to the group of participants who did not listen to Mozart's music.

(Continued)

(Continued)

Questions

1. What is the independent variable in this study? Specifically, what was the variable that was manipulated because it was hypothesized to produce a change?

2. What is the dependent variable in this study? Specifically, what was the variable that was observed and measured in this study?

3. According to Jones and Estell's (2007) results, was support for the Mozart effect found?

Answers

1. In this study, music was the independent variable. It was manipulated by having participants either listen to Mozart or no music at all. Researchers manipulated the variable of music because they hypothesized it would influence spatial abilities.

2. The dependent variable in this study was spatial reasoning skills. Remember, the dependent variable is the variable that is measured because it is believed to be impacted by the independent variable. In this particular study, the variable that was believed to be impacted by the music was a participant's spatial reasoning skills, which were tested by a series of spatial tasks.

3. Yes, based on the results obtained from Jones and Estell's (2007) study, the Mozart effect did occur. We mentioned earlier that the Mozart effect is the temporary increase in spatial reasoning following listening to Mozart. Upon listening to Mozart's music and completing the spatial tasks, participants who had listened to the music performed better than those who did not listen to the music. Therefore, in this experiment the Mozart effect was supported.

Subject Variables

SUBJECT VARIABLE

A characteristic or attribute of a participant that can impact a study.

There is another type of variable that we want to discuss that is used in research that has some of the same qualities as the independent variable. This variable is known as a subject variable. A **subject variable** is a characteristic or attribute of a participant that can impact the participant's behavior or thoughts within a study. Subject variables are often traits that are specific to a participant, such as gender, age, or ethnicity, and these traits can influence the dependent variable.

A subject variable is similar to an independent variable in that it is predicted to influence the dependent variable and cause a change. However, subject variables are not true independent variables. This is because a researcher can manipulate an independent variable and choose how the participant will be exposed to it. Yet, a researcher cannot truly manipulate a subject variable. For example, let's go back to the advertising study at the beginning of this chapter. In that study, the participants had a chance to be exposed to either a radio or television advertisement. On the other hand, if the researchers wanted to know the influence of participants' gender on interest in the toothpaste, the researchers could not have exposed participants to the variable of gender. Participants would have arrived to the study with the subject variable as part of their identities. Although you cannot directly manipulate a subject variable like a true independent variable, it is still possible to see if the responses on the dependent variable are influenced.

YOU TRY IT!

Questions

In the following mini-research studies, can you identify which variable is the independent variable or subject variable and which variable is the dependent variable?

1. A researcher is interested in determining if different exercise programs have an influence on the amount of weight that participants lose. Upon arriving to the experiment, the researcher assigns the participants to different exercise programs and measures the amount of weight lost over a two-month period.

2. You predict that people from different religious backgrounds will vary in terms of their racial tolerance. You have participants complete a survey that gathers information on their current religion and measures racial tolerance.

3. Your university wants to know if its graduates make more money when compared to high-school graduates. So, the university surveys a sample of college graduates and high-school graduates and asks participants to indicate their current salary.

4. A professor wants to know if the amount of time spent studying for a test influences test performance. She has participants study for either 30 minutes or 1 hour before taking the test.

Answers

1. The exercise programs are the independent variable. This is because the researcher manipulates the exercise program given and predicts it will influence weight loss. The dependent variable is the amount of weight lost. This is the dependent variable because it is observed and measured for change.

2. The variable of religion is a subject variable in this study. Religion is like an independent variable in that you can predict it will influence racial tolerance. However, you cannot directly manipulate a participant's religion. The dependent variable is racial tolerance.

3. The variable of level of education is a subject variable in this study. Researchers can examine the influence of a participant's educational level (e.g., whether they graduated from high school or college) but cannot directly manipulate this variable. The dependent variable is job salary. This is the variable that the university measured.

4. The independent variable is the amount of time spent studying. This is the independent variable because the researcher can manipulate how the participants are exposed to study time and because study time is predicted to influence test performance. The dependent variable is the scores on the test. This is where the researcher predicts the change can be observed.

Treatment Conditions

An independent variable will always have at least two conditions. These are referred to as **treatment conditions**. Typically, the treatment conditions are the experimental and the control group. The **experimental group** is the group that is exposed to the independent variable. In other words, the experimental group is the group of participants that is given the independent variable and is the group where we would expect to see a measureable change occur. The **control group** is

TREATMENT CONDITIONS

Levels or number of groups in the independent variable.

EXPERIMENTAL GROUP

The group that is exposed to the independent variable in a study.

CONTROL GROUP

The group that is not exposed to the independent variable.

the group of participants that is not exposed to the independent variable. This group does not receive the independent variable, and, therefore, we do not expect to see any measurable change in the participants.

In the study above on Mozart, the experimental group was the group of participants that was exposed to the independent variable. This was the group that listened to Mozart's music for 7.5 minutes before completing the spatial problems task. The control group was the group of participants who did not listen to any music for 7.5 minutes before completing the spatial problems task. The control group provided a comparison so that the researchers could determine if listening to Mozart influenced performance on the spatial problems task. (We will discuss treatment conditions further in Chapter 7 when we discuss levels of the independent variable.) It should be noted that although traditionally a control group is not exposed to the independent variable, there is an exception. If a researcher is comparing a new method to the current (or old) method then the current (or old) method is serving as the control group. The new method would serve as the experimental group. An example comes from one of our classes. Jenn wanted to know how teaching statistics in her traditional manner compared to a new method where students were to develop skits to explain the material. To see if there was a difference in student learning, she compared exam scores of those students in the traditional section to those students in the new method section. In this case, the traditional manner is serving as the control group. Scores from the new method group, experimental group, are then compared to the traditional group to examine the influence on learning. So even though we typically refer to the control group as the absence of exposure to the independent variable, in some cases the control group might involve exposure to the standard or typical level of the independent variable.

In addition to the experimental and control groups, there is another group that is often used as a treatment condition in research. This group is known as the **placebo control group**. The placebo control group is similar to the control group in that participants assigned to this condition are not exposed to the independent variable. However, the placebo control group is different from the control group because the participants are exposed to a placebo. A placebo is an inert substance or object that is similar to the independent variable but has no direct effect. Essentially, the placebo control group acts as an insurance policy. Sometimes researchers see measurable changes in the experimental group that are not due to the independent variable but to the participant's belief that a change will occur. Therefore, the placebo control group acts as a way for the researcher to determine how much measurable change is due to the independent variable and how much change is due to the participant's belief in a change occurring. For example, if you wanted to know if caffeine influences levels of alertness, you could have three treatment conditions. The first treatment condition, the experiment group, would receive the independent variable in the form of a caffeinated beverage. The second treatment group, the control group, would receive nothing. The third treatment group, the placebo control group, would receive a beverage believed to contain caffeine. However, in reality the beverage would not contain caffeine (such as a caffeine-free beverage). You could then measure participants' levels of alertness in all three groups. Having the placebo control group would allow you to see if alertness levels changed not due to caffeine, but due to the participants' belief in the influence of caffeine on behavior.

PLACEBO CONTROL GROUP

The treatment group which is exposed to an inert substance or object that is similar to the independent variable but has no effect.

YOU TRY IT!

There are many advertisements on television for antidepressants. Have you ever wondered how a researcher knows if these drugs will reduce symptoms of depression? Drug companies conduct research studies to determine the effectiveness of medications. Take a look at this scenario. A drug company wants to know if a new antidepressant is effective at reducing the symptoms of depression. The drug company has sampled people who are depressed and placed them into an experimental group and a control group. The participants in the experimental group will receive the new drug and the participants in the control group will receive nothing. For eight weeks, the experimental group will receive daily doses of the new drug and the control group will receive nothing. After eight weeks, the drug company measures the level of depression in the participants again. The results show that participants in the experimental group are less depressed compared to participants in the control group. Therefore, the drug company concludes that its drug is effective at reducing symptoms of depression.

Questions

Now that we have introduced the idea of a placebo control group, we want you to: (a) describe why having a placebo control group would be of benefit to this design and (b) describe what participants in the placebo control group would do during the experiment.

Answers

When looking at the scenario above, you might wonder if the drug really worked. It could easily be the case that those participants in the experimental group wanted the drug to work and that participants' belief alone in the drug reduced the symptoms of depression. Adding a placebo control group to the design ensures that observed changes in the symptoms of depression were due to the drug itself (independent variable) and not participants' belief in the drug's effectiveness. Participants in a placebo control group would have gone through the same events as participants in the experimental group, taking a pill every day for eight weeks. The pill given to the placebo control group would look exactly the same as the pill given to the experimental group, but would be an inert substance (e.g., a sugar pill). In other words, the participants in the placebo control group would have received something that looked like the independent variable but had no direct therapeutic effect. If, after eight weeks, the participants in the placebo control group showed the same reduced levels of depression as participants in the experimental group, the researchers should question if the drug alone is causing the change. However, if the participants in the placebo control group demonstrated similar levels of depression to participants in the control group after eight weeks, the researcher would have reason to believe that the drug is effective in reducing symptoms of depression. We will return to the topic of placebos and placebo control groups in Chapter 9.

Section Summary

- A *variable* is an event or characteristic that has at least two attached values (p. 76).
- When conducting a study, there are two important variables to be considered (pp. 76–77):
  - The *independent variable* is the variable in a study that is being manipulated by the researcher (pp. 76–77).

♦ The *dependent variable* is the variable within a study that is observed or measured (p. 77).
♦ A *subject variable* is a characteristic or attribute of a participant that can impact the participant's behavior or thought within a study (pp. 78–79).
  ♦ Subject variables are often traits that are specific to a participant, such as gender, age, or ethnicity (pp. 77–78).
♦ *Treatment conditions* refer to levels or number of groups in the independent variable (pp. 79–80).
  ♦ The *experimental group* is the group that is exposed to the independent variable (pp. 79–80).
  ♦ The *control group* is the group that is not exposed to the independent variable (pp. 79–80).
  ♦ The *placebo control group* is exposed to an inert substance or object that is similar to the independent variable but has no effect (pp. 79–80).

RELIABILITY AND VALIDITY

In the first part of this chapter, we introduced you to the concept of variables and discussed independent and dependent variables. When you read about independent and dependent variables, it is important to consider two measurement concepts. The first concept is reliability. Reliability deals with the consistency when measuring variables in a research study. The second concept is validity. Validity is concerned with the accuracy of the measurements used to assess different variables. In the remainder of this chapter, we will present you with specific techniques used to establish the reliability and validity of variables. We will begin with reliability.

Reliability

RELIABILITY

The consistency of your measure to produce similar results on different occasions.

TEST–RETEST RELIABILITY

A reliability assessment where your measure is tested on two different occasions for consistency.

Reliability of a variable is very important when conducting research. **Reliability** is the consistency of your measure to produce similar results on different occasions. Therefore, reliability is primarily concerned with being able to replicate or reproduce the findings. To make sure a measure is consistent in its ability to evaluate a variable, there are several types of reliability assessments.

The most common type of reliability assessment is known as **test–retest reliability**. When using a test–retest assessment, you give your measure to a sample of participants individually (*test*) and then again at a later date (*retest*). Usually, the testing is done a few weeks apart. In order to make sure the measure is reliable, you look at the two scores for each participant. If the measure is reliable, the individual will have comparable scores on the two points in time. For example, if we were to give an intelligence test to your class at the beginning of the semester and then again midway through the semester, we would expect to see similar scores for each person. We would not expect the scores to be exactly the same, just close. To determine whether the measure is reliable, you compute a correlation coefficient for the scores. A correlation coefficient of .80 in a measure is generally seen as very reliable. At this point, you do not need to know how to compute a correlation coefficient. Rather, the goal is to have you prepared to know what to look for when reading about this procedure in research articles. One disadvantage of the test–retest procedure is that it is time consuming.

Another method that does not require the same amount of time to assess reliability is known as the **split-half method**. The split-half method occurs when you administer a measure to a sample of participants. Unlike a test–retest method, where you would wait several weeks before giving the measure again, the split-half method uses only the results from the first collection of data. Specifically, you would split the measure in half. It might sound strange to split a measure in half. However, consider assessing the reliability of a 50-question multiple-choice exam. This could be done by randomly assigning questions from the exam to two groups, dividing the exam between odd and even questions, or by dividing the exam at the midpoint. You then compute scores for each half finding a correlation coefficient between the two halves. One concern is that the method in which you split the halves can impact the correlation. Specifically, if you unknowingly have several similar questions in the same half and none in the other half, the correlation will be low. Therefore, many researchers use a modified version of the split-half method known as internal consistency.

The **internal consistency** method is the same as the split-half method with one exception. In the internal consistency method, you repeat the split-half procedure multiple times, thus collecting multiple correlation coefficients. Then, you average the multiple correlation coefficients. This method counteracts the impact of having too many similar questions in only one-half of the split. A commonly used statistic for computing internal consistency is Cronbach's alpha (Aron, Aron, & Coups, 2009).

Another way to assess the reliability of a measure is to use the **parallel-forms method**. In this method of reliability assessment, you divide a measure into two parts. Questions from the original measure are randomly divided among the two parts. You then administer both of the parts to a sample of participants. Following the administration, you compute the correlation coefficient for the two parts. The higher the correlation between the parts, the more reliable the measure is said to be. The benefit to this approach is the brief amount of time it takes to assess reliability. However, one disadvantage is that you must generate a large number of questions in order to divide into two parts.

The last assessment of reliability that we want to discuss is **interrater or interobserver reliability**. The previous assessments of reliability were focused on how you would construct a measure (such as constructing an exam in a class). However, interrater or interobserver reliability is focused on using a measure consistently in research. Interrater reliability is used when a research design calls for observations of an event. This type of reliability assessment is used to ensure that the observations being made are consistent and not biased. For example, if you want to evaluate bullying behavior in children, you could observe 100 instances of bullying and categorize the bullying into one of four categories. If you were the only researcher making the observations, there is no way to know if you consistently categorized the 100 observations. However, if there is more than one observer, you can become more confident in the ratings. Interobserver reliability uses more than one observer and the observations of the observers are compared to assess the level of agreement. In the bullying example, two or more observers would compare the categorizations of the

SPLIT-HALF METHOD

A reliability assessment in which a measure is split in half and the two halves are compared. If the correlation is high, the measure is said to have high reliability.

INTERNAL CONSISTENCY

A reliability assessment similar to the split-half method. However, the splitting occurs more than once and an average of the correlations is taken.

PARALLEL-FORMS METHOD

A reliability assessment in which a measure is divided in half and given to two groups of people. The reliability is high if each measure given is highly correlated.

INTERRATER OR INTEROBSERVER RELIABILITY

A reliability assessment used when a research design calls for observations of an event. Two or more observers compare results from their observations. The higher the observer consensus, the higher the reliability.

100 instances of bullying. If the observers were to agree 92 times out of a 100, the reliability would be 92%, which is quite reliable. However, if the observers only agreed 48 times out of a 100, the reliability would be 48% and the measure would not be very reliable. Essentially, you are calculating a correlation coefficient between the degree of similarities in the observations of the observers. To be confident in the reliability of your results, you want to obtain a high degree of similarity.

Validity

As we have mentioned, selecting your variables is an important part to any research design, as is measuring them. In this section, we will talk about the concept of validity. **Validity** is defined as the ability of your measurement to accurately measure what it is supposed to measure. This is different from reliability, which is about being able to replicate scores on future instances. Let's begin with an example.

Recently, we had a student decide to pursue his graduate degree in psychology. In order to apply to graduate school, he had to take the Graduate Record Examination (GRE). In this example, the GRE score is the measurable variable. The GRE measures a person's verbal and quantitative skills. Our student took the test and did not do very well. Believing the score was an anomaly, he took the GRE a second time. Unfortunately, the student received a similar score. It was after this second exam that we discovered the student had been taking the wrong test. Specifically, the student had been studying for the GRE-General but had taken the GRE-Psychology (or GRE subject test). The GRE-Psychology exam tests a student's knowledge of the field of psychology. You can use this example to think about validity. The GRE-Psychology is not a valid measure of a person's verbal and quantitative skills. This is because the GRE-Psychology is designed to measure knowledge in the area of psychology. Thus, it makes sense why the student was complaining that the information he studied was not on the test. You can also use this example to compare the concepts of reliability and validity. The GRE-Psychology is a reliable measure. This is because the student received similar scores both times he took the test.

Internal, External, and Construct Validity

When measuring a variable, there are several types of validity to consider. The three most common types of validity are internal validity, external validity, and construct validity. Each of these types of validity deals with a different aspect of measurement. However, the commonality in all is that they are concerned with the accuracy of the measures used in a research design. The first type of validity we will discuss is internal validity. Internal validity is an important factor for independent variables. **Internal validity** is confidence in saying the observed change in the dependent variable is due to the independent variable and not due to any outside influences. This allows you to make a causal inference regarding the influence of the independent variable on the dependent variable. This is important when conducting a study because you want to be able to show that the manipulation had an impact.

Rothbaum, Anderson, Hodges, Price, and Smith (2002) examined different types of therapies to relieve fear of flying. Specifically, over a six-week period, participants were placed into one of three groups, where each group was exposed to a different type of therapy. After six weeks, the researchers measured participants' fear of flying. The interesting part to this study was that the researchers again assessed participants' fear of flying one year after the conclusion of the study. Results showed that the levels of fear had remained relatively stable since the end of the study. Therefore, the researchers concluded that the introduction of the independent variable (types of therapy) had caused a measurable change in the dependent variable (fear of flying). We mention this study to bring up the idea that researchers need to remain vigilant as to factors that might threaten the internal validity of their study. For example, do you think that the follow-up results (i.e., results after 12 months) would have been different had the events on September 11, 2001, occurred during that time? The answer is probably yes. Had the results been different and the fear level was higher, the researchers would not have been able to conclude that the independent variable had a lasting influence. There are many threats to internal validity that a researcher must be aware of when conducting research. We will discuss many of these threats later in Chapter 9.

The next type of validity we want to discuss is external validity. **External validity**, also known as ecological validity, is the extent to which the obtained results in a study can be generalized to other settings. When considering external validity, you examine if any changes in the dependent variable can be applied to similar events. Specifically, can the results you obtained in the laboratory occur in a real-world setting? Researchers are often confronted with problems due to external validity. This is because a large percentage of research is conducted in a laboratory environment, where the researcher can isolate a single independent variable to determine its influence on a dependent variable. However, since research is done in such controlled environments, it is sometimes difficult to know if the causal inference drawn in the laboratory will apply to the real world.

EXTERNAL VALIDITY

The extent to which the obtained results in a study can be generalized to other settings.

One way to combat threats to external validity is to design experiments as close to the real world as possible. For example, researchers in the area of cognitive psychology have done much research using microworld simulations and virtual computer games. Researchers continue to think outside of the box and design experiments that are as close to the real world as possible. This allows researchers to extend results obtained in the lab to the real world.

The final type of validity that we will discuss is construct validity. **Construct validity** is perhaps the most difficult to understand. **Construct validity** refers to the likelihood that the device or scale used to measure a variable actually is related to the topic or theory of interest. In other words, does the way we measure a variable accurately capture the theoretical construct behind that variable? If we are interested in measuring college student obesity, we could ask the following questions:

CONSTRUCT VALIDITY

The likelihood that the device or scale used to measure a variable actually is related to the topic or theory of interest.

Do you overeat?

    Not at all   1   2   3   4   5   6   7   All the time

How often do you eat fast food?

    Not at all   1   2   3   4   5   6   7   All the time

Do you eat vegetables?

    Not at all   1   2   3   4   5   6   7   All the time

On the surface, these questions might appear as though they will measure the variable of obesity. (This is known as face validity, where the device or scale has the superficial look to assess a variable's theoretical construct.) However, what is the likelihood that participants in your study would be truthful in their answers? In addition, just because you eat a lot of food or fast food does not necessarily mean that you are obese. Conversely, eating lots of vegetables does not mean you are skinny. If these were the questions you used to assess college student obesity, you might have low construct validity.

In order to have higher construct validity, you can assess two different components that are related to construct validity. The first component is **convergent validity**. The logic behind convergent validity is that your measure should converge or be similar to other measures of the same variable. Therefore, to have high construct validity your measure for a variable should show similar results to other valid measures of the same variable. Going back to the example on obesity, your measure should yield results similar to that of a valid measure of obesity. The second component that is related to construct validity is **divergent or discriminant validity**. This is the opposite of convergent validity. Whereas convergent validity argues that your measure of a variable should be similar to other valid measures of the same variable, divergent validity argues that your measure should be dissimilar to measures of different variables. Looking at the example of obesity again, your results from your measure should look similar to other obesity measures, but should not look similar to say a measure on diabetes. By using these two related components when developing measures of variables, researchers are able to increase construct validity in their study.

CONVERGENT VALIDITY

A type of construct validity that states that your measure should converge or be similar to other measures of the same variable.

DIVERGENT OR DISCRIMINANT VALIDITY

A type of construct validity that argues that your measure should be dissimilar to measures of different variables.

Section Summary

- *Reliability* is the consistency of your measure to produce similar results on different occasions. There are several ways to assess reliability (pp. 82–84):
  - *Test–retest reliability* is a reliability assessment where your measure is tested on two different occasions for consistency (p. 82).
  - *Split-half reliability* is a reliability assessment in which a measure is split in half and the two halves are compared. If the correlation is high, the measure is said to have high reliability (p. 83).
  - *Internal consistency* is a reliability assessment similar to a split-half method. However, the splitting occurs more than once and an average of the correlations is taken (p. 83).
  - The *parallel-forms* method is a reliability assessment in which a measure is divided in half and given to two groups of people. The reliability is high if each measure given is highly correlated (p. 83).
  - *Interrater reliability* is used when a research design calls for observations of an event. Two or more observers compare results from their observations. The higher the observer consensus, the higher the reliability (pp. 83–84).

- *Validity* is the accuracy of a measure to evaluate what it is supposed to measure. The three most common types of validity are internal, external, and construct validity (pp. 84–86).
  - *Internal validity* provides confidence in saying that the observed change in the dependent variable is due to the independent variable and not due to any outside influences (pp. 84–85).
  - *External validity* is the extent to which the obtained results in a study can be generalized to other settings (p. 85).
  - *Construct validity* refers to the likelihood that the device or scale used to measure a variable actually is related to the topic or theory of interest. Construct validity is composed of two components, convergent validity and divergent validity (pp. 85–86).
    - *Convergent validity* states that your measure should converge (or be similar) to other measures of the same variable (p. 86).
    - *Divergent validity* argues that your measure should be dissimilar to measures of different variables (p. 86).

Are You Equipped Now?

Part I

Do you ever talk on your cell phone while driving a car? It is ok to admit it! In fact, so many people talk on their cell phones while driving that researchers have studied how this can influence driving abilities. For the purposes of this exercise, we are going to give you a simplified version of an experiment conducted by Drews, Pasupathi, and Strayer (2008). Drews et al. wanted to manipulate driving conditions (i.e., driving while talking to a friend on the cell phone or driving while talking to a friend in the car) to see if this influenced the number of driving errors committed. Participants completed this task on a driving simulator that simulated 24 miles of driving. Results indicated that driving while talking on the cell phone produced more driving errors than driving while talking to a passenger.

For this experiment, answer the following questions:

1. What is the independent variable?
2. What is the dependent variable?
3. How did the researchers try to increase the ecological validity of the experiment?

Answers

1. The variable that the researchers manipulated is the driving condition. Specifically, the researchers varied if participants were driving while talking to a friend on the cell phone or driving while talking to a friend in the car. The researchers manipulated this variable because they predicted it would influence driving abilities.
2. The variable that the researchers measured was the number of driving errors. Thus, driving errors was the dependent variable. The researchers did find that the dependent variable was influenced by the independent variable, with the highest driving errors occurring in the cell phone condition.
3. The researchers increased the ecological validity of the experiment by having participants drive on the simulator. This increases the likelihood that the results can be generalized to the real world.

Part II

As mentioned above, we are simplifying the actual experiment for the purposes of this exercise. However, we want to tell you about one more part to the experiment. In addition to recording driving errors, the researchers also recorded the conversations between the driver and the friend on the cell phone and in the car. The researchers wanted to know if the driving condition influenced the number of references made to traffic conditions. The conversations were transcribed and two observers reviewed the conversations, documenting the number of references made to traffic. The interrater reliability was .92. Results indicated that the driving condition did influence the number of references made to traffic conditions. Specifically, more references were made to the traffic when the driver was talking with the friend in the car compared to when the driver was talking on the cell phone.

Based on this new information, answer the following questions:

1. What is the independent variable?
2. What is the new dependent variable?
3. Why did the researchers use interrater reliability and was the level obtained appropriate?

Answers

1. Just as in part I, the variable that the researchers manipulated was the driving condition. Specifically, the researchers varied if participants were driving while talking to a friend on the cell phone or driving while talking to a friend in the car. The researchers manipulated this variable because they predicted it would influence the number of references made to traffic.
2. The variable that the researchers measured was the number of references made to traffic in the participants' conversation. Therefore, the number of references made about traffic was the dependent variable. The researchers did find that the dependent variable was influenced by the independent variable, with the highest number of references regarding traffic occurring while talking to a passenger.
3. The researchers used interrater reliability to increase the probability that the results could be replicated in the future and would be consistent across researchers. The level that the researchers obtained was appropriate and indicated a high degree of similarity between the two observers.

Chapter Summary

- A *variable* is an event or characteristic that has at least two possible values (p. 76).
- When conducting a study, there are two important variables to consider: (pp. 76–77).
    - The *independent variable* is the variable in a study that is being manipulated (pp. 76–77).
    - The *dependent variable* is the variable within a study that is observed or measured (p. 77).

- A *subject variable* is a characteristic or attribute of a participant that can impact the participant's behavior or thought within a study (pp. 78–79).
    - Subject variables are often traits that are specific to a participant, such as gender, age, or ethnicity (pp. 77–78).
- *Treatment conditions* refer to the levels or the number of groups in the independent variable (pp. 79–80).
    - The *experimental group* is the group that is exposed to the independent variable (pp. 79–80).
    - The *control group* is the group that is not exposed to the independent variable (pp. 79–80).
    - The *placebo control group* is exposed to an inert substance or object that is similar to the independent variable but has no effect (pp. 79–80).
- *Reliability* is the consistency of your measure to produce similar results on different occasions. There are several ways to assess reliability: (pp. 82–84)
    - *Test–retest reliability* is a reliability assessment where your measure is tested on two different occasions for consistency (p. 82).
    - *Split-half reliability* is a reliability assessment in which a measure is split in half and two halves are compared. If the correlation is high, the measure is said to have high reliability (p. 83).
    - *Internal consistency* is a reliability assessment similar to a split-half method. However, the splitting occurs more than once and an average of the correlations is taken (p. 83).
    - The *parallel-forms* method is a reliability assessment in which a measure is divided in half and given to two groups of people. The reliability is high if each measure given is highly correlated (p. 83).
    - *Interrater reliability* is used when a research design calls for observations of an event. Two or more observers compare results from their observations. The higher the observer consensus, the higher the reliability (pp. 83–84).
- *Validity* is the accuracy of a measure to evaluate what it is supposed to measure. The three most common types of validity are internal, external, and construct validity (pp. 84–86).
    - *Internal validity* is confidence in saying the observed change in the dependent variable is due to the independent variable and not due to any outside influences (pp. 84–85).
    - *External validity* is the extent to which the obtained results in a study can be generalized to other settings (p. 85).
    - *Construct validity* refers to the likelihood that the device or scale used to measure a variable actually is related to the topic or theory of interest. Construct validity is composed of two components, convergent validity and divergent validity (pp. 85–86).
        - *Convergent validity* states that your measure should converge (or be similar) to other measures of the same variable (p. 86).
        - *Divergent validity* argues that your measure should be dissimilar to measures of different variables (p. 86).

APA Learning Goals Linkage

- **Goal 1.** *Knowledge Base of Psychology*

  Students will demonstrate familiarity with the major concepts, theoretical perspectives, empirical findings, and historical trends in psychology.

  Sections Covered: Are You Equipped?, An Introduction, Are You Equipped Now?

  Explanation of the Goal: The field of psychology uses specific concepts to account for psychological phenomena. This chapter introduced concepts such as independent, dependent, and subject variables. The exercises at the beginning and the end of the chapter helped you practice identifying these variables.

- **Goal 2.** *Research Methods in Psychology*

  Students will understand and apply basic research methods in psychology, including research design, data analysis, and interpretation.

  Sections Covered: An Introduction, Reliability and Validity, Are You Equipped Now?

  Explanation of the Goal: This chapter covered two areas in basic research methods. First, we introduced different research methods used by psychologists. The methods included the use of an experimental group, a control group, and a placebo control group. Next, we introduced two important terms in research: validity and reliability. After learning about these terms, you should be able to: (a) evaluate the validity of conclusions presented in research reports, (b) select and apply appropriate methods to maximize internal and external validity and reduce plausibility of alternative explanations, and (c) use reliable and valid measures of variables of interest.

- **Goal 3.** *Critical Thinking Skills in Psychology*

  Students will respect and use critical and creative thinking, skeptical inquiry, and, when possible, the scientific approach to solve problems related to behavior and mental processes.

  Sections Covered: Are You Equipped?, An Introduction, Are You Equipped Now?

  Explanation of the Goal: Critical thinking skills are needed to identify variables of interest presented in research scenarios. This chapter contained many exercises requiring you to identify independent, dependent, and subject variables, in addition to explaining how and why placebo control groups are utilized.

(Continued)

- **Goal 4.** *Application of Psychology*

  Students will understand and apply psychological principles to personal, social, and organizational issues.

  Sections Covered: Are You Equipped?, An Introduction, Reliability and Validity, Are You Equipped Now?

  Explanation of the Goal: In our discussion of concepts in research methods such as variables, reliability, and validity, we used examples from everyday life and examples that can be applied to personal and social issues. These examples were also diverse in scope to appeal to a wide range of students. We began the chapter with an example on computer advertising. We also presented examples on the influence of listening to classical music and ways to reduce the fear of flying, and concluded the chapter with an example on cell phone use while driving cars.

- **Goal 5.** *Values in Psychology*

  Students will be able to weigh evidence, tolerate ambiguity, act ethically, and reflect other values that are the underpinnings of psychology as a discipline.

  Sections Covered: An Introduction

  Explanation of the Goal: Psychological explanations are complex in nature. Thus, to answer research questions, more sophisticated designs (e.g., use of a placebo control group) are sometimes needed. In addition, to ensure that explanations are correct, reliability and validity are key.

Experimental Research Methods

Hypothesis Testing

CHAPTER OUTLINE

Are You Equipped?

Over the past 10 years, we have had an ongoing discussion about our writing abilities. This stems from the fact that we disagree over who is the better writer. During graduate school, our professors confirmed that Jenn was the better writer. However, John's writing skills significantly improved during graduate school and this accomplishment was recognized at his dissertation defense. So, this brings us to today. As we begin to write chapters that students traditionally find more problematic, Jenn insists that she should do the majority of the writing, while John insists that he is equally qualified. In other words, John is arguing there is *no difference* in writing abilities and Jenn is arguing that there *is a difference* in writing abilities and that she is a *better* writer than John.

We are telling you about our ongoing discussion to illustrate research and statistical hypotheses. In this chapter, we will present the topics of null and research hypotheses. You will then be able to see how our discussion presented above actually relates to hypothesis testing.

As you go through this chapter, we also want you to keep in mind how the material relates to the APA goals for psychology majors. Specifically, this chapter will address the following goals:

- **Goal 1. Knowledge Base of Psychology**
  Students will demonstrate familiarity with the major concepts, theoretical perspectives, empirical findings, and historical trends in psychology.
- **Goal 2. Research Methods in Psychology**
  Students will understand and apply basic research methods in psychology, including research design, data analysis, and interpretation.
- **Goal 3. Critical Thinking Skills in Psychology**
  Students will respect and use critical and creative thinking, skeptical inquiry, and, when possible, the scientific approach to solve problems related to behavior and mental processes.
- **Goal 4. Application of Psychology**
  Students will understand and apply psychological principles to personal, social, and organizational issues.
- **Goal 6. Information and Technological Literacy**
  Students will demonstrate information competence and the ability to use computers and other technology for many purposes.

FORMULATING A RESEARCH QUESTION

To introduce this topic, we would like for you to take a moment and recall a famous psychology experiment. This could be an experiment that you learned about in a General Psychology course. Can you describe some of the details of the experiment? Now, what if we asked you tell us what the research question for that experiment was? All of a sudden, this task has taken on a more complex nature. What we have just demonstrated to you is that there is a difference between a research topic and a research question.

RESEARCH TOPIC

A broad concept or idea.

A **research topic** consists of an idea that is not very well defined. We will discuss a little later where to get started in research and where ideas come from. However, generating research ideas at this point might seem intimidating. Below are some examples that we received from students when we asked them to generate research ideas in class:

Student 1
    Eating disorders and athletes

Student 2
    Texting and college students

Student 3
    Sexual abuse by teachers

Student 4
    Sexual orientation and religion

Although the students were providing us research ideas, they were not giving us research questions. If you were to take any of these research topics above, you could go in one of a thousand different directions. For example, look at student number one from the previous page. This student could be interested in males or females, anorexia or bulimia, amateur or professional athletes, and so on.

On the other hand, a **research question** is a better-defined idea. Specifically, research questions are written generally as a structured sentence expressing some amount of clarity. Additionally, a research question helps you to narrow your idea from being broad to something more specific. This is in stark contrast to a research topic which is broad in scope and is full of ambiguity. Hence, how would you take the aforementioned research topics of our students and represent them in a research question? Below are some examples of how our students moved their research topics into a specific research question.

RESEARCH QUESTION

States a research idea in a clearly defined manner that is testable.

Student 1

Are female high-school athletes at greater risk of acquiring an eating disorder than female college athletes?

Student 2

What is the prevalence of using text messaging in inappropriate situations (e.g., in class) by college students?

Student 3

Do female high-school teachers who engage in sexual activities with their students receive lighter sentences as compared to male teachers?

Student 4

Do homosexuals who attend regular religious services have higher or lower self-esteem?

The research questions above are far more direct and narrow than the topics that were originally proposed by the students. The research questions are stated in such a way that a project can be clearly identified and executed as opposed to the ambiguous nature of identifying a research topic.

We want to relate the concepts of research topics and questions to experiments conducted in the field of psychology. First, we will talk about the research of Albert Bandura. Possibly the most famous study conducted by Bandura (1965) was on observational learning. Bandura (1965) utilized a video that recorded adults playing with Bobo dolls in an aggressive manner. (FYI—a Bobo doll is a large inflated balloon that generally has a character like a clown on it and is filled with sand at the bottom so that it stands upright.) Following the adult's play, the adults were either: (a) positively reinforced with sweets for their behavior, (b) punished with scolding or spanking for their behavior, or (c) received no consequence for their behavior.

This video was then shown to preschool children who observed either the reinforcement, punishment, or no consequences condition. After viewing the video, the children were allowed to play in a room full of toys. In addition to all the toys, the room contained a Bobo doll. Results showed that the children who viewed the video with the adults receiving punishment following their interaction with the Bobo doll engaged in far less aggressive behaviors toward the doll than the other two groups (i.e., the reinforcement and no consequences). In Bandura's experiment, what was the research topic(s) and what was the research question?

As a reminder, a research topic is very broad and general in scope. The research topics in this experiment were observational learning, reinforcement, punishment, and children. All of these topics were present in the study. Yet, the research question for this experiment was more specific. This is because a research question provides some level of clarity and directionality to research. Thus in this experiment, the research question was extremely detailed and thorough in its content: Does the type of reinforcement or punishment given to the model influence the observer's aggressive behaviors? It still encompasses the research topics, in addition to providing the readers (and researcher for that matter) with direction.

To further illustrate the point, here is another example. Elizabeth Loftus conducted one of the most influential studies in memory distortion and eyewitness recall over three decades ago. In her study, Loftus and Palmer (1974) showed a video of the two cars involved in a car wreck. After the video, Loftus and Palmer had people recall the events and then answer several questions. One of the questions asked the participants to estimate the speeds of the two cars. However, the groups of people received questions that were worded slightly differently. Loftus and Palmer asked one group, "About how fast were the cars going when they *hit* each other?" For other groups, they replaced the word *hit* with *smashed, collided, bumped,* and *contacted.* As you might have predicted, the type of verb used changed participants' perceptions of speed. For this experiment, what were the research topic(s) and the research question?

For this experiment, the research topics were eyewitness recall, leading questions, and memory. These are very broad and can encompass a wide range of possible research ideas. However, the research question for this experiment was more detailed. Specifically, Loftus and Palmer's (1974) research question sought to determine if leading questions had long-term consequences on what a person remembers about an eyewitness event. Once more, this adds a level of clarity to the research project that the research topics alone do not. Now that we have discussed the difference between research topics and research questions, and have covered examples in psychological research, we can turn our attention to an earlier identified problem: Where do research ideas come from?

Getting Your Research Idea

We have just gone through two classic experiments in psychology, and while both had a large impact on their field, each researcher started at the same place: What am I going to investigate? Before the first participant is selected, methodology decided upon, and piece of data collected, all researchers must first develop an idea. One of the fundamental questions that we routinely get from undergraduates surrounds this very concept. Students ask us questions including: (a) what are we going to do a project on, (b) where do we get ideas from, or (c) how do I start a research project? Most research ideas are developed from one of four areas: everyday experiences, functional problems, prior research, and theory.

The most basic place where ideas come from is **everyday experiences**. Generally, when asked by a student for help in coming up with an idea, we ask the student what interests him or her? By our nature, humans are curious about the world around us and we all enjoy explaining the things we experience (Piaget, 1954). For example, how many times have you walked by something and thought why did that occur or why did that person do that? This is an excellent start for a research idea. Asking those questions have led to the development of psychology as a science and to some of the greatest discoveries in the field. After all, where would the field of psychology be if Ebbinghaus (1885) hadn't asked "why do we forget," Pavlov (1926) hadn't asked "why are those dogs salivating when they hear my footsteps," or Loftus (1997) hadn't asked "are people's eyewitness accounts accurate."

You might be thinking that it cannot be that simple. Those researchers we mentioned were big names with big brains. However, it is that simple. They all started out as a student like you. For example, all of you are planning on a career in the near future after graduation. So, how are you going to decide on which job you are going to take? This practical question could become a research question. In fact, one of our undergraduates asked this very question and designed a study to determine what factors contribute to a college student selecting a job. You can try this too. Think about a topic that you find interesting from an aspect of everyday life. It could have to do with buying products, choosing where to eat, selecting a pet, or even asking why people behave in a certain way. Think about how that aspect of everyday life could become a research question.

Other times, research is born from people attempting to solve **functional problems**. Functional problems are real-world situation in which a solution is needed. For instance, researchers who developed medication to reduce the symptoms of depression were tackling a functional problem (i.e., depression). Previous researchers had identified the symptoms of depression, but these researchers decided to do something about this problem.

Likewise, a major problem in professional sports is the use of steroids. Recently, countless athletes in football, baseball, track and field, as well as other sports have been charged with anabolic steroid use. Therefore, it is no surprise that professional sports organizations spend millions and millions of dollars every year to combat this problem. Nearly all of this money is spent on research. This research is conducted to detect steroids, determine the results of steroid use, and develop effective ways to curb use among athletes and teenagers in general. Thus, research is often born from the need to solve functional problems that exist in the world.

Have you ever read the last part of a scholarly research article? Generally, near the end of a journal article, the author(s) lists several possible extensions to the research presented in the manuscript. This is an excellent place to get new ideas for research. Often, people will take the recommendations of authors and proceed with the suggested research from this **prior research**. This will in turn produce additional research. Once you start doing research, any research you conduct will inevitably produce new ideas. In other words, research leads to more research. Throughout the research process, you will always think of an additional twist to

EVERYDAY EXPERIENCES

Using experience from life to obtain a research idea.

FUNCTIONAL PROBLEMS

Using real-world problems as a source for a research idea.

PRIOR RESEARCH

Using what others have done as a starting point to obtain a research idea.

your current research project. Although you may want to change your current idea, this is a time to write down your idea and use it for your next project.

For example, past work by Asch (1955) on conformity has led to years of research and published articles by many other people. You probably talked about Asch's (1955) studies on conformity in your General Psychology class, in which he presented people with a *standard line* and three *comparison lines.* Then each participant had to verbally indicate which comparison line was equal to the standard line. The basic tenet is that people will conform (i.e., change their opinion or behavior in response to real or imagined pressure) in a social situation. In Asch's study, three-quarters conformed at least once by indicating a wrong response. This work led to Asch and others conducting additional research on why people conform, the causes of conformity, and how to reduce conformity.

THEORY

Using an interrelated set of concepts to explain a body of data to obtain your research idea.

Finally, many people develop research ideas by using a previous **theory** in a novel way. Take for instance the movie *A Beautiful Mind.* For those who are unfamiliar with this movie, it is a movie about a famous mathematician, Dr. John Nash, who develops a new theory about mathematical relationships often called the Nash equilibrium theory. The catch is that Dr. Nash has schizophrenia and battles with this illness throughout the movie. In real life, Dr. Nash's schizophrenia is under control and he is a brilliant mathematician. Originally, Dr. Nash's theory was only used sparingly and only in the field of mathematics. However, his theory was later applied to many different areas, including economics. It was this application in economics that won Dr. Nash a Nobel Prize many years later. Thus, it was due to the use of Nash's theory in a novel way that led to new research and applications.

In cognitive psychology, Information Integration Theory (IIT) has been applied to a number of topic areas. Developed by Norman Anderson (1979) in the 1960s and 1970s, IIT accounts for decisions made in a complex world. Anderson proposed that people follow algebraic rules when making decisions. Specifically, IIT allows researchers to determine how people make decisions and the way they combine information about a decision to arrive at a choice. IIT has been used to determine how people make decisions in sports (Rulence-Pâques, Fruchart, & Dru, V., & Mullet, E. 2005), in social interaction (Christiansen, Kaplan, & Jones, 1999), on smoking and alcohol use (Hermand, Mullet, & Lavieville, 1997), and in groups (Graesser, 1990). Again, this is an example of a theory being used in a variety of different ways and not only within a specific area of psychology.

As can be seen, research ideas are everywhere. There is no set formula that should be used to develop a research idea. It is not a secret that only the extremely bright and intelligent are privileged to know. Rather, you as a potential researcher or consumer of research should be open to the idea that research can come from anywhere and everywhere. Just focus on the things that you know and find interesting, and we guarantee a research question will develop.

Conducting Searches

Now that we have discussed ways to generate research ideas, it is time to explore how you would gather information on your selected topic. Not too long ago, researchers had to physically go to a library and search through a card catalog for information on their topic. Thankfully, the tools for these types of searches have been updated and can now be done over the Internet. Most universities have access to electronic databases where you can search for information on a given topic. In psychology, the most commonly accessed databases are PsycINFO and PsycARTICLES. Both of these databases have been developed and are maintained by APA. Each database has its advantages and disadvantages.

PSYCINFO®. PsycINFO is an abstract database maintained by APA that contains over 2.7 million records dating back to the 1600s. It is called an abstract database because according to APA, it contains the abstracts or summaries from over 2,500 journals, books, book chapters, and dissertations. This database is the most comprehensive source for published psychological content. The biggest drawback to this database is that the information is not always available in full-text. However, PsycINFO contains all the information you will need to locate an article, including the authors, place of publication, and year of publication. Once an article is located by PsycINFO as being relevant to your search, it is then up to you to decide if you would like that source. Once you decide, you will need to get the article through your university library. Although this database does not always offer full-text, it does contain nearly every record on anything that is psychological in nature. Therefore, the odds of finding relevant information are extremely likely.

PSYCINFO®
Largest electronic psychological abstract database by APA.

PSYCARTICLES®. The other commonly accessed database for searching the psychological literature is PsycARTICLES. Unlike PsycINFO, PsycARTICLES only contains a relatively small number of records—according to APA, around 135,000 in 60+ journals. Like PsycINFO, PsycARTICLES does offer the abstract citation with all the relevant information. However, PsycARTICLES is known as a full-text database. Specifically, PsycARTICLES provides direct access to all the research articles that are contained within the database. Therefore, some researchers prefer searching through PsycARTICLES because of the convenience of having access to the entire article. The big disadvantage to using this database is the limited number of records it contains. With a small group of articles to search, you limit the likelihood of finding the information you may need.

PSYCARTICLES®
A full-text electronic psychological database by APA.

THE INTERNET AS A SOURCE. In addition to the aforementioned search engines, the Internet offers many more. Search engines on the **Internet** such as Google and Yahoo! are becoming an increasingly popular way to collect information. However, unlike PsycINFO and PsycARTICLES, the information on the Internet is not always (a) verifiable or (b) reliable. Simply, the information people find on the Internet is *not always* regulated. Anyone with access to a computer could potentially put anything on the Internet. When searching the Internet, you need to be careful about the quality of the information you are reading. For example, information from sites that end in .com or .net is often not regulated. These sites may put information on the Internet, but who is to say it is valid? Often people behind the sites are selling something, so you need to question the information presented. Some websites end in .org. This ending usually represents sites that are for organizations or foundations. Many of these sites are nonprofit and are putting information on the Internet as a service to the public. However, it is important to be aware of the fact that the creators of websites can have agendas and may skew information presented to serve their needs. Websites may also end in .edu (like that of your university) and

INTERNET
A worldwide, publicly accessible network containing vast amounts of information.

these are education websites. The information obtained here is for the most part considered legitimate. However, again there is little accountability for the information provided. Finally, some websites are .gov. These represent websites hosted by government agencies, which are generally reliable. The lesson about the Internet is simple. Although there is a wealth of information to be found, the validity (i.e., the accuracy of information) is not always high. If you find information on the Internet, it is always best to find the actual research the claims are based on in order to be sure that each website is reporting information correctly.

Starting a Search

Everyone reading this book has conducted a search on the Internet for something. Usually, you just type in the topic and the Internet responds with millions of websites. If you were to conduct a search in one of the psychological databases, the same event would occur. The two biggest problems that students encounter when searching for information is finding either too much or too little information. Each of these problems is easily remedied if you search properly. Specifically, when searching, you do not want to be too broad in your search or too narrow. Below is an example in which we will walk you through the process.

Let's say that your research question for an upcoming class project is this: "Does viewing violent pornography influence men's attitudes toward women?" As we mentioned previously, many students get frustrated because they do not search properly. In this example, students will either do one of two things. First, they will type into their search engine (say PsycINFO) the word "pornography" (see Figure 6.1). This will yield a **large number of records** (or hits), over 1,100. No one really wants to sift through 1,100+ abstracts trying to find relevant information on a topic. Here, students are being too broad in their search. After this attempt, students usually take the extreme opposite approach. Specifically, students will input the entire research question into the search engine, "Does viewing violent pornography influence men's attitudes toward women?" Not too surprisingly, the PsycINFO search returns with **0 records** (or hits). Too often, this is where we hear students indicate there is nothing on their topic. However, as we have indicated, this is a result of not searching properly.

So how do you search properly? For any search, you should first identify the main topic areas. In this case, the main topics are violent pornography and attitudes. It is not the topics individually that are of interest. Rather, it is the overlap (see Figure 6.2). By searching "attitudes" or "pornography" alone, you will get a large number of records, 250,000+ and 1,100+, respectively. However, it is the common ground between the two topics that contains the desired information. Therefore by searching pornography *and* attitudes together, PsycINFO will only return those records that contain information on both pornography and attitudes, 330+ results. By simply adding the word *and*, you have narrowed your search considerably (see Figure 6.3 on page 104). Yet, this search could be refined even further. Specifically, the type of pornography is vital in this research question: violent. Therefore, you can redo your search by adding violent to the search criteria. Now your search is for pornography AND attitudes AND violent. The result is that you have narrowed your search to a little over 40 records that have the search criterion you used (see Figure 6.4 on

LARGE NUMBER OF RECORDS

Occurs when a researcher uses terms in a search engine that are too broad.

SMALL NUMBER OF (OR NO) RECORDS

Occurs when a researcher uses terms in a search engine that are too specific.

FIGURE 6.1 View of PsycINFO Search Engine.

FIGURE 6.2 Search Overlap.   Topic Overlap

page 104). This is a manageable number of records to search through and should give you an idea of what research has been done previously on your topic.

In addition to searching properly, you need to be flexible in the words you use when searching. Changing your search words such as "pornography" to "x-rated" or using another **synonym** can yield records that your previous search did not include. Remember, there is always more than one way to identify a topic. You might use one set of terminology and someone else who has done work on your topic might use a different set of terminology. As a searcher, you need to be flexible and think of other ways to articulate your research question.

USING SYNONYMS

When conducting searches, you may need to think of a synonym for your research topic.

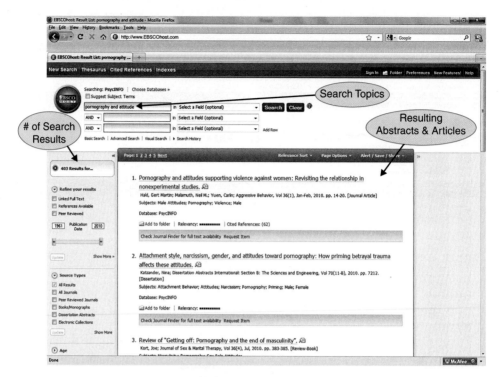

FIGURE 6.3 Search Window Results for Overlapping Topics.

FIGURE 6.4 Search Window Results When Further Narrowing Topic.

We have just gone through several concepts related to acquiring your research topic as well as your research question. Once you have identified these factors, finding information is relatively straightforward. As soon as you have a research question and know what has been done on your topic, it is time to develop your hypotheses. The next section will walk you through this process.

Section Summary

- A *research topic* is a very broad idea or set of ideas that are ambiguous (pp. 96–98).
- A *research question* states your research idea in a clearly defined manner that is testable (pp. 97–98).
- Research ideas can be generated from (a) everyday experiences, (b) functional problems, (c) prior research, and (d) theories (pp. 98–100).
- Psychological databases such as PsycINFO and PsycARTICLES are great places to search for information on your research topic (p. 101).
- Internet resources can be helpful in finding information. However, the accuracy of these sources must be confirmed (pp. 101–102).
- When searching for previous research on a topic, make sure your topics are not too broad or too narrow (pp. 102–104).

GENERATING HYPOTHESES

How many of you grab a soft drink out of the vending machines before class or grab a cup of coffee before an early morning class? We remember taking a night class in graduate school that definitely required such a beverage to stay awake. We probably have all reached for a beverage with caffeine to keep us awake or "make it through" those days when we are extremely tired. If we wanted to test the idea that drinking caffeine actually helps to keep us awake, we would first need to form a research question. Our research question would be, "Does caffeine influence levels of alertness?" The next step for us to test the research question would be to generate hypotheses.

You might have been taught in elementary school that a hypothesis is an educated guess. We would like to elaborate on that definition and add that a **hypothesis** is a statement about the relationship between variables. In our example, we need hypotheses that make statements about the relationship between the variables of caffeine and alertness. More specifically, we need two hypotheses which are mutually exclusive and exhaustive. This means that of our two hypotheses only one can be true *and* that these hypotheses are the only two possibilities. Take a look at the two hypotheses below regarding the variables of caffeine and alertness.

HYPOTHESIS
A statement about the relationship between variables.

Hypothesis 1: Caffeine *does not* have an influence on levels of alertness.

Hypothesis 2: Caffeine *does* have an influence on levels of alertness.

As you read Hypotheses 1 and 2, you will notice that they are mutually exclusive. If Hypothesis 1 is correct, Hypothesis 2 can't be correct. If Hypothesis

2 is correct, Hypothesis 1 can't be correct. Furthermore, these hypotheses are the only possibilities.

When researchers go to test their hypotheses, they refer to Hypothesis 1 as the **null hypothesis**. The null hypothesis always states that there is *no difference* or relationship among the scores of the dependent variables being studied. In other words, there is no influence of the independent variable on the dependent variable. In our example, the null hypothesis is stating that the independent variable (i.e., caffeine) does not influence the dependent variable (i.e., levels of alertness). The null hypothesis is generally expressed in the following symbols.

$$\text{Hypothesis 1 in symbols: } H_0 \quad \mu_1 = \mu_2$$

H_0 stands for the null hypothesis. The symbol μ stands for the mean of the population. Thus, this symbol means that the mean of population 1 *is equal to* the mean of population 2. In our example, we would state the mean levels of alertness of the population of individuals who consumed caffeine *is equal to* the mean levels of alertness of the population of individuals who did not consume caffeine. So we are specifying who group 1 is and who group 2 is.

$$H_0 \quad \mu_{(\text{participants who consumed caffeine})} = \mu_{(\text{participants who did not consume caffeine})}$$

It may seem awkward that the null hypothesis which states that caffeine does not influence alertness uses the words "is equal to." However, reasoning through this helps to understand why this is the case. If caffeine does not influence alertness, people who consume caffeine have the same levels of alertness as people who do not consume caffeine.

Hypothesis 2 is referred to as the **research hypothesis** (or alternative). The research hypothesis always states the opposite of the null. This means the research hypothesis always states that there *is a difference* on the scores of the dependent variables. In other words, there is an influence of the independent variable on the dependent variable. In our example, the research hypothesis is stating that the independent variable (i.e., caffeine) does influence the dependent variable (i.e., alertness). The research hypothesis is generally expressed in the following symbols.

$$\text{Hypothesis 2 in symbols: } H_1 \quad \mu_1 \neq \mu_2$$

H_1 stands for the research hypothesis. The symbol μ stands for the mean of the population. Thus, this symbol means that the mean of population 1 *is not equal to* the mean of population 2. In our example, we would state the mean levels of alertness of the population of individuals who consumed caffeine *is not equal to* the mean level of alertness of the population of individuals who did not consume caffeine.

$$H_1 \quad \mu_{(\text{participants who consumed caffeine})} \neq \mu_{(\text{participants who did not consume caffeine})}$$

It may seem awkward that the research hypothesis which states that caffeine does influence alertness uses the words "is not equal to." However, reasoning through this helps to understand why this is the case. If caffeine does influence alertness, people who consume caffeine will have different levels of alertness as compared to people who do not consume caffeine.

Researchers have some options when selecting the research hypothesis. In the example above, we selected a **nondirectional research hypothesis**. A nondirectional hypothesis states that the independent variable (i.e., caffeine) has an influence on the dependent variable (i.e., alertness), but it does not give the specific direction the influence might have. In other words, it does not specify if caffeine will increase or decrease levels of alertness. If researchers wanted to be more specific in their research hypothesis, they could form a **directional research hypothesis**. A directional research hypothesis predicts a specific direction that the results will occur. In our example, we could have predicted that caffeine increases levels of alertness and the symbols would be as follows:

$$H_1 \quad \mu_{(\text{participants who consumed caffeine})} > \mu_{(\text{participants who did not consumecaffeine})}$$

This would mean that the participants who consumed caffeine had higher levels of alertness than the participants who did not consume caffeine. It is important to realize that a researcher only has *one* research hypothesis. The researcher must pick from one of these three options: there is a difference (nondirectional), there is an increase in the dependent variable (directional), or there is a decrease in the dependent variable (directional).

To further illustrate the point, here is another example. Think back to the Are You Equipped section at the beginning of this chapter, where your textbook authors were having a discussion about who is the better writer. The research question for this discussion would be, "Does textbook author influence writing quality?" In response to this question, John stated that there is no difference in writing abilities. More specifically, John stated that the textbook author who was writing the majority of the chapter (Jenn versus John) did not influence the writing quality. However, Jenn stated that there is a difference in writing abilities and that she is the better writer. More specifically, Jenn stated that the textbook author who was writing the majority of the chapter (Jenn versus John) did influence the writing quality and that Jenn's writing was of higher quality than John's writing.

In this example, who is stating the null hypothesis? In other words, we want to know who is stating that the independent variable (i.e., the authors of the textbook) does not influence the dependent variable (i.e., writing quality). If you said John, you are correct. John is stating Jenn's writing is equal to John's writing and this is expressed in symbols in the following way:

$$H_0 \quad \mu_{(\text{Jenn's writing})} = \mu_{(\text{John's writing})}$$

On the other hand, Jenn is stating the research hypothesis that the independent variable (i.e., the authors of the textbook) does influence the dependent variable (i.e., writing quality). Jenn is stating that Jenn's writing is not equal to John's writing and this would be stated in symbols in the following way:

$$H_1 \quad \mu_{(\text{Jenn's writing})} \neq \mu_{(\text{John's writing})}$$

NONDIRECTIONAL RESEARCH HYPOTHESIS

A hypothesis that does not make a prediction about the direction that the results will occur in.

DIRECTIONAL RESEARCH HYPOTHESIS

A hypothesis that predicts a specific direction that the results will occur in.

When Jenn says that the writing abilities are not equal (as in the symbols above), is she stating a nondirectional research hypothesis or a directional research hypothesis? If you said nondirectional, you are correct. Jenn is stating there is a difference in writing abilities but has not yet specified who is the better writer.

Next, Jenn specifies that she believes she is the better writer and this would be expressed in symbols in the following way:

$$H_1 \quad \mu_{(Jenn's\,writing)} > \mu_{(John's\,writing)}$$

Now when Jenn says that her writing abilities are better than John's (as in the symbols above), is she stating a nondirectional research hypothesis or a directional research hypothesis? If you said directional, you are correct. Jenn is stating the specific direction she is predicting for the results.

YOU TRY IT!

We want you to practice generating null and research hypotheses. Below we have given you three research questions. For each, you are to: (a) state the null hypothesis in words and in symbols, (b) state the research hypothesis in words and in symbols, and (c) say if your research hypothesis is nondirectional or directional.

1. Not too long ago Heinz Ketchup started producing ketchup in different colors besides the traditional red. For example, they produced green ketchup. The research question for this example is, "Does color of ketchup (traditional red versus green) influence people's willingness to buy ketchup?"

2. We have a graduate student who shared the following hypothesis. Our graduate student believes that you can determine a woman's arrogance by the size of her sunglasses. The research question for this example is, "Is there a relationship between size of sunglasses (regular versus extra large) and a woman's arrogance?"

3. We are relatively young professors. Sometimes our age works to our benefit in that we can relate well to our students. However, other times our age works against us. Occasionally, students might not realize that although we are young we still have expertise in our areas. This leads us to wonder if age of professor can have an influence on the class. The research question for this example is, "Does age of professor (young versus mature) influence students' participation in class?"

Answers

Below are the answers to these practice exercises. Take a look at our answers and see how you did at generating null and research hypotheses.

1. In the Heinz Ketchup example, the first thing you need to do is reread the research question: "Does color of ketchup (traditional red versus green) influence people's willingness to buy ketchup?" When forming the null hypothesis for this research question, be sure you are stating that the independent variable (i.e., color of ketchup) does not influence the dependent variable (i.e., a person's willingness to buy ketchup). Your null hypothesis could state, "Color of ketchup does not influence people's willingness to buy ketchup." It is also equally correct to word your null hypothesis in the following way: "There is no influence of the color of ketchup

(Continued)

on people's willingness to buy ketchup." Both of these wordings are correct because they mean the same thing (i.e., the independent variable does not influence the dependent variable). Your null hypothesis would be expressed in symbols in the following way:

$$H_0\ \mu_{(red\ ketchup)} = \mu_{(green\ ketchup)}$$

More specifically, these symbols mean that people's willingness to buy red ketchup is equal to people's willingness to buy green ketchup. (Remember the null hypothesis, which states there is no influence of the independent variable on the dependent variable, uses the equal to sign in the equation).

As you picked your research hypothesis, you had three options. The options were (1) a nondirectional research hypothesis, (2) a directional research hypothesis with a prediction in one direction, and (3) a directional research hypothesis with a prediction in the opposite direction. Any of the three research hypotheses would have been correct. Let's further investigate each of these three hypotheses.

If you had selected a nondirectional hypothesis you might have said, "Color of ketchup does influence people's willingness to buy ketchup" or "There is an influence of the color of ketchup on people's willingness to buy ketchup." This nondirectional research hypothesis would be expressed in symbols as follows:

$$H_1\ \mu_{(red\ ketchup)} \neq \mu_{(green\ ketchup)}$$

These symbols mean that people's willingness to buy red ketchup is not equal to people's willingness to buy green ketchup.

If you had formed a directional research hypothesis, you might have said, "People are more willing to buy red ketchup than green ketchup," and this would be expressed in symbols as:

$$H_1\ \mu_{(red\ ketchup)} > \mu_{(green\ ketchup)}$$

Finally, if you had formed a directional research hypothesis in the opposite direction, you might have said, "People are more willing to buy green ketchup than red ketchup," and this would be expressed in symbols as:

$$H_1\ \mu_{(red\ ketchup)} < \mu_{(greenketchup)}$$

2. In the sunglasses example, the research hypothesis was, "Is there a relationship between size of sunglasses (regular versus extra large) and a woman's arrogance?" Your null hypothesis, stating that the independent variable of sunglass size does not predict the dependent variable of a woman's arrogance, could have been stated as, "The size of a woman's sunglasses is not related to her arrogance" or "There is no relationship between the size of a woman's sunglasses and her arrogance." The null hypothesis would be symbolized as:

$$H_0\ \mu_{(regular)} = \mu_{(extra\ large)}$$

This would mean that the arrogance level of a woman wearing regular-size sunglasses is equal to the arrogance level of a woman wearing extra-large sunglasses.

Again, as you picked your research hypothesis, you were faced with the option of selecting a nondirectional research hypothesis or a directional research

(Continued)

hypothesis. Your nondirectional research hypothesis would state, "The size of a woman's sunglasses is related to her arrogance" and would be symbolized as:

$$H_1 \ \mu_{(regular)} \neq \mu_{(extra\ large)}$$

This would mean that the arrogance level for a woman wearing regular-sized sunglasses is not equal to the arrogance level of a woman wearing extra-large sunglasses.

If you selected a directional research hypothesis, you could have stated, "A woman who wears regular-sized sunglasses is more arrogant than a woman who wears extra-large sunglasses"

$$H_0 \ \mu_{(regular)} > \mu_{(extra\ large)}$$

or that "A woman who wears extra-large sunglasses is more arrogant than a woman who wears regular-sized sunglasses."

$$H_0 \ \mu_{(regular)} < \mu_{(extra\ large)}$$

3. In the final example, the research hypothesis was, "Does age of professor (young versus mature) influence students' participation in class?" The null hypothesis would state, "Age of professor does not influence students' participation in class" or "There is no influence of age of professor on students' participation in class." In symbols, this would be stated as class participation of students with a young professor is equal to class participation of students with a mature professor:

$$H_0 \ \mu_{(young)} = \mu_{(mature)}$$

For the research hypothesis, you had three options. The nondirectional research hypothesis would state in words, "Age of professor does influence students' participation in class," represented in symbols as

$$H_0 \ \mu_{(young)} \neq \mu_{(mature)}$$

If you picked a directional research hypothesis, it would have stated either that "Young professors have more student participation in class than mature professors"

$$H_0 \ \mu_{(young)} > \mu_{(mature)}$$

or that "Mature professors have more student participation in class than young professors."

$$H_0 \ \mu_{(young)} < \mu_{(mature)}$$

How did you do? As you may have noticed above, your hypotheses might not have been worded exactly like ours. What is important, though, is that the meaning is the same. Ask yourself, does my null hypothesis say there is no influence of the independent variable on the dependent variable? If so, you are on the right track. Likewise, ask yourself, does my research hypothesis say that there is an influence of the independent variable on the dependent variable? If so, you are on the right track. If you have a question about whether or not the hypothesis you generated is saying the same thing as ours, be sure to ask your professor.

We want to mention two final topics on generating null and research hypotheses before moving on. First, most of the time when you read research articles the authors will state their research hypothesis and not mention the null hypothesis. This is because researchers are most interested in the research hypothesis and it is assumed that the reader knows the null hypothesis is the hypothesis being tested. Second, you may be wondering how to decide whether or not to use a nondirectional or directional research hypothesis. This is a great question, because the type of research hypothesis you select can influence the way you analyze your data. For right now, though, we will keep it simple. Unless you have a really good reason to believe your results will come out in a specific direction, you should use a nondirectional research hypothesis. However, if you are basing your research hypothesis off of previous research, you might have enough evidence to suggest your results will come out in a specific direction and you should use a directional research hypothesis.

TESTING THE HYPOTHESIS

When you test your hypotheses, you are actually testing the null hypothesis. If your results are so extreme that they could not likely be due to chance, then you can reject the null hypothesis and conclude that the independent variable did have an influence on the dependent variable. We will explain this in more detail in Chapter 14.

We also want to point out that results of a study are never used to *prove* a research hypothesis or a null hypothesis. Psychologists avoid saying that results of an experiment prove a research hypothesis to be true. Rather, depending on the outcome, psychologists say either that results *support* a research hypothesis or that the study is inclusive.

Section Summary

- The *null hypothesis* states there is *no* difference between the groups of scores on the dependent variables (p. 106).
- The *research hypothesis* states that there *is* a difference between the groups of scores on the dependent variables (pp. 106–107).
- Research hypotheses can be either directional or nondirectional (pp. 107–108).
  - A *nondirectional hypothesis* makes no specific prediction as to the direction the results will occur (pp. 107–108).
  - A *directional research* hypothesis makes a specific prediction as to the direction the results will occur (pp. 107–108).

Are You Equipped Now?

Think about a time when you have been sick. Did it influence your ability to perform even the simplest of tasks let alone a full-time job? Research conducted by Smith, Tyrrell, and Willman (1987) sought to investigate this exact problem. Although we all know intuitively that sickness can have a negative impact on human performance, Smith et al. decided to test this experimentally. Specifically, the researchers in this experiment wanted to know what influence the exposure to minor illness has on the efficiency of human performance. The researchers believed that illness would negatively impact human performance. In order to test this hypothesis, Smith et al. infected people with influenza and the common cold. Following infection, the researchers kept the participants quarantined for 10 days while they studied the effects. The results indicated that while the cold affected eye–hand coordination, influenza only affected a person's ability to detect and respond to stimuli. In other words, there were differences between participants' performance before and after being infected.

Questions

From this example, can you identify the following elements:

1. The research question.
2. The null hypothesis in symbols and words.
3. The research/alternative hypothesis in symbols and words.

Answers

1. In this experiment, the research question was, "What influence does the exposure to minor illness have on the efficiency of human performance?" To visit an earlier topic, the research topics were illness and human performance.

2. Hypothesis 1: Exposure to minor illness *does not* have an effect on human performance. The null hypothesis can be symbolized as:

$$H_0 \ \mu_{(before\ infection)} = \mu_{(after\ infection)}$$

3. Hypothesis 2: Exposure to minor illness *does* have an effect on human performance (nondirectional).

    In this experiment, the researchers chose a directional research hypothesis in that they believed exposure to minor illness would have a negative affect on human performance. The nondirectional and directional hypotheses can be symbolized as follows:

    The nondirectional hypothesis:

$$H_1 \ \mu_{(before\ infection)} \neq \mu_{(after\ infection)}$$

    The directional hypotheses:

$$H_1 \ \mu_{(before\ infection)} > \mu_{(after\ infection)}$$

$$OR$$

$$H_1 \ \mu_{(before\ infection)} < \mu_{(after\ infection)}$$

Chapter Summary

- A research topic and a research question are distinctly different. Everyone starts off with an idea in mind. This idea is usually not very well formed and quite ambiguous. When your research idea is in this form, it is a *research topic*. However, once you have refined this idea into a question that exhibits clarity and concreteness, you have developed a *research question* (pp. 96–98).

- Research ideas can be developed at anytime, in any place, and by anybody. Research ideas generally are developed from one of four areas: (a) everyday experiences, (b) functional problems, (c) prior research, and (d) theory (pp. 98–100).
  - The most basic place that ideas can come from is *everyday experiences*. All throughout your daily life, questions can arise that lead to a research idea (p. 98).
  - Another area that can lead to a research idea is when someone tries to solve a *functional problem*. Research ideas are born from problems in the world because people search for a solution (p. 98).
  - Many times, research is an extension of *prior research*. One research study often generates new problems and ideas that are an excellent starting point for the development of a new research idea (pp. 99–100).
  - Finally, new research ideas can be developed by taking a *theory* and applying it in a novel way (p. 100).
- Most searches in the field of psychology are conducted with search engines. The two most commonly accessed search engines are PsycINFO® and PsycARTICLES® (pp. 100–101).
  - PsycINFO is a psychological database that contains abstracts (i.e., short summaries about the research). PsycINFO contains nearly 2.7 million citations dating back to the 1800s. Once a citation is found to be useful, you will most likely have to find the full-text article by visiting your university library (p. 101).
  - PsycARTICLES is a full-text psychological database. The advantage is that you do not have to go to your university library to get the article you find relevant. However, this database only contains citations from roughly 135,000 articles. This is far fewer than that of PsycINFO (p. 101).
- In addition to PsycINFO and PsycARTICLES as a source for finding information, you can use Internet search engines. However, information on the Internet is not always peer reviewed or verified for accuracy. If you are going to use the Internet, you need to make sure the information you obtain is accurate (pp. 101–102).
- When gathering information about your research idea, it is best to identify the underlying topics. Searching a topic that is too broad will yield too much information on your topic. However, by searching a topic that is too narrow, very little information will be obtained on your idea (pp. 102–104).
- A hypothesis is a statement about the relationship between two or more variables. When conducting research, you should state your null hypothesis as well as your research hypothesis (pp. 105–108).
  - A null hypothesis indicates that there is *no* difference in scores on the dependent variables between groups in a study (p. 106).
  - A research hypothesis indicates that there *is* a difference in scores on the dependent variables between groups. A research hypothesis can be stated as either nondirectional (i.e., no direction is predicted) or directional (i.e., a direction is predicted) (pp. 106–108).

- ◆ Each hypothesis can also be represented symbolically (pp. 106–108).
  - ◆ Null Hypothesis: H_0 $\mu_1 = \mu_2$
    where scores from population 1 are equal to scores from population 2 and they are not different (p. 106).
  - ◆ Research Hypothesis: H_1 $\mu_1 \neq \mu_2$
    where scores from population 1 are not equal to scores from population 2 and differences exist (p. 106).
  - ◆ Directional Research Hypothesis: H_1 $\mu_1 < \mu_2$ or $\mu_1 > \mu_2$
    where scores from population 1 are greater or less than scores from population 2 (p. 107).

APA Learning Goals Linkage

- **Goal 1.** *Knowledge Base of Psychology*

  Students will demonstrate familiarity with the major concepts, theoretical perspectives, empirical findings, and historical trends in psychology.

  Sections Covered: Formulating a Research Question

  Explanation of the Goal: Although the main focus of this chapter was on hypothesis testing, we also learned about some of the classical research studies in the history of psychology. For example, we discussed the work of Bandura at the beginning of the chapter when differentiating between research topics and research questions. Later on, we covered how to get research ideas and mentioned Asch's work on conformity. Even if you have heard of these researchers before in an introduction course, it is helpful to revisit pivotal studies in the field from a research methods perspective.

- **Goal 2.** *Research Methods in Psychology*

  Students will understand and apply basic research methods in psychology, including research design, data analysis, and interpretation.

  Sections Covered: Are You Equipped?, Formulating a Research Question, Generating Hypotheses, Are You Equipped Now?

  Explanation of the Goal: To conduct research, you must know how to locate and use relevant databases. The first part of this chapter was devoted to this topic. We explored how to use PsycINFO, PsycARTICLES, and the Internet as databases. The second part of the chapter was devoted to another essential skill in research, which is formulating testable research hypotheses. Specifically, we learned how to generate null and research hypotheses.

- **Goal 3.** *Critical Thinking Skills in Psychology*

  Students will respect and use critical and creative thinking, skeptical inquiry, and, when possible, the scientific approach to solve problems related to behavior and mental processes.

(Continued)

Sections Covered: Are You Equipped?, Formulating a Research Question, Generating Hypotheses, Are You Equipped Now?

Explanation of the Goal:

This chapter opened with a discussion of research topics versus research questions. Knowing the difference between the two provided you with experience in approaching problems effectively by recognizing ill-defined and well-defined problems. Next, we used critical thinking to develop research ideas. These ideas can be obtained from everyday experiences, functional problems, prior research, and theory. Finally, we used critical thinking skills in generating multiple possible solutions to research questions when forming null and research hypotheses.

• **Goal 4.** *Application of Psychology*

Students will understand and apply psychological principles to personal, social, and organizational issues.

Sections Covered: Formulating a Research Question, Generating Hypotheses, Are You Equipped Now?

Explanation of the Goal: We presented numerous examples of how psychological principles can relate to personal and social issues in everyday life. A few examples were violence and observational learning, memory distortions and eyewitness recall, and conformity. We also practiced forming research questions with everyday topics such as willingness to buy different colors of ketchup and the relationship between human performance and sickness.

• **Goal 6.** *Information and Technological Literacy*

Students will demonstrate information competence and the ability to use computers and other technology for many purposes.

Sections Covered: Formulating a Research Question

Explanation of the Goal: APA states that psychology majors should be able to demonstrate information competence at each stage in the following process: (a) formulate a researchable topic that can be supported by database search strategies, (b) locate and choose relevant sources from appropriate media, and (c) use selected sources after evaluating their suitability. Furthermore, psychology students are expected to demonstrate these computer skills in using databases and searching the Internet for high-quality information. The information provided in the chapter on conducting searches will assist you in achieving the needed competence at each stage.

Selection of Variables, Operational Definitions, and Measurement Issues

Are You Equipped?

Do you know how much you weighed when you were born? We just read an article from the news looking at the relationship between birth weight and adolescent depression. The news article was summarizing research findings of Costello and colleagues (2007). Specifically, the researchers used 1,420 participants who were assessed yearly for depression between the ages of 9 and 16, and participants' mothers provided the researchers with the birth weight information. The birth weights were divided into two levels. Those participants weighing less than 5.5 pounds at birth were considered to be of low birth weight, and those weighing more than 5.5 pounds were considered to be of normal birth weight. Results indicated that for female participants there were differences in rates of depression based on birth weights. Here are the results:

- 38.1% of female participants of low birth weight experienced at least one episode of depression during adolescence compared to 8.4% of female participants of normal birth weight.
- 23.5% of female participants of low birth weight reported being depressed each year compared to 3.4% of female participants of normal birth weight.

As you read this example, you might be wondering lots of things—what was my birth weight, why is birth weight related to depression, what other factors could be causing the depression besides the birth weight, and so on. However, for the purposes of this chapter, we would like to draw your attention to identifying the independent variable and the dependent variable. Remember from Chapter 5 that the independent variable is the variable thought to produce a change and the dependent variable is the variable that is being measured to look for this change. In this study, the researchers were looking at the relationship between birth weight and adolescent depression. Therefore, the variable being measured for change was rates of adolescent depression. Now, what variable was thought to influence rates of adolescent depression? The answer is birth weight. Keep in mind that birth weight is actually a subject variable being treated as an independent variable.

As you go through this chapter, we also want you to keep in mind how the material relates to the APA goals for psychology majors. Specifically, this chapter will address the following goals:

- **Goal 2. Research Methods in Psychology**
  Students will understand and apply basic research methods in psychology, including research design, data analysis, and interpretation.
- **Goal 3. Critical Thinking Skills in Psychology**
  Students will respect and use critical and creative thinking, skeptical inquiry, and, when possible, the scientific approach to solve problems related to behavior and mental processes.
- **Goal 4. Application of Psychology**
  Students will understand and apply psychological principles to personal, social, and organizational issues.
- **Goal 7. Communication Skills**
  Students will be able to communicate effectively in a variety of formats.
- **Goal 8. Sociocultural and International Awareness**
  Students will recognize, understand, and respect the complexity of sociocultural and international diversity.

SELECTING THE LEVELS OF THE INDEPENDENT VARIABLE

LEVELS OF THE INDEPENDENT VARIABLE

The number of conditions for a specific independent variable.

So far we have just been reviewing definitions we hope you already feel comfortable with. We now want to introduce how to select the **levels of the independent variable**. In the example above, there are two levels of the subject variable of birth weight: there is level number one (i.e., low birth weight) and level number two (i.e., normal birth weight). In this chapter, we are going to practice identifying the levels of an independent variable and discuss how to decide the number of levels that is needed for a given independent variable.

Think back to Chapter 6 where we looked at the research question, "Does caffeine influence levels of alertness?" In this research question, the independent variable was caffeine and the dependent variable was levels of alertness.

We briefly discussed that to actually test this research hypothesis you would need two groups: one group of participants that would get a caffeinated beverage and one group of participants that would get a noncaffeinated beverage.

Group 1: Participants who would get a caffeinated beverage

Group 2: Participants who would get a noncaffeinated beverage

Then you could compare the alertness levels of the two groups to see if there was a difference. If you were to really test this research question, your design would not be quite that simple. The reason is because you would probably need more than two levels of the independent variable. Currently, the two levels are caffeine and no caffeine. However, you might want to consider varying the amount of the caffeinated beverage participants consume to see if there is a certain amount of caffeine that participants need in their system before alertness levels are changed. You could have the following design:

Group 1: Participants who get 8 ounces of a caffeinated beverage

Group 2: Participants who get 24 ounces of a caffeinated beverage

Group 3: Participants who get no caffeine

You could then compare the levels of alertness of the three groups to see if there was a difference. It might be the case that it takes 24 ounces of a caffeinated beverage before we see an increase in alertness. The main point is that by adding multiple levels of the independent variable you are better able to see the influence of the independent variable.

Here is another example. This idea came from a group of undergraduate students that we worked with at Kansas State University. They wanted to know if the type of clothes that a faculty member wore influenced students' perceptions of that faculty member's competence. In other words, do students perceive professors who wear dress clothes as more competent than professors who wear jeans? These students designed an experiment and had a professor guest lecture to two sections of General Psychology students. The guest professor wore dress clothes (nice dress slacks) to one section of General Psychology and casual clothes (blue jeans) to another section of General Psychology. In other words:

Group 1: One section of General Psychology with guest professor in dress clothes

Group 2: One section of General Psychology with guest professor in casual clothes

The General Psychology students were then asked to evaluate the guest professor and rate his or her competence in the discipline of psychology.

In this example:

What is the independent variable (i.e., what is being manipulated or thought to produce a change)?

> The independent variable is type of clothes, because it is what is being manipulated (or varied) in the experiment.

How many levels of the independent variable are there?

There are two levels of the independent variable: dress clothes and casual clothes.

What is the dependent variable (i.e., what is being measured for change)?

The dependent variable is competence of the guest professor, because it is what is being measured.

The results were as follows. In short, the competence ratings depended on the sex of the guest professor. If the guest professor was a woman, she was judged to be equally competent wearing dress slacks as blue jeans. However, if the guest professor was a man, he was judged to be less competent when he wore blue jeans than when he wore slacks.

To further help you with understanding levels of the independent variable, here is another example. What about the research question, "Does size of computer monitor influence reaction time?" John and some colleagues have tested if varying the size of a computer monitor (i.e., 17 inch, 19 inch, and 21 inch) will influence how quickly participants perform a task. John and his colleagues wanted to know if bigger computer screens would always lead to faster reaction time. They had three groups of participants.

Group 1: Participants who completed a task on a 17-inch computer monitor

Group 2: Participants who completed a task on a 19-inch computer monitor

Group 3: Participants who completed a task on a 21-inch computer monitor

They then compared the reaction times of participants in each of the three groups to see if there was a difference.

In this example:

What is the independent variable?

What are the levels of the independent variable?

What is the dependent variable?

Here are the answers:

The independent variable is size of computer monitor.

It has three levels—17 inch, 19 inch, and 21 inch.

The dependent variable is reaction time.

Results for this experiment found that bigger is not always better in terms of size of computer monitors. This research demonstrated that the best size for a computer monitor is 19 inches. Believe it or not, 21 inches is actually too big and participants spend extra time turning their heads to look at all parts on the screen. (We bet Dell would not want these results to become well known.)

Here is one last example on identifying levels of independent variables. As you are reading the example, try to pick out the independent variable, its levels, and what is being measured. There are many different types of bosses in a workplace setting, and each boss has his or her own leadership style or way of treating employees. Some bosses treat all employees as equals and value the input of each employee (democratic leadership style), whereas other bosses treat employees as workers who do not have input in how things are done (autocratic leadership style). Researchers have been interested in knowing if leadership style of a boss (i.e., democratic versus autocratic) influences employees' satisfaction with their jobs.

In this example:

> What is the independent variable?
>
> What are the levels of the independent variable?
>
> What is the dependent variable?

Here are the answers:

> The independent variable is leadership style of a boss.
>
> It has two levels—democratic and autocratic.
>
> The dependent variable is employees' satisfaction with their jobs.

Before moving on to the topic of selecting dependent variables, we want to mention one more thing about selecting the levels of an independent variable. You may be wondering how does someone know how many levels is the correct amount to select. The answer is that there is no magical number of levels for an independent variable. Sometimes you start with levels that are far apart such as 8 ounces of a caffeinated beverage and 32 ounces of a caffeinated beverage. If there is a difference in these two levels, you could conduct another experiment with the levels of 16 ounces and 24 ounces to better understand the exact amount of a caffeinated beverage needed to influence alertness.

YOU TRY IT!

It is now time for you to practice selecting levels of an independent variable. For the purposes of this example, we would like you to come up with three levels of the independent variable.

Questions

Here is your research question: "Does type of sport a student plays in college influence his or her class attendance rates?" Since you are going to pick the levels of the independent variable, we will save you some work and tell you the independent variable is type of sport and the dependent variable is class attendance rates. Now you need to think of at least three levels of the independent variable type of sport. In other words, what are three different levels or types of sports that college students could play? Take a look at our answers below, after thinking about the question:

Answers
Example 1:

> IV: Type of Sport
>
> Levels of IV: football, baseball, soccer

(Continued)

(*Continued*)

In Example 1, you would compare the attendance rates for students who played football, baseball, and soccer to see if a difference in attendance rates existed among the three sports.

Example 2:

IV: Type of Sport

Levels of IV: softball, basketball, and tennis

In Example 2, you would compare the attendance rates for students who played softball, basketball, and tennis to see if a difference in attendance rates existed among the three sports.

Example 3:

IV: Type of Sport

Levels of IV: cheerleading (yes we think it is a sport), rugby, and no sport

In Example 3, you would compare the attendance rates for students who were cheerleaders, played rugby, and did not belong to a sports team at all to see if a difference in attendance rates existed among the three. (Note: These three examples are not the only possibilities. There are many other different types of sports that you could have listed as levels of your independent variable and been correct.) How did you do?

Section Summary

- An *independent variable* is the variable that is being manipulated. It is believed to produce a change in the dependent variable (pp. 118–122).
- *Levels of the independent variable* are the number of conditions in an independent variable. All independent variables will have at least two conditions (i.e., the presence of a treatment and the absence of a treatment). However, an independent variable can have as many conditions as is necessary for the particular study you are conducting (pp. 118–122).
- A *dependent variable* is the variable that is being measured or observed for a change. It is believed to change because of the independent variable (pp. 118–122).

MEASURING THE DEPENDENT VARIABLE AND NUMBER OF DEPENDENT VARIABLES

Universities across the country offer Supplemental Instruction (SI) for many historically difficult general education courses. SI is a program where a junior or senior student serves as a teaching assistant for an introductory level course by attending class regularly and holding study sessions outside of class time. We both participated in this program a few years ago along with about 10 other faculty members. When we looked at the results, John had the most students who attend SI study sessions outside of class. As an SI program, we wanted to better understand how John was promoting SI to his students so that we could do the same thing in the other classes. We could measure the way John's students responded to his promoting of SI (the dependent variable) in numerous ways. In other words, there are different types of measures for a dependent variable.

The first type of measure we have already mentioned. We could measure students' behavior, which would be called a **behavioral measure**. In this example, the behavioral measure would be the number of students who attended SI sessions outside of class. Another type of measure that we could take is an **attitudinal measure**. We could survey the class to see if they had a positive or negative attitude toward the use of the SI program. It is probably the case that John's students held a more positive (or favorable) attitude toward the SI program than students in other classes. Third, we could also take a **cognitive measure** of John's students. It could be the case that John's students knew more about the SI program. For example, his students may have known more facts about the program including on what days the outside study sessions met, where the outside study sessions met, and by how much attending SI sessions improved their exam grades. Finally, we could measure the way John's students responded to how he promoted SI by taking a **physiological measure**. It is possible that his students were less stressed (lower heart rates, slower rates of breathing) at the idea of attending SI than students in other classes. This example illustrates that when measuring a dependent variable there are many types of measures, such as behavioral, attitudinal, cognitive, and physiological that you can utilize.

Let's look at another example on types of measures. Currently, we are conducting research on how the social context of an audience influences perceptions of humor of racial jokes. Specifically, we want to know how the racial makeup of the audience influences whether or not a racial joke is perceived to be humorous. For example, we will have participants watch an African American comedian (e.g., Dave Chapelle) perform jokes about race relations and vary whether the audience is of mixed races, all Caucasians, or all African Americans. Next, we will have participants watch a Caucasian comedian (e.g., Ralphie May) perform jokes about race relations and vary whether the audience is of mixed races, all Caucasians, or all African Americans. We could measure perceptions of humor using behavioral, attitudinal, cognitive, and physiological measures.

For a behavioral measure, we could look to see if the participant laughed at the jokes. For an attitudinal measure, we could see if the participant reported liking or not liking the comedian. We could measure the participant's knowledge or understanding of the jokes for a cognitive measure. Finally, we could measure the participant's pulse rate for a physiological measure.

BEHAVIORAL MEASURE

A measure to investigate a person's behaviors.

ATTITUDINAL MEASURE

A measure assessing a person's attitudes on the topic.

COGNITIVE MEASURE

A measure of one's mental ability or knowledge of a topic.

PHYSIOLOGICAL MEASURE

Measures that are biological in nature (heart rate, pulse, blood pressure, etc.)

YOU TRY IT!

We want you to think of examples using behavioral, attitudinal, cognitive, and physiological measures. Pretend that you put together a 15-minute video presentation that highlights the benefits of attending a public college or university. You show this video to parents of high-school students. You want to measure if this video influences viewers' (i.e., parents) perceptions of public universities. How could you measure viewers' perceptions in each of the following ways: behavioral, attitudinal, cognitive, and physiological? After you have generated examples for each, take a look at our answers below.

(Continued)

(Continued)

There are many possible answers to this question. Here are some examples.

a. **Behavioral Measure**—One type of behavioral measure would be following up with viewers a few months later to see if they had requested information from a public university. Another type of behavioral measure would be following up with the viewers to see if their son or daughter had applied to or was now attending a public university.

b. **Attitudinal Measure**—Measuring viewers' willingness to attend a public university themselves would be one type of attitudinal measure. A second type of attitudinal measure would be measuring viewers' willingness to send their son or daughter to a public university.

c. **Cognitive Measure**—Measuring viewers' knowledge about facts related to public universities (e.g., average cost, faculty to student ratio, resources available) would be an example of a cognitive measure.

d. **Physiological Measure**—You could measure parents' biological response (e.g., heart rate, pulse) after having them imagine their child was attending a public university.

Again, these are just a few examples. You may have come up with other answers that were equally correct. If you are unsure about your answer, be sure to ask your professor.

These different types of measures (i.e., behavioral, attitudinal, cognitive, and physiological measures) can be assessed in different ways. Ways to assess the measures include: **percentage correct**, **frequency of responding**, and **degree of response**. Let's look at an example of each type of measure.

PERCENT CORRECT

Average of correct responses to overall responses represented as a percentage.

PERCENT CORRECT. In the example of SI above, we could assess what percentage of John's students were correct in knowing the days of the week study sessions were held on and the location. We could compare the percentage of students who were correct in John's class to the percentage of students who were correct about this same information in other classes.

FREQUENCY OF RESPONDING

A sum of the number of times a person/group responds to a question.

FREQUENCY OF RESPONDING. In the humor research example above, we could assess how many of the participants responded to the comedians by laughing. We could then compare the frequency of laughing across the audience conditions to determine if the racial makeup of the audience influences rates of laughing.

DEGREE OF RESPONSE

A measure of intensity of a response.

DEGREE OF RESPONSE. In the humor research example above, we could assess how hard the participants laughed at the jokes. We could then compare how hard people laughed at the jokes across the audience conditions to determine if the racial makeup of the audience influences degree of laughing.

Before we move on to operational definitions, we want to mention a few more considerations about dependent variables. Similar to the levels of independent variables, you might be wondering how many dependent variables you should have. Again, there is not a magical number of dependent variables to have. However, it can be beneficial to have more than one dependent variable. **Multiple dependent variables** allow you to see if you have converging results on a topic (remember this back from Chapter 4?). In addition to thinking about the number of dependent variables, you should also be cautious in selecting the difficulty level of the dependent variables. Sometimes the task is too difficult for people to complete, causing scores to pile up at the bottom. If scores pile up at the bottom of the dependent variable, you will not be able to see the effect of the independent variable. This is known as a **floor effect**. The opposite can also happen. The task can be too easy causing results to pile up at the top of the distribution. This is known as a **ceiling effect**. One way to prevent floor and ceiling effects is to have your friend complete the task and give feedback on the difficulty level.

Jenn had a group of students in Iowa looking at how memories for traumatic events change over time. Her students surveyed people over their memories for the events surrounding Hurricane Katrina immediately after the event and a few weeks later. However, the questions on the survey were so difficult to answer that nobody did well at all. The students were then unable to see how memories change over time because people scored equally poorly on the task immediately after the event and a few weeks later. Finally, it can be beneficial to use preexisting scales because properties (validity and reliability) have been established.

MULTIPLE DEPENDENT VARIABLES

Most studies have more than one dependent variable. Having multiple dependent variables increases the amount of information collected.

FLOOR EFFECT

When scores fall primarily at the lower range of a response option.

CEILING EFFECT

When scores fall primarily at the upper range of a response option.

YOU TRY IT!

Question

Take a look at Figures 7.1 and 7.2 . In these figures, we have fictitious grade distributions for an General Psychology class and an upper-level Physiological Psychology class. Can you identify which figure illustrates the floor effect and which illustrates the ceiling effect?

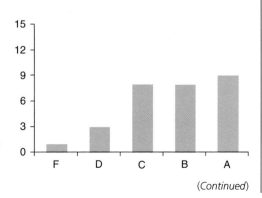

FIGURE 7.1 Final Grade Distribution for General Psychology.

(Continued)

(*Continued*)

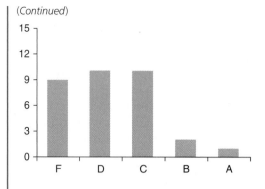

FIGURE 7.2 Final Grade Distribution for Physiological Psychology.

Answer

Figure 7.2 of the upper-level Physiological Psychology class illustrates the floor effect. This is because the scores piled up at the bottom of the distribution, which in this case is the final grade. On the other hand, Figure 7.1 illustrates a ceiling effect with scores clustered at the top of the distribution.

Section Summary

- The dependent variable can be measured in four different ways (pp. 122–124).
  - *Behavioral measures* are those measures that assess an individual's behavior (p. 123).
  - *Attitudinal measures* are those measures that assess an individual's attitudes toward the research topic of interest (p. 123).
  - *Cognitive measures* assess an individual's mental ability (p. 123).
  - *Physiological measures* are used to gather information that is biological in nature (p. 123).
- There are several different ways in which you can assess your dependent variable (pp. 124–125).
  - *Percent correct* is an average of correct responses to overall responses represented as a percentage (p. 124).
  - *Frequency of response* is a sum of the number of times a person or group responds to a question (p. 124).
  - *Degree of response* is a measure of the intensity of the response an individual has to a question (p. 124).
- For any study, most researchers use more than one dependent variable. This is done to collect more information as to the effect of the independent variable (p. 125).
- Sometimes, dependent variables that are used can experience either a ceiling or floor effect. A *ceiling effect* occurs when responses primarily fall on the upper limit of a response option. A *floor effect* is the opposite, in that scores primarily fall on the lower range of a response option (pp. 125–126).

OPERATIONAL DEFINITIONS

Do you watch any animated TV shows? If so, which one is your favorite? We admit that we have many favorites such as *The Simpsons*, *Family Guy*, and *King of the Hill*. We have a fun assignment for you. Pick your favorite animated TV show and go watch 15 minutes of it. You read that correctly. We want you to go watch TV. While you are watching this 15 minutes worth of TV, take a piece of paper and pen with you and count the number of violent acts that you see. What you determine to be a violent act is up to you. We will be here when you get back.

So, how many violent acts did you find in the 15 minutes worth of TV that you viewed? Do you think that we would have found the same number of violent acts if we were watching the TV show with you? We doubt it. But, why would we not have counted the same number of violent acts as you? Probably because we all have different definitions of what violence is. For example, if watching *The Simpsons*, we would count Homer trying to strangle Bart as a violent act. But you might not. This is because everybody has their own definition of violence.

It is important when we conduct research or read about research findings of others that we know how the variables are being operationally defined. Think about the following example. We read an article that reports a positive relationship between childhood aggression and viewing violent cartoons. Of course, we would want to know more about these results because we have two children who watch cartoons on Saturday mornings. Specifically, we would want to know what is meant by "violent cartoons." How was violence defined and measured? What is meant by childhood aggression? How was it defined and measured? In both these cases, we want to know the operational definitions of the variables. Sometimes variables can be very broad in scope. Violence and aggression are two examples of broad variables that could encompass many different meanings. By knowing the **operational definition**, we can make a broad concept more specific. This allows us to replicate research findings and extend research findings.

Sometimes it is not easy to operationally define a variable. It may take time to think about what is exactly being manipulated or measured. However, it is important that you do not skip over defining your variables. Without defining your variables, it will be very difficult to interpret results. Similarly, be sure to look for operational definitions of variables when you read research. In some cases, you may agree with the definitions the authors used, and in other cases, you may not. This will help you in interpreting the results.

Here is an example. Consider the following statement: College classroom performance can be increased by attending study sessions. You would want to know how "college classroom performance" and "study sessions" are operationally defined before you start investing time in attending the study sessions. What if it turns out that "college classroom performance" is defined as the number of times students participate in classroom discussions? Would you be willing to attend study sessions to increase your participation in discussions? Maybe not. But what if "college classroom performance" was defined as overall grade point average? Would you be willing to attend study sessions to increase your overall grade point average? The purpose of this example is to illustrate

OPERATIONAL DEFINITION

Defines how a concept or idea will be measured.

the importance of operational definitions. By knowing what is meant by "college classroom performance," you can determine how you will interpret the results.

Section Summary

♦ In order to properly assess your variables, you must make sure that they are properly defined. An operational definition is used to define how a concept or idea will be measured (p. 128).

TYPES OF SCALES

We would like for you to read the scenario below and tell us what you would do if you were in this situation.

Imagine that the United States is preparing for the outbreak of an unusual Asian disease, which is expected to kill 600 people. Two alternative programs to combat the disease have been proposed. Assume that the exact scientific estimates of the consequences of the program are as follows:

• If Program A is adopted, 200 people will be saved.
• If Program B is adopted, there is a one-third probability that 600 people will be saved and a two-thirds probability that no people will be saved.

Which program would you select? Would you select Program A or Program B? This scenario is from a research conducted by Tversky and Kahneman (1981). They found that most people selected Program A (72% of participants) over Program B (28% of participants). The results support the idea that participants are risk averse. In other words, participants will select the for-sure option of Program A that saves 200 lives over the gamble of Program B. Did your choice of program indicate that you preferred the sure bet over the gamble?

The purpose of this example is to get you thinking about how researchers measure variables. Tversky and Kahneman (1981) decided to measure people's likelihood of selecting a program by having them essentially say "yes" or "no." By having participants say yes or no to the programs, they were using a nominal scale. A **nominal scale** is a scale used when participants select options that name things. Examples of nominal scales include: ethnicity, religion, sex, and school classification. In all of these examples, the variable being measured is a category or name. For example, your school classification can be freshman, sophomore, junior, or senior, or your sex can be male or female. Nominal scales are beneficial when you want to gather information on the percentage of people who belong to, or who selected, a particular option (as Tversky and Kahneman did). However, it should be noted that there are limits to the type of statistical procedures that can be conducted with nominal scales, and therefore in these cases another scale should be selected (see a statistics book for further information).

NOMINAL SCALE

Classification of data into one of two or more categories.

Ordinal scales put items in order. Class rankings are examples of ordinal data. When you graduated from high school, you probably had a valedictorian and salutatorian. These were the students with the highest and second-highest grade point averages, respectively. When we were in graduate school, we were also ranked. At the end of every semester, we were given a class rank (e.g., 3rd out of 12) to let us know where we stood in relation to other graduate students in our class. A final example is the result of a National Association for Stock Car Auto Racing (NASCAR) race. It is typically reported which driver came in first, second, third, and so forth. In Tversky and Kahneman's research, they could have used an ordinal scale instead of a nominal scale. Specifically, they could have changed the instructions and asked participants to rank their preferences by indicating their first choice and second choice. (Note: Ordinal scales are typically used when there are more than two items to rate. We are only using this two-item scenario to carry out the example from the beginning of this section and to illustrate that changing how the question is worded will change the type of scale you are using.)

ORDINAL SCALE

Classification of data into an order or rank of magnitude.

Although ordinal scales provide information as to the order of preference, it does have drawbacks. Specifically, it does not tell you how far apart the options are or the distance between the options. For example, if John tells Jenn that Dale Earnhardt Jr. won the NASCAR race and Tony Stewart came in second, Jenn does not know by how much Dale Earnhardt Jr. won the race. Was it a close race or did Jr. win by a good distance? Similarly, what does a ranking of 3rd out of 12 in a graduate course really mean? If the student ranked 3rd has a final course grade of 96% and the student ranked 10th has a final course grade of 93% then there is not much difference between them. Thus, while ordinal scales can provide information on individuals' ranking, ordinal scales do not provide information on the distance between the rankings. Another drawback is that similar to a nominal scale, the type of analysis that can be conducted with an ordinal scale is limited.

Interval scales measure a variable on a scale assuming equal distance between the numbers. For example, we could ask you to rate how much of a morning person you are from 1 (not much a morning person) to 10 (very much a morning person). In this example, the distance between 1 and 2 is assumed to be equal to the distance between 3 and 4, and so forth. In Tversky and Kahneman's research, they could have used an interval scale instead of a nominal scale. Specifically, they could have changed the instructions and asked participants to rate how likely they would be to adopt each program ranging from 1 (not very likely to adopt) to 100 (very likely to adopt).

INTERVAL SCALE

Classification of data on a scale that assumes equal distance between numbers.

A large percentage of psychological research uses interval scales because it lends itself to more advanced statistical procedures than nominal and ordinal scales. Yet, interval scales do not have a true zero value to represent the absence of a variable. Take temperature for example. Temperature is an interval scale. It has assumed equal distance between numbers. There is also zero degrees on the temperature scale. However, zero degrees in temperature does not represent an absence of temperature. In fact, we know after living in the Midwest that zero degrees is very cold. Thus, the number zero is not representing the true amount of zero. Rather, the number zero is just an arbitrary number on the scale. If the variable you are measuring has a true zero value, the variable would use a ratio scale.

RATIO SCALE

Classification of data on a scale that assumes equal distance and has a true zero value.

A **ratio scale** assumes equal distances between the numbers on the scale but also has a true zero value. We like to give the following example of how many time per week you exercise. The answer to the question could in fact be zero and indicate an absence of working out. Because there is a true zero, a person who works out eight times per week is working out twice as much as a person who works out four times per week. Can you think of how Tversky and Kahneman could have used a ratio scale? Remember, to use a ratio scale equal distance is assumed and an absolute zero is possible. Tversky and Kahneman could have a scale that ranges from 0 to 100, where 0 is equal to "would not adopt at all" and 100 is equal to "would definitely adopt."

YOU TRY IT!

We want you to practice writing questions and varying the response scales. First, here is a review of the types of scales.

Nominal scales	=	name things
Ordinal scales	=	put things in order
Interval scales	=	equal intervals
Ratio scales	=	equal intervals, true zero value

Practice 1

For Practice Problem 1, we will use the research question, "Are students satisfied with the advising process on their campus?" How could you measure student satisfaction with advising using a *nominal scale*?

Answer

You could ask students, "Are you satisfied with the advising you receive?" and students could respond "yes" or "no." We could then look at the percentage of students who responded yes and no. You might have a slightly different answer than us and that is perfectly acceptable. Maybe you asked students, "Are you satisfied or not satisfied with the advising that you receive?" and students could respond "satisfied" or "not satisfied." In trying to determine if your answer is correct, just be sure that the way you asked the questions resulted in students responding on a scale that named something.

Practice 2

For Practice Problem #2, we will use the research question, "What type of foods do college students prefer?" You are interested in the following types of food: pizza, lasagna, steak, chicken, and seafood. How could you measure food preferences using an *ordinal scale*?

Answer

You could give students the list of foods (pizza, lasagna, steak, chicken, and seafood) and ask the students to rate the foods from their most favorite to their least favorite (or from their least favorite to their most favorite). This would provide us with a ranking of food preferences. But remember that this ordinal scale would not tell us how far

(Continued)

apart the preferences were. So, for example, you would not know by how much the student preferred the most favorite food of pizza to the second favorite food of steak.

Practice 3

For Practice Problem 3, we will use the research question, "To what extent, do people prefer salty snacks?" How could you measure snack preference on an interval scale?

Answer

You could ask people to rate on a scale from 1 to 7 (with 1 indicating "do not prefer" and 7 indicating "greatly prefer") what type of snack they prefer. This interval scale would assume equal distance between the 7 numbers on the scale.

   To what degree do you prefer salty snacks?
   Do Not Prefer   1 2 3 4 5 6 7   Greatly Prefer

Practice 4

For Practice Problem 4, we will use the research question, "How often do college students read books other than those assigned in classes?"

Answer

You could ask students the number of non–class related books they have read in the past month. It is possible that the students have read zero books, and therefore a true zero exists. In addition, you would be able to say that someone who has read 10 books has read twice as many as someone who has read 5 books.

How did you do? If you found this exercise to be a little difficult that is normal. Wording questions to use different types of scales is a type of survey construction that takes practice. The "Are You Equipped Now?" section below will help you at identifying types of scales rather than constructing them. You should find this much easier.

Section Summary

- The way in which researchers measure their variables is important. There are four types of scales that can be used to properly measure a dependent variable (pp. 128–131):
    - A *nominal scale* is used when data are classified into one of two or more categories (pp. 128–129).
    - An *ordinal scale* is used when data are classified into an order or rank of magnitude (p. 129).
    - An *interval scale* is used when data are classified on a scale that assumes equal distance between numbers (p. 129).
    - A *ratio scale* is used when data are classified on a scale that assumes equal distance and has a true zero value (p. 130).

Are You Equipped Now?

In the early part of 2000, we began collecting data on the Olympics. Specifically, we took the approach of evaluating the amount of time people spent watching the Olympics, where they watched the Olympics, with whom they watched the Olympics, and what people got out of watching the Olympics. In order to investigate this topic and collect exploratory data, we designed a survey. Below is a list of questions directly from that survey for the Summer Olympics. Try and determine the type of data being collected from each question. In other words, is the scale being used nominal, ordinal, interval, or ratio?

1. What time of day did you primarily watch the Olympic Games?

   a) Morning   b) Afternoon   c) Evening   d) Late night

2. In general, where did you most often watch the Olympic Games?

   a. Your home
   b. Someone else's house
   c. Bar/Restaurant
   d. Other, please indicate ___

3. Among those who watched the sporting event with you, was at least one family member present?

   a) Yes   b) No

4. The events that I wanted to watch/see **should** have been covered more.

   Strongly agree   1   2   3   4   5   6   7   Strongly disagree

5. I would like to have seen more coverage of **men's** sports:

   Strongly agree   1   2   3   4   5   6   7   Strongly disagree

6. I would like to have seen more coverage of **women's** sports:

   Strongly agree   1   2   3   4   5   6   7   Strongly disagree

7. Estimate the percentage of broadcasting time in Olympic coverage for each below (total equaling 100%):

   _____ Opening ceremony/Closing ceremony
   _____ Actual coverage of sporting event
   _____ Summaries and Highlights of events and competitions
   _____ Commentator/analysis of sporting events
   _____ Human interest stories about athletes
   _____ Background stories about participating countries
   _____ Background stories about past Olympics
   _____ Stories about Australia and specific Olympic sites

8. Approximately how many hours of the Olympic coverage did you watch: ___

9. Take a moment to think about the events you watched. In the first column next to the events listed on the following page, check all those events that you watched during the Olympics. After completing that, go back and rank the ones that you checked; assign or give a rank of 1 for the event you most enjoyed.

✓	Rank	Event	✓	Rank	Event
____	____	Men's Archery	____	____	Men's Sailing
____	____	Women's Archery	____	____	Women's Sailing
____	____	Men's Badminton	____	____	Men's Shooting
____	____	Women's Badminton	____	____	Women's Shooting
____	____	Baseball	____	____	Men's Soccer
____	____	Men's Basketball	____	____	Women's Soccer
____	____	Women's Basketball	____	____	Softball
____	____	Boxing	____	____	Men's Swimming
____	____	Men's Canoeing	____	____	Women's Swimming
____	____	Women's Canoeing	____	____	Men's Table tennis
____	____	Closing ceremony	____	____	Women's Table Tennis
____	____	Men's Cycling	____	____	Men's Tennis
____	____	Women's Cycling	____	____	Women's Tennis
____	____	Men's Diving	____	____	Men's Track & Field
____	____	Women's Diving	____	____	Women's Track & Field
____	____	Men's Gymnastics	____	____	Men's Triathlon
____	____	Women's Gymnastics	____	____	Women's Triathlon
____	____	Opening ceremony	____	____	Men's Volleyball
____	____	Men's Rowing	____	____	Women's Volleyball
____	____	Women's Rowing			

Answers

1—3

These questions all rely on a nominal scale. Each one of the questions asks participants to put themselves into a category. Whether that category is yes/no or asks about location of watching the Olympics with a predefined set of responses, each is a selected category.

4—6

The next three questions are all interval data. Here, participants are to rate themselves along a predetermined scale from 1 to 7. This scale assumes that between each number there is equal distance in value.

7—8

These two questions are ratio-scale questions. The participants can answer with any value they choose, even a zero value. It is the fact that this scale can have a true zero value that makes it a ratio scale.

9

The final question is both ordinal and nominal in scale. The participants are asked to select all that apply to them, which is a nominal scale (i.e., selecting yes or no). However, what makes the scale ordinal is the rank order of those selections that participants are asked to make. By putting a ranking to their data participants are using an ordinal scale.

Chapter Summary

+ An *independent variable* is the variable in a study that you are manipulating. You are manipulating this variable because you believe it will cause a change in the participant (pp. 118–122).
+ The *levels of an independent variable* is the number of conditions that are being manipulated. All independent variables will have at least two levels. For example, the first level could be the presence of a manipulation or treatment. The second level could be the absence of a manipulation or treatment. Of course, an independent variable can have more than two levels but it should always have at least two (pp. 118–122).
+ A *dependent variable* is the variable that is being measured in a study. This is the variable that the researcher believes will change in response to the independent variable (pp. 118–122).
+ Four different types of dependent variables are commonly used in psychology. The four types are behavioral measures, attitudinal measures, cognitive measures, and physiological measures. Depending on your design, you can use only one or all of these measures (pp. 122–124).
  + *Behavioral measures* are those measures that assess an individual's behavior (p. 123).
  + *Attitudinal measures* are those measures that assess an individual's attitudes toward the topic (p. 123).
  + *Cognitive measures* assess an individual's mental ability (p. 123).
  + *Physiological measures* are used to gather information that is biological in nature such as blood pressure, pulse, and so on (p. 123).
+ In addition to deciding on the type of dependent variable that you will collect, you must also decide how you are going to assess each measure. Below are the three most common ways a dependent variable is assessed (pp. 124–125).
  + *Percent correct* is an average of correct response to overall responses represented as a percentage (p. 124).
  + *Frequency of response* is a sum of the number of times a person or group responds to a question (p. 124).
  + *Degree of response* is a measure of the intensity of the response an individual has to a question (p. 124).
+ Good research will assess more than one dependent variable. By collecting data on more than one measure, you will maximize the likelihood of detecting a difference between the levels of your independent variable (p. 125).
+ In order to properly assess your variables, you must make sure that they are adequately defined. An *operational definition* is used to define how a concept or idea will be measured. It does not define the concept or idea but rather how it will be assessed (p. 128).
+ Once you have decided on the measure you will be taking and the way you want to assess each, you have to decide on the type of scale you want to use.

There are four types of scales that can be used. Each collects information on a dependent variable in a different way (pp. 128–131). As a researcher, you must decide which scale is appropriate for your study.

- A *nominal scale* is used when data are classified into one of two or more categories (pp. 128–129).
- An *ordinal scale* is used when data are classified into an order or rank of magnitude (p. 129).
- An *interval scale* is used when data are classified on a scale that assumes equal distance between numbers (p. 129).
- A *ratio scale* is used when data are classified on a scale that assumes equal distance and a true zero value (p. 130).

APA Learning Goals Linkage

- **Goal 2.** *Research Methods in Psychology*
  Students will understand and apply basic research methods in psychology, including research design, data analysis, and interpretation.

  Sections Covered: Are You Equipped?, Selecting the Levels of Independent Variables, Measuring the Dependent Variables and Number of Dependent Variables, Operational Definitions, Types of Scales, Are You Equipped Now?

  Explanation of the Goal: In this chapter, we added to our understanding of the basic characteristics of the science of psychology by addressing the topic of selecting the levels of the independent variables. Next, we examined research methods used by psychologists. In doing so, we first listed how the dependent variables could be measured by behavioral, attitudinal, cognitive, and physiological means. Second, we covered the different ways to assess the dependent variables such as percent correct, frequency of responding, and degree of response and how the level of difficulty should be appropriate to avoid floor and ceiling effects. The importance of operational definitions as well as the types of scales (i.e., ordinal, nominal, interval, and ratio) concluded the chapter.

- **Goal 3.** *Critical Thinking Skills in Psychology*
  Students will respect and use critical and creative thinking, skeptical inquiry, and, when possible, the scientific approach to solve problems related to behavior and mental processes.

  Sections Covered: Are You Equipped?, Selecting the Levels of Independent Variables, Measuring the Dependent Variables and Number of Dependent Variables, Types of Scales, Are You Equipped Now?

  Explanation of the Goal: To help you enhance your critical thinking skills, you completed numerous exercises. In addition, to the Are You Equipped exercises at the beginning and the end of the chapter, you also completed

(Continued)

(Continued)

You Try It! exercises for many of the sections in the chapter. These exercises required you to think critically as you selected the levels of an independent variable, generated ways to measure perceptions of parents after viewing a college recruitment video, and learned to write questions that have participants utilize the different types of psychological scales.

- **Goal 4.** *Application of Psychology*
Students will understand and apply psychological principles to personal, social, and organizational issues.

    Sections Covered: Are You Equipped?, Selecting the Levels of Independent Variables, Measuring the Dependent Variables and Number of Dependent Variables, Operational Definitions, Types of Scales, Are You Equipped Now?

    Explanation of the Goal: The material in this chapter can be applied easily to everyday life. In fact, we have used examples that apply to you and society in each section. It might not have surprised you that the psychological principles could be related to violence in cartoons, leadership styles, and factors that contribute to depression such as birth weight. However, you might have found it interesting that the material in the chapter could be applied to the Olympics, size of computer monitor, perceptions of humor, and results of a NASCAR race.

- **Goal 7.** *Communication Skills*
Students will be able to communicate effectively in a variety of formats.

    Sections Covered: Measuring the Dependent Variables and Number of Dependent Variables

    Explanation of the Goal: APA recommends that students be able to communicate effectively in a variety of formats. Although we might typically think of communication in terms of oral and written forms, you will also need to be able to communicate and interpret quantitative visual aids accurately. To this end, you gained experience in interpreting graphical depictions of floor and ceiling effects. This skill will be important as a researcher in creating graphics to represent psychological findings and as a consumer in interpreting them.

- **Goal 8.** *Sociocultural and International Awareness*
Students will recognize, understand, and respect the complexity of sociocultural and international diversity.

    Sections Covered: Operational Definitions

    Explanation of the Goal: Individual differences can influence beliefs, values, and interactions with others. In our discussion of operational definitions, we have illustrated how individual differences can influence the perception of violence. Thus, it is important as psychologists that we define how a concept or idea will be measured in a study.

Selection and Assignment of Participants

CHAPTER OUTLINE

Are You Equipped?

In 1963, Stanley Milgram published a research article in the *Journal of Abnormal and Social Psychology* that has become famous within the field of psychology. We are sure that you have heard about Milgram's research somewhere along the way, probably in General Psychology. Much discussion surrounding Milgram's research has focused on if the experiment was ethical to conduct. However, we are going to tell you about Milgram's research again. This time we want you to focus on how Milgram obtained participants for his experiment.

Milgram's research came from looking at how blind obedience can be destructive. Milgram reflected on the people killed in concentration camps by soldiers who were being obedient to an authority figure. Milgram wanted to study this obedience experimentally.

Milgram obtained his sample in the following way: "The subjects were 40 males between the ages of 20 and 50, drawn from New Haven and the surrounding communities. Subjects were obtained by a newspaper advertisement and direct mail solicitation." Participants who responded to the newspaper advertisement or the mail solicitation believed they were participating in an experiment on memory and learning.

Participants arrived two at a time. One participant was an individual obtained from the procedure described above and the other participant was actually a confederate involved in the research experiment who was a trained actor. Participants were told that the researchers were investigating the role of punishment on learning. Participants drew from a hat to see who would be the teacher and who would be the student. However, the drawing was fixed so that the true participant was always the teacher and the trained actor was always the learner. The learner was then strapped to an instrument that would provide electric shock (in reality the learner never received any shocks). In the other room, the teacher faced an instrument allowing them to administer shock ranging from 15 to 450 volts. The teacher was instructed to give the student a shock for each incorrect response given and to increase the shock level for each subsequent mistake. Milgram wanted to see if participants would administer shock for incorrect responses and how many volts of electricity they would administer. Results indicated that two-thirds of participants administered the full 450 volts! In addition, no participants refused to administer shock before 300 volts. As mentioned earlier, the learner did not receive any shocks. Rather, the trained actors played tape recorded responses for each level of shock. Milgram reported that nobody could have predicted the obtained results. These results provide very interesting information as to human nature. As you are reading this chapter on how to obtain samples, think about what procedure Milgram used to obtain his sample. Also, consider the advantages and disadvantages to the sampling procedure Milgram utilized.

As you go through this chapter, we also want you to keep in mind how the material relates to the APA goals for psychology majors. Specifically, this chapter will address the following goals:

- **Goal 1. Knowledge Base of Psychology**
  Students will demonstrate familiarity with the major concepts, theoretical perspectives, empirical findings, and historical trends in psychology.
- **Goal 2. Research Methods in Psychology**
  Students will understand and apply basic research methods in psychology, including research design, data analysis, and interpretation.
- **Goal 3. Critical Thinking Skills in Psychology**
  Students will respect and use critical and creative thinking, skeptical inquiry, and, when possible, the scientific approach to solve problems related to behavior and mental processes.
- **Goal 4. Application of Psychology**
  Students will understand and apply psychological principles to personal, social, and organizational issues.
- **Goal 7. Communication Skills**
  Students will be able to communicate effectively in a variety of formats.

POPULATION

The entire group of individuals in which you are interested in studying.

POPULATIONS VERSUS SAMPLES

When we conduct research, we are interested in studying **populations** of people. We might want to know how men and women best lose weight or how children respond to different types of parenting styles. In these examples, we are interested in different populations. In the first example, men and women are the populations of interest. In the second example, children are the population of interest. So, if we were to try to answer these research questions, how would we go about testing the population? Would it be possible to test all people belonging to the population? In other words, could we logistically survey *all* men and women or *all* children? Probably not. However, we can still determine answers to the research questions by surveying a sample of the population. A **sample** is a group of people representative of the population who are selected to participate in the research.

SAMPLE

Smaller group of individuals that is representative of the larger population.

PROBABILITY SAMPLING PROCEDURES

There are many different sampling techniques or ways to go about selecting individuals from the population. The two main procedures are probability sampling and nonprobability sampling. With a **probability sampling procedure**, individuals from the population have a known probability (or chance) of being selected. We will discuss the use of four types of probability sampling procedures: simple, systematic, stratified, and cluster. With a nonprobability sampling procedure, each individual does not have a known chance of being selected to participate. Examples of nonprobability sampling procedure include: convenience, snowballing, and quota. To better understand probability sampling procedures, consider the following example.

PROBABILITY SAMPLING PROCEDURE

A procedure where individuals from the population have a known probability (or chance) of being selected for a study.

Parking is a hot topic on our campus. It feels as though every student complains about the parking situation and lack of spaces available. It causes students to be late for class and puts them in a bad mood. What if our university decided to better understand students' attitudes toward the parking situation? The population of interest would be all university students who have parking permits (the university would not be interested in how students feel that are parking without registered permits). In this situation, we would have a list of individuals in the population and therefore a probability sampling technique could be used. We could get a list from the controller's office of students in our population.

If we used a **simple probability sampling** procedure, each individual with a registered parking pass would have an equal probability of being selected to complete the study. We would then use an unbiased method of selecting people from the list. This could be putting all the names in a hat and randomly drawing out 100 names. We could also use a random number table to select individuals from the list. A random number table is a table of numbers that is usually produced by a computer program. Numbers are presented in rows and columns. In a random number table, the numbers are always random no matter whether you view them as a row, column, or diagonally. Thus, the numbers listed have no symmetrical or discernable order.

SIMPLE PROBABILITY SAMPLING

All individuals in a population have an equal probability of being selected.

In order to use a random number table, you would give all individuals a number ranging from 1 to the total number of participants you have in your population. Next, you would pick a random spot on the table and select respondents with matching numbers from the table. Therefore, if you had started at Column *F*, Row *6* from the Table 8.1, you would begin by selecting the 24th individual in your population for inclusion in your study. You would continue this process

TABLE 8.1   Random Number Table Created in Excel.

		Column									
		A	**B**	**C**	**D**	**E**	**F**	**G**	**H**	**I**	**J**
	1	394	904	979	468	121	380	438	147	197	592
	2	666	297	139	512	989	308	478	680	782	834
	3	402	792	805	885	102	538	22	585	519	925
	4	413	371	472	788	268	537	70	550	669	473
Row	**5**	38	641	24	18	409	815	837	535	568	259
	6	1	820	702	456	695	24	956	839	543	240
	7	293	535	128	498	159	503	651	354	530	713
	8	405	577	208	783	632	183	294	138	647	134
	9	911	255	141	383	688	923	739	749	557	782
	10	816	561	818	312	267	748	335	760	437	373

BIASED SAMPLE

A sample in which not everyone in the population has an equal or known chance of being selected.

SAMPLING WITH REPLACEMENT

Individuals are selected one at a time with each individual being replaced before the next is sampled. Here, each selection has exactly the same probability of being selected.

SAMPLING WITHOUT REPLACEMENT

Individuals are selected and are not replaced before the next is sampled. Here, the probability of being selected changes with each removal.

until you have a large enough sample. This is just one example of how the table can be used. Many computer programs (such as Excel or SPSS) can produce a table for use in a given experiment.

By any of these methods, each student with a registered parking pass (the population of interest) is equally likely to be selected to participate in the study. However, would it be an unbiased method to have the first 100 people who paid for parking permits this academic year to be our sample? Ask yourself, if we use only the first 100 students, then do all students have an equal chance of being selected? The answer is no. Taking the first 100 students who get parking permits to be the sample is a **biased sample**. A biased sample may produce different results. This is because students who are the first ones to buy their parking permits are probably also the ones who will arrive to campus early everyday to ensure a good parking spot. Thus, the students arriving early and getting good parking spots would not be representative of all students and their parking experiences.

With the simple probability sampling procedure, we can sample with replacement or without replacement. Think back to the method of putting names in a hat. After we draw out the first name, we can either put the name back in the hat before drawing the second name (with replacement) or put the name to the side and not put it back in the hat (without replacement). If you use the simple probability **sampling procedure with replacement**, it is possible that the same person could be selected more than once. However, each person in the population would have an equal probability of being selected. If you **sampled without replacement**, then the probability of being selected would change with the removal of each individual. Researchers can decide if it is acceptable for a person to be selected more than once depending on the nature of the study.

Another type of probability sampling is **systematic probability sampling**. In this technique, we would select individuals from a list in a systematic manner (i.e., selecting every k^{th} person). For example, we would select every 10th person on the list. This would give us a sample of 600 students (assuming there are 6,000 students in the population). If we wanted a smaller sample, we could select every 100th person on the list. This would give us a sample of 60 students. Systematic sampling gives us an unbiased sample in an efficient manner.

An additional type of probability sampling procedure is stratified. In a **stratified probability sampling** procedure, you begin by identifying subgroups (or strata) and then randomly sample from the subgroups. When it comes to the issue of parking on a college campus, can you think of subgroups of students whose membership to the group might influence their attitudes toward parking? We can think of a few important subgroups to consider. The first subgroup is day students (students who attend classes primarily during the day) and the second subgroup is night students (students who attend classes primarily at night). At least on our campus, day students have a much more difficult time finding parking spaces than night students. Therefore, we might want to sample from these subgroups in such a way that the numbers in the subgroup reflect the numbers in the population. In other words, if our population is composed of 80% day students and 20% night students, then our sample should be of a similar composition. We would identify our subgroups of day and night students and sample from each subgroup in an unbiased manner. Other subgroups that might be important to identify are students who live on-campus and students who live off-campus. It might be the case that students who live on-campus do not have problems with parking and students who live off-campus do have problems with parking. If you selected to use these subgroups, you would identify the students in each subgroup and sample in an unbiased manner from each.

Cluster sampling is the last type of probability sampling. In a cluster procedure, we would identify naturally occurring clusters of individuals within a population. Then, we would randomly select individuals from the clusters of individuals to be included in the sample. In our study on students' attitudes toward parking on campus, we could identify many clusters of students: for example, those who park on the north side of campus and the south side of campus. We would need to be sure that the same student does not participate twice. Specifically, it could occur that one student varies his or her parking pattern and parks on both the north and the south side of campus given one's classes on a particular day. In this case, we would want this student to only participate one time.

It is important to note that following these unbiased sampling procedures described previously does not guarantee an unbiased sample. In other words, an unbiased sampling procedure has the possibility of producing a biased sample. However, this possibility is highly unlikely. In addition, the benefit of using a random sampling technique or procedure increases the external validity of the design.

SYSTEMATIC PROBABILITY SAMPLING

Random sampling in which a systematic approach is used.

STRATIFIED PROBABILITY SAMPLING

A probability sampling technique where a researcher begins by identifying subgroups (or strata) and then randomly samples from each subgroup.

CLUSTER SAMPLING

Involves identifying naturally occurring clusters of individuals from the population to select from to be included in the sample.

YOU TRY IT!

It is time for you to practice the four types of probability sampling procedures (i.e., simple, systematic, stratified, and cluster) using the following example. A high school on the east coast recently went under reorganization. Specifically, the high school divided into separate schools known as academies. In all, there are now six different academies including: (a) Business, Finance, and Marketing; (b) Engineering and Skilled Trades; (c) Health Sciences; (d) Math, Science, and Technology; (e) Leadership and Public Service; and (f) Visual and Performing Arts. This move has been very controversial. Government grant money to continue this program will run out soon; therefore, decisions need to be made about continuing the program or merging the high school back into one unified structure. One measure that might be used to make decisions about the future of the program is student satisfaction with the academies. We want you to explain how you would sample the population of all students in the high school with each of the four types of probability sampling procedures. You try it and then compare your results to our answers below.

Simple

If we were to use a simple probability sampling procedure, we would need a list of all students at the high school. We could then use a random number table or put all the names in a box and draw names. This would give us our sample of students selected from the population in an unbiased manner.

Systematic

In a systematic sampling procedure, we would select participants for the sample in a systematic way. One way would be to get an alphabetical list of all students and select every 50th student on the list. You could also select every 50th student as they walked through the front doors one school morning.

Stratified

The six different academies (Business, Finance, and Marketing; Engineering and Skilled Trades; Health Sciences; Math, Science, and Technology; Leadership and Public Service; and Visual and Performing Arts) could be our subgroups. We would need a list of students in each academy and then we would randomly select students from each of the six academies. Other subgroups that you might identify are class ranking such as freshman, sophomore, junior, and senior. The same procedure with these subgroups would be used. You would need a list of all students who are freshman, sophomores, juniors, and seniors. You would then select students from each subgroup in an unbiased manner.

Cluster

Finally, with a cluster procedure, we would identify naturally occurring groups in the population. We could identify clusters of students such as those who live in different areas of the county. As before, we would want to be sure that no single student participated more than once (e.g., has parents who live in more than one area).

Before moving on to the topic of nonprobability sample procedures, we want to try one more example of probability sampling procedures with you. Our local obstetrics and gynecology (OBGYN) office had received many complaints. The complaints were mainly about poor office organization and extremely long waits (which were especially undesired for the pregnant clients). The doctors decided to hire a new office manager, reorganize how the office was run on a day-to-day basis, and schedule office visits in a different fashion. For the purposes of this example, we want you to pretend that the doctors want to find out how the clients are responding to this new system. The doctors do not have time to survey all their clients (the population of interest), so they decided to take a sample. The doctors are also interested in how the pregnant clients are responding to the changes because these clients compose a large percentage of their repeat business. How could the doctors take a simple, systematic, stratified, and cluster sample? When you have thought about each, compare your answers to ours below.

Simple

If we wanted to construct a sample using a simple probability procedure, we could get a list of all the clients and use a random method to select our sample from the population.

Systematic

For the systematic probability sample, we would take our alphabetical list and select the participants for the sample in a systematic (regular, methodical) manner. This could be selecting every 25th client on the list.

Stratified

The subgroups of importance to our doctors are the pregnant and non-pregnant clients. We could get a list of all the pregnant clients and non-pregnant clients and randomly select from each. In this case, we would want to have more clients selected from the pregnant subgroup because the doctors are very interested in their responses.

Cluster

Clusters of individuals from our population could be found in the waiting room of the doctor's office or on the maternity floor of the hospital. We would select which of the clusters we wanted to survey and do so.

Section Summary

- *Probability sampling procedures* are used to ensure that every individual within a population has a known probability or likelihood of being selected for a study. There are four types of probability sampling procedures (pp. 139–143).
    - With *simple probability sampling*, all individuals in a population have an equal probability of being selected (pp. 139–140).
    - With *systematic probability sampling*, a random sample taken in a systematic approach is used (p. 141).
    - *Stratified probability sampling* is a sampling technique where a researcher begins by identifying subgroups (or strata) and then randomly sample from each subgroup (p. 141).
    - *Cluster probability sampling* involves identifying clusters of individuals from the population. These clusters are then sampled from to obtain the sample (pp. 141–142).

NONPROBABILITY SAMPLING PROCEDURES

NONPROBABILITY SAMPLING PROCEDURE

A procedure where not all individuals within the population of interest have an equal likelihood or known probability of being selected.

CONVENIENCE

A procedure which involves using those participants who are readily available or will volunteer to participate.

SNOWBALLING

A procedure where a sample is acquired by a referral process among similar individuals.

QUOTA

A convenience sample is selected that is comprised of subgroups similar in number to the population.

If a probability sampling procedure is not possible, a **nonprobability sampling procedure** can be used. In these procedures, *not all* individuals within the population of interest have an equal or known likelihood of being selected. These nonprobability sampling procedures include convenience, snowballing, and quota. **Convenience** nonprobability sampling (sometimes referred to haphazard) involves using participants who are readily available or who will volunteer to participate. Many experiments in psychology are conducted on General Psychology students. Those students are readily available and volunteer to participate to receive partial course credit or a monetary stipend. **Snowballing** is when you select initial participants who meet some set of criteria and then acquire other participants through a referral from your initial participants. Jenn used a snowballing procedure when she was in graduate school. Jenn was conducting research on married couples. She selected people to participate who met the criteria of being married. These married couples then gave Jenn the names of married couples they knew who would also be interested in participating. Her sample grew in size as a snowball grows when you add more snow to it.

The last nonprobability sampling procedure is **quota**. In quota sampling, you select a convenience sample that is comprised of subgroups similar in number to the population. You could recruit General Psychology students to form a sample that matches the population (all university students) in terms of percentage of students for each ethnic group. If Caucasian students make up 53% of the student population, then a quota sampling procedure would have a sample with 53% Caucasian participants. The disadvantage to all nonprobability sampling procedure is an increased likelihood of a biased sample. The biased sample can occur due to the self-selecting process of the procedure. In other words, individuals who self-select to participate could be different in nature than individuals who do not self-select. Ways to minimize this disadvantage will be discussed later.

YOU TRY IT!

Text messaging has become very popular. We are currently investigating how popular text messaging is among college students and why it is so popular. Help us with our study by answering the question. Then, compare your ideas on obtaining the sample to the answers below.

Questions:

Explain how we could obtain our sample using the following procedures: (1) convenience, (2) snowballing, and (3) quota.

1. Convenience—You might have recommended that in the convenience procedure we post the opportunity to our General Psychology students to participate in the experiment.

(Continued)

2. Snowballing—You might have recommended for the snowballing procedure that we find students who use text messaging, survey them, and ask if they know other students who text message that might be willing to participate.

3. Quota—Finally, with the quota procedure you might have recommended that we get a convenience sample, paying attention to the numbers of individuals that comprise the subgroups. For example, we would want to be sure that we have a sample comprised of 50% men and 50% women.

Section Summary

♦ The alternative to probability sampling procedures is using *nonprobability sampling* procedures. In this type of procedure, not all individuals within the population of interest have an equal likelihood or known probability of being selected, and biases may be a problem (pp. 144–145).
   ♦ A *convenience sample* involves using those participants who are readily available or who will volunteer to participate (p. 144).
   ♦ A *snowballing sampling* procedure is where a sample is acquired by a referral process among similar individuals (p. 144).
   ♦ A *quota sample* is similar to stratified sampling, where subgroups are identified which are similar in number to the population. However, this is a nonrandom sample (p. 144).

RANDOM ASSIGNMENT TO CONDITIONS

We mentioned previously that many studies in psychology (and other social sciences) use the nonprobability sampling technique of a convenience sample by having General Psychology students as participants. You might wonder if using a convenience sampling procedure creates a biased sample. This is a good question because it certainly could. Nonprobability sampling procedures can cause threats to external validity. However, no matter whether you use a probability or nonprobability sampling procedure, it is always a good idea to use **random assignment** of participants to the treatment condition. This will control for threats to internal validity.

Take for instance the following example. Students in our Research Methods class want to know if listening to classical music improves academic performance. This is known as the Mozart effect and students in psychology are always interested in the topic, especially with the popularity of the recent Baby Einstein series. The Research Methods class decides they need two groups of participants. Group one will listen to Mozart and group two will not listen to music. Jenn tells the Research Methods class that they can use her 8 am and 10 am sections of General Psychology classes and she will offer extra credit to those students willing to serve as participants. This is a nonprobability sampling technique, because the Research Method class is merely using students who are readily available and willing to volunteer. Next, General Psychology students wanting to participate

RANDOM ASSIGNMENT

A procedure in which a selected participant has an equal probability of being placed into each group of a study.

could come to the research lab one afternoon and be randomly assigned to treatment conditions. For example, they could then be divided into two groups by flipping a coin. However, would it be random assignment to flip a coin and assign an entire class to the treatment conditions? In other words, can we randomly assign the 8 am class to one group and the 10 am class to the other group? Although this may seem like an easy alternative, it is not a random process. This is because the classes differ as a whole. At our institution, students who register on time fill up the 10 am classes, while students who wait until the last minute are stuck registering for the 8 am class. This means that the two groups are not the same (are not equal) prior to the introduction of the variable of interest. It is important then that each student, not the class as a whole, be randomly assigned.

YOU TRY IT!

We want you to get comfortable with using random assignment. Read the following paragraph about a recent Stanford study by Dr. Dena Bravata and colleagues (2007). We would like for you to help us decide how to do our similar study.

A Stanford study recently found that pedometers help people stay active. A pedometer is a small device that counts the number of steps you take per day. (You might remember that not too long ago McDonald's gave away pedometers when you purchased salads.) Results indicated that those wearing pedometers increased physical activity by about 2,000 steps (equivalent to one mile) per day. We want to replicate this study with our General Psychology students. We will offer those students willing to participate in the study extra credit (and an alternative for extra credit for those not wanting to participate in research). We will have two groups of participants. One group of participants will wear pedometers allowing them to see the number of steps taken per day, and another group will wear pedometers not allowing them to see the number of steps taken per day. In this situation, how would you assign the participants to each of the two groups?

You probably decided to randomly assign participants to the two groups. Did you flip a coin, use the random number chart, or come up with another unbiased method of your own? We would like to mention one last word on random assignment before we change topics. It is not always possible to use random assignment. For example, a recent study in the news conducted by Dartmouth researchers found that rural patients are diagnosed earlier for colorectal and lung cancer than urban patients (Paquette & Finlayson, 2007). In this study, it would not be possible to randomly assign participants to being urban patients or rural patients. However, if you cannot randomly assign participants to the conditions, you can be sure to control for other factors across the two groups. In the study described above, the researchers controlled for factors such as age, race, gender, marital status, income, and education level.

Section Summary

♦ *Random assignment* is the procedure in which a selected participant has an equal probability of being placed into each group of a study (p. 145).

DETERMINING SAMPLE SIZE

One of the most difficult questions to answer when you are conducting a study is regarding the number of participants needed—in other words, "How big of a sample do I need?" Simply, there is no one way to determine sample size completely. Oftentimes, people rely on past precedent and do what others have done.

Sample size, the number of individuals that participate in a study, is important to consider because you want to know how much data need to be collected to see a change in the dependent variable, if one truly exists. No one wants to collect more data than are needed to demonstrate the independent variable "worked." Fortunately, there is a known relationship between the sample size of a study and the ability of statistical tests to determine an effect. This relationship is known as power and is thus an important piece to the puzzle.

SAMPLE SIZE

The number of individuals needed or that are selected for a study.

POWER

The probability of rejecting the null hypothesis when it is indeed false or the probability of accepting the alternative when it is true is the definition of **power**. In other words, we want to know the probability of seeing an effect when there is really an effect to be seen. As mentioned earlier, there is a positive correlation between power and sample size in that as one increases so does the other. So, should we just sample a large number of people to obtain high power? The answer is no. As you increase your sample size, other factors increase as well, such as time and money. Therefore, we try to achieve sufficient power while minimizing sample size. Cohen (1965) recommended that the baseline for power be .80. Cohen indicated that this was a sufficient enough level to decrease the probability of a Type II error or failing to reject the null hypothesis when it is indeed false. (We will learn about Type I and Type II Errors later in Chapter 14.)

POWER

The probability of rejecting the null hypothesis when it is indeed false.

In addition to determining sample size through power, you must also consider the effect size of the study. The **effect size** is the amount of overlap between populations. Specifically, effect size speaks to the magnitude of the treatment. The larger the overlap between population, the smaller the difference on the dependent variable. Contrarily, the smaller the overlap between the population, the greater the difference on the dependent variable. Effect size can be determined by looking at previous research and be calculated post hoc. When estimating effect size, we rely on past research where effect size is noted to make a determination for our study. By using the combination of desired power and effect size, a person can easily narrow in on the needed sample size. For example, look at Table 8.2. This is a table of the relationship between power and effect size. If you were conducting a study where you wanted to obtain power of .80 and past research had shown your variables should yield an effect size of .60, then you would need only 18 participants. Typically, you would want power to be at least .80 to indicate you had sufficient strength in rejecting the null hypothesis when it is indeed false.

EFFECT SIZE

The amount of overlap between populations.

TABLE 8.2 Power Table.

		Effect Size								
		0.10	0.20	0.30	0.40	0.50	0.60	0.70	0.80	0.90
	0.25	167	42	20	12	8	6	5	4	3
	0.50	385	96	42	24	15	10	7	6	4
	0.60	490	122	53	29	18	12	9	6	5
	0.67	570	142	63	34	21	14	10	7	5
Power	0.70	616	153	67	37	23	15	10	7	5
	0.75	692	172	75	41	24	17	11	8	6
	0.80	783	194	85	46	28	18	12	9	6
	0.85	895	221	97	52	32	21	14	10	6
	0.90	1047	259	113	62	37	24	16	11	7
	0.95	1294	319	139	75	46	30	19	13	8
	0.99	1828	450	195	105	64	40	27	18	11

Source: Cohen, J. (1988). *Statistical power analysis for the behavioral sciences*, (2nd. ed.). Hillsdale, NJ: Lawrence Erlbaum.

Section Summary

- The number of individuals needed or that are selected for a study is known as the *sample size* (p. 147).
- The probability of rejecting the null hypothesis when it is indeed false is known as *power* (p. 147).
- The amount of overlap between populations is known as *effect size* (p. 147).

Are You Equipped Now?

At the beginning of this chapter, we reviewed Milgram's research on obedience. As our last activity for this chapter, we want to replicate Milgram's research. (By the way, Milgram's research has been replicated lately while controlling for ethical concerns.) For our replication study, we will use the students at our university as the population. Therefore, we have a known list of all people within the population. We would like for you to explain how you could use the four probability sampling techniques and three non-probability sampling techniques to get our sample.

Probability Sampling Procedures

a. Simple—If we wanted to use a simple probability procedure, we could get list of all students at the university. We would then put the names in a big box and pull out 50 names of students to serve as participants.

b. Systematic—For the systematic procedure, we would again need a list of all university students. We would then select every 120th participant to get 50 names of students to serve as participants.

c. Stratified—We would identify the subgroups and randomly sample from the subgroups. Our subgroup could be sex and we would randomly sample from the men and women attending the university.

d. Cluster—The cluster procedure involves identifying clusters of students. These clusters might come from students who are from different parts of the state or those who live in different dormitories on campus. After identifying clusters of students to participate in the study, we would want to be sure that each student only participates one time

Nonprobability Sampling Procedures

a. Convenience—If we wanted to use a convenience sampling technique, we would use students enrolled in our classes (say our General Psychology classes). We would offer extra credit to those students willing to participate.

b. Snowballing—When using the snowballing procedure, we would go to the cafeteria and ask students, who we know, to participate in the study. We would then ask these students if they had friends who might also be willing to participate.

c. Quota—When using the quota procedure, we would want the subgroups in our sample to be numerically similar to subgroups in the population. Our sample would come from General Psychology classes and our subgroups (sex, day versus night student, ethnicity) would be equivalent to that of the population.

Chapter Summary

- A *population* is the entire group of people from which the results of a study are generalized. On the other hand, a *sample* is a smaller group that is representative of the larger population (pp. 138–139).
- When conducting a study, it is not always feasible to use the entire population. Therefore, researchers use samples. There are two types of procedures that you can use: probability sampling and nonprobability sampling. *Probability sampling* ensures that everyone in the larger population has a known probability of being selected for the study. In contrast, *nonprobability sampling* is used when everyone in the larger population does *not* have a known probability of being selected for the study (pp. 139–145).
- There are four common types of probability sampling. These four types can be used to ensure that participants in a larger population have an equal or known probability of being selected for a study (pp. 139–143).
  - In *simple probability sampling*, all individuals in a population have an equal probability of being selected. You can use this type of probability sampling with or without replacement (pp. 139–140).
    - In sampling with replacement, individuals are sampled one at a time, with each individual being replaced before the next is sampled. Here, each person has exactly the same probability of being selected (p. 139).

- ◆ In sampling without replacement, individuals are sampled and are not replaced before the next is sampled. Here, the probability of being selected changes with each removal (p. 139).
  - ◆ In *systematic probability sampling*, a random sample is taken in a systematic approach is used (p. 141).
  - ◆ *Stratified probability sampling* is a sampling technique where a researcher begins by identifying subgroups (or strata) and then randomly samples from each subgroup (p. 141).
  - ◆ *Cluster probability sampling* involves identifying clusters of individuals from the population. These clusters are then included in the sample (pp. 144–142).
- ◆ Nonprobability sampling does *not* ensure that all members of the larger population have an equal or known probability of being selected for a study. Many times it is not possible to sample all members. Therefore, a more commonly used alternative to the four types of probability sampling are the three types of nonprobability sampling (pp. 144–145).
  - ◆ A *convenience sample* involves using those participants who are readily available or who will volunteer to participate (p. 144).
  - ◆ A *snowballing sampling* procedure is where a sample is acquired by a referral process among similar individuals (p. 144).
  - ◆ A *quota sample* is similar to stratified sampling, where subgroups are identified. However, this is a nonrandom sample (p. 144).
- ◆ One way to reduce bias to internal validity is by *randomly assigning* individuals in the sample to conditions. We take the individuals in our sample and give each one an equal chance of being assigned to one of the two or more levels of the independent variable (p. 145).
- ◆ Deciding how many individuals to use in a study is not a simple task. In other words, sample size is the number of individuals that participate in a study. Sample size is a function of power and effect size. If you know the desired power for a study and the effect size that can be achieved, you can use a power table to determine the sample size that you need (pp. 147–148).
  - ◆ *Power* is represented by a probability ranging from 0 to 1 (p. 147).
  - ◆ The amount of overlap between populations is known as effect size. Effect size estimates are determined by looking at past research (p. 147).

APA Learning Goals Linkage

- **Goal 1.** *Knowledge Base of Psychology*
  Students will demonstrate familiarity with the major concepts, theoretical perspectives, empirical findings, and historical trends in psychology.

  Sections Covered: Are You Equipped?

  Explanation of the Goal: Psychological research today has been greatly influenced by key experiments from the past. One such experiment in the

(Continued)

history of psychology was that of Milgram's on obedience. This chapter opened with an overview of Milgram's 1963 experiment with special attention given to how individuals were recruited for participation.

- **Goal 2.** *Research Methods in Psychology*

Students will understand and apply basic research methods in psychology, including research design, data analysis, and interpretation.

Sections Covered: Are You Equipped?, Populations versus Samples, Probability Sampling Procedures, Nonprobability Sampling Procedures, Random Assignment to Conditions, Determining Sample Size, Power, Are You Equipped Now?

Explanation of the Goal: As we proceed through the textbook, we are learning more about the basic research methods utilized by psychologists. This chapter focused on how individuals are selected for participation in psychological research and how the participants can be assigned to treatment conditions. In order to discuss these topics, the chapter began with a discussion on the difference between populations and samples. Next, we outlined probability and nonprobability sampling procedures, articulating the strengthens and weaknesses of each sampling method. It is essential to recognize how biases may shape design, and therefore this chapter included information on biased samples and the use of random assignment to treatment conditions to reduce systematic differences. Finally, we equipped you to interpret basic statistical conclusions through the topics of determining sample size, effect size, and power.

- **Goal 3.** *Critical Thinking Skills in Psychology*

Students will respect and use critical and creative thinking, skeptical inquiry, and, when possible, the scientific approach to solve problems related to behavior and mental processes.

Sections Covered: Are You Equipped?, Probability Sampling Procedures, Nonprobability Sampling Procedures, Random Assignment to Conditions, Are You Equipped Now?

Explanation of the Goal: This chapter was unique in that the You Try It! exercises all required you to generate multiple possible solutions to a problem. For example, you were asked to explain how to utilize the types of probability sampling procedures in obtaining a sample from a high school and how to utilize the types of nonprobability sampling techniques in obtaining a sample to study text messaging. Thus, your critical thinking skills were needed in creatively deciding how to solve a situation by using different approaches.

- **Goal 4.** *Application of Psychology*

Students will understand and apply psychological principles to personal, social, and organizational issues.

(Continued)

(*Continued*)

Sections Covered: Are You Equipped?, Probability Sampling Procedures, Nonprobability Sampling Procedures, Random Assignment to Conditions, Are You Equipped Now?

Explanation of the Goal: As with almost every chapter in the textbook thus far, we have applied psychological principles to everyday examples. In this chapter, we included examples of text messaging, parking on college campuses, and the use of pedometers. However, we also took time to examine how ethically complex situations can arise when psychological principles are applied to societal issues. Specifically, Milgram conducted his research on obedience to understand the issue facing society of how individuals committed such violent acts to other humans in concentration camps. However, designing an experiment to understand human behavior like obedience is not simple and involves many ethical considerations.

• **Goal 7.** *Communication Skills*

Students will be able to communicate effectively in a variety of formats.

Sections Covered: Power

Explanation of the Goal: In continuing to improve your ability to communicate quantitative information, we included in this chapter a section on appropriate statistical analyses needed for interpretation purposes. Power and effect size are both needed to interpret measurements and thus we supplied information on the conventionally accepted levels for both.

Controls and Threats to Internal Validity

CHAPTER OUTLINE

Are You Equipped?

Do you ever watch *American Idol*? Your textbook authors must admit that we have been avid fans of the show since the very first season. We will even record *American Idol* so we do not miss a single episode. If you are not a fan of the show, let us tell you the basic format. Singers compete on stage one at a time and then a panel of "expert" judges weigh in on their performances. At the end of the show, the phone lines open and the audience can call in to vote for their favorite singer. Each week, the singer with the fewest votes is kicked off the show. The process sounds harmless and fair to the performers. However, we have noticed that we tend not to form our own opinions until the judges have given theirs. Basically, we wait until we hear what the judges are saying before we decide on if we liked the performance of the singer. Do you think there is a potential problem with the judges throwing in their two cents? In other words, does this method influence how viewers vote?

Answer

If you think that this could influence how people perceive the performance of the contestants and how people vote, we would agree with you. You can think of this example as an experiment with the viewers as participants and the judges as researchers. By giving their "expert" opinions, the judges (or researchers) are subtly communicating to the viewers (or participants) how they should behave. This could be a problem. We will describe in this section of the textbook why researchers should be careful not to influence participants' responses and avoid biasing the results.

As you go through this chapter, we also want you to keep in mind how the material relate to the American Psychological Association's goals for psychology majors. Specifically, this chapter will address the following goals:

- **Goal 2. Research Methods in Psychology**
  Students will understand and apply basic research methods in psychology, including research design, data analysis, and interpretation.
- **Goal 3. Critical Thinking Skills in Psychology**
  Students will respect and use critical and creative thinking, skeptical inquiry, and, when possible, the scientific approach to solve problems related to behavior and mental.
- **Goal 4. Application of Psychology**
  Students will understand and apply psychological principles to personal, social, and organizational issues.
- **Goal 8. Sociocultural and International Awareness**
  Students will recognize, understand, and respect the complexity of sociocultural and international diversity.

CONTROL

EXTRANEOUS VARIABLE

Variable that is not controlled for in the experiment that may have an effect on the dependent variable.

NUISANCE VARIABLE

A variable that is not controlled for in the experiment that influences all participants in the same manner.

As discussed in Chapter 5, an experiment involves many variables, including an independent variable and a dependent variable. Researchers devote a substantial amount of time in selecting these two variables and deciding how they will be defined and measured. However, it is important to be aware of other variables that could influence (and potentially bias) research findings. Extraneous variables and nuisance variables are two examples. **Extraneous variables** are variables not controlled for in the experiment that may have an effect on the dependent variable. However, when a variable varies systematically with the independent variable, making it difficult to determine the effect of the independent variable, it is said to be confounding. **Nuisance variables** are unwanted variables that can influence all groups of participants, causing the results to be less clear. We are going to give you examples for each to demonstrate these definitions and illustrate how these variables can influence the interpretation of results from an experiment. Let us start by reading the following example from a recent news story.

The news headline reads, "Study Suggests Possible Link between TV Viewing and Autism in Children." This news article describes research conducted at Cornell University by Michael Waldman examining rain, cable TV subscriptions, and autism. Researchers looked at two factors leading them to their conclusions about TV viewing and autism in children. First, the researchers looked at autism rates in counties of California, Oregon, and Washington. Results indicated that as rainfall increased, so too did rates of autism, and conversely as rainfall decreased, so too did rates of autism. The researchers found this interesting because prior research conducted by U. S. Bureau of Labor Statistics reported that children watch more TV when it is raining. Second, the researchers looked at the percentage of households with cable TV subscriptions in the states of California and Pennsylvania. Results indicated that as cable TV subscriptions increased, so too did rates of autism, and, conversely, as cable TV subscriptions decreased, so too did rates of autism. The researchers combined these two results to conclude there is a link between watching TV and autism. The researchers further justified this link by stating that they can think of no other obvious factor correlated with both rain and cable TV subscriptions, except TV viewing.

From this example, can you think of an extraneous variable that could be influencing the interpretation of the results? In other words, is there another variable besides TV viewing that relates to cable TV subscriptions and rain? Here are a few hints:

1. You are looking for a variable that the researchers did not mention controlling for in their results.

2. You are looking for a variable that potentially varies with both cable TV subscriptions and rain amounts.

Answer

We think that a possible extraneous variable is population size. Our reasoning is as follows. As the population size increases in a particular area, the number of cable TV subscriptions also increases. Therefore, it is more likely that a city with 100,000 residents will have more cable TV subscriptions than a city with 2,500 residents. Similarly, as population size increases, the number of children within that area increases. The more children there are in an area, the more likely it is that cases of autism will be found in that area. Here is an example to understand this argument using fictitious data. Pretend that in any given city, children comprise 10% of the population. So in a city of 100,000 people, there will be 10,000 children. Similarly, in a city of 2,500 people, there will be only 250 children (see Figure 9.1 *top*). Therefore, as population size increases, the number of children increases. This works the same for rates of autism. Let's say for simplicity sake, that 1 out of every 100 children is diagnosed with autism. In the larger city with 10,000 children, there would be 100 cases of autism, and in a smaller city with 250 children, there would be 2.5 cases of autism (see Figure 9.1 *bottom*). Thus, the larger city will exhibit more cases of autism (100 versus 2.5) and more cable TV subscriptions, not due to TV viewing but due to population size. Furthermore, the possibility exists that more people live in areas with greater amounts of rain. It could be the case that

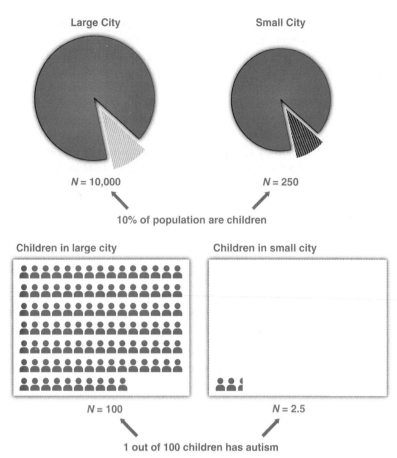

FIGURE 9.1 Fictitious Population of a Large and Small City with Children who Have Autism.

the counties receiving the most rain are also the counties with the most residents. Thus, we cannot confidently conclude that TV viewing (which occurs most frequently when it rains) causes autism. This is because the extraneous variable of population size varies with cable TV subscriptions, number of children with autism in a given area, and possibly counties receiving the most rain.

Now that we have seen how extraneous variables can make it difficult to determine the effect of the independent variable in an experiment, let us discuss nuisance variables. Like extraneous variables, nuisance variables are important to consider when interpreting research findings. Specifically, nuisance variables are variables that are not controlled for in the experiment that influences all participants in the same manner. It is important to note the similarities and differences between extraneous variables and nuisance variables. Typically, both extraneous variables and nuisance variables are unwanted. This means that research findings can be influenced by both extraneous variables and nuisance variables in unwanted ways. Furthermore, we are not normally interested in the effect of extraneous and nuisance variables, except to understand how it might be influencing our research results. However, extraneous variables and nuisance variables are also different. Extraneous variables vary with the independent variables (so it is different between groups), whereas nuisance variables are the same for all groups.

This next example on nuisance variables comes from our own research. We have noticed over the past two years that our students are spending more and more time on friend networking sites such as MySpace and Facebook. Until recently, we had never even heard of such sites. So, in case you are not familiar with these sites either, here is some information. These friend networking sites have a number of features that allow individuals to communicate with others. For example, these sites allow users to post information about themselves, post pictures, leave messages for friends about upcoming events, and link (i.e., provide a hyperlink) their sites to friends' sites. Because our students were always talking about these sites, we were interested in learning more about MySpace and Facebook. We selected these sites because they appeared to be the two most popular friend networking sites for our students. In the spring of 2007, we recruited participants for an experiment on "Student Internet Usage" with no mention made of friend networking sites. We were interested in how many students use friend networking sites and how many students do not use friend networking sites, and therefore, we did not mention friend networking sites in the title of the experiment so all students would participate in the experiment. Our results were very interesting and did demonstrate that friend networking sites were popular among our students. In fact, 87.1% of participants indicated having either a MySpace or Facebook account and 74.3% of participants had accounts in both sites. We also were surprised at the amount of time students spend per day on their accounts. We found that students reported spending an average of 1.46 hours on their accounts and 1.10 hours on others' accounts. Finally, we were shocked at the average number of friends students reported having linked to their account. Specifically, the mean number of friends linked was 235.51.

We are currently in the process of designing a second survey to gather more information about friend networking sites. Now that we know college students are using friend networking, it is important to understand why some college students use friend networking sites while other college students do not. Specifically for students who are using friend networking sites, we want to know what needs are being met for students by interacting with friends in this venue. We have our survey complete and are set to administer it in the beginning of the fall semester. However, we realized there could be a potential problem with that plan. Specifically, our original data were collected at the end of the spring semester and now we are thinking about collecting data at the beginning of the fall semester. How could time of the year (spring semester versus fall semester) be a nuisance variable for us? In other words, how could the time of the year when we ask students about their usage of friend networking sites make the results less clear?

We think time of the year might be a nuisance variable for the following reasons. The data that we will collect will primarily be from college freshmen. It is possible that students do not create (or even learn about) friend networking sites until they have been in college a semester. Therefore, the data we collected in the spring would show how popular friend networking sites are for college students, but data collected in early fall on college freshmen might more accurately describe high-school students' use of friend networking sites. Thus, time of the year is an unwanted variable. We are not interested in how usage of friend networking sites varies with the seasons (although that could be true) and we are also not interested in how popular these sites are among high-school students (although that might warrant future research). We just want to know in general how college students use friend networking sites. In order to do so, we must be aware of nuisance variables (like time of the year) that might make our results less clear.

An important take-home message from these examples of extraneous variables and nuisance variables is that research should be designed so that it controls for as many variables as possible. Although we might not normally think of control as a good thing, with regard to research, control can be a positive. When you read research findings or hear them presented in the media, you should ask yourself if the research experiment was designed to control for extraneous and nuisance variables. However, if the research was not designed to control for these variables, be sure to ask yourself how this might have influenced the results. Maybe it does not significantly influence the results or maybe it does, like in the examples of TV viewing and autism discussed earlier.

Section Summary

- When designing and conducting research, you must take into account variables that can potentially influence and/or bias results (pp. 154–158).
- Two types of variables that could potentially influence and/or bias results are (pp. 154–155):
    - *Extraneous variables* are variables not controlled for in the experiment that vary with the independent variables (p. 154).
    - *Nuisance variables* are variables that are not controlled for in the experiment that influences all participants in the same manner (p. 154).

THREATS TO INTERNAL VALIDITY

As mentioned in Chapter 5, internal validity is being able to say with confidence that the independent variable caused the observed change in the dependent variable. Now, whether you are going to conduct your own research or you are consuming research findings presented in the media, you should be aware of threats to internal validity. Threats to internal validity are threats to saying that the manipulated variable (i.e., the independent variable) caused the change in the measured or observed variable (i.e., the dependent variable). In other words, a threat means that something else could have caused the change observed besides the variable that was manipulated. Campbell and Stanly (1969) outlined threats to internal validity many years ago. In order to help you determine if any threats to internal validity are present in an experiment, you can ask yourself the following 10 questions. Depending on your answers, you will know if threats to internal validity are an issue.

- **Question # 1**   Could the change in the dependent variable be due to an event beyond the researcher's control?

When an event beyond the researcher's control can explain the change in the dependent variable, **history** is a threat to internal validity. Let us pretend that the U. S. Department of Agriculture does regular surveys on mature Americans to see what concerns they have with foodborne illnesses. You hear on the news one night that mature Americans are now 50 times more likely to worry about Mad Cow disease than they were five years ago. You happen to remember that there was an outbreak of Mad Cow disease last year (at around the same time the data were collected). It is possible that the increase in concern over Mad Cow disease is partially due to the recent outbreak. This is an example of history being a threat to internal validity. The outbreak of Mad Cow disease was an event beyond the researcher's control, yet it influenced the results.

HISTORY

An event beyond the researcher's control that can explain the change in the dependent variable.

YOU TRY IT!

Here is another example for you to try. Within the past five years, there was an outbreak of salmonella in peanut butter. Imagine you were conducting a study evaluating the safety of peanut butter use in family households for a major peanut butter producer. Would this salmonella outbreak have an impact on your results?

If you asked people before and after this outbreak how safe peanut butter was to eat, you might see a change in response immediately after the outbreak. Specifically, after the outbreak of salmonella, people would probably report that peanut butter was less safe to eat than they would have reported before the outbreak. In this example, the change in the dependent variable (peoples' perceptions of the safety of peanut butter) is partially influenced by the recent outbreak of salmonella. In conclusion, always ask yourself if events going on beyond the researcher's control could have influenced the way participants responded in the experiment.

- **Question # 2**   Could the change in the dependent variable be due to internal changes within the participant that have occurred over time?

If so, **maturation** could be a threat to internal validity. Maturation means that the change in the dependent variable is not solely due to the independent variable, but to internal changes within the participant that occurred over time.

For example, when our oldest daughter was younger, she greatly enjoyed playing hide-and-seek. Unfortunately, she was not very good at the game because she was very egocentric. Egocentrism is the inability to see another person's point of view. When we would play hide-and-seek, she would hide under a small end table that had a short tablecloth. She was easy to find because her feet would inevitably be sticking out from under the tablecloth. From her point of view, she could not see us (i.e., she only saw the back of the tablecloth) and therefore we could not see her. Yet, when we found her quickly, she would become quite upset

MATURATION

The change in the dependent variable is due to internal changes within the participants over time.

and insist that we had cheated. We cannot tell you how many countless hours we worked trying to get her to understand that her feet were out in the open. After several months of working with her, one day she pulled her feet under the table cloth. Of course, we did not find her quickly and became concerned. After all, she was always so easy to spot. However, we eventually found her under the table cloth and naturally assumed that we were great hide-and-seek teachers. However, shortly after this episode we began to realize that it had nothing to do with us and that rather it was a result of a change in her internal state. She was maturing and outgrowing egocentrism. Although we deeply wanted to believe that it was our teaching (independent variable) that caused the change in her egocentrism (dependent variable), it was more than likely the effects of maturation. Therefore, you should always ask yourself if a change in the observed behavior (dependent variable) is due to your manipulation (independent variable) or just an internal change within the participant. Now, you try one on your own.

YOU TRY IT!

Many colleges and universities offer a freshman seminar/introduction to college class to prepare and equip students for college life. In these freshman seminar classes, instructors work with incoming students on a variety of topics such as time management, money management, and study skills. Because colleges and universities put a great deal of money into these classes, they want to know if the freshman seminar classes (the independent variable) have an influence on students' attitudes and behaviors (the dependent variable). This is commonly measured by conducting a survey at the end of the first year about information covered in the classes. Could there be a problem with this methodology related to maturation?

As you may have guessed, before concluding that the freshman seminar class was responsible for the changes demonstrated on the survey, we must consider the fact that the students matured over time. In other words, the changes at the end of the year could be due to students' maturation during that time period. Think about your first year in college. You probably encountered many challenges and experiences that required you to grow up. Being away from parents for the first time, managing your own money, and figuring out a class schedule that works for you are just a few examples of activities that may have lead to your own maturation. Therefore, it may not be the freshman seminar class itself causing the change in the student, but the fact that the student is growing up and maturing. In sum, be sure to ask yourself if changes within the individual due to the participant simply maturing may have caused the change in the dependent variable. This is an important threat to internal validity to consider with research on children, whose internal states are constantly changing and developing.

REGRESSION TO THE MEAN

The change in the dependent variable is due to extreme scores moving toward the mean on later measures.

• **Question # 3** Could the change in the dependent variable be due to extreme scores moving toward the mean?

This is an example of a threat to internal validity known as **regression to the mean.** In regression to the mean, the change in the dependent variable is not due to the independent variable, but due to extreme scores moving toward the mean. Let's take a look at an everyday example. Have you ever noticed that two extremely attractive people can have an average-looking or unattractive child?

Or have you ever noticed that two extremely unattractive people can have an average-looking or attractive child? (As a disclaimer, we believe that all children are cute, especially our own!) However, if you think about this example, you will realize you have seen this before. This is an example of regression to the mean. Think about this example with attractiveness on a scale ranging from not at all attractive to very attractive. Two very attractive people (e.g., the extreme scores) have a less attractive child (e.g., regression toward the mean), or two very unattractive people (e.g., extreme scores) have an attractive child (e.g., regression to the mean).

For those of you needing a less controversial example of regression to the mean, think about playing a video game. Have you ever played a video game breaking the all-time high score only to find that you were never able to duplicate that performance? This is another example of regression to the mean. You will most likely always follow up any extreme score (i.e., your all-time high score) with regression to the mean (i.e., a lower score). Therefore, anytime in research results where participants with extreme scores have subsequent scores which have moved up or down, be sure to ask yourself if the change was due to the independent variable or regression to the mean? This is an important threat to consider when individuals score very high or low on a first test and in the opposite direction on a second test. The change in performance could be due to regression toward the mean rather than a change in any variable.

- **Question # 4**   Could the change in the dependent variable be due to how the participants were selected or assigned to groups?

If **selection** of participants is a threat to internal validity, the change in the dependent variable could be due to how the participants were selected for the experiment or how they were assigned to groups. Here is an example from our own campus. All over the campus, blasted on signs and coffee mugs are the results of a survey on the number of alcoholic beverages students at our university consume when they drink. In fact, as we write this example, we are looking at a coffee mug that states, "Most university students make healthy choices. 69% have 0–4 drinks when they drink." Our university is not alone in advertising such results. We remember a similar slogan from our graduate university. However, there is a lot to consider when you look at these results. We will ignore the issues all together as to whether or not this is a healthy choice or whether or not participants are in fact telling the truth. Instead, just think about how the participants were selected for the survey. In other words, where did they come from or how were they selected? Were participants selected depending on if they lived on- or off-campus? Were all the participants in a sorority or fraternity? Were non–traditional age students included in the survey? Were men and women equally sampled? Did they only sample those students over the age of 21? It is possible that the answers to these questions might change the results. For example, do you think that members of a Greek affiliation drink more or less than the average college student? If they do drink different amounts compared to other college students, then having too many or too few Greek-affiliated students in the survey could bias the results. It is important to ask yourself if all

SELECTION

Change in the dependent variable is due to how participants were selected for the experiment or how they were assigned to groups.

students had the opportunity to be selected for the study and, if appropriate, were participants randomly assigned to treatment groups. If participants were *not* randomly selected/assigned and a convenience sample was used (e.g., whatever students walked by the university cafeteria), selection could be a threat to internal validity.

- **Question # 5**   Could the change in the dependent variable be due to participants systematically dropping out of the experiment?

ATTRITION

Participants systematically drop out of an experiment, thus changing the experimental results.

Attrition occurs when participants systematically drop out of an experiment and therefore change the results of the experiment. We can use the Atkins diet as an example. In case you are not familiar with this diet, the Atkins diet involves eliminating all carbohydrates from your diet (i.e., breads and starches). We decided to give the diet a try ourselves because some of our friends had lost weight successfully using it. However, the diet was not as successful for us. Not because it did not work per se, but because we dropped out or stopped the diet. (Although we enjoyed the meats and cheeses, we greatly missed breads and, of course, chocolate.) Think of a research experiment designed to test which diet is best at helping people lose weight—Atkins, Jenny Craig, or Weight Watchers. The results could show that the average weight lost on Atkins was 6 pounds per week and on Jenny Craig and Weight Watchers was 2 pounds per week. Based on such fictitious results, we might all start the Atkins diet immediately. However, you must ask yourself if the results in weight loss are due to the independent variable (type of diet) or participants systematically dropping out of the experiment. It could in fact be the case that a significant number of participants on the Atkins diet dropped out. Maybe 8 of the 10 people on the Atkins diet dropped out of the experiment leaving only two participants the diet really worked for in the group. On the other hand, the dropout rate for the Jenny Craig and Weight Watchers groups was much lower (e.g., only one dropout per condition), and therefore contained participants with varying degrees of weight-loss success. Thus, it is important to ask yourself if participants are dropping out of a study in a manner that might influence the results. If the answer is yes, attrition could be a threat to internal validity.

- **Question # 6**   Could the change in the dependent variable be due to participants' familiarity with the test?

TESTING

Change in the dependent variable is due to the participants becoming more familiar with the test or testing procedures.

Testing is a threat to internal validity when the change in the dependent variable is not due to the independent variable, but rather is due to the participant becoming more familiar with the test or testing procedures. In academic settings, this is why instructors give practice quizzes or why students take practice SATs and ACTs. In sports, athletes run drills or practice plays over and over. In short, you get better at something when you practice it. Think about the example below on testing as a threat to internal validity. We both teach classes that historically students do not normally enjoy taking (Research Methods, Statistics, and Physiological Psychology). It happens occasionally that a student who is in one of our classes has previously taken the class from another instructor either at our institution or another. The repeater students will comment that the class is so much easier with us as instructors. Now, we might want to believe that we are such great instructors that student learning (the dependent variable) has drastically improved because of us (the independent variable). However, it is probably more likely that the increase in student learning (dependent variable) is due to testing (practice or familiarity). Specifically, the student has become familiar with the course material as well as how material in the course will be tested. Therefore, practice and familiarity can, at least partially, explain the increase in student learning we hear students reporting. When reading about research findings be sure to ask yourself if the participant improved from the first test to the second test because of practice.

- **Question # 7**   Could the change in the dependent variable be due to participants in one group talking to participants in another group?

Typically, in research we have more than one group of participants. For example, one group of participants is given one level of the independent variable and the second group of participants is given a second level of the independent variable. Therefore, the participants in the two groups are given different instructions and different treatment levels. Similarly, in teaching, we sometimes teach two sections of the same course. This is a great opportunity to try different teaching strategies or different activities. The different teaching strategies serve as the independent variable and student learning serves as the dependent variable. We have used a similar situation to test teaching methods and student learning. For example, in the past we each taught two sections of General Psychology and played jeopardy with our students the class period before the exam. Traditionally, we have offered five points bonus on the exam to the winning team, four points to the second place team, and two points to all students who attended class the day we played jeopardy. However, we noticed that students were not studying for jeopardy because they were happy just receiving the two bonus points. We wanted to create an environment where students had studied prior to arriving to class on the day of jeopardy. One semester, we changed our approach so one section of our General Psychology classes was treated in the traditional manner (as described above), while the other section was told that the wining team would receive five bonus points and the second place team would receive four bonus points. There would be no bonus points for other students. We wanted to see if the bonus points offered (independent variable) would influence students' preparedness for the game (dependent variable). This worked as predicted for the first exam. The students in the traditional form of bonus points were not as prepared as students in the new format of bonus points. However, for the second exam this trend did not persist. Students in both sections were arriving to jeopardy unprepared. It turns out that students in the two classes were talking and assumed that they would all receive the two bonus points just for attending class on the jeopardy day. In other words, **diffusion of treatment** conditions had occurred. Be sure that changes in the dependent variable are not due to participants in different groups communicating with each other. If they are communicating, this shared information could cause a change in the dependent variable.

DIFFUSION OF TREATMENT

Change in the dependent variable is due to participants in different groups communicating with each other.

- **Question # 8**   Could the change in the dependent variable be due to changes in how the dependent variable was measured?

When a change in how the dependent variable was measured can explain the change in the dependent variable, **instrumentation** is a threat to internal validity. Pretend that we told you to go watch an episode of the *Simpsons* and count the number of violent acts that you see. You could even pick an episode of *The Family Guy* or *American Dad.* Now, pretend even further that we asked your friend to also watch the same episode you were watching and count the number of violent acts they saw. Do you think at the end of the episode that you and your friend would have counted a similar number of violent acts? Probably not. But, why not? The reason is you and your friend probably have different definitions of violence. Therefore, you may count Homer trying to choke Bart as a violent act, but your friend may not. Having an operational definition (see Chapter 7) would allow you and your friend to measure violent acts in the same way. Similarly, it is important for researchers to be sure that the dependent variable is always measured in exactly the same way. Changes in how the dependent variable is measured from one occasion to the next can produce a change in the dependent variable itself, as well as the interpretation of the results for the study.

- **Question # 9**   Could the change in the dependent variable be due to the participant's expectation that change will occur?

Sometimes just thinking a change will occur is enough to produce a change. This is known as a **placebo effect.** At our undergraduate university, a famous (or infamous) study had been conducted demonstrating the placebo effect. Well, let us clarify that it was famous only within our university and some of the details have probably been distorted as the story has been verbally passed along. Apparently, several years before we arrived at the university, a professor and a few psychology students designed an experiment to see if expectations alone really could change behavior. The psychology students recruited participants for an experiment to examine the effects of alcohol consumption on reaction time. Participants were given Jell-O shots to consume before participating in experiments where reaction time was measured. The students genuinely believed they were consuming Jell-O shots containing alcohol and their behavior in the experiments demonstrated this with impaired reaction time, slurred speech, and so on. However, to the participant's surprise, the Jell-O shots were not made with alcohol. In fact, it was just plain, regular Jell-O. When the participants were debriefed and told that the Jell-O contained no alcohol, some participants were in disbelief and actually refused to drive home until they had time to "sober up." This is a great example of how the participant's expectations (thinking the Jell-O shots contained alcohol) can influence the dependent variable (reaction time). You can imagine that this is an important threat to control for when testing the effectiveness of a new drug. Therefore, be sure participants' expectations are not influencing their behavior.

- **Question # 10**   Could the change in the dependent variable be due to the researcher's hypotheses or the participant's hypotheses?

If participants believe they should act or behave in a certain way during an experiment or if a researcher somehow communicates to participants how they should act or behave, **demand characteristics** could be a threat to internal validity. Demand characteristics are various hints and cues that participants use to tell them how the researcher wants them to behave, or at least how they think the researcher wants them to behave. If participants are responding to these demand characteristics, rather than the independent variable, this could explain the changes in the dependent variable. Think about the *American Idol* example in the Are You Equipped? section at the beginning of the chapter. By the judges giving their expert opinions on contestants' performances, they are communicating to the audience how we should vote. Sometimes, on *American Idol*, this is done very subtly by the judges reminding the audience that it is a singing competition and not a popularity contest or by reminding the audience to vote for contestants who have given consistently good performances. However, other times, the message is not so subtle. But no matter how this is done, the audience sometimes responds to the judges (demand characteristics) rather than the performances (the independent variable).

Be sure to keep in mind that in a laboratory experiment, researchers purposely do not tell participants how to respond nor are participants being bad by trying to figure out how they should act. It is only natural for participants to try to figure out the experiment and, in some cases, try to help the researcher by acting the way they think they should. Likewise, the researcher should never purposely bias results by treating participants in such a way that his or her hypothesis is confirmed. However, researchers are only human and this can occur without them knowing it. In short, research should be designed to prevent demand characteristics from changing the dependent variable.

MINIMIZING THREATS

If you are thinking that there must be ways to control for threats to internal validity, you are correct. In later chapters, we will discuss how threats to internal validity can be controlled for based on the research design that is used. However, we do want to mention in this section two simple techniques that can control many of the threats to internal validity. The two simple techniques are the use of a double blind study and the use of a placebo as a control.

When conducting research, a researcher can have a single or double blind study. In a **single blind study,** the participant has no knowledge of which group he or she has been assigned to—only the researcher knows. Although it is advantageous that the participant does not know which group he or she has been assigned to, there is a drawback. Specifically, the threat of demand characteristics may affect your study results. However, in a **double blind study** neither the participant nor the researcher interacting with the participant knows which experimental group the participant has been placed into. Thus, you reduce the likelihood of the participant or experimenter behaving in a way that can influence the study, because neither knows which group the participant is in.

The other type of basic control is the use of a placebo. A **placebo** is an inert substance that mimics the independent variable but has no effect. Think back to the threat we discussed called the placebo effect. The participants who received

DEMAND CHARACTERISTICS

The change in the dependent variable is due to the researcher somehow communicating to participants how they should act or behave.

SINGLE BLIND STUDY

A study in which the participant has no knowledge of which experimental group he or she may be participating within—only the researcher knows.

DOUBLE BLIND STUDY

An experiment in which neither the participant nor the researcher knows which experimental group the participant has been placed into.

PLACEBO

An inert substance that has no effect.

regular Jell-O were receiving a placebo (i.e., it had no effect). However, they still displayed a behavior change. Without the use of the placebo, researchers would not have been able to identify the internal threat of a placebo effect.

In addition to the aforementioned controls, think back to the beginning of the chapter when we discussed techniques. At the beginning of the chapter, we were discussing how controlling for extraneous variables and nuisance variables is a good thing. Hopefully, now you can see that controlling for threats to internal validity is also a good thing to do. We will investigate other controls in later chapters.

Section Summary

- When an event beyond the researcher's control explains the change in the dependent variable *history* is a concern (p. 159).
- *Maturation* occurs when internal changes in the participant cause the change in the dependent variable (p. 159).
- In *regression to the mean*, the change in the dependent variable is not due to the independent variable but due to extreme scores moving toward the mean on later measures (pp. 160–161).
- In *selection*, the change in the dependent variable is due to how the participants were selected for the experiment or how they were assigned to groups (pp. 161–162).
- *Attrition* occurs when participants systematically drop out of an experiment and therefore change the results of the experiment (p. 162).
- *Testing* is a threat to internal validity when the change in the dependent variable is not due to the independent variable, but rather due to the participant becoming more familiar with the test or testing procedures (pp. 162–163).
- *Diffusion of treatment* occurs when changes in the dependent variable are due to participants in different groups communicating with each other (p. 163).
- When a change in how the dependent variable was measured can explain the change in the dependent variable, *instrumentation* is a threat to internal validity (p. 164).
- Sometimes just thinking a change will occur is enough to produce a change. This is known as a *placebo effect* (p. 164).
- If participants believe they should act or behave in a certain way during an experiment or if a researcher somehow communicates to participants how they should act or behave, *demand characteristics* could be a threat to internal validity (p. 165).
- A *single blind study* is a study where the participant does not know which experimental group he or she has been placed into, but the researcher knows (p. 165).
- A *double blind study* is a study where neither the participants nor the researcher interacting with the participants knows which experimental group the participant has been placed into (p. 165).
- A *placebo* is an inert substance that has no effect (p. 165).

Are You Equipped Now?

A popular news channel summarized research findings stating that "Acupuncture may ease hip and joint pain from osteoarthritis, the most common type of arthritis." The news source went on to describe the experiment conducted by Witt and colleagues in the following way. More than 3,500 participants from Germany with osteoarthritis of the hip and/or knee participated in the experiment. Most participants were in their early 60s. In addition, 11% of participants reported having acupuncture in the year prior to the experiment. Upon arriving to the experiment, participants were asked to select which joint (i.e., the hip or the knee) was producing the most pain and then to rate that pain on the provided scale. Of the participants, around 3,200 participants received acupuncture treatments during a three-month time period and about 300 participants served as a control group (i.e., they were put on a waiting list and received no treatment). Results indicated that about a third of participants in the group receiving the acupuncture treatments reported less pain as compared to their initial visit and an increase in overall quality of life. However, only 6% of participants in the control group reported a decrease in pain and an increase in quality of life.

This article was a very compelling one. We might even be tempted to tell everyone we know with osteoarthritis that they should run out and receive acupuncture treatments. However, you have just learned about threats to internal validity. In other words, you have learned about factors that might be a threat to saying that the independent variable (i.e., acupuncture treatments) caused the change in the dependent variables (i.e., perceived pain and quality of life). Think about the 10 questions presented in this chapter. Could any of these be threats to internal validity? If so, explain. (Hint: As you read through the questions and look for threats to internal validity, we want you to focus on factors that were very likely to be threats to internal validity. Sometimes, for example, a factor might be a possible threat to internal validity, but one that is highly unlikely. Do not include such a factor in your list.)

Answer

When we looked through the 10 questions, we found 6 factors that could be threats to the internal validity of the experiment. They are: maturation, regression to the mean, selection, attrition, placebo effect, and demand characteristics. We will explain why below.

- *Maturation* means that the change in the dependent variable is not solely due to the independent variable, but to internal changes within the participant that occurred over time. It is possible that the decrease in pain reported by participants was not due to the acupuncture treatments alone, but to an internal change that occurred within the participant over the three-month time period. It might have been possible in milder cases of osteoarthritis for the pain to ease over time by itself. For example, maybe the seasons changed during the three-month time period and the change in temperatures helped to alleviate some of the pain. If this occurred, the decrease in pain reported by participants would be due to maturation rather than the independent variable (acupuncture treatments).

- In *regression to the mean*, the change in the dependent variable is not due to the independent variable, but due to extreme scores moving toward the mean. It is our hypothesis that the participants who received the acupuncture treatments were in pain, not just minor discomfort. We think this for two reasons. First, we would have to be in severe pain to sign up for an experiment that used a treatment that may or may not work. Second, participants were instructed to select the joint that caused the most pain. Both of these factors create a situation that would cause participants at the beginning of the experiment to rate the pain as very high. If the pain is rated on the upper end of a pain scale on the first occasion, subsequent ratings after treatment could inherently go down, creating regression to the mean.

- If *selection* of participants is a threat to internal validity, the change in the dependent variable could be due to how the participants were selected for the experiment. In this experiment, no information was given about how participants were selected to participate. For example, no information was given regarding how participants were recruited or if a financial stipend was given to participants. However, we are most concerned with a self-selection problem. Participants who believed the acupuncture treatments would relieve pain are those who self-selected to participate in the experiment. In other words, those participants with osteoarthritis who agreed to participate could somehow be different from those participants with osteoarthritis who did not participate. Specifically, those individuals who did not think acupuncture treatments would work did not participate in the experiment. To support our hypothesis that selection could be a threat to internal validity, the article even stated that about 11% of participants had already received acupuncture in the year before the experiment, potentially demonstrating that participants open to the idea in the first place participated in the study.

- *Attrition* occurs when participants systematically drop out of an experiment and therefore change the results of the experiment. Attrition could have been a threat to internal validity in the current experiment. For example, what if some participants did not believe that the acupuncture treatments were working for them? They may have decided to drop out of the experiment before it ended. This would leave a greater number of participants remaining in the experiment who believed the acupuncture treatments were decreasing their pain. Thus, at the conclusion of the experiment, the acupuncture treatments could look more effective in relieving osteoarthritis pain because those participants the acupuncture treatments did not work for had dropped out of the experiment.

- Sometimes just thinking a change will occur is enough to produce a change. This is known as a *placebo effect*. Remember, participants in this study were experiencing enough pain that they were actively searching for relief. It may be such that the participants wanted so strongly for this new treatment to alleviate their pain that they experienced pain relief. Therefore, it may not be the effectiveness of the independent variable (acupuncture treatment), but the expectation the participant held for the effectiveness of the independent variable, that led to a decrease in pain.

- *Demand characteristics* are various hints and cues that participants use to tell them how the researcher wants them to behave, or at least how they think the researcher wants them to behave. It is possible that during the acupuncture treatments the doctors interacting with the participants could have given various cues that caused the participants to believe the treatments would help. This seems only logical. The doctors participating in this study certainly believed in the effectiveness of acupuncture to relieve pain associated with osteoarthritis. If they did not, they would not be willing to administer this treatment. Therefore, it is only natural to believe that their positive attitudes toward acupuncture treatments might be conveyed to the participants in the experiment. And, it is this positive attitude that the participants could have used to determine the manner in which they should behave (i.e., experiencing the relief of pain).

How did you do? Did you find the same threats to internal validity that we did? Did you find other threats to internal validity that we did not? If so, bring them up to a friend or your professor and discuss them.

Chapter Summary

- Control is at the heart of all research. Researchers need to make sure that there are not unaccounted-for variables in a study that could influence or bias results (pp. 154–158).
- Two common types of variables that can lead to biased results are extraneous and nuisance variables (pp. 154–155):
    - *Extraneous variables* are variables not controlled for in the experiment that vary with the independent variables (p. 154).
    - *Nuisance variables* are variables that are not controlled for in the experiment that influences all participants in the same manner (p. 154).
- When conducting a study, a researcher needs to consider threats to internal validity. *Internal validity* is ensuring that the observed change in behavior/mental process is due to the variable(s) that is/are being manipulated. However, there are factors that can threaten internal validity in a study (pp. 159–165).
    - For each, the observed change might not be due to the independent variable but rather due to an unaccounted-for aspect (p. 159).
        - *History*—change due to outside events during the study (p. 159).
        - *Maturation*—change due to internal changes in the participant (pp. 160–161).
        - *Regression to the mean*—change due to the extreme scores moving toward the mean on later measures (pp. 161–162).
        - *Selection*—change due to how the participants were selected for the experiment or how they were assigned to groups (p. 162).
        - *Attrition*—change due to of participants dropping out of a study systematically (pp. 162–163).
        - *Testing*—change due to the participant becoming more familiar with the test or testing procedures (p. 163).
        - *Diffusion of treatment*—change due to participants in different groups communicating with each other (p. 164).
        - *Instrumentation*—change due to how the dependent variable was measured (p. 164).
        - *Placebo* effect—change due to participants thinking/believing a change will occur (p. 165).
        - *Demand* characteristics—change due to participants believing they should act or behave in a certain way during an experiment or if a researcher somehow communicates to participants how they should act or behave (p. 165).
- It is better to use a *double blind study* as opposed to a *single blind study*. A double blind offers the benefit of neither the researcher nor the participant knowing which group the participant has been placed into (p. 165).
- A *placebo* is an inert substance that has no effect (p. 165).

APA Learning Goals Linkage

• **Goal 2.** *Research Methods in Psychology*

Students will understand and apply basic research methods in psychology, including research design, data analysis, and interpretation.

Sections Covered: Are You Equipped?, Control, Threats to Internal Validity, Minimizing Threats, Are You Equipped Now?

Explanation of the Goal: This chapter adds to our knowledge of research methods in numerous ways. To begin, information was provided on limitations to inferences that can be drawn from research designs. The first example of this was provided at the beginning of the chapter when we observed how nuisance and extraneous variables can influence outcomes. The second example was later in the chapter when we scrutinized how single versus double blind studies can lead to different outcomes in a study, thereby changing the inferences that are drawn. We also addressed how to select and apply appropriate methods to maximize internal validity. In order to do so, we outlined threats to internal validity that should be avoided or minimized. These measures are taken in research design so that alternative explanations for the findings can be reduced. Finally, through our discussion of threats to internal validity such as selection of participants, demand characteristics, and placebo effect, we recognized how personal biases may shape the research process.

• **Goal 3.** *Critical Thinking Skills in Psychology*

Students will respect and use critical and creative thinking, skeptical inquiry, and, when possible, the scientific approach to solve problems related to behavior and mental processes.

Sections Covered: Are You Equipped?, Control, Threats to Internal Validity, Are You Equipped Now?

Explanation of the Goal: Critical thinking involves weighing support for conclusions and using the scientific method to solve problems related to behavior and mental processes. The exercises in this chapter were designed to practice these skills of critical thinking. In particular, you were often asked to evaluate how conclusions from a study might be limited due to threats to internal validity. This uses the critical thinking skill of weighing support for conclusions. You also practiced controlling for threats to internal validity to answer questions on important topics like the relationship between TV viewing and rates of autism. This exemplifies the critical thinking skill of using the scientific method to solve problems related to behavior and mental processes.

• **Goal 4.** *Application of Psychology*

Students will understand and apply psychological principles to personal, social, and organizational issues.

(Continued)

Sections Covered: Are You Equipped?, Control, Threats to Internal Validity, Are You Equipped Now?

Explanation of the Goal: When psychological principles are applied to key societal issues, the inferences drawn become crucial. As social scientists, we must be very cautious when drawing conclusions on topics (e.g., autism, health-care options) that influence the public. This chapter also illustrated how relaxing activities like watching *American Idol* and using social networking sites are not exempt from relating to psychological concepts.

- **Goal 8. *Sociocultural and International Awareness***
  Students will recognize, understand, and respect the complexity of sociocultural and international diversity.

  Sections Covered: Threats to Internal Validity, Are You Equipped Now?

  Explanation of the Goal: Individual differences can influence behavior and mental processes and thus the outcome of a study. Through our coverage of threats to internal validity, we saw how changes within an individual over time, maturation, can influence psychological findings. Awareness of this topic allows threats to be minimized and consequently the number of alternative explanations reduced.

Types of Designs

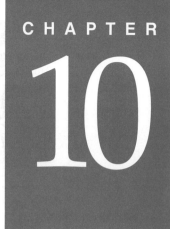
Between Subjects Designs

CHAPTER OUTLINE

Are You Equipped?

A report available on HealthOrbit (*http://healthorbit.ca/abtus.asp*) summarized findings conducted by researchers at Brigham and Women's Hospital on the relationship between deep sleep and learning a specific visual task. In this study, the researchers trained participants on a visual task. This task required participants to look at a computer screen and report the orientation of dashes, which were embedded in horizontal dashes. The researchers wanted to know if deep sleep would improve participants' performance on this new task.

In this example, the independent variable would be deep sleep. It would have two levels: deep sleep and no deep sleep. The dependent variable would be accuracy on the new visual task. If you were the researcher and had 50 participants who had volunteered for your study, how would you go about deciding how the participants would be exposed to the two levels of the independent variable?

There is more than one correct answer to this question. However, in this chapter we are going to focus on one way to expose participants to the levels of the independent variable. Specifically, we will discuss between subjects designs. It just so happens that the researchers at Brigham and Women's Hospital used a between subjects design. This means that one group of participants was allowed to experience deep sleep, while the other group of participants was deprived of deep sleep. Next, participants in both groups completed the visual task. Results indicated that performance did improve on the visual task for participants in the group that experienced deep sleep.

What makes this a between subjects design? This is a between subjects design because the participants only received one of the levels of the independent variable. The participants served either in the deep sleep condition or no deep sleep condition. But, the participants never served in both conditions. In this chapter, we will talk more about between subjects designs and discuss advantages and disadvantages of its use in research.

As you go through this chapter, we also want you to keep in mind how the material relates to the American Psychological Association's goals for psychology majors. Specifically, this chapter will address the following goals:

- **Goal 1. Knowledge Base of Psychology**
  Students will demonstrate familiarity with the major concepts, theoretical perspectives, empirical findings, and historical trends in psychology.
- **Goal 2. Research Methods in Psychology**
  Students will understand and apply basic research methods in psychology, including research design, data analysis, and interpretation.
- **Goal 3. Critical Thinking Skills in Psychology**
  Students will respect and use critical and creative thinking, skeptical inquiry, and, when possible, the scientific approach to solve problems related to behavior and mental processes.
- **Goal 4. Application of Psychology**
  Students will understand and apply psychological principles to personal, social, and organizational issues.

We will relook at these goals again at the end of the chapter.

INTRODUCTION TO BETWEEN SUBJECTS DESIGNS

In this chapter, we are going to begin by building on a concept that we introduced to you in Chapter 7. Specifically, we are talking about levels of an independent variable. We introduced this topic to you with the example of birth weights and adolescent rates of depression. The two levels of the subject variable birth weight were low birth weight and normal birth weight. Next, we discussed the example of caffeine influencing levels of alertness. In that example, we had three levels of the independent variable: no caffeine, 8 ounces of a caffeinated beverage, and 24 ounces of a caffeinated beverage. In other words, the levels of the independent variable are the specific conditions of that variable. When you have levels of an independent variable, a decision must be made as to how participants will be exposed to those levels. There are different ways this can be done. This chapter will focus on one way.

BETWEEN SUBJECTS DESIGN

Participants will be exposed to only one level of the independent variable.

The first way that participants can be exposed to the levels of the independent variable is through a between subjects design. This can also be referred to as a between participants design or an independent groups design. In a **between subjects design,** your research participants will be exposed to only one level of the independent variable. Thus, your participants will only serve in one group and would never be exposed to more than one condition of your independent variable.

Examples from Chapter 7

In the quasi-experimental birth weight study described in Chapter 7, the birth weight was the subject variable. (Although we will discuss it as an independent variable, it is important to remember that the researchers did not actually manipulate the birth weights.) Participants born were of either low birth weight or normal birth weight. Low birth weight was defined as babies weighing less than 5.5 pounds and normal birth weight was defined as babies weighing 5.5 pounds or more. For this study, babies could only be placed into one of two groups. Furthermore, babies could not be in both groups at the same time. This would make the subject variable of birth weight a between subjects variable.

In Chapter 7, we also used a between subjects design to see if caffeine influenced levels of alertness. We had three groups of participants: participants who received 8 ounces of a caffeinated beverage, participants who received 24 ounces of a caffeinated beverage, and participants who received no caffeine. In this example, a total of 30 participants were exposed to only one of the three levels. There was never a participant who was exposed to more than just one condition.

Take a look at Table 10.1. This is known as a **research matrix**. It is a visual representation of a research design.

RESEARCH MATRIX

A visual representation of a research design.

TABLE 10.1   Research Matrix.

No Caffeine	8 Ounces	24 Ounces
10 participants	10 participants	10 participants

Another example from Chapter 7 was also a between subjects design. Remember John's research on monitor size and reaction time? He had three groups of participants too. Each group was exposed to a different monitor size and the reaction times were measured. Here is what this research design would look like visually (Table 10.2).

TABLE 10.2   Research Matrix for Monitor Size.

17 inch	19 inch	21 inch
25 participants	25 participants	25 participants

YOU TRY IT!

We know we have only just started this chapter but we want to see how you are doing. Here are some questions for you to try regarding John's study on monitor size. Pretend you are a researcher working with John on the study.

(Continued)

(Continued)

Questions

1. You want to give every participant in the study a piece of paper with the contact information of the researchers. How many pieces of paper will you need or how many total participants do you have?

2. Your friend Joe wants to know about your study because he is thinking of participating. Tell Joe how many groups it is possible for him to participate in as per the design.

Answers

1. If you wanted to give each participant a piece of paper with the researchers' contact information, you would need 75 pieces of paper. This is because 25+25+25=75. In other words, there are three groups with 25 participants in each group yielding a total of 75 participants.

2. You would tell Joe that it would be possible for him to be assigned to one of the three groups. Joe would be allowed to use either the 17-inch, 19-inch, or 21-inch monitor. However, he would not get to use more than one of the monitor sizes due to the type of research design being used.

A Classic Research Example

Now that we have looked at some examples from Chapter 7, we want to take a look at a classic research experiment within the field of psychology that also decided to use a between subjects design for one of the independent variables. This study was conducted in 1973 by researchers Darley and Batson. The study was on situational and dispositional variables in helping behavior. As you might be able to gather from the title, the researchers got their research idea from the Bible, in particular the Good Samaritan parable. The researchers set out to design a study to examine the influence of situational and personality variables on helping behavior. The variable that we want to mention in this chapter is the independent variable of degree of hurry.

The participants used in this experiment were Princeton Theological Seminary students. The participants began the experiment in one building and were then asked to go to another building for the second part of the study. The participants then passed a "victim" placed by the researchers between the two buildings. The victim was slumped in a doorway and coughed twice and groaned as the participants passed. The independent variable was the degree to which the participants were instructed to hurry to the other building (i.e., high-hurry, intermediate-hurry, and low-hurry) and the dependent variable was the amount of help offered to the victim.

This is in fact how Darley and Batson exposed participants to the independent variable. Participants in the first group were told they were running late and the research assistant in the next building would be waiting for them (high-hurry). Participants in the second group (the intermediate group) were told the research assistant was ready for them and they could go to the next building. Finally, the last group of participants in the low-hurry condition

YOU TRY IT!

Question

Based on what you have learned to this point, can you determine how the independent variable of hurry was used as a between subjects variable?

Answer

The independent variable was a between subjects variable because participants were exposed to only one of the three levels. This means that a given student could have served in the high-hurry, intermediate-hurry, or low-hurry condition. However, students would not have served in more than one condition.

was told it would be a few minutes before the research assistant would be ready for them in the next building, but to go ahead and head over. In case you are wondering the results, the researchers found that participants who were in the high-hurry condition were the least likely to offer help to the victim.

Contemporary Research Examples

Although Darley and Batson's design was used in the 1970s, it does not mean that this type of design is outdated. In fact, researchers continue to use between subjects designs to investigate current topics of interest. Take for example a research study by Barlett, Harris, Smith, and Bonds-Raacke. This study was published in 2005 with the purpose of determining whether action figures contribute to negative body image in young adult men who handled them. Barlett was interested in this idea because previous research had examined the relationship between girls' body image and playing with Barbie dolls that have unrealistic figures. For Barlett's study, the independent variable was muscularity of action figures handled and the dependent variable was body image. The study had three groups of male participants.

Group 1

This group served as the control group. The group did not handle any action figure. The group only received measures of body image to complete.

Group 2

This group was one of the experimental groups. This group manipulated highly muscular action figures. After handling the highly muscular action figures, the participants completed the body images measures.

Group 3

This group was the second experimental group. This group manipulated moderately muscular action figures. After handling the moderately muscular action figures, the participants completed the body image measure.

Below you will find a visual representation of the research design (Table 10.3).

TABLE 10.3 Research Matrix for Bartlett and Colleagues (2005).		
Control	**Experimental 1**	**Experimental 2**
No action figures	Highly muscular figures	Moderately muscular figures
32 participants	22 participants	28 participants

As you can see from the visual representation, there were a total of 82 participants. Each participant only received one level of the independent variable and thus would have only been assigned to one of the three groups. Results did find that participants in the experimental group that handled the highly muscular action figures had a decrease in body esteem after handling the action figures.

Barlett has continued to investigate the influence of media on users. In a more recent study, Barlett, Harris, and Bruey (2008) examined the influence of the amount of blood in a violent video game on aggression, hostility, and arousal. The amount of blood was the independent variable and the dependent variables were aggression, hostility, and arousal.

Participants were randomly assigned to one of four groups. Each group of participants played a video game for 15 minutes (*Mortal Kombat: Deadly Alliance*). However, the blood level varied for each of the groups. For group number one, the blood level was set on maximum. For group number two, the blood level was set on medium. For group numbers three and four, the blood levels were set to low and no, respectively. After playing the violent video game, participants completed measures of aggression, hostility, and arousal.

This too was a between subjects design. Participants served in one of the four groups. In other words, participants would have been exposed to high, medium, low, or the no blood condition.

TABLE 10.4 Research Matrix for Barlett and Colleagues (2008).			
Group 1	**Group 2**	**Group 3**	**Group 4**
Maximum blood	Medium blood	Low blood	No blood

Results indicated that there were differences in hostility and physiological arousal based on the amount of blood level the participant was exposed to in the video games. Specifically, participants in the maximum and medium blood levels had a significant increase in both hostility and physiological arousal. However, participants in the low blood and no blood levels did not have a significant change in these dependent variables.

There are advantages as well as some drawbacks to the between subjects design. Before we discuss them, we want to tell you about one more contemporary research study that utilized a between subjects variable. This study was developed on the observation that men and women often disagree about the meaning of women's nonverbal cues. Farris, Treat, Viken, and McFall (2008) wanted to see if this was in fact the case. Men and women participants were asked to view photo images of women for varying amounts of time. After viewing the images, the participants were asked to place the photos into one of four categories: friendly, sexually interested, sad, or rejected. The researchers then compared the accuracy of responses for men and women. Results indicated that men were more likely than women to misidentify friendly targets as indicating sexual interests and to misidentify sexually interested targets as indicating friendliness.

This was a between subjects design. The researchers were interested in if men and women were equal in their ability to judge women's nonverbal cues. The between subjects variable was participants' sex. This is a between subjects design because the participants were either men or women. The participants could not be both and therefore were in either one of the two levels of the variable of sex.

We used this example to bring up the variable of sex (or gender) of the participants. Sex is an example of a subject variable which is always a between subjects variable. Anytime researchers are interested in comparing responses of men to women, you have a between subjects variable. There are other variables that by nature are between subjects variables. In Chapter 8, we mentioned a study that examined the relationship between where one lives (urban or rural location) and when a specific form of cancer is diagnosed. For this research, the independent variable was where one lives and it had two levels, urban or rural. Participants either lived in an urban or rural setting. However, the participants could not live in both. Hence, this would be another example of a variable that is between subjects. Can you think of any others? If so, mention them to your professor and see if you are correct.

Section Summary

- A *between subjects design* occurs when participants in a study are exposed to only one level of the independent variable (pp. 176–181).
- A *research matrix* is a visual representation (in table form) of your research design (pp. 177–178).

FACTORS TO CONSIDER

When using a between subjects design, you will need to consider factors such as the advantages and disadvantages of this approach. In order to accomplish this, we are going to do several things. First, we will discuss the advantages and disadvantages of this type of design listed in Figure 10.1. Next, we will examine these within the context of two research experiments that we already discussed in this chapter. Finally, we will let you practice with an example. Take a look at Figure 10.1. Keep in mind that just because there are more reasons listed as advantages than as disadvantages, this does not make this design the best one for all research experiments. You will see in later chapters that other research designs have numerous benefits as well.

Advantages to the between subjects design include the fact that you do not have to worry about **attrition** (e.g., participants not retuning for a second part of the experiment and dropping out); little fatigue; the opportunity to collect multiple dependent measures because of available time; and no **carry over**, **order**, or

ATTRITION

Participants dropping out of a study or not returning to complete additional parts to a study.

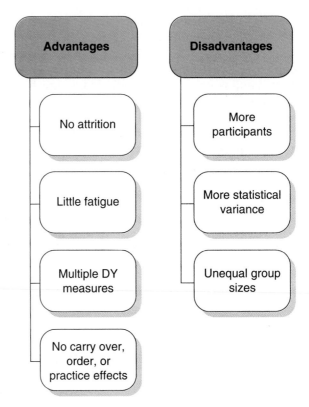

FIGURE 10.1 **Advantages and Disadvantages of a Between Subjects Design.**

STATISTICAL VARIANCE

The degree of spread among data when surrounding the mean.

practice effects. The downsides to this design include the fact that you will need more participants, you will have more **statistical variance** (making it more difficult to see differences between groups), and your groups could be unequal in size.

We want to explain how these pros and cons could have influenced researchers' decisions to select a between subjects design in experiments that we discussed previously. The first experiment we will look at again is the one by Barlett et al. (2005), examining the influence of action figures on body image of males. Recall that this experiment had three groups of participants. The first group served as a control group by participants not handling any action figures and completing measures on body image. The second group was the first experimental group, handling highly muscular action figures before completing the body image measures. The final group was the second experiment group that handled moderately muscular action figures before completing the scales. The design for this study had many benefits. First, the researchers did not have to require participants to come back to the experiment a second time (possibly on another day) to complete another level of the independent variable. Because the participants completed their one level of the independent variable within the one-hour time frame, the researchers did not have to consider the issue of attrition. Second, the researchers did not have to worry about the participants becoming tired and fatigued, thus influencing participants' performance. Participants in the two experimental conditions were required to handle the action figures for a maximum time period of 45 minutes. This amount of time would not result in participants being severely tired. Third, because the participants were only in one of the three conditions, there was additional time to collect more than one dependent variable. In fact, the researchers had participants complete three scales to measure body image. This included self-esteem, body esteem, and body satisfaction. Finally, the researchers were not concerned about carryover, order, or practice effects.

A **carryover effect** is when the effect of a treatment condition is literally carried over into a second treatment condition. For example, if participants completed the first experimental condition of handling highly muscular action figures first and the second experimental condition of handling moderately muscular action second, you would wonder about the possibility of a carryover effect. This is because after handling the highly muscular action figures, the male participant's body image would decrease. As the male participant started the second condition and handled the moderately muscular action figures, his body image would still be decreased due to the first condition. In this situation, we would be unable to determine if the decrease in body image in the second condition was actually due to the moderately muscular action figures or the highly muscular action figures. This is because it is difficult to undo what a participant has already seen. An **order effect** could have occurred if participants completed all three levels of the independent variable and always completed them in the same order. You would not be able to determine if the condition caused the influence on the dependent variable or the order of the presentation. For example, scores on body image may always decrease on the third condition presented. This may be due to the fact that participants are ready to complete the experiment and go home. Therefore, it would be difficult to determine if the third condition alone decreased scores or if it was just the fact that it was the third (and last) condition. Finally, the researchers did not have to consider in their design the fact that the participants could improve their performance on subsequent trials and so **practice effects** were nonissue.

Even with these numerous benefits, the researchers did have a few cons to consider when they selected their approach. First, by using a between subjects design, the researchers needed more participants. Instead of 25 participants being exposed to all three levels of the independent variable, the researchers needed at least 75 participants to have a minimum of 25 participants in each of the three levels. Second, because different participants served in each of the three conditions, there needed to be a greater difference in the treatment effect for the results to be significant. Had it been the same participants in each of the three levels, the within group differences would have been reduced and the difference between the levels would not need to be as great. Finally, the researchers had to be careful when gathering data to ensure that the groups were relatively close in numbers.

There were similar advantages and disadvantages to using a between subjects design when used in the later research conducted by Barlett and colleagues, examining the effect of the amount of blood in a violent video game on aggression, hostility, and arousal. Participants were randomly assigned to one of four groups. Each group of participants played a video game for 15 minutes. However, the amount of blood varied for each of the groups. For group number one, the blood level was set on maximum. For group number two, the blood

CARRYOVER EFFECTS

These occur when the effects of a prior treatment condition influence a subsequent treatment condition.

ORDER EFFECTS

Effects of a study are due to the participants experiencing the same order of presentation of the levels of the independent variable.

PRACTICE EFFECTS

Participants improve performance due to subsequent experiences on the same task.

level was set on medium. For group numbers three and four, the blood levels were set to low and no, respectively. After playing the violent video game, participants completed measures of aggression, hostility, and arousal.

Benefits of this design include the fact that, first, participants did not have to return for a second (or third) part of the study and therefore did not have the opportunity to drop out. Second, participants only played the video game for 15 minutes (rather than 60 minutes if they had been in all four levels of the independent variable). Since this time span was brief, the researchers did not have to consider fatigue as a variable influencing aggression, hostility, and arousal. Also, since the participants only served in one level of independent variable requiring 15 minutes, the participants had time to complete three dependent measures. Third, participants' exposure to one treatment condition did not influence their response to another treatment condition. In other words, no influence was carried over to another condition. Similarly, the order of presentation did not influence responses and participants did not improve over time as they completed four conditions. The disadvantages, however, included the need for more participants to have a minimum number in each of the four conditions, more statistical variance, and the possibility of unequal group sizes.

YOU TRY IT!

Think back to the research experiment by Darley and Batson on level of hurry and helping behavior. This research experiment had three groups of participants. Participants in the first group (the high-hurry group) were told they were running late and the research assistant in the next building would be waiting for them. Participants in the second group (the intermediate group) were told the research assistant was ready for them and they could go to the next building. Finally, the last group of participants in the low-hurry condition was told it would be a few minutes before the research assistant would be ready for them in the next building, but to go ahead and head over.

Question

Can you describe one advantage of this between subjects design for Darley and Batson and one disadvantage?

Answer

There is not just one correct answer to the question above. In fact, you could have selected any of the reasons listed in the table that we previously discussed. However, probably the most obvious disadvantage is that Darley and Batson had to recruit more participants for the between subjects design that they utilized than if the participants had served in all of the three conditions. Yet, this disadvantage is outweighed by numerous advantages. Preventing a carryover effect was a huge advantage for this being a between subjects variable. This prevented the helping behavior from being influenced by the previous treatment condition. It takes time in becoming comfortable with thinking critically about the advantages and disadvantages of research designs. After you complete Chapter 11 (which is also on types of research designs), this type of thinking about pros and cons to research designs will get easier with practice.

Section Summary

- Between subjects designs have several advantages which make it an appealing design to use. Advantages include: no attrition; very little participant fatigue; the collection of multiple dependent variables; and no order, carryover, or practice effects (pp. 181–184).
    - When participants drop out of studies or fail to complete all parts of a study, it is known as *attrition* (p. 181).
    - A *carryover effect* occurs when a prior treatment condition from an experiment influences current or future treatment conditions (p. 183).
    - If all participants experience the same order of treatment conditions in an experiment, then any obtained results may be due to the order and not the conditions themselves. This is known as an *order effect* (p. 183).
    - An improvement in performance by a participant on subsequent stimuli independent of the variable being manipulated is known as a *practice effect* (p. 183).
- Even though between subjects designs have several advantages, there are disadvantages to using this methodology. Disadvantages include the use of a large number of participants and higher statistical variance between conditions (pp. 183–184).
    - *Statistical variance* is the degree of spread among scores from the mean of the group of scores. This can make it more difficult to determine if group differences exist (p. 182).

WAYS TO MINIMIZE DISADVANTAGES

It is possible to minimize the disadvantages of the between subjects design that we previously described. If you know that you are going to use a between subjects design, you could reduce the number of levels of the independent variable (if possible). This way you might only need three groups instead of four groups. Reducing the number of groups that you need will in turn reduce the number of participants that you need. You can also reduce statistical variance by randomly assigning participants to the groups and using sound methodology. Finally, it is a fairly simple task to keep track of the number of participants in each group as you collect data. The number of participants in each group does not have to be exactly the same. However, it should be fairly close.

We would like to mention one final note before wrapping up this chapter. You may be wondering how to decide when to use a between subjects design. This will depend on the specific variables you are interested in and how easily the disadvantages could be overcome for your particular study. It could be the case that you need to employ a different research design. We will talk about within subjects designs and factorial designs in the next two chapters, respectively.

Are You Equipped Now?

Dr. Rosebud Roberts with the Mayo Clinic in Rochester, Minnesota, conducted the following study, which was summarized on HealthOrbit.com. Roberts collected data on 2,050 individuals between the ages of 70 and 89. Data were collected through interviews, examinations, and cognitive tests. Results indicated that 15% of the sample exhibited mild cognitive impairment. Dr. Roberts also found that men were one and a half times more likely than women to exhibit cognitive impairment.

In this design, the subject variable was sex of participants and the dependent variables were performance on interviews, examinations, and cognitive tests used to assess cognitive impairment.

Question

Why did Dr. Roberts use a between subjects design in this experiment?

Answer

We hope this was a relatively easy Are You Equipped Now section. Dr. Roberts used a between subjects design because the participants were either men or women. The participants could not be both and therefore were only exposed to one level of the independent variable.

Chapter Summary

- A *between subjects design* occurs when participants in a study are exposed to only one level of the independent variable. Therefore, participants only participate in one group of the study (pp. 176–181).
- A *research matrix* is a visual representation (in table form) of your research design. Typically, a research matrix allows a participant to "see" the type of treatment each group will receive in a research study (pp. 177–178).
- Between subject designs have several *advantages* which make it an appealing design to use. Advantages include: no attrition; very little participant fatigue; the collection of multiple dependent variables; and no order, carryover, or practice effects (pp. 181–184).
  - When participants drop out of studies or fail to complete all parts of a study, it is known as *attrition* (p. 181).
  - Since participants in this methodology are exposed to only one level of the independent variable, they are less likely to be fatigued in completing the experiment (pp. 182–183).
  - A between subjects design allows multiple dependent variables to be collected in a study due to the participants only being in one treatment condition (p. 183).
  - A *carryover effect* occurs when a prior treatment condition from an experiment influences current or future treatment conditions (p. 183).
  - If all participants experience the same order of treatment conditions in an experiment, then any obtained results may be due to the order and not the conditions themselves. This is known as an *order effect* (p. 183).

♦ An improvement in performance by a participant on subsequent stimuli independent of the variable being manipulated is known as a *practice
effect* (p. 183).

♦ Even though between subjects designs have several advantages, there are
disadvantages to using this methodology. Disadvantages include the use
of a large number of participants and higher statistical variance between
conditions (pp. 183–184).

♦ In order to obtain sufficient sample sizes for the levels of the independent variable, more participants are used. Specifically, a relatively
equal number of participants has to be utilized for each treatment
condition, which increases the number of participants as compared
with designs where each participant goes through all treatment
conditions (p. 183).

♦ *Statistical variance* is the degree of spread among scores from the mean
of the group of scores. This can make it more difficult to determine if
group differences exist (p. 182).

APA Learning Goals Linkage

• **Goal 2.** *Research Methods in Psychology*
Students will understand and apply basic research methods in psychology,
including research design, data analysis, and interpretation.

Sections Covered: Introduction to Between Subject Designs, Factors to
Consider, Ways to Minimize Disadvantages

Explanation of the Goal: As a psychology major, you will be expected to
explain different research methods commonly used within the field.
The between subjects design discussed in this chapter is a popular
methodology. In articulating the strengths and limitations of the
between subjects design, we also introduced major research concepts
such as attrition; fatigue; and carryover, order, and practice effects. By
knowing the advantages and disadvantages of this design, you will be
able to select and apply appropriate methodologies to answer your
research questions.

• **Goal 3.** *Critical Thinking Skills in Psychology*
Students will respect and use critical and creative thinking, skeptical
inquiry, and, when possible, the scientific approach to solve problems
related to behavior and mental processes.

Sections Covered: Are You Equipped?, You Try It!, Are You Equipped
Now?

Explanation of the Goal: After explaining the concepts in this chapter, we
have tested your knowledge and comfort level with the material. In particular, we have asked you to evaluate problems and generate a solution

(Continued)

for that problem. To generate solutions, you need to have an open but critical mind and link the problem to the specific material learned. This allowed you to select the best solution to the problem. It is through the use of critical thinking skills that we can investigate areas of interest such as differences between men and women in: (a) cognitive impairments with age and (b) ability to judge women's nonverbal cues.

• **Goal 4.** *Application of Psychology*
Students will understand and apply psychological principles to personal, social, and organizational issues.

Sections Covered: Are You Equipped?, A Classic Research Example, Contemporary Research Examples, Are You Equipped Now?

Explanation of the Goal: In each of the aforementioned sections, we have presented research examples by which we have illustrated the use of between subjects designs. These examples have been chosen to help you apply the psychological principles in this chapter to either personal, social, or organizational issues. For example, in the section "Contemporary Research Examples," we discussed how between subjects designs have been used to study the relationship between violent video games and aggression. Given the prevalence of these games in our society, it has become important to apply our knowledge in research design to this social issue. Without the application of psychological principals to this issue, we are left with an inability to determine the scientific impact that violent video games may have on aggression.

CHAPTER

11

Within Subjects Designs

CHAPTER OUTLINE

Are You Equipped?

Back in the late 1980s and early 1990s, the soda wars were in full force. In particular, the Pepsi Cola Co. and the Coca Cola Co. were competing for the crown of top soda producers. Although both companies had several variations of sodas, the two main rivals for this crown were each company's number one brand, Pepsi and Coke, respectively. To determine the overall champion, the Pepsi Cola Co. went around the country with a contest known as "The Pepsi Challenge." During the challenge, participants would have the opportunity to taste a sample of cola from each contender, Pepsi and Coke. Once the participant had tasted each of the contenders, he or she would then make a judgment about which one tasted better. Typically, these taste tests occurred at events with large crowds surrounding a Pepsi Co. booth. Not too surprisingly, the results of the Pepsi Co.challenge indicated that a vast majority of people preferred the taste of Pepsi over Coke. In fact, this led the Pepsi Co. to make several commercials in which they showed people choosing Pepsi over Coke followed by crowds cheering. However, the interesting aspect of this story is that whether the Pepsi Cola Co. intended it or not, they were utilizing a popular research methodology.

For this methodology, there was one independent variable (i.e., type of cola). The independent variable had two levels, Coke and Pepsi. The dependent variable for this methodology was the judgment of which cola tasted better. Now think about how the participants were exposed to the two levels of the independent variable. Was this procedure a between subjects design as described in the previous chapter or something a little different?

This methodology is different from the between subjects design we discussed in Chapter 10. Probably the most obvious difference is that the participants were exposed to all levels of the independent variable and not just one level. This is known as a within subjects design and will be the focus of this chapter.

As you go through this chapter, we also want you to keep in mind how the material relates to the American Psychological Association's goals for psychology majors. Specifically, this chapter will address the following goals:

- **Goal 1. Knowledge Base of Psychology**
  Students will demonstrate familiarity with the major concepts, theoretical perspectives, empirical findings, and historical trends in psychology.
- **Goal 2. Research Methods in Psychology**
  Students will understand and apply basic research methods in psychology, including research design, data analysis, and interpretation.
- **Goal 3. Critical Thinking Skills in Psychology**
  Students will respect and use critical and creative thinking, skeptical inquiry, and, when possible, the scientific approach to solve problems related to behavior and mental processes.
- **Goal 4. Application of Psychology**
  Students will understand and apply psychological principles to personal, social, and organizational issues.

INTRODUCTION TO WITHIN SUBJECTS DESIGNS

WITHIN SUBJECTS DESIGNS

Design in which participants are exposed to all levels of the independent variable.

This chapter will build on information regarding the levels of an independent variable that we discussed in Chapters 7 and 10. Specifically, we will be discussing the use of a **within subjects design.** A within subjects design is a methodology in which each participant is exposed to all levels of the independent variable. This is very different from the previous chapter on the between subjects design in which participants were exposed to only one level of the independent variable. Within subjects designs are also referred to as repeated measures designs (or within participant designs). This is because the participants literally repeat the dependent measures under all the conditions of the independent variable.

Examples from Chapter 7

As we did in the last chapter, let's go back and look at an earlier example to help explain this topic. Think about the study John conducted on monitor size. In that study, John wanted to determine if monitor size (independent variable) had an effect on performance (dependent variable) within a microworld simulation. For that example, there were three groups of participants and three different monitor sizes, 17 inch, 19 inch, and 21 inch. This study used a between subjects design, where each participant was exposed to only one of the three levels of the independent variable (monitor size). This is represented visually in Figure 11.1.

Design	17 inch	19 inch	21 inch
Between Subjects	25 participants	25 participants	25 participants

FIGURE 11.1
Research Matrix for Between Subjects Design.

In reality, John and his colleagues carried out a different methodology. The methodology consisted of a within subjects design and not a between subjects design. Rather than having three separate groups each experience working on a different size monitor, this study had one group of individuals experience working on all three monitor sizes. Thus, the size of the monitor was a within subjects variable. The research matrix resembled what is in Figure 11.2.

Design	17 inch	19 inch	21 inch
Within Subjects	< -------------------- 25 Participants	-------------------- >	

FIGURE 11.2
Research Matrix for Within Subjects Design.

What you need to remember is that in a within subjects design each participant is exposed to all levels of the independent variable. Therefore, each person in this study was exposed to all three types of monitor size (i.e., 17, 19, and 21 inches). So, 25 total participants were needed. This is a smaller number than the 75 participants needed for when a between subjects design was utilized.

In addition to John's monitor study, we also discussed in a previous chapter a study on caffeine and alertness. We explained how each of the participants was given 0, 8, or 24 ounces of a caffeinated beverage. Again, this is an example of a between subjects design because each participant was exposed to only one level of the independent variable. However, this study could have been conducted as a within subjects design. In order to change this study to a within subjects design, what needs to be done?

If you said that each participant should be exposed to all levels of the independent variable, you were correct. In order to conduct this study as a within subjects design, each participant would have his or her alertness tested after receiving 0, 8, and 24 ounces of a caffeinated beverage. Therefore, there would be only one group of participants receiving all three levels of the independent variable (caffeine).

YOU TRY IT!

Pretend that you are a research assistant working on John's study about monitor size using a within subjects design. Before data collection begins, you will need to answer the questions below.

Questions

1. You want to give every participant in the study a piece of paper with the contact information of the researchers. This is in case the participants have questions after the study is complete. How many pieces of paper will you need? In other words, how many total participants do you have?

2. Your friend Sara wants to know about your study because she is thinking of participating. Tell Sara how many conditions she will be exposed to.

(Continued)

(Continued)

Answers

1. If you wanted to give each participant a piece of paper with the researcher's contact information, you would need only 25 pieces of paper. This is because you have only one group of 25 participants.

2. You would tell Sara that she would be exposed to a total of three conditions. Specifically, Sara would use the 17-, 19-, and 21-inch monitors because of the within subjects design.

A Classic Research Example

Classic research experiments within the field have utilized within subjects designs. For example, in Stroop's (1935) experiment, he wanted to know what would occur when a person was presented a color word (e.g., red) written in an incongruent ink color (e.g., green). In order to test the effects on an individual, Stroop developed three types of stimuli that can be seen below. The first type of stimuli consisted of color words printed in black ink. The second type of stimuli consisted of color words printed in an ink different from the color expressed by the word's semantic meaning. The final stimuli consisted of blocks in different colors. Stroop conducted two different experiments with these stimuli. The independent variable in each experiment was the type of stimuli to which the participants were exposed. The dependent variable was the amount of time it took for the participants to complete the task.

The first experiment involved a comparison between Stimuli 1 and Stimuli 2. Specifically, Stroop had two levels to the independent variable (task type). In this experiment, the time to complete the task was the dependent variable and was measured by how quickly the participants could correctly read the word in each stimuli.

In the second experiment, a comparison between Stimuli 2 and Stimuli 3 was made. Again, Stroop had two levels to the independent variable (task type). However, the dependent variable was measured by how quickly the participants could name the colors in each of the stimuli. If you are wondering what Stroop's results were, we are going to tell you in the next section.

Stimuli 1:

Red	Blue	Green	Yellow	Blue	Green	Red	Green	Yellow

Stimuli 2:

Red	Blue	Green	Yellow	Blue	Green	Red	Green	Yellow

Stimuli 3:

■■■■■■■	■■■■■■■	■■■■■■■	■■■■■■■	■■■■■■■	■■■■■■■	■■■■■■■	■■■■■■■	■■■■■■■

YOU TRY IT!

Question

We want you to think about how to conduct these two experiments discussed above using a within subjects design. Specifically, how would you conduct a within subjects experiment to make a comparison between the levels of the independent variable in the first experiment? And, how would you conduct a within subjects experiment to make a comparison between the levels of the independent variable in the second experiment? Also, do you have a hypothesis about the results Stroop obtained?

Answer

Here is what Stroop did. For the first experiment, Stroop had a group of participants read the words for Stimuli 1 (black ink) and Stimuli 2 (incongruent ink). Participants in this experiment would be exposed to both sets of stimuli (e.g., both levels of the independent variable). Interestingly, results showed no difference between these two types of stimuli in terms of reaction time. Participants did not show a difficulty in reading the color words when printed in black or in a color inconsistent with the semantic meaning of the word.

In the second experiment, Stroop had a group of participants indicate the color of the ink used for each word (Stimuli 2) and for each set of blocks (Stimuli 3). The participants were to say the color independent of the word that was written for Stimuli 2 and indicate the color of the set of blocks. Again, participants in this experiment would be exposed to both sets of stimuli (levels of the independent variable). Unlike the first experiment, results for the second experiment showed a large difference between Stimuli 2 and Stimuli 3 in terms of reaction time. Specifically, participants had a difficult time saying the color of the ink for Stimuli 2 as compared to saying the color of the ink for Stimuli 3 leading to longer reaction times. Stroop reasoned that the automatic response of reading was interfering with the identification of the printed word's ink color.

Stroop's study has seen many variations since its original publication almost 80 years ago. In fact, researchers have used some version of the Stroop Task in over 700 research experiments. The most common replication occurs with the second experiment. This experiment shows the usefulness of a within subjects research design. However, the within subjects research design is not only a tool of the past but is one that is quite useful to researchers today.

Contemporary Research Examples

Recently, researchers choose to conduct a within subjects research design to examine music preference while playing computer games (Tamir, Mitchell, & Gross, 2008). This study was a within subjects design with the independent variable of music condition. The within subjects variable had three levels: angry, exciting, and neutral. Tamir et al. wanted to see what impact the music had on the participants playing the computer games. Participants in the experiment were exposed to all three levels of the music condition while they were playing the same computer games. The research matrix for this study looked like the one in Figure 11.3 on the following page.

As you can see from the matrix, every participant played a computer game while listening to all three types of music: angry, exciting, and neutral. We will discuss this study in more detail and provide the results in Chapter 12. At that time, we will tell you more about the research design and the findings.

IV:	Angry Music	Exciting Music	Neutral Music
	< --- All Participants Experience Each Music Type --- >		

FIGURE 11.3   Research Matrix for Tamir et al. (2008).

YOU TRY IT!

We have explained several different studies to you in this chapter, each one using a within subjects design. In a recent study, researchers wanted to determine if the type of scenario given influenced a participant's adjustment from an anchor (Janiszewski & Uy, 2008). An anchor in psychology has very little to do with a boat and how to keep it from moving in a body of water. Rather, when speaking of anchor and adjustment, psychologists are usually referring to the work by Tversky and Kahneman (1974). This is a psychological heuristic in which people use a starting point (an anchor) as the basis to make judgments about a given scenario (adjustment).

In Janiszewski and Uy's (2008) experiment, they had 43 participants read 10 scenarios in which they wanted to determine the impact of the scenario type on the anchoring and adjustment of the participants. The researchers anchored the participants by supplying the retail price for a product. A scenario in this study read similar to the one below:

> Imagine that you have just earned your first paycheck as a highly paid executive. As a result, you want to reward yourself by buying a large-screen, high-definition plasma TV. As you browse through a store, you see a plasma TV from Sony that you like because of its attractive carbon-fiber finish. Its WEGA 50-inch screen has been rated by a panel of electronics experts as the "clearest and sharpest in the market today, because of a new technology that doubled its resolution and increased it contrast ratio to 4,000:1."
>
> If you were to guess the plasma TV's actual cost to the retailer (i.e., how much the store bought it for), what would it be? Because this is your first purchase of a plasma TV, you have very little information with which to base your estimate. All you know is that it should cost less than the retail price of $5,000. Guess the product's actual cost. This electronics store is known to offer a fair price. Most of their items are priced very close to their actual cost because they compete on volume. The only reason that this particular plasma TV is expensive is that it uses a new technology, and the picture quality is outstanding. So the actual cost would be only slightly less than $5,000.

Participants made ratings for 10 scenarios. Specifically, participants provided ratings of a plasma TV, as described above, and the following items: beach house, beverage, cheese, context-free, basketball, figurine, hummer, pen, and pet rock (see Figure 11.4) .

Question

Why was this a within subjects design? What were the participants exposed to that lead you to this conclusion?

Answer

Because the independent variable is scenario type, there were 10 levels of the independent variable. Typically, most independent variable do not reach double digits like this

(Continued)

study. A visual representation of this design is provided below. The 43 participants in this study received all levels of the independent variable. This means that each participant read and made judgments on all 10 scenarios that were available.

IV:	Scenarios									
	1	2	3	4	5	6	7	8	9	10
	< ---------------------- 43 Participants ---------------------- >									

FIGURE 11.4   Sample Research Matrix for Janiszewski and Uy (2008).

Section Summary

- A *within subjects design* occurs when participants in a study are exposed to all levels of the independent variable. This design is also known as a repeated measures design or within participants designs (pp. 190–195).

FACTORS TO CONSIDER

So far in this chapter, we have presented you with several classic and contemporary examples of within subjects designs. However, as with any research design there are advantages and disadvantages to the use of a within subjects designs. We will discuss the advantages and disadvantages to within research designs that are listed in Figure 11.5. After which, we will use examples from this chapter to illustrate how each advantage and disadvantage could influence a design. Let's begin by looking at Figure 11.5.

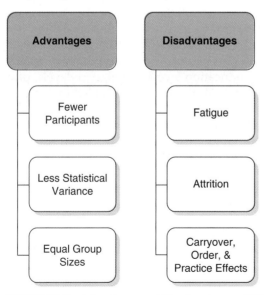

FIGURE 11.5   **Advantages and Disadvantages of Within Subjects Designs.**

There are two main advantages to using a within subjects design. The first advantage is the use of a small number of participants in your study. Unlike a between subjects design, where there are different groups of participants for each level of the independent variable, within subjects designs have only one group of participants. For example, look at Figures 11.6 and 11.7. Imagine you were conducting an experiment where you had an independent variable with four levels and you desired to have 30 people complete each level. If you were to conduct the experiment as a between subjects design, then you would have four groups (each representing a level of the independent variable) with 30 participants in each group. This would yield a total sample size of 120 participants. However, if you conducted this study as a within subjects design, then you would have one group with 30 participants, each experiencing all four levels of the independent variable.

Design	Level 1	Level 2	Level 3	Level 4	
Between Subjects	30	30	30	30	Total: 120

FIGURE 11.6   **Between Subjects Design.**

Design	Level 1	Level 2	Level 3	Level 4	
Within Subjects	< --- Same 30 participants for each level --- >				Total: 30

FIGURE 11.7   **Within Subjects Design.**

Thus, a within subjects design can greatly reduce the number of participants you need for a given study. This is important to consider when conducting research with special populations, where the recruitment of participants may be difficult.

STATISTICAL VARIANCE

The degree of spread among data surrounding the mean.

The second advantage to a within subjects design is that these designs have less statistical variance. **Statistical variance** occurs in part because of differences between participants. For example, participants arrive to experiments with varying education levels, intelligence levels, prior knowledge, and so on. However, in a within subjects design, these differences are reduced because the same participants are exposed to each level of the independent variable. This is extremely beneficial because a researcher can see how the change in the independent variable influenced a participant's score on the dependent variable. This is a distinct advantage over a between subjects design. A within subjects design reduces the variance (or differences between people), making it easier to see differences in the levels of the independent variable. Finally, a within subjects design has the advantage of each level of the independent variable having group sizes that are equal. The same participants partake in each condition, so you do not have to worry about conditions having unequal numbers.

FATIGUE

Occurs when participants become tired during an experiment.

However, there are some disadvantages to using a within subjects design. The first disadvantage is the development of **fatigue** in participants. Unlike a between subjects design, where participants are exposed to only one level of the independent variable, participants in a within subjects design are exposed to all levels of the independent variable. Therefore, by the end of the experiment, participants can become fatigued. The more levels (conditions) that a within subjects design has, the more likely it is that a participant can get tired of taking part in the study. This can easily influence scores on the dependent variables, because participants begin to lose focus. Oftentimes, this leads to another disadvantage, attrition.

Attrition occurs when participants withdraw from or drop out of a study before it has ended. Here is an example of attrition that you might have noticed. A researcher is looking to assess the impact of using a new teaching technology. On the first day of class, the researcher takes measurements about the new teaching technology using all 50 students in the class. The researcher then plans to take other measurements at the midpoint and at the end of the semester. However, as is the case in many college classes, the student population drops during the semester. Therefore, the researcher collects data on only 36 students at the midpoint and only 28 students at the end of the study. Rather than having 50 participants in his or her study, the researcher now only has full data for 28 students. This is a perfect example of how attrition can influence the results obtained. Specifically, we would not hear about the new technology from the students who dropped out of the class. Participants systematically dropping out of the experiment (or in this example the class) causes attrition to influence the interpretation of the results. The students dropping out of the class may be the ones who are struggling with the new teaching technology. This would leave primarily those students in the class who liked the new technology.

ATTRITION

Participants dropping out of a study or not returning to complete additional parts to a study.

The other major disadvantages are **carryover, order,** and **practice effects.** These effects were covered in Chapter 10. However, we have included a short review here. A carryover effect occurs when the effect of a treatment condition is literally carried over into a second treatment condition. An order effect occurs when a participant completes all levels of the independent variable and always completes them in the same order. This is a problem because a researcher would not be able to determine if the different levels of the independent variable caused the influence on the dependent variable or if it was the order of the presentation. Finally, a practice effect occurs when a participant improves his or her performance on subsequent trials of a study. Be sure to refer back to Chapter 10 if you would like specific examples of each.

CARRYOVER EFFECTS

These occur when the effects of prior treatment conditions influence subsequent treatment conditions.

ORDER EFFECTS

Effects of a study are due to the participants experiencing the same order of presentation of the levels of the independent variable.

PRACTICE EFFECTS

Participants improve performance due to subsequent experiences on the same task.

Ways to Minimize Disadvantages

Although within subjects designs come with disadvantages, there are ways to minimize and even negate these problems. The best way to fight fatigue is to not expose your participants to all levels of the independent variable in one sitting. Rather, it might be beneficial for researchers to have the participants complete part of a study in the first session and finish the second part at another time. This can also aid in reducing any practice effect that may occur between trials in an experiment. However, this suggestion should be balanced with the likelihood of increasing attrition.

	Combination 1	Combination 2	Combination 3	Combination 4
Subject 1	Condition A	Condition B	Condition C	Condition D
Subject 2	Condition B	Condition C	Condition D	Condition A
Subject 3	Condition C	Condition D	Condition A	Condition B
Subject 4	Condition D	Condition A	Condition B	Condition C

FIGURE 11.8 **Sample Counterbalancing with Four Levels of the Independent Variable.**

COUNTER-BALANCING

Involves making sure that all combinations of the order of presentation occur in a study.

Attrition can be combated with the offer of an incentive for participation in a study. For example, when John was in graduate school, he conducted several eight-week longitudinal studies. John retained participants in the study by the use of money. By offering a financial incentive, participants were more willing to come back and participate because there was a benefit to them personally. There are some special ethical considerations with the use of financial incentives. For more information on ethics refer back to Chapter 3.

Lastly, carryover and order effects are usually reduced by **counterbalancing** conditions between subjects. Rather than always presenting the conditions in the same order, a researcher changes the order such that all combinations are possible in a study. This will allow a researcher to observe any effect that may be a result of the order of the conditions. For example, a researcher has a within subjects design in which there were four levels of the independent variable, A, B, C, and D. The researcher presents to all participants the four conditions in the same order (i.e., A–D). The results of this study are such that there was a difference between level A and level D. Can the researcher be sure that A and D are truly different? Not necessarily because it could be the case that the participants experienced fatigue, carryover, or order effects that led to A and D being different. Rather, had the researcher used counterbalancing (see Figure 11.8), he or she could be confident that any differences between the levels are due to the independent variable and not the order in which the levels were presented.

YOU TRY IT!

We have discussed the advantages and disadvantages to within subjects designs and we want you to practice identifying these factors. Take a look at the scenario below.

A professor wants to investigate the impact of different types of studying habits on an algebra test. She decides to conduct a within subjects design in which she has 25 General Psychology students participate. The professor has four levels to her independent variable: no studying, studying with the aid of notes only, studying with the aid of the textbook only, and studying with the aid of notes and a textbook. Her study involves each of the 25 participants spending two hours in each condition followed by a 30-minute algebra task. The professor conducts this study on a Saturday, making sure that each participant receives the same order for each level of the independent variable. In addition, the same exam was given after each condition so that the

(Continued)

researcher was able to compare scores. Surprisingly, her results indicated that students did best in the no studying condition followed by conditions two, three, and four.

Questions

1. Do you believe that not studying is the best method? If not, what are some possible limitations to this within subjects design that could have lead to these odd results?

2. How would you conduct this study to minimize disadvantages?

Answers

1. The researcher's results could be due to participant fatigue or an order effect. The design required the participants to complete two hours in each of the four conditions, followed by four 30-minute exams. This would mean that each participant would participate for 10 total hours. By the end, the participants might not care about the test and put down any answer to be done. In this case, the participant's fatigue in the study influenced the last condition. In addition, each participant followed the same order. So, an order effect could have taken place in which the last condition received the poorest score because of its position and not the actual level of the independent variable (Figure 11.9).

Participant	Condition 1	Condition 2	Condition 3	Condition 4
1	No studying	Studying with the aid of notes only	Studying with the aid of the textbook only	Studying with the aid of notes and a textbook
2	Studying with the aid of notes only	Studying with the aid of the textbook only	Studying with the aid of notes and a textbook	No studying
3	Studying with the aid of the textbook only	Studying with the aid of notes and a textbook	No studying	Studying with the aid of notes only
4	Studying with the aid of notes and a textbook	No studying	Studying with the aid of notes only	Studying with the aid of the textbook only

FIGURE 11.9   Example of Counterbalancing for You Try It!

2. There are ways to conduct the study such that you minimize disadvantages. First, rather than having each level of the independent variable conducted in succession on one day, we would suggest spacing out the study over several weeks. This would limit any fatigue and carryover effects. In addition, we would recommend offering some kind of incentive to make sure participants complete all parts of the study. This would minimize attrition. Next, we would reduce the study time from two hours to one hour and use different versions of the algebra test. This would help to reduce the impact of fatigue as well as reduce the practice effect. Lastly, we would use counterbalancing to reduce the likelihood of order effects.

Section Summary

- Within subjects designs have several advantages which make it an appealing design to use. Advantages include: fewer participants, less statistical variance, and equal group sizes (pp. 195–197).
  - By having each participant partake in each level of the independent variable, you reduce the number of participants needed (p. 196).
  - *Statistical variance* is the degree of spread among scores from the mean of the group of scores. A within subjects design reduces this variance making it easier to determine if differences exist among the levels of the independent variable (p. 196).
  - The group sizes are equal because each participant is exposed to all levels of the independent variable (p. 196).
- Even though within subjects designs have several advantages, there are disadvantages to using a within subjects design. These include: attrition, carryover, order, and practice effects (pp. 196–197).
  - Participants are more likely to become tired in a within subjects design and suffer from *fatigue* because they are exposed to all levels of the independent variable (p. 196).
  - When participants drop out of studies or fail to complete all parts to a study, this is known as *attrition* (p. 197).
  - A *carryover effect* occurs when a prior treatment condition from an experiment influences current or future treatment conditions (p. 197).
  - If all participants experience the same order of treatment conditions in an experiment, any obtained results may be due to the order and not the conditions themselves. This is known as an *order effect* (p. 197).
  - An improvement in performance by a participant on subsequent stimuli independent of the variable being manipulated is known as a *practice effect* (p. 197).
- *Counterbalancing* conditions between participants is a good way of minimizing order and carryover effects. Counterbalancing involves making sure that all combinations of order of presentation occur in a study (pp. 197–199).

MATCHED SUBJECTS DESIGNS

MATCHED SUBJECTS DESIGN

A methodology where participants are matched on a particular characteristic before being assigned to the different levels of the independent variable.

Sometimes, it is not feasible to conduct a within subjects design even though you may want to due to its advantages. However, a similar design, which retains many of the within subjects design advantages, is a **matched subjects designs.** A matched subjects design is a type of research methodology in which participants are matched on a particular characteristic before being assigned to the different levels of the independent variable. In other words, instead of having the same participant complete all levels of the independent variable (as you would in a within subjects design), you would match or pair participants so that each level of the independent variable has a different but characteristically similar participant. This matching of participants across levels of an independent variable affords you the benefit of a within subjects design without having the same participant in each condition. Therefore, you can compare dependent variables across the conditions as if you had conducted a within subjects design.

To illustrate the matched subjects design, we will walk you through an example. You want to know how successful children are in school based on the amount of homework given. The independent variable would be the amount of homework given and its levels could be meets requirements and exceeds requirements. The dependent variable would be the children's scores on the end of grade tests. One factor that might influence these findings is the children's excitement about school work in general. So, you match the children on their excitement level. In order to do this, you must test their base level of excitement. After getting the scores, you rank order the children in terms of highest excitement level to lowest. Next, you take the scores of the first two children with the highest scores, randomly assigning each to one of the two groups (meets or exceeds). Subsequently, you take the next two children with the highest scores and match them before placing them into one of the two groups. You continue this process until all children are matched and assigned to the two homework groups. This is how a matched subjects design works. In essence, you have made sure that each group is equal in terms of the matched variable you have chosen (i.e., each group has the same number of high– and low–level excitement children). You should be able to detect results between the groups because you have reduced the effect of individual differences, just as you would had you used a within subjects design.

As you may have figured out, matched subjects designs also come with disadvantages. The introduction of an additional step, the matching step, can become time consuming. Depending on the intricacy of the match, you may have to spend additional time and, possibly, resources to ensure the match is complete. When considering this design, you will need to think about the limitations of making the match in comparison to the benefit offered by controlling for the variable.

Are You Equipped Now?

Have you ever watched the show *Mythbusters*? *Mythbusters* is a show on the Discovery Channel in which two guys, Jamie and Adam, attempt to debunk myths that exist in the world. Although this show is intended to be for entertainment, there is a lot of science that goes into the busting of myths. For each myth, the guys set up a study or experiment in which they test the details of the myth. During the third season of the show, the guys set out to debunk "Seasickness Cures." Many people get easily seasick or motion sick. There are a number of cures, some urban myths, which can be used to get rid of seasickness. Jamie and Adam decided to look at the five most common cures to seasickness: homeopathic tongue tingle (a spray you squirt under your tongue), wrist straps, ginger pills, acupuncture, and the use of over-the-counter pharmaceuticals. The type of cure in this case was the independent variable and the level of sickness was the dependent variable. If you were to conduct this as a within subjects design, how would you do it? And, what would be the biggest disadvantage you might face with this study?

Answer

There are a number of ways to conduct this study. However, as long as each person was exposed to all levels of the independent variable (the cures) you conducted the study correctly. The Mythbusters actually utilized a within subjects design to test these cures. Specifically, Jamie and Adam developed a model of NASA's seasickness chair, in which a chair rotates in a circle at 7 revolutions per minute (rpm) and a blindfolded participant sits in the chair. During the rotation of the chair, the participant is to lean his or her head forward, back, and to the left and right, touching tennis balls on the chair. This is to simulate seasickness. The Mythbusters had two participants who were exposed to all levels of the independent variable. Results showed that the ginger pills and the over-the-counter pharmaceuticals were the most effective at preventing seasickness (although the pharmaceuticals made the participants extremely drowsy). In addition, as you may have figured out, the biggest disadvantage in this study was that the participants were getting sick during each condition. However, it is not the getting sick that was the disadvantage but rather the desire to quit the experiment, attrition.

Therefore, the Mythbusters might have been better served using a matched subjects design for this experiment. By matching subjects on their susceptibility to seasickness and attempting to get them sick only once (i.e., five matched subjects exposed to only one level of the independent variable), the Mythbusters might have been more merciful to their participants. However, we doubt it would have made good television.

Chapter Summary

- A *within subjects design* occurs when participants in a study are exposed to all levels of the independent variable. It is also known as a repeated measures design and within participants design (pp. 190–195).
- Within subjects designs have several advantages which make it an appealing design to use. Advantages include: fewer participants, less statistical variance, and equal group sizes (pp. 195–197).
  - By having each participant partake in each level of the independent variable, you reduce the number of participants needed (p. 196).
  - *Statistical variance* is the degree of spread among scores from the mean of the group of scores. A within subjects design reduces this variance, making it easier to determine if differences exist among the levels of the independent variable (p. 196).
  - Since each participant is exposed to all levels of the independent variable, the group sizes are equal (p. 196).
- Even though within subjects designs have several advantages, there are disadvantages to using a within subjects design. These include: attrition, carryover, order, and practice effects (pp. 196–197).
  - Since each of the participants is being exposed to all levels of the independent variable, they are more likely to tire in the study and suffer from *fatigue* (p. 196).
  - When participants drop out of studies or fail to complete all parts to a study, this is known as *attrition* (p. 197).
  - A *carryover effect* occurs when a prior treatment condition from an experiment influences current or future treatment conditions (p. 197).

- ◆ If all participants experience the same order of treatment conditions in an experiment, then any obtained results may be due to the order and not the conditions themselves. This is known as an *order effect* (p. 197).
    - ◆ An improvement in performance by a participant on subsequent stimuli independent of the variable being manipulated is known as a *practice effect* (p. 197).
- ◆ *Counterbalancing* conditions between participants is a good way of minimizing order and carryover effects. Counterbalancing involves making sure that all combinations of order of presentation occur in a study (pp. 197–199).
- ◆ A *matched subjects design* occurs when participants are matched on a particular characteristic before being assigned to the different levels of the independent variable. This type of design is an alternative methodology to a within subjects design without many of the disadvantages (pp. 200–201).

APA Learning Goals Linkage

- • Goal 1. *Knowledge Base of Psychology*
  Students will demonstrate familiarity with the major concepts, theoretical perspectives, empirical findings, and historical trends in psychology.

    Sections Covered: Introduction to Within Subjects Designs

    Explanation of the Goal: Stroop's research conducted in 1935 is a classic in the field of psychology. In one of the experiments, participants were asked to read the words displayed in black ink and incongruent ink. In the second experiment, participants indicated the color of the ink used for each incongruent word and for each set of blocks. These experiments were included in this chapter as Stroop utilized a within subjects design and exposed participants to all levels of the independent variable within the experiments.

- • Goal 2. *Research Methods in Psychology*
  Students will understand and apply basic research methods in psychology, including research design, data analysis, and interpretation.

    Sections Covered: Are You Equipped?, Introduction to Within Subjects Designs, Factors to Consider, Matched Subjects Designs, Are You Equipped Now?

    Explanation of the Goal: Within subjects designs and matched subjects designs are two types of research methods. In this chapter, we examined these two methods and the types of questions and hypotheses associated with each. In addition, we articulated the strengths of the within subjects design (i.e., fewer participants, less statistical variance, and equal group sizes) and the limitations (i.e., fatigue, attrition, carryover, order, and practice effects). In the coverage of reducing limitations, special attention was given to the use of counterbalancing.

(Continued)

- **Goal 3.** *Critical Thinking Skills in Psychology*
  Students will respect and use critical and creative thinking, skeptical inquiry, and, when possible, the scientific approach to solve problems related to behavior and mental processes.

  Sections Covered: Are You Equipped?, Introduction to Within Subjects Designs, Factors to Consider, Are You Equipped Now?

  Explanation of the Goal: You engaged in critical thinking in this chapter by approaching problems effectively. Specifically, you were asked to design studies so that participants were exposed to all levels of the independent variable. We practiced this skill with classic and contemporary research examples. In addition, you utilized creative thinking when you were asked to improve the design of studies so that disadvantages due to the nature of the within subjects design would be minimized.

- **Goal 4.** *Application of Psychology*
  Students will understand and apply psychological principles to personal, social, and organizational issues.

  Sections Covered: Are You Equipped?, Introduction to Within Subjects Designs, Are You Equipped Now?

  Explanation of the Goal: The examples from this chapter that applied to everyday life were both novel and continuations from previous chapters. New examples included the Coke versus Pepsi dual presented at the opening and the *Mythbusters'* testing of motion sickness remedies presented at the end. Monitor size and reaction time and caffeine and alertness were reexamined in the context of within subjects designs.

Factorial Designs

CHAPTER OUTLINE

Are You Equipped?

This preview is a little different from previous chapters. We will not be asking you to try something new. Rather, we will be telling you about something new. Specifically, we are going to introduce a new type of research design.

A recent study by Dommeyer (2008) examined what factors influence whether or not people respond to a mail survey. In other words, are there factors that can influence if a person responds to a survey that he or she received in the mail? Dommeyer wanted to know if the attractiveness of the researcher in a cover letter would influence if people responded to the mail survey. Dommeyer also wanted to know if the sex of the researcher (male or female) in the cover letter would influence if people responded to the mail survey.

This quasi-experimental study described above was a factorial research design. It was a factorial research design because it had more than one independent variable. The first independent variable was attractiveness of the researcher in the cover letter. This independent variable had two levels: attractive and not attractive. The second independent variable (or subject variable in this case) was sex of the researcher in the cover letter. It also had two levels: male and female. Participants in this experiment would have received one of four cover letters. The first cover letter had an attractive female researcher. The second cover letter had an unattractive female researcher. The third and fourth cover letters had an attractive male researcher and an unattractive male researcher, respectively. These four cover letters can be viewed in a research matrix as seen in Table 12.1.

TABLE 12.1 Factorial Design Research Matrix.		
	IV #2 **Level 1**	**IV #2** **Level 2**
IV #1 **Level 1**	Attractive Female	Attractive Male
IV #1 **Level 2**	Unattractive Female	Unattractive Male

This experiment would be referred to as a 2 × 2 between subjects factorial research design. In this chapter, we will discuss why this experiment is a factorial research design. We will also discuss how to understand a research matrix. Finally, we will discuss three types of factorial research designs. These are between subjects, within subjects, and mixed subjects factorial research designs.

As you go through this chapter, we also want you to keep in mind how the material relates to the American Psychological Association's goals for psychology majors. Specifically, this chapter will address the following goals:

- **Goal 2. Research Methods in Psychology**
  Students will understand and apply basic research methods in psychology, including research design, data analysis, and interpretation.
- **Goal 3. Critical Thinking Skills in Psychology**
  Students will respect and use critical and creative thinking, skeptical inquiry, and, when possible, the scientific approach to solve problems related to behavior and mental processes.
- **Goal 4. Application of Psychology**
  Students will understand and apply psychological principles to personal, social, and organizational issues.
- **Goal 7. Communication Skills**
  Students will be able to communicate effectively in a variety of formats.

INTRODUCTION TO FACTORIAL DESIGNS

Before we begin this chapter, we should tell you the results of Donneyer's (2008) study. The only variable that influenced people's response to the survey was that of sex of the researcher. Interestingly, people were more likely to respond to a mail survey if the researcher was a female than a male.

FACTORIAL RESEARCH DESIGN

A research design that uses more than one independent variable.

In this chapter, we are going to discuss different types of factorial designs. Factorial designs are important to cover in a research methods course because many psychological studies employ them. **Factorial research designs** have more than one independent variable. If you think back to the examples we have covered previously, the examples had only one independent variable. However, there were generally two or three levels of the independent variable. Take for example sex of participant as a variable. Sex has two levels (male and female). It is also a between subjects variable. Another example we have discussed was size of computer monitor. It had three levels (i.e., 17 inch, 19 inch, and 21 inch). This chapter will focus on research designs that have more than one independent variable and each independent variable will typically have two or three levels.

A factorial research design can be one of three types. It can be a completely **between subjects factorial research design.** In this situation, all of the independent variables in the research design are between subjects variables. Participants are, therefore, only exposed to one level of each of the independent variables (think back to Chapter 10). Next, is a completely **within subjects factorial research designs.** In this situation, all of the independent variables in the research design are within subjects variables. Hence, participants are exposed to all levels of each of the independent variables (think back to Chapter 11). Finally, you could have a **mixed subjects factorial research design.** In this situation, not all of your independent variables would be of the same type. You might have one between subjects variable and one within subjects variable. To help better illustrate these three types of factorial designs, we will now walk you through examples of each.

Between Subjects Factorial Designs

In Chapter 10, we talked about the research study on situational and dispositional variables in helping behavior. At the time, we presented the results to you of one of the between subjects variables. It was the variable of hurry. As you might recall, the variable of hurry had three levels: high, intermediate, and low. Participants were assigned to one of these three levels. Results indicated that participants in the high-hurry condition were least likely to help the person they passed on their way from one building to the next. In actuality, this study conducted by Darley and Batson (1973) had a second independent variable. Remember how in the experiment, participants began the experiment in one building and then were asked to go to another building for the second part of the study? Well, participants were told that when they arrived at the second building they would be giving a three-to-five-minute talk based on the message of a passage that they received. The second independent variable was the message of the passage. It had two levels. The levels were task-relevant condition (i.e., these participants were to give a talk on professions of seminary students) and helping-relevant condition (i.e., these participants were to give a talk on the Good Samaritan parable from the Bible). This second variable of message was a between subjects variable. This is because participants were assigned to only one of the two conditions.

Up to this point, we have just been reviewing information on between subjects variables that we covered in Chapter 10. However, if we combine the two independent variables into one study, we can discuss our new topic of this chapter. Specifically, Darley and Batson (1973) used a between subjects factorial research design. It was a between subjects factorial research design because it had more than one independent variable. Participants in the experiment would have actually been assigned to one of six conditions. These six conditions can be viewed in the research matrix in Table 12.2 on the following page. This research matrix illustrates a 3 × 2 between subjects factorial research design.

BETWEEN SUBJECTS FACTORIAL RESEARCH DESIGN

A research design in which all independent variables are between subjects.

WITHIN SUBJECTS FACTORIAL RESEARCH DESIGN

A research design in which all independent variables are within subjects.

MIXED SUBJECTS FACTORIAL RESEARCH DESIGN

A research design in which not all of the independent variables are the same type (i.e., one independent variable is between subjects and the other is within subjects).

TABLE 12.2   Research Matrix for "Jerusalem to Jericho" Study.

	IV#2 Level 1	IV #2 Level 2
IV #1 **Level 1**	High hurry Helping relevant	High hurry Task relevant
IV #1 **Level 2**	Intermediate hurry Helping relevant	Intermediate hurry Task relevant
IV #1 **Level 3**	Low hurry Helping relevant	Low hurry Task relevant

YOU TRY IT!

We know we have just started this chapter but we want to see how you are doing. Below are a few questions based on the research matrix above. Try them out.

Questions

1. Why is this a factorial research design?
2. Why is this a between subjects factorial research design?
3. What does the 3 stand for in the 3 × 2 design?
4. What does the 2 stand for in the 3 × 2 design?
5. How do you determine how many total conditions there are in this study?

Answers

1. This is a factorial research design because it had more than one independent variable. Specifically, it had two independent variables: hurry and message.

2. This is a between subjects design because both of the independent variables were between subjects variables. The first variable, hurry, was a between subjects variable with participants being assigned to only one of the three conditions. The second variable, message, was also a between subjects variable with participants being assigned to only one of the two conditions. In any between subjects design, participants are only assigned to one level of each of the independent variables.

3. In this particular design, the 3 represents the three levels of the first independent variable of hurry. The three levels were high, intermediate, and low.

4. The 2 represents the two levels of the second independent variable, message. The two levels were task relevant and helping relevant. In a factorial research design, researchers discuss the design by using this standard format. If the research design has two independent variables, the format would be _____ × _____. The number of levels of the first independent variable goes in the first blank and the number of levels of the second independent variable goes in the second blank. By the way, when you say this format, the " × " reads as "by." So, you would say "a 3 by 2 design" (not "3 times 2 design").

(Continued)

5. You can figure out how many total conditions there are by multiplying the number of levels of each of the independent variables. In this case, we had 3 times 2, which equals 6 (i.e., high hurry/task relevant, intermediate hurry/task relevant, low hurry/task relevant, high hurry/helping relevant, intermediate hurry/helping relevant, and low hurry/helping relevant).

How did you do? Some of the questions that we asked you over the research study were ones we had not talked about yet. Therefore, if you did not know the answers to these questions, do not worry. We will practice these again later.

Next, we want to tell you about another study that was also a between subjects factorial research design. This was a 2 × 2 between subjects factorial design. Based on this little amount of information, you already could answer many questions including:

- *Why is this a factorial research design?*
- *What does the first 2 represent in the 2 × 2 design?*
- *What does the second 2 represent in the 2 × 2 design?*
- *How many total conditions are there?*

You could even answer these questions without knowing the exact names of the independent variables. However, we want to tell you more about the study. The researchers Brescoll and Uhlmann (2008) wanted to know if men and women were judged the same for expressing similar emotions in the workplace. Participants in this experiment watched a video of a job candidate. The job candidates were being interviewed while sitting at a table. The job candidates were describing an incident in which they and a colleague lost an important account and how it made them feel. The first independent variable was sex of job candidate. Sex had two levels—male and female. This was a between subjects variable because participants were either male or female. The second independent variable was emotion displayed. Emotion displayed had two levels—anger and sadness. This was also a between subjects variable. So, participants viewed one of four job candidates. A research matrix is given in Table 12.3.

After viewing one of the four job candidates, the participants were asked many questions about the candidates, including how much they would pay them and their competence levels. Because both of the independent variables

TABLE 12.3 Sample Research Matrix for Between Subjects Design.

	IV#2 Level 1	IV #2 Level 2
IV #1 Level 1	Male Anger	Male Sadness
IV #1 Level 2	Female Anger	Female Sadness

were between subjects variables, the overall research design was also between subjects. By now, you are probably getting the hang of between subjects designs. If you would like one last example, go back to the beginning of the chapter and read the Are You Equipped? section again.

Within Subjects Factorial Designs

It is now time to talk about the second type of factorial research designs. This is a within subjects factorial research design. In this design, participants are exposed to all levels of the independent variables of interest. In Chapter 11, we talked about the research conducted by Tamir, Mitchell, and Gross (2008), and music preference while playing computer games. At that time, we told you about the within subjects variable of music condition. This independent variable had three levels of angry, exciting, and neutral. Participants in the experiment were exposed to all three levels of the music condition while they were playing computer games. However, this was just one of the independent variables that the study actually investigated. Another independent variable of interest was type of game. Type of game had two levels that were confrontational and nonconfrontational. The researchers wanted to know if the type of computer game, in addition to the type of music, influenced performance. By adding this second variable, we now have a 3 × 2 within subjects factorial research design. If we were to think about this design visually, it would look like the research matrix in Table 12.4. However, keep in mind that because this is a within subjects design, all participants would at some point be in each of the six conditions.

Before we move on and discuss the last type of factorial research design, we want to talk about one more example of a completely within subjects factorial research design. This next study was adapted from Desrumaux, Bosscher, and Léoni (2009) to determine how evaluating a job applicant varies by the applicant's gender and physical appearance. For our purposes, we are going to focus on two of the independent variables, making this a 2 × 2 within subjects design.

TABLE 12.4   Research Matrix for Tamir et al. (2008).

	IV #2 Level 1	IV #2 Level 2
IV #1 Level 1	Angry Nonconfrontational	Angry Confrontational
IV #1 Level 2	Exciting Nonconfrontational	Exciting Confrontational
IV #1 Level 3	Neutral Nonconfrontational	Neutral Confrontational

YOU TRY IT!

Before we tell you more about this experiment, we want to see what you can already figure out based on the little information we have given you. Try these questions:

Questions

1. Why is this a factorial research design?
2. How many levels does the first independent variable have?
3. How many levels does the second independent variable have?
4. How many total conditions will there be in the research matrix?

Answers

1. This is a factorial research design because it has more than one independent variable.

2. The first independent variable has two levels. You can tell this because the standard format for a factorial research design is _____ × _____, where the number of levels for the first independent variable is in the first blank.

3. The second independent variable also has two levels. You can tell this because the standard format for a factorial research design is _____ × _____, where the number of levels for the second independent variable is in the second blank.

4. This research matrix will have four conditions. You can figure this out because $2 \times 2 = 4$.

Now we will tell you more about the research design. The first independent variable was the gender of the applicant and the two levels were male and female. The second independent variable was the physical appearance of the applicant. The two levels were attractive and unattractive. Both of these variables were within subjects variables, meaning that participants were in all of the four conditions represented visually in Table 12.5.

Specifically, participants viewed four resumes. Characteristics on the resume such as age, marital status, interests, and work experience were kept constant across the conditions. However, the picture presented with the resume was varied. The four pictures were attractive male, unattractive male, attractive female, and unattractive female. After viewing each resume with the accompanying picture, participants rated the applicants on numerous factors including hireability. Results indicated that although gender had no influence on ratings of

TABLE 12.5   Sample Research Matrix for a Within Subjects Factorial Design.

	IV #2 Level 1	IV #2 Level 2
IV #1 Level 1	Male Attractive	Male Unattractive
IV #1 Level 2	Female Attractive	Female Unattractive

hireability, physical appearance did. As predicted, the attractive applicants were more likely to be hired than the unattractive applicants.

Mixed Subjects Factorial Designs

Finally, there are mixed subjects factorial research designs. In a mixed subjects factorial research design, the independent variables are not all of the same type. In other words, some variables are between subjects and others are within subjects. Therefore, the design is mixed in terms of the types of variables. We want to tell you about two research studies that used a mixed subjects design.

The first study was conducted by Cameron and Rutland (2006). The purpose of the study was to determine if extended contact through story reading in school could reduce children's prejudice toward the disabled. This was a 3 × 2 mixed subjects design. The first independent variable was type of extended contact. It had three levels. The levels were neutral, decategorization, and "intergroup." In other words, the children heard stories that portrayed friendships between disabled and nondisabled children. In some of the stories, there was no emphasis placed on the individual qualities of the children (neutral). In other stories, the qualities were emphasized little (decategorization) or stressed (intergroup).Participants were placed into one of the three conditions. The children either heard neutral, decategorization, or "intergroup" stories.

The second independent variable was time of interview. It had two levels. The levels were preextended contact and postextended contact. This was a within subjects variable, meaning that all children were interviewed before and after the extended contact. When you have a mixed subjects design, you still determine the total number of conditions in the same way. For the study we have just described, you would have 3 × 2 = 6.

YOU TRY IT!

How would you draw the research matrix? Give it a try and compare your matrix to our matrix given in Table 12.6.

TABLE 12.6   Research Matrix for Cameron and Rutland (2006).

	IV #2 Level 1	IV #2 Level 2
IV #1 Level 1	Neutral Precontact	Neutral Postcontact
IV #1 Level 2	Decategorization Precontact	Decategorization Postcontact
IV #1 Level 3	"Intergroup" Precontact	"Intergroup" Postcontact

Remember that the second independent variable is a within subjects variable, so all children complete the precontact and postcontact conditions. The extended contact did lead to more positive attitudes toward the disabled, especially for the intergroup condition.

The second mixed subjects design we want to discuss was conducted by Janiszewski and Uy (2008). We will describe the first of the five studies conducted. In Chapter 11, we told you about one of the independent variables that the researchers used. This was the within subjects variable of scenario. Specifically, participants in this experiment all read 10 scenarios and then estimated a number based on the information given in the scenario. The 10 scenarios were the following: beach house, beverage, cheese, context free, basketball, figurine, hummer, pen, pet rock, and plasma TV. When we talked about this experiment in Chapter 11, it may have seemed strange to have participants estimate numbers in these 10 scenarios. However, now we are going to tell you about the second independent variable used in the experiment and the task will make more sense.

The researchers' second independent variable was type of anchor. This was a between subjects variable with three levels. The three levels were rounded anchor, precise under anchor, and precise over anchor. Participants were assigned to one of the three levels. The researchers wanted to know if precise or rounded anchors influenced judgments of numbers. An example might make this research design clearer. In the context-free scenario, participants read something like the following: "There is a number saved in a file on this computer. It is slightly less than _____. Can you guess the number?" In the rounded condition, the _____ would have been a number like 5,000. In the precise under, the _____ would have been a number like 4,989 and in the precise over, the _____ would have been a number like 5,012. This was a mixed subjects design because the independent variables were not all of the same type. The first independent variable of scenario was a within subjects variable and the second independent variable of anchor type was a between subjects variable. The results found that participants in the rounded condition gave larger adjustments than the two precise conditions. If you like to think about things visually, the research matrix for this design is given in Table 12.7.

TABLE 12.7 Sample Research Matrix for a Mixed Subjects Design.

	IV #2 Level 1	IV #2 Level 2	IV #2 Level 3	IV #2 Level 4	IV #2 Level 5	IV #2 Level 6	IV #2 Level 7	IV #2 Level 8	IV #2 Level 9	IV #2 Level 10
IV #1 Level 1	Rounded Beach house	Rounded Beverage	Rounded Cheese	Rounded Context-free	Rounded Basketball	Rounded Figurine	Rounded Hummer	Rounded Pen	Rounded Pet rock	Rounded Plasma TV
IV #1 Level 2	Precise under Beach house	Precise under Beverage	Precise under Cheese	Precise under Context-free	Precise under Basketball	Precise under Figurine	Precise under Hummer	Precise under Pen	Precise under Pet rock	Precise under Plasma TV
IV #1 Level 3	Precise over Beach house	Precise over Beverage	Precise over Cheese	Precise over Context-free	Precise over Basketball	Precise over Figurine	Precise over Hummer	Precise over Pen	Precise over Pet rock	Precise over Plasma TV

Section Summary

- A *factorial research design* is a design where there is more than one independent variable. Typically, a factorial research design has two or three independent variables with each variable having multiple levels (pp. 206–207).
- In a *between subjects factorial research design*, there is more than one independent variable. However, since this design is between subjects, participants are only exposed to one level of each independent variable. In this design, the number of groups of participants are determined by multiplying the total number of levels for each variable (i.e., 3 × 2 design yields 6 distinct groups, each receiving one level of each independent variable) (pp. 207–210).
- In a *within subjects factorial research design*, there is more than one independent variable. However, since the design is within subjects, participants are exposed to all levels of each independent variable. In this design, you have one group of participants who experience all treatment conditions (pp. 210–212).
- In a *mixed subjects factorial research design*, there is more than one independent variable. However, in this design both between and within subjects variables are used (pp. 212–213).

RESULTS OF FACTORIAL DESIGNS

We want to briefly mention how to understand the results of a factorial research design. The benefit of a factorial design (no matter what type) is that you can get the answer to three questions with just one experiment. You can find out (a) if there was an influence of the first independent variable on the dependent variable(s), (b) if there was an influence of the second independent variable on the dependent variable(s), and (c) if the influence of the first independent variable depended on the second independent variable.

Main Effects

MAIN EFFECT

Determining if an independent variable has had an effect on the dependent variables while ignoring or collapsing across the other independent variables in the factorial research design.

Finding out if each of the independent variables influenced the dependent variable(s) is referred to as **main effects.** There could be a main effect for each independent variable that you have in a factorial research design. We will talk about main effects using the 2 × 2 between subjects factorial design from the preview of this chapter. In this study the the researchers wanted to know if attractiveness of the researcher in the cover letter (IV#1) and sex of the researcher in the cover letter (IV#2) influenced response rates from mail surveys. To begin, the researcher would have looked for a main effect for the first independent variable of attractiveness. Let's call the first independent variable A. When you are looking for a main effect of A, you need to ignore B (sex). Put another way, you will look at A while collapsing across B. Take a look at the Table 12.8. If we were looking to see if attractiveness had an influence on the number of responses received, we would compare all of the responses from participants who received the letter from the attractive researcher to all of the responses from participants who received the letter from the unattractive researcher. The × in the table

TABLE 12.8 Example of the Main Effect for Independent Variable A.

	Male	Female	
Attractive			X
Unattractive			X

represents the mean number of responses received. Therefore, we would need to average across the male and female condition to determine the mean number of responses for the attractive researcher and for the unattractive researcher.

Subsequently, we would look to see if there was a main effect of B. In other words, we want to know if sex of researcher in the cover letter influenced response rate while ignoring or collapsing across attractiveness. In Table 12.9, the × again represents the mean number of responses. We would need to average across the attractive and unattractive condition to determine the mean number of responses for the male and female researcher.

TABLE 12.9 Example of the Main Effect for Independent Variable B.

	Male	Female
Attractive		
Unattractive		
	X	X

We can look to the study by Darley and Batson (1973) for another example. The researchers wanted to know if the independent variable of hurry (high, intermediate, and low) and the independent variable of message of passage (task-relevant and helping-relevant) influenced willingness to help. To begin, the researchers would have looked for a main effect for the first independent variable of hurry. When you are looking for a main effect of A, you need to ignore B (message). Put another way, you will look at A while collapsing across B. Take a look at Table 12.10. If we were looking to see if hurry had an influence on willingness to help, we would compare the willingness to help from participants in the high, intermediate, and low conditions. The × in the table represents the mean number of people willing to help. So, we would need to average across the task-relevant and helping-relevant condition to determine the mean helping response for the high, intermediate, and hurry levels.

TABLE 12.10 Main Effect for Darley and Batson's (1973) Independent Variable #1.

	Task Relevant	Helping Relevant	
High Hurry			X
Intermediate Hurry			X
Low Hurry			X

Next, we would look to see if there was a main effect of B. In other words, we want to know if message of passage influenced willingness to help while ignoring or collapsing across hurry. In Table 12.11, the $\times$ again represents the mean number of responses. So, we would need to average across the hurry conditions to determine the mean number of responses for the task relevant and helping relevant conditions.

TABLE 12.11   Main Effect for Darley and Batson's (1973) Independent Variable 2.

	Task Relevant	Helping Relevant
High Hurry		
Intermediate Hurry		
Low Hurry		
	X	X

Interactions

INTERACTION

Occurs when the effect of one independent variable depends on another independent variable.

The final question that a factorial design answers is if the influence of the first independent variable depends on the influence of the second independent variable. This is referred to as an **interaction.** In an interaction, you obtain results that would not have been produced from either independent variable alone. These results literally tell you how your independent variables interact with one another. We like to have students think about interactions using the following example. We want to know how sex and exercise condition influences weight lost. Our first independent variable is the subject variable of sex of participant (male and female), and our second independent variable is exercise condition (exercise, peer support, and control) as is displayed by the matrix in Table 12.12.

To begin, we would look for main effects of A and B to see if sex and exercise condition each had an influence on weight lost. It is probably the case that men lose more weight than women. This could be determined by evaluating the difference between X_{Women} and X_{Men}. And, it is also probably the case that exercise yields the most weight lost. This can be determined by evaluating the difference between $X_{Exercise}$, $X_{Peer\ Support}$, and $X_{Control}$.

TABLE 12.12   Research Matrix for Interaction.

	IV #2 Male	IV #2 Female	
IV #1 Exercise			X
IV #1 Peer Support			X
IV#1 Control			X
	X	X	

We would also then want to know if the independent variables interacted in some way on the dependent variable. For example, it could be the case that women will lose more weight with peer support than men, and men will lose more weight with exercise than women. In order to make this determination, we must now evaluate each of the six conditions to see where differences exist and not average across independent variables. If this concept is still a little unclear, don't worry. We will return to this idea of factorial interactions in a later chapter.

Section Summary

- A *main effect* is the effect that an independent variable had on the dependent variables in a given research design (pp. 214–215).
- An *interaction* occurs when the effect on the independent variables for a given study is due to the other independent variables in that study (pp. 216–217).

Are You Equipped Now?

Let us see how you are doing with all the material that we have discussed in this chapter. We will describe part of an experiment that we have not previously told you about. As you read about the experiment, keep looking for the independent variables and you will be able to answer our questions. (Hint: there are two independent variables.)

Researchers at the Center for AIDS Intervention Research conducted an experiment with 207 individuals taking HIV medications (Catz, Kalichman, Benotsch, Miller, & Suarez, 2001). Participants were randomly assigned to read one of six vignettes. The vignettes varied by medical situation and physician prescription action. For medical situation, participants were randomly assigned to one of three levels. In the first medical situation, participants were informed that the HIV viral load had increased. In the second medical situation, participants were informed that the HIV viral load had decreased. In the third medical situation, participants were informed that the HIV viral load had remained the same. For physician prescription action, participants were randomly assigned to one of two levels. The first action was a medication change, while the second action was continued monitoring. After reading one of these vignettes, participants rated their affective anticipated response (i.e., how they would predict they would feel if these were their test results).

Questions
1. Why was this a factorial research design?
2. What was the first independent variable?
3. What was the second independent variable?
4. What type of factorial research design was this (i.e., between, within, or mixed)?
5. What does the research matrix look like?

Answers
1. This was a factorial research design because there was more than one independent variable. In fact, there were two independent variables.
2. The first independent variable was medical situation. This independent variable had three levels. The three levels were increased viral load, decreased viral load, and no

change. This was a between subjects variable because the participants were randomly assigned to be in only one of the three levels.

3. The second independent variable was physician prescription action. It had two levels. The levels were medication change and continued monitoring. This was a between subjects variable because the participants were randomly assigned to be in only one of the two levels.

4. It is a between subjects factorial design because both of the independent variables are between subjects variables.

5. The research matrix looks like the following.

	IV 2 Level 1	IV 2 Level 2
IV #1 Level 1	Viral load increase medication change	Viral load increase continued monitoring
IV #1 Level 2	Viral load decrease medication change	Viral load decrease continued monitoring
IV #1 Level #3	Viral load no change medication change	Viral load no change continued monitoring

Chapter Summary

- A *factorial research design* is a design where there is more than one independent variable. Typically, a factorial research design has two or three independent variables, with each variable having multiple levels. Rarely do factorial designs have more than three variables. This is because if the researcher manipulated too many variables, he or she would be unable to tell which independent variable was producing the observed change in the dependent variable (pp. 206–207).
- In a *between subjects factorial research design*, there is more than one independent variable. However, since this design is between subjects, participants are only exposed to one level of each independent variable. In this design, the number of groups of participants are determined by multiplying the total number of levels for each variable (pp. 207–210).
  - For example, in a research design with an independent variable that has three levels and another independent variable with two levels, there are a total of six distinct conditions. However, participants would only be placed into one of the six conditions as the study is a between subjects factorial design (p. 208).
- In a *within subjects factorial research design*, there is more than one independent variable. However, since the design is within subjects, participants are exposed to all levels of each independent variable. In this design, you have only one group of participants who experience all treatment conditions (pp. 210–212).
  - For example, in a research design with an independent variable that has three levels and another independent variable with two levels,

there are a total of six distinct conditions. Each participant would participate in all six distinct conditions as the study is a within subjects factorial design (p. 210).

◆ In a *mixed subjects factorial research design*, there is more than one independent variable. Specifically, in a mixed design there are between and within variables (pp. 212–213).

　◆ For example, in a research design with a between subject independent variable that has three levels and another within subject independent variable with two levels, there are a total of six distinct conditions. The participants would participate in only one of the levels of the first independent variable but all of the levels of the second independent variable (p. 212).

◆ A *main effect* is the effect that an independent variable has on the dependent variables in a given research design. In other words, this evaluates the impact of manipulating a single independent variable while ignoring or collapsing across all other independent variables (pp. 214–215).

◆ An *interaction* occurs when the effect on the independent variables for a given study is dependent upon other independent variables in that study. In other words, this evaluates whether the presence of each independent variable has an effect on the other independent variables as seen by a change in the dependent variable (pp. 216–217).

APA Learning Goals Linkage

• **Goal 2. *Research Methods in Psychology***
Students will understand and apply basic research methods in psychology, including research design, data analysis, and interpretation.

Sections Covered: Are You Equipped?, Introduction to Factorial Designs, Results of Factorial Designs, Are You Equipped Now?

Explanation of the Goal: This chapter introduced us to different types of factorial research designs. First, we talked about between subjects factorial research designs. This is a research design where all independent variables are between subjects variables. The second factorial design that we covered was the within subjects factorial research design. In this case, all of the variables are within subjects variables. Another research design, mixed subjects factorial design, occurs when not all independent variables are the same type. As factorial designs are very common in psychological research, it is imperative that they are included in a discussion of research methods. In addition to types of research designs, this chapter furthered our knowledge in interpreting basic statistical conclusions related to factorial designs with information given on main effects and interactions of variables.

(Continued)

(Continued)

- **Goal 3.** *Critical Thinking Skills in Psychology*
  Students will respect and use critical and creative thinking, skeptical inquiry, and, when possible, the scientific approach to solve problems related to behavior and mental processes.

    Sections Covered: Are You Equipped?, Introduction to Factorial Designs, Are You Equipped Now?

    Explanation of the Goal: Psychologists recognize that human behaviors and mental processes are complex. As a result, the research methods utilized must take into account the fact that multiple factors might be influencing an individual. You engaged in critical and creative thinking by completing exercises in this chapter that required you to design studies to understand the influence of these multiple factors. For example, we discussed how the gender of a job applicant and the physical appearance of a job applicant can both contribute to ratings of hireability. Similarly, we saw how more than one factor plays a role when an individual is deciding whether or not to help someone else.

- **Goal 4.** *Application of Psychology*
  Students will understand and apply psychological principles to personal, social, and organizational issues.

    Sections Covered: Are You Equipped?, Introduction to Factorial Designs, Results of Factorial Designs, Are You Equipped Now?

    Explanation of the Goal: Factorial research methods can be applied to personal, social, and organizational issues. In fact, every section in this chapter contained an example of a factorial design that was related to understanding thoughts and behaviors of individuals in everyday life situations. Applying psychological principles to common situations allowed us to understand why men and women's emotions are judged differently in the workplace and how we can work to reduce prejudice behavior.

- **Goal 7.** *Communication Skills*
  Students will be able to communicate effectively in a variety of formats.

    Sections Covered: Are You Equipped?, Introduction to Factorial Designs, Results of Factorial Designs, Are You Equipped Now?

    Explanation of the Goal: Quantitative communication skills are needed to exhibit factorial research designs in graphical form. Consequently, we practiced how to construct and interpret a research matrix to display information about the variables manipulated in a factorial design. We also used graphical information to illustrate how factorial designs tell us the influence that each independent variable has on the dependent variable (main effects) and if the independent variables interact to produce a result on the dependent variable (interaction).

CHAPTER

13

Single Case Designs

CHAPTER OUTLINE

Are You Equipped?

In the early 1920s, two researchers took a child under the age of one and used classical conditioning techniques to condition an emotional response. Specifically, Watson and Rayner (1920) took a young child, *Little Albert*, and conditioned him to associate the appearance of a white rabbit with being scared. On its own the rabbit did not elicit any response from *Little Albert*. However, in the experiment the researchers paired the white rabbit with the hitting of a hammer on a metal bar (which naturally caused the child to become frightened). Within seven pairings of the white rabbit with the hammer and bar, *Little Albert* was conditioned so that each time he saw the white rabbit he displayed a fearful response. Interestingly, this fear in *Little Albert* transferred over to anything white and fluffy. Although this is one of the most famous studies in psychology, many do not know that this was a specialized type of research design. Can you determine what is different about this study than many of the other studies we have discussed thus far?

What is unique about this design is that it involved only one participant. This type of design is known as a single case or a N = 1 design. Watson and Rayner's (1920) study became one of the most important research findings in early psychology. And, unlike other designs in which numerous subjects are used, the researchers had a single participant. Yet, the impact in the field of psychology was significant. Watson and Rayner are not alone in their use of a single case design. Additional findings in the field of psychology were the result of single case designs. These designs will be the focus of our discussion in this chapter.

As you go through this chapter, we also want you to keep in mind how the material relates to the American Psychological Association's goals for psychology majors. Specifically, this chapter will address the following goals:

- **Goal 1. Knowledge Base of Psychology**
  Students will demonstrate familiarity with the major concepts, theoretical perspectives, empirical findings, and historical trends in psychology.
- **Goal 2. Research Methods in Psychology**
  Students will understand and apply basic research methods in psychology, including research design, data analysis, and interpretation.
- **Goal 3. Critical Thinking Skills in Psychology**
  Students will respect and use critical and creative thinking, skeptical inquiry, and, when possible, the scientific approach to solve problems related to behavior and mental processes.
- **Goal 4. Application of Psychology**
  Students will understand and apply psychological principles to personal, social, and organizational issues.
- **Goal 5. Values in Psychology**
  Students will be able to weigh evidence, tolerate ambiguity, act ethically, and reflect other values that are the underpinnings of psychology as a discipline.

AN INTRODUCTION TO SINGLE CASE DESIGNS

SINGLE CASE DESIGN

A design that focuses on a single participant, single group of participants, or a small group of participants.

Historically, a design in which the focus is on a (a) single participant, (b) small group of individuals, or (c) single group of participants was known as a single subject design (Shadish, Cook, & Campbell, 2002). Today, researchers refer to these types of designs as **single case designs.** We will examine specific examples later in the chapter. For now, it is important to know that the focus of a single case design is the individual. Specifically, researchers are attempting to show the impact an experimental condition has on a single participant. Oftentimes, these designs are mistaken as case studies. Remember from Chapter 4, a case study is an in-depth observation of an individual, animal, event, or treatment method. In truth, a case study is a type of single case design. However, not all single case designs are case studies.

The field of psychology has used single case designs from the beginning. In fact, one of the earliest users of single case designs was Wilhelm Wundt, regarded by most as the *father of psychology*. Wundt developed a technique known as introspection, which is a type of single case methodology. In his methodology, a single participant was trained to become consciously aware of his or her inner thoughts and feelings. Wundt believed that this was the best way to explore the human mind. From participants' reported experiences, Wundt attempted to extrapolate a picture of the working mind. Although Wundt used several individuals in his research with introspection, his work focused on the individual and his or her own personal experience. This type of methodology does not sample from a large population as do many of the designs we have discussed thus far. Rather, the individual is the focus of interest.

Early on, the area in which single case designs were utilized the most was in behavioral psychological research. For example, we have already discussed the study with Little Albert, in which conditioning was used to elicit an emotional response. Furthermore, researchers such as Pavlov and Skinner used single case designs to explore classical and operant conditioning. Today, researchers are using single case designs to explore work in clinical, counseling, educational, cognitive, physiological, and other applied research setting.

YOU TRY IT!

One of the earliest research experiments on child development involved the use of a chimpanzee named Gua. Gua was raised by two researchers, Winthrop Kellogg and Luella Kellogg (1933). The Kelloggs were interested in how life experiences with the environment impacted early-stage development. Therefore, the Kelloggs decided to raise Gua side by side with their own infant child for nine months. Over the time period, the researchers systematically assessed the differences between their human child and the adopted chimp. The results showed that much of the early experiences that Gua was afforded resulted in a modification of traditionally instinctive behaviors. Specifically, Gua showed great maturation in nearly all areas of development including speech comprehension. The only exception was in the area of speech production.

Questions

1. Why is this considered to be a single case design?
2. What is the independent variable that the Kelloggs were manipulating? In other words, what was the experimental manipulation the Kelloggs were trying to show had a direct impact on development?

Answers

1. The use of the single chimp makes this an example of a single case design. All the data collected and conclusions that the Kelloggs (1933) developed from their study centered on their systematic observation of a single participant, Gua. The study focused on the chimp and how her behavior changed over a nine-month period.
2. The independent variable the researchers were trying to manipulate was the early-life experiences with the environment. Specifically, the Kelloggs (1933) wanted to see if manipulating the early experiences with the environment had a direct impact on the chimp's rate of development. As it turned out, this was indeed the case, with Gua maturing at a quick rate.

Interestingly, one of the theorized reasons as to why the study was stopped was that the Kelloggs' own infant son began developing many characteristics of the chimp. This would only further strengthen the Kelloggs' claim that early-life experiences can modify development. For many years, this study was the basis for illustrating how maturation is impacted by learning. Again, what is unique about this study is that the results were obtained by examining the change in a single participant and was not achieved with a large group of participants.

Although we have started this chapter by illustrating the impact and usefulness of single case designs, these types of designs cannot be used carte blanche. Rather, these designs are preferred by researchers when large group designs using inferential statistics are not possible or desired. Specifically, in large group designs the researchers rely on averages across all participants which can lead to individual differences becoming lost within the data. However, single case designs focus solely on detecting these differences within the individual (or small group).

Previously, we mentioned the prevalence of single case designs in a number of areas in psychology. However, single case designs are most likely to occur in three specific situations. The first situation is in clinical research where the patient with a specific disorder is the focus of interest. Referring back to the beginning of this chapter, this case would be an example of a single case design that focuses on a single participant. Second, single case designs are preferred when investigating unique or specialized populations where large numbers either (a) do not exist or (b) access is limited. These populations might include using Fortune 500 CEOs (Chief Executive Officers) or experts in a given domain for a research study. This is an example of a single case design with a small group of individuals. Lastly, single case designs are useful in group or team research, where the single unit of analysis is that of the group or team. In particular, single case research is often used when examining juries or business work teams where the jury or a work team itself is the single case. This is an example of a single case design focusing on a single group of participants.

Section Summary

- Single case designs are a special classification of research designs where the focus is on a
    - single participant,
    - small group of individuals, or
    - single group of participants (pp. 222–223).
- Single case designs are most likely to occur
    - in clinical research,
    - with specialized or unique populations where large numbers (a) do not exist or (b) access is limited, and
    - in group or team research (p. 224).

WHY USE SINGLE CASE DESIGNS?

Until now, we have only introduced and made suggestions about when to use a single case design. However, it is important to know why it may be appropriate to use a single case design and what the benefits are to using a single case design over other types of designs. Surprisingly, the use of a single case design has nothing to do with limiting the amount of data collected. Instead, there are two main reasons to use a single case design:

- Single case designs can have high internal validity.
- Single case designs avoid problems with obtaining control groups.

First, single case designs can have high internal validity (see Chapter 5). Internal validity is the power of a design to isolate the independent variable as being responsible for any experimental effects. Thus, single case designs are good at showing that any manipulation of the independent variable had an impact on the dependent variable. This allows the researcher to establish practical significance between variables. For example, everyone knows that when you deprive someone of water they become dehydrated. However, what does "become dehydrated" actually mean? This is a generalization of what happens. Rather in a single case design you would take a single participant and deprive him or her of water. This would give you a firsthand glimpse as to the practical relationship between water and the impact that it has on a participant. Ethically, you could not do this experiment but it is a great example of what is meant by establishing a practical relationship. Therefore, with single case designs, individual effects are not masked by group averages as they can be in a large design. Instead, you see directly the impact of the independent variable on the dependent variable, thereby establishing the exact relationship between those variables.

Second, single case designs avoid problems with obtaining control groups. As with most experiments in which a researcher manipulates a variable, you have two groups: a control and experimental group. However, in a single case design the participant of interest serves as his or her own control group and therefore acts as his or her own baseline for comparison. Thus, there is no need for a second group for comparison. Rather, a researcher observes behavior before and after the introduction of the independent variable.

YOU TRY IT!

Arguably, the most important research on memory occurred back in the late 1800s. Herman Ebbinghaus (1885) was a pioneer in human memory research. In order to investigate human memory, Ebbinghaus devised a set of experiments in which he was the participant. His research focused on how quickly humans learn information. In his experiments, Ebbinghaus developed lists of nonsense syllables. These lists would consist of multiple consonant-vowel-consonant groups such as JEZ, FIQ, and YOT. Next, he would learn the same list of syllables at two different occasions, with varying time intervals in between. He would then learn the list again, noting how long it took to learn the list each time. From this difference in time (i.e., the first time to learn and the second time to learn), Ebbinghaus was able to calculate what he called a savings. For example, when learning a list for the first time it took Ebbinghaus an average of 952 seconds. When relearning that list 19 minutes later, it took him an average of 452 seconds. This yields a savings of 57% of the information. Ebbinghaus repeated this experiment with different lists for intervals of 19 minutes, 1 hour, 8.8 hours, 24 hours, 48 hours, 6 days, and 31 days (levels of his independent variable). From this, Ebbinghaus was able to illustrate a forgetting curve.

(Continued)

(Continued)

The curve shows that retention of information takes the biggest hit in the first 20 minutes and then gradually flattens out over several days. See Figure 13.1 for a visual representation.

Questions

1. What makes this study a single case design?
2. Why is it that Ebbinghaus' study could have high internal validity?
3. When did Ebbinghaus serve as the control group in the study?

Answers

1. The only participant in Ebbinghaus' study was himself. He served as the control group to establish a baseline and then served in the experimental group by varying the time period between sessions.

2. Ebbinghaus' study could have had high internal validity because he was able to demonstrate how time influenced learning and retention of information. By developing the forgetting curve, he was able to show empirically how his independent variable (time) had an impact on his dependent variable (learning). Specifically, because Ebbinghaus served in both the control and experimental group, he reduced any threats to internal validity (see Chapter 9).

3. Again, Ebbinghaus' use of himself as his participant allowed other researchers to see firsthand the relationship between the variables in his study. He served as the control group in the study during the initial phase of learning. The learning of the list the first time through was the control condition. At this point, the independent variable of time had not been introduced. Therefore, the initial learning phase served as the control for the study.

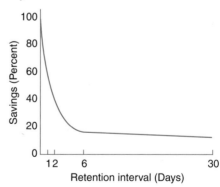

FIGURE 13.1 Ebbinghaus' Forgetting Curve.

Section Summary

- Single case designs can have high internal validity (pp. 224–225).
- Single case designs avoid problems with obtaining control groups (p. 225).

CONDUCTING SINGLE CASE DESIGNS

There are several ways in which you can develop and carry out a single case design. In other words, there are specific types of methodologies used in single case designs. We are going to discuss the three most common types of method-ologies used in single case design research: (a) AB or pretest–posttest designs, (b) ABA or reversal designs, and (c) multiple baseline designs.

AB Designs (Pretest–Posttest)

Thus far, we have mentioned this design several times in this chapter without actually giving it a name. An **AB design,** also known as a pretest–posttest design, involves taking measurements before and after the administering of an independent variable. For example, when testing a new drug for schizophrenia, the researchers would take an initial baseline assessment of the symptoms (A). After which, the researchers would administer the drug for a certain period. Then, the researchers would bring the participant back following that period and conduct a follow-up assessment of the symptoms (B).

AB DESIGN

A methodology where measurements are taken before and after the administering of an independent variable.

    This type of design occurred in the research by Ebbinghaus (1885). He attempted to learn the information as quickly as he could, thereby establishing a baseline (A). Then, he administered the independent variable (time) followed by a follow-up session of learning (B). However, the use of an AB design does not always allow the researcher to fully see the impact of the independent variable. There are other designs which are better able to show the impact of the inde-pendent variable on a participant.

ABA Designs (Reversal Designs)

Remember, the purpose of a single case design is to detect the impact of an inde-pendent variable. With an AB design, this is accomplished by looking at the change from point A to point B. However, the most powerful methodology that exists in single case designs to show the impact of the independent variable is the **ABA or reversal design.** This methodology initially proceeds just like an AB design. However, once measurement information is collected after exposure to the inde-pendent variable is collected (B), the independent variable is then removed. At this point, the participant is exposed to a time period (same amount as the independent variable) where nothing occurs in terms of manipulation. After that time is up, the researcher conducts another measurement (A). Once the independent variable is removed, the participant should return to a baseline state. Thus, the third assess-ment is also called measure (A).

ABA DESIGNS

A methodology where measurements are taken before and after the administering of an independent variable as well as after the removal of the independent variable.

    For example, Kuoch and Mirenda (2003) conducted a single case study in which they looked at the influences of a social story on the behavior of autistic chil-dren. A social story is a story that is used to teach specific social skills as an alternative to a problem behavior (i.e., problems with sharing toys). Kuoch and Mirenda used an ABA design to assess the social story impact on specific behavioral problems. During the initial baseline phase, the researchers would observe the participant in certain problem situations and record the number of behavioral prob-lems (A). Following the initial baseline, the intervention stage was administered (B). In this stage, the researchers would read to the participant a social story before a problem situation was presented. Afterwards, the researcher would count the num-ber of behavioral responses the participant displayed in the corresponding problem situation. Finally, the researchers removed the use of the social story and collected data in a follow-up baseline (A). This is a great example of the use of an ABA design in single case research. Interestingly, participants' behavior was permanently changed following the intervention. In particular, the initial baseline results showed higher numbers of behavioral problems as compared with the follow-up baseline.

Even with the usefulness of an ABA design, instances exist when it is not possible to conduct an ABA design. Reasons for not using an ABA design usually fall into two categories, ethical concerns or feasibility concerns. The first category deals with the ethical consequences of removing an independent variable after it has had a positive effect. For example, if a researcher developed a new drug that cured cancer in his or her patient, is it ethical of that researcher to withdraw the drug? Should the researcher go through a reversal, knowing that it could increase the chances that the patient would develop cancer again? The answer is obviously no. Therefore, an ABA design could not be used in this particular case. The other category surrounds the feasibility of truly removing the independent variable. In particular, it may not be possible to fully remove the effects of the independent variable, thereby reverting the participant's behavior to baseline. This often happens in research where the independent variable involves learning or the development of skill. In these situations, the removal of a learned skill is not practical, resulting in the participant being unable to revert to his or her baseline performance. This category was evident in the example used earlier, where Kuoch and Mirenda (2003) had participants who did not revert back (or reverse) to their initial baseline performance.

Multiple Baseline Designs

MULTIPLE BASELINE DESIGNS

A methodology where researchers have a small number of participants receive the independent variable at varying times.

A multiple baseline design is a stronger version of an AB or ABA design that allows a researcher to more clearly see the impact of an independent variable. Researchers use this type of design to ensure that the change that is seen is due to the independent variable and not something else. When using **multiple baseline designs,** researchers have a small number of participants receive the independent variable at varying times. This allows the researcher to see how outside events might influence the participant.

For example, over the last few decades high schools have been grappling with educating students about sexual activity. Imagine a new program has been developed to educate these students. However, since this program is still unproven, a county superintendent chooses to conduct a study. The superintendent selects three schools in his or her county to participate in the study. In order to minimize outside effects and fully determine the likelihood of the program to be successful, the superintendent decides to use a multiple baseline methodology. Specifically, the superintendent introduces the program in each school at varying times. The following results are based on reported sexual activity of students. The first school in this program received the program after 4 weeks of classes, the second school after 8 weeks of classes, and the third school after 12 weeks of classes. As can be seen from the results, all schools showed similar levels of baseline sexual activity. However, immediately following the introduction of the program, sexual activity changed in all schools. These results show that the program had an effect (see Figure 13.2). The researcher (in this case the superintendent) can argue that the program led to the change and that the change was not due to outside influences such as a history effect or maturation (threats to internal validity).

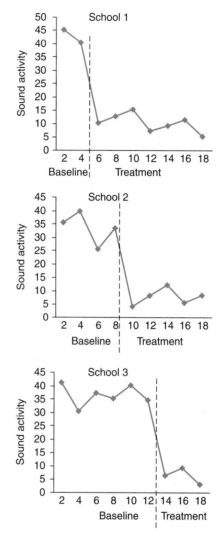

FIGURE 13.2 Hypothetical Data for High-School Intervention.

YOU TRY IT!

We are looking to conduct a single case design. We want to look at the influence of mental imagery on performance in elite athletes. Mental imagery occurs when a person mentally rehearses events in his or her mind before performing them in reality. We have a small population of elite swimmers who have never used mental imagery. Since this is a small and specialized population, we know that we will be using a single case design. What type of methodology would you use to conduct a study on this topic—an AB design, an ABA design, or a multiple baseline approach?

(Continued)

(Continued)

Answer

You could have conducted this research study using any of the aforementioned designs. For this study, an AB design would collect data for the initial baseline (A) of swimming performance. This would then be followed by the administering of the independent variable of mental imagery and the collection of data again on swimming performance (B). If you chose to conduct an ABA design, you would follow the same procedure as the AB design. However, after the administering of the mental imagery, you would remove that independent variable before collecting the follow-up baseline on swimming performance (A).

The last type of method you could have chosen is a multiple baseline approach. Casby and Moran (1998) used this approach when studying this exact topic. They used a multiple baseline approach with four swimmers. Each swimmer was assessed for varying amounts of time to establish baseline performance followed by the administering of the independent variable of mental imagery. Results showed that regardless of when the independent variable was implemented, none of the swimmers significantly improved their performance. Therefore, the researchers concluded that the use of mental imagery had no direct impact on performance.

Section Summary

- When conducting single case designs, several methodologies can be used (pp. 226–230).
  - *AB designs* are also known as pretest–posttest designs. These designs involve taking measurements before (A) and after the introduction of the independent variable (B) (p. 227) .
  - *ABA designs* are also known as reversal designs. In this methodology, measurements are taken before (A), after the introduction of the independent variable (B), and after the removal of the independent variable (A) (pp. 227–228).
  - A *multiple baseline design* involves introducing the independent variable in a study at varying times to a small group of participants. With this design, the participants all experience a varying amount of time in the baseline and treatment conditions (pp. 228–229).

LIMITATIONS OF SINGLE CASE DESIGNS

Even with all of the benefits that can be gained by using a single case design, there are several limitations to these types of designs. First, because single case designs use within subject methodologies, the design faces the same limitations that we discussed in Chapter 12. These include carryover, order, and practice effects. In addition, with single case designs, a researcher has to be very aware of fatigue influencing the participant. However, the most glaring limitation to single case designs has to do with the generalizability of the results to large populations. While single case designs have high internal validity, they have low external validity. In other words, single case designs cannot be used to predict behavior beyond the participant or small group within the study. This is a major limitation. Nonetheless, many (if not most) single case designs are only useful to the participant being studied and are not concerned with generalizing to a larger population. Therefore, single case designs are very useful to advancing knowledge when used appropriately.

Are You Equipped Now?

Over the past several years, there has been a developing story in major sports involving the National Football League (NFL). During the off-season, several teams look to improve their rosters by bringing in high-priced talent. Recently, the teams follow a trend of bringing in one particular player. The name of the player is Terrell Owens. After starting his career with the San Francisco 49ers, Terrell moved on to play for the Philadelphia Eagles, Dallas Cowboys, and, most recently, the Buffalo Bills. An interesting trend has been discussed throughout the sports world for years about this player: Does he have a positive impact on a team? The question has risen due to the nature of events that transpires with each team. In particular, each team starts with the player not on their roster, followed by two to three years of the player on their roster, followed by a time when the player is no longer on the team.

Questions

Can you explain how this could be an example of a single case design? Specifically, can you identify the participants, the independent variable, and the type of methodology used here?

Answers

In this example, the participants are the teams that have acquired Owens and the independent variable is Terrell Owens. This may seem counterintuitive but Owens is what is being manipulated in this scenario (i.e., his presence on the team or his absence). If you said that the approach being used was an ABA design, you are partially right. Actually, this single case design would be using a multiple baselines approach. The methodology follows like an ABA design with a baseline assessment (A), the administering of the treatment (B), and the removal of the treatment (A). However, since the participants are the different teams, this becomes a multiple baseline approach. Specifically, each team acquired Owens (the independent variable) at different times. This allows each team to have a varying amount of time to establish a baseline before the independent variable is administered (i.e., the acquisition of Owens). With this approach, the answer to the question of impact on a team could be seen.

Chapter Summary

- A *single case design* focuses on a (1) single participant, (2) single group of participants, or (3) small group of participants (pp. 222–223).
- Single case designs are most likely to occur in three areas (p. 224).
  - Single case designs are most popular when conducting clinical research (p. 224).
  - Single case designs are used when investigating specialized or unique populations where large numbers (1) do not exist or (2) access is limited due to availability (p. 224).
  - Finally, single case designs are used in research that investigates group or team research where the group or team is the focus (e.g., jury studies) (p. 224).
- Single case designs have several advantages (pp. 225–226):

- ◆ Single case designs have been shown to have high internal validity (p. 225).
- ◆ Single case designs avoid problems with obtaining control groups (p. 225).
- When conducting single case research, there are several methodologies that can be used (pp. 226–230).
  - ◆ *AB designs* are also known as pretest–posttest designs. These designs involve taking measurements before (A) and after the introduction of the independent variable (B) (p. 227).
  - ◆ *ABA designs* are also known as reversal designs. In this methodology, measurements are taken before (A), after the introduction of the independent variable (B), and after the removal of the independent variable (A) (pp. 227–228).
  - ◆ A *multiple baseline design* involves introducing the independent variable in a study at varying times to a small group of participants. With this design, the participants all experience a varying amount of time in the baseline and treatment conditions (pp. 227–229).

APA Learning Goals Linkage

- **Goal 1.** *Knowledge Base of Psychology*
  Students will demonstrate familiarity with the major concepts, theoretical perspectives, empirical findings, and historical trends in psychology.

  Sections Covered: Are You Equipped?, An Introduction to Single Case Designs, Conducting Single Case Designs

  Explanation of the Goal: Many psychological studies in the history of the field used a single case design. The chapter started with a single case design conducted by Watson and Rayner to condition fear in a child. Ebbinghaus experimented with forgetting with only himself as a participant. We also mentioned the work of Wundt, often considered the father of psychology, and the Kelloggs, who were interested in early developmental experiences. These examples demonstrate that the individual is a relevant level of analysis within the field.

- **Goal 2.** *Research Methods in Psychology*
  Students will understand and apply basic research methods in psychology, including research design, data analysis, and interpretation.

  Sections Covered: Are You Equipped?, An Introduction to Single Case Designs, Why Use Single Case Designs, Conducting Single Case Designs, Limitations of Single Case Designs, Are You Equipped Now?

  Explanation of the Goal: Single case designs focus on a single participant, single group of participants, or small group of participants. In this chapter, we introduced you to this design, along with the different types of single

(Continued)

case designs commonly used (AB designs, ABA designs, multiple baseline designs). We articulated the strengths and limitations of the design in the corresponding sections on advantages and disadvantages of the approach. One major limitation was regarding the ability to generalize conclusions from single case designs to other populations. By discussing this limitation, you gained the skills needed to recognize how individual differences may influence the applicability of research findings.

- **Goal 3.** *Critical Thinking Skills in Psychology*
  Students will respect and use critical and creative thinking, skeptical inquiry, and, when possible, the scientific approach to solve problems related to behavior and mental processes.

  Sections Covered: Are You Equipped?, Introduction to Single Case Designs, Why Use Single Case Designs, Conducting Single Case Designs, Are You Equipped Now?

  Explanation of the Goal: The exercises that you completed in this chapter entailed recognizing the use of single case designs in classical (e.g., Ebbinghaus, Kelloggs) and current research examples (e.g., mental imagery and swimmers). You used critical thinking skills to then explain how the designs of the studies yielded both advantages and disadvantages.

- **Goal 4.** *Application of Psychology*
  Students will understand and apply psychological principles to personal, social, and organizational issues.

  Sections Covered: Are You Equipped?, Introduction to Single Case Designs, Why Use Single Case Designs, Conducting Single Case Designs, Are You Equipped Now?

  Explanation of the Goal: To begin, we identified appropriate applications of psychology in solving problems at the beginning of the chapter when we outlined how different areas of psychology all use single case designs. The examples provided continued to relate to societal issues such as autism and applying psychological principles to personal issues such as mental imagery for swimmers.

- **Goal 5.** *Values in Psychology*
  Students will be able to weigh evidence, tolerate ambiguity, act ethically, and reflect other values that are the underpinnings of psychology as a discipline.

  Sections Covered: Limitations of Single Case Designs

  Explanation of the Goal: APA states that psychology majors should recognize and respect human diversity. In the section on the limitations of single case designs, we learned to anticipate how psychological explanations may vary across populations.

Hypothesis Testing Continued and Interpreting Results

CHAPTER

14

Hypothesis Testing Revisited and Interpreting Results

Are You Equipped?

Researchers Dunn, Huntsinger, Lun, and Sinclair (2008) conducted a study to explain how individuals interpret gift giving in new acquaintance situations. The researchers obtained their participants from another study that had paired members of the opposite sex and required them to engage in social interactions for fewer than five minutes. Afterwards, the researchers separated these new acquaintances and asked them to rank order their own preferences for $20 gift cards to 12 stores and restaurants. Participants were then asked to select a gift card for their new acquaintance and were told their new acquaintance would be doing the same for them. Participants were informed that they had a small chance of actually winning the gift card in a lottery. Next, the participants were told what gift card their new acquaintance had selected for them. However, in reality, the researchers randomly assigned participants to receive either a good gift card (the participant's first choice) or a bad gift card (the participant's eleventh choice).

After learning what their new acquaintance had allegedly selected for them, participants completed a survey and indicated how similar they were to the acquaintance in terms of interests and ways they spend their free time.

The researchers had predicted that men and women would respond differently to receiving good and bad gifts from new acquaintances. The results indicated that women reported the same degree of similarity between themselves and the new acquaintances whether they received a good gift or a bad gift. Men, on the other hand, reported different levels of similarity between themselves and the new acquaintances based on the type of gift. Specifically, men reported higher levels of similarity after receiving a good gift and lower levels of similarity after receiving a bad gift.

In Chapter 6, we introduced the topic of hypothesis testing and discussed how researchers design experiments to answer questions. Dunn et al. (2008) conducted a study to test a hypothesis. The null hypothesis was that men and women would not be different in how they responded to the good and bad gifts; whereas, the research hypothesis was that men and women would differ in how they responded. We want to add to your knowledge of hypothesis testing by discussing how researchers decide whether to reject the null hypothesis or fail to reject the null hypothesis. Dunn et al. would reject the null hypothesis because they found differences in how men and women responded to the gift selected. In this chapter, you will learn how to look at statistical outcomes for a study and decide the appropriate action in regard to the null hypothesis.

As you go through this chapter, we also want you to keep in mind how material relates to the American Psychological Association's goals for psychology majors. Specifically, this chapter will address the following goals:

- **Goal 2. Research Methods in Psychology**
  Students will understand and apply basic research methods in psychology, including research design, data analysis, and interpretation.
- **Goal 3. Critical Thinking Skills in Psychology**
  Students will respect and use critical and creative thinking, skeptical inquiry, and, when possible, the scientific approach to solve problems related to behavior and mental processes.
- **Goal 4. Application of Psychology**
  Students will understand and apply psychological principles to personal, social, and organizational issues.
- **Goal 7. Communication Skills**
  Students will be able to communicate effectively in a variety of formats.

EXAMINING THE RESULTS—REJECTING THE NULL OR FAILING TO REJECT THE NULL HYPOTHESIS

Previously, we introduced the concept of hypothesis testing. For the current chapter, we will be revisiting this topic and adding to your understanding of hypothesis testing. In particular, we will discuss how a researcher decides whether the null hypothesis should be rejected or not at the conclusion of the study. In order to provide continuity, we will start by reviewing some of the earlier examples.

Heinz Ketchup Example Revisited

In Chapter 6, we discussed the introduction of ketchup in a variety of colors by Heinz Ketchup in the early 2000s. For example, the Heinz Ketchup company developed ketchup in the colors of green and purple. In this example, we formed the research question, "Does the color of ketchup (traditional red versus green) influence people's willingness to buy ketchup?" From this research question we were able to identify both the null and the research hypotheses. Can you remember how to identify each in words and symbols?

The null hypothesis could be stated as, "The color of ketchup *does not* influence people's willingness to buy ketchup" or as "There is *no* influence of the color of ketchup on people's willingness to buy ketchup." In symbols, the null hypothesis would be represented like this:

$$H_0 \; \mu_{(red\ ketchup)} = \mu_{(green\ ketchup)}$$

The research hypothesis could be stated as, "The color of ketchup *does* influence people's willingness to buy ketchup" or as, "There *is* an influence of color of ketchup on people's willingness to buy ketchup." In symbols, the research hypothesis would be represented like this:

$$H_1 \; \mu_{(red\ ketchup)} \neq \mu_{(green\ ketchup)}$$

You could also form a directional research hypothesis where you hypothesize that one color of ketchup will be viewed more favorably when compared to the other color of ketchup. In this case, your directional research hypothesis could be stated as, "People will be more willing to buy green ketchup as opposed to red ketchup." In symbols, the directional research hypothesis would be represented like this:

$$H_1 \; \mu_{(red\ ketchup)} < \mu_{(green\ ketchup)}$$

Once you have developed the appropriate hypotheses, you can conduct your study. The question then becomes, "What do we do once we have the results?" We mentioned at the end of Chapter 6 that researchers never say that they have *proved* a result. Rather, researchers are more likely to say that the results support a particular hypothesis or that the results are inconclusive. In order to make any causal inference about the results of a study, the researcher has two options they must consider: to reject the null hypothesis or to fail to reject the null hypothesis.

In order to do this, researchers test the null hypothesis. The logic behind testing the null hypothesis is quite elegant. It is easier to disprove the null hypothesis than it is to disprove the research hypothesis. Therefore, researchers are looking to disprove the null hypothesis or the likelihood that the means of the groups are equal.

As we have mentioned, when researchers have conducted a study and analyzed their data, they have a decision to make regarding the null hypothesis. The researcher can either reject the null hypothesis or fail to reject the null hypothesis. If a researcher **rejects the null hypothesis,** the results have indicated that there is a statistically significant difference between the means of the groups

REJECTING THE NULL HYPOTHESIS

Indicates that there is a statistically significant difference between the means of the groups in the study.

FAILING TO REJECT THE NULL HYPOTHESIS

Indicates that there is not a statistically significant difference between the means of the groups in the study and that the means are equal.

LEVEL OF SIGNIFICANCE

The level of significance is indicated by the alpha level (α).

(i.e., the means of the groups are not equal). If the researcher **fails to reject the null hypothesis,** the results have indicated that the means of the groups are equal (i.e., there is no difference in the means of the groups).

To determine if the groups are statistically different from one another, researchers perform statistical procedures and examine the level of significance. The **level of significance** is known as the alpha level (α) and is determined prior to conducting an experiment. Alpha is the probability of obtaining data assuming the null hypothesis is true. In psychological research, most researchers accept an alpha level of .05 as the desired level of significance.

The lower the *p*-value, the less likely the obtained differences in the results are due to chance and the more likely the obtained differences in the results are due to the manipulation of the study. If the *p*-value obtained from a study is less than the conventional alpha level of .05 (i.e., $p < .05$), we reject the null hypothesis. In other words, the results are so extreme that they are unlikely due to chance and have indicated a statistically significant difference between the means of the groups. If the *p*-value obtained from a study is greater than the conventional alpha level of .05 (i.e., $p > .05$), we fail to reject the null hypothesis. If a researcher fails to reject the null hypothesis, the results have indicated that there is not a statistically significant difference between the means of the groups. This does not imply that the researcher has proved the null hypothesis. Rather, it just means the researcher is unable to reject it.

YOU TRY IT!

Below are two examples of research studies. We provide you with the research question and the results of the study. To complete this You Try It! you will need to use your knowledge gained from Chapter 6 in addition to the information covered thus far in the chapter. We would like for you to state (a) the null hypothesis; (b) the null hypothesis in symbols; (c) the research hypothesis, indentifying if it is directional or nondirectional; (d) the research hypothesis in symbols; and (e) whether, based on the results, you should reject the null hypothesis or fail to reject the null hypothesis.

Questions

1. A researcher has designed a study to answer the question, "Do men or women drink more coffee?" The researcher conducts the study by observing the coffee consumption of men and women during a one-week time period. The researcher hypothesizes that men will consume *more* coffee than women. After the study has concluded, the researcher finds that there is no difference between men and women ($p > .05$).

2. You want to know whether typed or handwritten papers are graded differently by professors. So, you have professors read and evaluate papers of both types. You hope to show that there is a *difference* in the way typed and handwritten papers are evaluated. After the study has concluded, you find that there is a difference between the typed and handwritten papers in the grades received. This result is statistically significant at the $p < .05$ level.

(*Continued*)
Answers

1. The null hypothesis for this question could be stated as, "There is *no* difference between the amount of coffee consumed by men and women." In symbols this would be represented like this:

$$H_o \, \mu_{(men)} = \mu_{(women)}$$

   The research hypothesis in this study is a directional research hypothesis. This is evident by the researcher indicating men would consume *more* coffee than women would consume. The directional research hypothesis could be stated as, "Men will consume more coffee than women." In symbols:

$$H_1 \, \mu_{(men)} > \mu_{(women)}$$

   Based on the results of this study ($p > .05$), the researchers would fail to reject the null. In other words, the results did not indicate a statistically significant difference between men and women in their consumption of coffee. Additionally, the results were counter to what the researcher predicted.

2. The null hypothesis in this question could be stated as, "There is *no difference* in the evaluation of typed and handwritten papers." In symbols this would be represented like this:

$$H_o \, \mu_{(typed \ papers)} = \mu_{(handwritten \ papers)}$$

   The research hypothesis in this study is a nondirectional research hypothesis. This is evident by indicating a difference should occur and not specifying which type of paper will receive higher grades. The nondirectional research hypothesis could be stated as, "There is a *difference* in the evaluation of typed and handwritten papers." In symbols:

$$H_1 \, \mu_{(typed \ papers)} \neq \mu_{(handwritten \ papers)}$$

   Based on the results of this study ($p < .05$), you would reject the null hypothesis. Specifically, the results of the study showed a statistically significant difference in the evaluation of typed and handwritten papers.

Type I and Type II Errors

Given the information presented so far, it would appear as though all you need to do is look at the *p*-value to make a determination of whether to reject or fail to reject the null hypothesis. However, there is more to the decision. As can be seen from Table 14.1, there are four possible outcomes to a study. First, you can make the decision to reject the null when the null hypothesis is false. This would be a correct decision. The other correct decision would be to fail to reject the null when the null hypothesis is true. However, there are occasions when decision errors are made.

As can be seen from the table, there are times where you reject the null hypothesis when the null is in fact true. This is known as a **Type I Error.** This first type of error, Type I Error, occurs when a researcher finds the groups to be different when they are really the same. The probability of making a Type I Error in an experiment is related to the level of significance set at the beginning. Conventionally, there is a 5% chance or less of rejecting the null when it is in fact

TYPE I ERROR

It occurs when a researchers rejects the null when the null is in fact true.

TABLE 14.1   Hypothesis Testing Conclusions.

		Researcher's Decision	
		Reject the Null Hypothesis	Fail to Reject the Null Hypothesis
True State of Affairs	Null hypothesis is true.	Type I Error Probability $= \alpha$	Correct Decision Probability $= 1-\alpha$
	Null hypothesis is false.	Correct Decision Probability $= 1-\beta$	Type II Error Probability $= \beta$

TYPE II ERROR

It occurs when a researcher fails to reject the null even though the null hypothesis is false.

true. If the alpha level is set more stringent (.01), the probability of committing a Type I Error is lower. There is a 1% chance or less of rejecting the null hypothesis when it is in fact true. Therefore, the lower the alpha level, the lower the probability that a researcher will commit a Type I Error. The second error that can be made is known as a **Type II Error.** A Type II Error occurs when a researcher fails to reject the null hypothesis even though the null hypothesis is false. This is a situation when the researcher finds the groups to be the same when they are really different. A Type II Error occurs when statistical power is low. Back in Chapter 8 we mentioned power. Power is the probability of rejecting the null hypothesis when it is indeed false or the probability of accepting the research hypothesis. The formula for power is represented by 1-β. The chances of committing a Type II Error are directly related to the power level of a study. The lower the power a study has, the greater the chance of committing a Type II Error. Likewise, the stronger the power a study has, the less of a chance of committing a Type II Error. A more thorough review of power can be found in a statistic book.

Some examples will help in thinking about Type I and Type II Errors. Just like researchers, juries can make two correct decisions. These would be to find an innocent person not guilty of a crime and to find a guilty person guilty of a crime. However, juries can also make decision errors. For example, a jury might find an innocent person guilty of a crime. Or, a jury might find a guilty person innocent of a crime. However, just as juries do not make decision errors on purposes, neither do researchers. Nor do only bad researchers make errors. Rather, the errors made by researchers are due to the use of probability in hypothesis testing.

The Role of Replication

The last topic we would like to mention on hypothesis testing is the role that replication plays in research. The results and conclusions drawn from research studies must be verified. One of the best ways to ensure a result is accurate and not a product of an error is by replicating the study. A study replication occurs when another researcher (or the same researcher) recreates a study using the same methodology as is in the original study. Study replication allows researchers to verify results. If a study is replicated and the results are the same as the original, researchers can be confident a decision error was not committed.

However, if a study is replicated and results are different from the original study, an error might have been committed. If this were to occur, the conclusions from the original study would need to be reevaluated. The next time you conduct a research study, think about conducting a follow-up study to ensure your results are not an error.

Section Summary

- *Rejecting the null hypothesis* indicates that there is a statistically significant difference between the means of the groups in the study (pp. 238–240).
- *Failing to reject the null hypothesis* indicates that there is not a statistically significant difference between the means of the groups in the study and that the means are equal (pp. 238–240).
- The *level of significance* is indicated by the alpha level (α) (p. 240).
  - Traditionally, psychologists accept an alpha level of .05 (p. 240).
  - If the obtained *p*-value in a study is less than the conventional alpha level, we reject the null hypothesis (p. 240).
  - If the obtained *p*-value in a study is more than the conventional alpha level, we fail to reject the null hypothesis (p. 240).
- When conducting research, there are four possible decision outcomes. The first two are to reject the null when it is false or to fail to reject the null hypothesis when it is true (pp. 241–243).
  - A *Type I Error* occurs when a researcher rejects the null hypothesis when the null is in fact true (pp. 242–243).
  - A *Type II Error* occurs when a researcher fails to reject the null hypothesis even though the null hypothesis is false (pp. 242–243).

INTRODUCTION TO INTERPRETING STATISTICAL RESULTS

Most psychology departments require that students take a research methods course. This is because the skills and knowledge obtained through the course material are foundations for working in any area of psychology. At some universities, research methods and statistics are taught together in one course, while at other universities, the two subject areas are taught as different courses. Our goal for the next section is not to teach you how to conduct statistical procedures. Rather, we want to provide suggestions for how to draw conclusions when you read statistical outcomes. This information will benefit you no matter which approach your university takes to teaching research methods and statistics.

We will discuss two branches of statistics known as descriptive and inferential statistics. The purpose of descriptive statistics is to describe the data; whereas, the purpose of inferential statistics is to allow you to draw conclusions about the population of interest from the sample used. In the following subsections on these two branches of statistics, we will cover common procedures for each and implications that you should consider when interpreting them.

Drawing Conclusions from Descriptive Statistics

DESCRIPTIVE
STATISTICS
───────────
Statistics used by
researchers to
describe data sets.

MEASURES OF
CENTRAL
TENDENCY
───────────
Numbers that
represent the scores
in the data set.

MEAN
───────────
The average of the
scores in the data set.

MEDIAN
───────────
The number in the
middle of a data set.

MODE
───────────
The most frequently
occurring number in
a data set.

Descriptive statistics are used by researchers to describe data sets. Specifically, descriptive statistics summarize data sets by providing numbers which are representative or typical for the set. This is helpful because most of the time you do not have access to a researcher's full data set. It is also a quick way to obtain an overview of the scores in the set.

A frequent way of summarizing a data set is to give measures of central tendency. **Measures of central tendency** are numbers that represent the scores in the data set. Three commonly used measures of central tendency are the mean, median, and mode. The **mean** is the average of the scores in the data set. To obtain the mean, you add up all the scores in the data set and divide by the total number of scores. The **median** can be found by arranging all the scores in the data set from highest to lowest (or lowest to highest) and locating the number in the middle. If there is an even number of scores in the data set, you will need to calculate the mean for the two numbers in the middle. The **mode** is the most frequently occurring number in the data set and it is possible to have more than one mode.

Here is a data set:

$$10, 20, 30, 40, 40, 50$$

To find the *mean*, you would add up the scores and divide by the total number of scores.

$$10 + 20 + 30 + 40 + 40 + 50 = 190$$

$$\frac{190}{6} = 31.66$$

To find the *median*, you arrange the scores from lowest to highest and locate the middle value.

$$10, 20, 30, 40, 40, 50$$

NORMAL
DISTRIBUTION
───────────
A normal
distribution of scores
occurs when most
scores cluster around
the middle and few,
but equal, numbers
cluster on the
extremes.

Note: Because there is an even number of scores, the average of the two numbers in the middle (30 and 40) is taken. The median is 35.

To find the *mode*, you look for the number that occurs most frequently. The mode for this example would be 40 because it is the only score that occurs more than once.

You can infer much about a data set by knowing if the mean, median, and mode are the same (or about the same). If these three measures are similar, the data set has a **normal distribution** (see Figure 14.1 on the following page). You can see

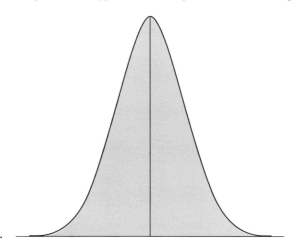

FIGURE 14.1   A Normal Curve.

from the illustration that when a data set has a normal distribution, most of the scores cluster around the center. Few scores occur at the high and low ends of the distribution. One way to think about this concept is using the distribution of exam scores from a psychology course. If scores from the exam follow a normal distribution, it would mean that most of the students earned a C on the exam. Fewer students would have earned Bs and Ds and even fewer students would have earned As and Fs. Normal distributions are also symmetrical, meaning that there would be an equal number of high scores and low scores.

If you know that a data set has a normal distribution, there are conclusions that you can draw about the scores. The first implication for any data set with a normal distribution is that most of the participants gave responses that fell in the middle of the distribution. It is also the case that extreme scores, in either direction, are less frequent. Therefore, any measure of central tendency would be a good representation for the data set. Specifically with a normal distribution, the mean, median, and the mode all are the same value. However, the conclusions that you draw about a data set change when the distribution is not normal. A distribution that is not normal is said to be skewed. A **skewed distribution** is one in which the most frequently occurring scores are not in the middle. In other words, the scores pile up at one end of the distribution or the other end (see Figures 14.2A and B on the following page). With a skewed distribution, the mean, median, and mode are not the same.

One issue to consider with a skewed distribution is which measure of central tendency best represents the data set. In their statistics book, Aron, Aron, and Coups (2009) provide a wonderful illustration of this situation by using data from Miller and Fishkin (1997), who surveyed male and female participants regarding how many partners they ideally wanted to have in the next three decades. If you compare responses of men and women by looking at the means, men (64.3) desired to have a far greater number of partners than did women (2.8).

However, Aron et al. point out that because the data set is not normal, the mean is not the most representative number. This is because means are easily

SKEWED DISTRIBUTION

A distribution in which the most frequently occurring scores are not in the middle.

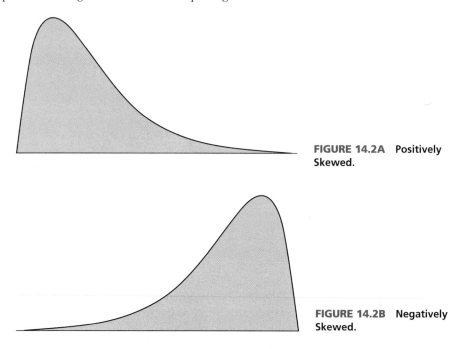

FIGURE 14.2A   Positively Skewed.

FIGURE 14.2B   Negatively Skewed.

influenced by extreme scores. This occurred in the Miller and Fishkin data set because a few of the male respondents gave very high numbers in the thousands, thus increasing the mean. In this situation, it is helpful to look at the median. The median indicated that the score in the middle for both men and women was 1. Thus, looking at either the mean or the median in this study can lead you to draw different conclusions about the number of partners that men and women want in the future. The take-home message is that when you see a skewed distribution, you have to be careful about conclusions that you make by looking at the mean. If there are extreme scores in the data set, the median might be the more representative score.

Before moving on to the topic of inferential statistics, we would like to briefly mention two measures of variability that can also be used to summarize data. These two measures are variance and standard deviation. While variance provides information on the spread of scores in a set, standard deviation is used most frequently to provide information on how much scores vary from the mean. A large standard deviation would indicate that scores vary widely from the mean and are spread out in the data set. A small standard deviation would indicate that most scores are located around the mean. Knowing the amount of standard deviation can help to determine if the mean is a representative score for the data set.

INFERENTIAL STATISTICS

Used to draw inferences about a population from the sample used.

Drawing Conclusions from Inferential Statistics

Inferential statistics are used so that inferences can be drawn about a population from the sample used. As we discussed earlier in this textbook, it is not feasible or practical to conduct research on entire populations. However, we can obtain a representative sample of individuals from the population of interest. We can then use inferential statistics to make generalizations about our population. Hence, inferential statistics allow us to make generalizations that go beyond our sample.

One of the most basic inferential statistics is the t-test. There are three types of t-tests. The **one-sample t-test** is used to determine when a mean is significantly different from a constant. This constant can be obtained from previous research, chance level, or the midpoint on a scale. The **dependent or paired-samples t-test** is used to determine if the mean difference between the pairs is significantly different from zero. The pairs for this t-test can be from repeated-measures designs or matched subjects designs. Finally, the **independent t-test** evaluates whether or not means from two different groups are significantly different from one another.

The first issue to consider when a researcher uses a t-test is whether or not the researcher used the correct t-test when analyzing his or her data. Although there are similarities among the three t-tests, each one actually evaluates a different assumption. The correct t-test needs to be used for the specific application. For example, we would use a t-test if our university wanted to assess the effectiveness of a faculty development workshop. We could have students evaluate the same group of faculty members on their teaching before and after they attend the workshop. In order to determine if the workshop influenced the ratings, we would use a dependent samples t-test. This is because we have the following conditions: one independent variable with two levels, a repeated measures design, and an intervention. You would not use a one-sample or independent t-test. If you have not had statistics yet, you may not know when to use each of the t-tests. This is ok. The important thing to remember is that when you do learn the information, the first step in evaluating this inferential statistics is to ensure the correct one was used.

A second issue to consider with the use of a t-test is the probability of committing a Type I Error (or rejecting the null hypothesis when it is in fact true). This is an issue to have in mind if the researcher uses more than one t-test. This is referred to as multiple t-tests. For each t-test conducted, the alpha level is at .05. But, with each additional t-test, the alpha level increases. For example, if you have two t-tests, the p-value would be .10 (i.e., .05 + .05 = .10). One way the researchers can reduce the probability of making a Type I Error when conducting multiple t-tests is to make the alpha level more stringent. Specifically, you take .05 and divide by the number of t-tests you plan on conducting. To be significant, each t-test should be less than the new p-value. In an example with 5 t-tests, you would take .05 and divide by 5, which equals .01. Thus, for each t-test the new alpha level would be .01. This process is known as the **Bonferroni correction.**

Another type of inferential statistics is **analysis of variance** (commonly abbreviated ANOVA). When you have one independent variable with three or more levels, you can use a one-way ANOVA. The results will tell you if there are differences between the levels, and follow-up analyses will tell you where the particular differences occurred. If you have more than one independent variable as with a factorial design, you could perform a more advanced ANOVA,

*ONE-SAMPLE
t-TEST*

Used to determine when a mean is significantly different from a constant.

*DEPENDENT
t-TEST*

Used to determine if the mean difference between pairs is significantly different from zero.

*INDEPENDENT
t-TEST*

Evaluates whether or not two means are significantly different from one another.

*BONFERRONI
CORRECTION*

The correction used when conducting multiple statistical tests to limit the possibility of making a Type I Error.

*ANALYSIS OF
VARIANCE
(ANOVA)*

Used when you have an independent variable with three or more levels or when you have multiple independent variables.

allowing all variables to be examined. For example, if you had two variables, you would perform a two-way ANOVA and if you had three variables you would perform a three-way ANOVA. These more complex ANOVAs can tell you if there are differences for each independent variable (main effects) and if the independent variables interact with one another (interactions).

If a researcher has conducted any type of ANOVA, he or she should provide you with some basic information to help you interpret the results. First, you should look to see if there were any missing data points, and if so, how the researchers handled the situation. Systematically missing data points would warrant further explanation. Second, you should look to see if there were outliers (or extreme scores) in the data set. As we discussed earlier, extreme scores can influence the shape of the distribution. This leads us to the third suggestion of assessing the shape of the distribution. If a distribution is severely skewed, it might not be possible to conduct inferential statistics without data transformation. Finally, you have to see if the variables being studied have a linear relationship.

In this brief section on drawing conclusions from inferential statistics, we have only mentioned a few common procedures. Many other inferential statistics are available to address particular research questions, such as Pearson correlations which examine the extent to which two variables are related. However, with each inferential statistics utilized, you should always be cautious when drawing conclusions. For example, with the Pearson correlation, you should not imply cause and effect, as the procedure only provides information on relationships between variables of interest. APA-style recommends that for any inferential statistics used, the following information should be provided when possible: the sample size of each condition, means and standard deviations for each condition, the obtained statistical value, degrees of freedom, the obtained p-value, effect size, and confidence intervals.

YOU TRY IT!

Questions

1. When we return exams in our classes, we find it beneficial to share with students information on the distribution of scores. We provide this information so that students will have an idea of how they scored on the exam in comparison to their peers. However, deciding which descriptive information to provide to the class is not always an easy decision. To illustrate this example, take a look at the graph given in Figure 14.3. These are modified grades from one of Jenn's statistics classes. For this data set, the mean is 77, the mode is 92, and the median is 86. If you were the professor of the class, do you think sharing the mean scores on the exam with the class is a representative score of the data set? Why or why not?

2. If a researcher is conducting a study and wants to perform a series of seven t-tests to evaluate the research hypotheses, what would you recommend the alpha level to be for each test? Why would you recommend this level?

(Continued)

FIGURE 14.3   Hypothetical Exam Grades.

3. We found a news report that summarized research findings from Lawlor, Timpson, Harbord, and Leary (2008). These researchers were looking at the relationship between a mother's weight during pregnancy and the child's fat mass at ages 9 or 11. The researchers predicted that the more a mother weighed during pregnancy, the higher the fat mass would be in the child. Such findings would support the developmental overnutrition hypothesis, which states that overeating during key developmental times has an influence on the offspring. The results of the study found that (a) prepregnancy material weight (BMI) was positively associated with the child's fat mass and (b) the relationship between maternal BMI and the child's fat mass was stronger than the relationship between paternal BMI and the child's fat mass. This study reported on the *relationships* between variables. If you are drawing conclusions from these results, what caution should you have in mind?

Answers

1. In looking at the distribution of scores on the exam, we would argue that the mean would not be the most representative number. If the class was only given the mean of 77, it might be inferred that most students earned a C. However, this is not the case at all. By providing students with the mode of 92 and the median of 86, students get a better picture of the distribution of scores. It is actually the case that most students did well on the exam, with a few low scores pulling down the mean. This example relates back to the section on drawing conclusions from descriptive statistics. Our purpose in using this example was to illustrate how knowing if a distribution is skewed or normal aids in interpreting the scores.

2. If a researcher is conducting multiple t-tests, the alpha level should be more conservative. In this situation, the researcher should take .05 and divide by 7, equaling the new alpha level of .007. This procedure, known as the Bonferroni correction, reduces the likelihood of committing a Type I Error or rejecting the null hypothesis when it is in fact true.

3. The results from Lawlor et al. (2008) on maternal BMI and child fat mass are very interesting and have implications for the biological basis of weight. However, the inferential statistics used only provides information on relationships. Thus, you should not infer cause and effect.

Statistical Significance versus Practical Significance

At the beginning of this chapter, we discussed when to reject the null hypothesis and when to fail to reject the null hypothesis. When we reject the null hypothesis, we are saying that the results are statistically significant and the differences observed are not due to chance or error. It is important now to bring up the distinction between statistical significance and practical significance. This is because not all results that are found to be statistically significant are of practical use in the everyday world. For example, you could survey 1,000 undergraduate students and ask them if they preferred to have class at 8:00 am or 8:15 am. You might find that students significantly prefer starting class at 8:15 over 8:00. However, the practical use of this information for a university might be limited. Class might need to start on the hour so as not to interfere with the schedule for the remainder of the day. But, does the fact that students prefer to start class 15 minutes later really warrant a change? Many reviewers and editors are aware of the fact that large sample sizes can produce significant results despite relatively small differences between groups. Therefore, it is becoming a common practice for authors to explain in the discussion section of a manuscript how the results are of practical use in the field of psychology. For that reason, obtaining statistically significant results might not be the end goal after all. The ideal combination would be to find significant results that contribute to the field in a meaningful way.

Section Summary

- *Descriptive statistics* are used by researchers to describe data sets (pp. 244–246).
  - *Measures of central tendency* are numbers that represent the scores in the data set (p. 244).
    - The *mean* is the average of the scores in the data set (p. 244).
    - The *median* is the number in the middle of a data set (p. 244).
    - The *mode* is the most frequently occurring number in a data set (p. 244).
  - A *normal distribution* of scores occurs when most scores cluster around the middle, and few, but equal, numbers cluster on the extremes (pp. 244–245).
  - A *skewed distribution* is one in which the most frequently occurring scores are not in the middle (pp. 244–246).
- *Inferential statistics* are used so that inferences can be drawn about a population from the sample used (pp. 246–249).
  - There are three types of t-tests (p. 247).
    - The *one-sample t-test* is used to determine when a mean is significantly different from a constant (p. 247).
    - The *dependent t-test* is used to determine if the mean difference between pairs is significantly different from zero (p. 247).
    - The *independent t-test* evaluates whether or not two means are significantly different from one another (p. 247).

- *Bonferroni correction* can be used when conducting multiple statistical tests. The correction is used to limit the possibility of making a Type I Error (p. 247).
  - *Analysis of variance (ANOVA)* is used when you have an independent variable with three or more levels or when you have multiple independent variables (pp. 247–248).
- In the field of psychology, many times researchers achieve results which are statistically significant. However, researchers should also be aware of the practical significance their results carry. In other words, does a statistically significant result have a practical impact on society (p. 250)?

Are You Equipped Now?

Researchers Feldman, Weller, Zagoory-Sharon, and Levine (2007) conducted a study to examine the relationship between a mother's oxytocin levels during and after pregnancy with bonding behaviors. The participants were 62 women. The women participated in three assessments. The first assessment was during the first trimester, the second assessment was during the third trimester, and the final assessment was postpartum (after birth). At each session, blood was taken to measure oxytocin levels. At the final session, the women (a) completed questionnaires, (b) were videotaped during a 15-minute time period interacting with the infants, and (c) were interviewed for at least half an hour regarding thoughts and behaviors. The researchers wanted to know if oxytocin levels were related to maternal behaviors (e.g., gaze, affect, touch, and vocalization), attachment, and checking behaviors. To begin, the researchers found no relationship between oxytocin levels and demographic factors. However, there were correlations between oxytocin levels in early pregnancy and maternal behaviors ($p < .05$), attachment ($p < .05$), and checking behaviors ($p < .01$) and there were correlations between oxytocin levels postpartum and maternal behaviors ($p < .05$), attachment ($p < .01$), and checking behaviors ($p < .001$). For the purposes of this activity, we briefly summarized Feldman et al.'s work. If you are interested in learning more about this study, we encourage you to read the full article. From the brief information we provided on the study, we would like you to apply the information that you learned in this chapter. Take a look at the following questions.

Questions

1. The researchers found no relationship between oxytocin levels and demographic factors. In this situation, would the researchers reject the null hypothesis or fail to reject the null hypothesis?

2. The researchers found correlations between oxytocin levels in early pregnancy and maternal behaviors ($p < .05$), attachment ($p < .05$), and checking behaviors ($p < .01$) and there were correlations between oxytocin levels postpartum and maternal behaviors ($p < .05$), attachment ($p < .01$), and checking behaviors ($p < .001$). In this situation, would the researchers reject the null hypothesis or fail to reject the null hypothesis?

3. Why might the researchers want to replicate their findings? (Hint: be sure to address what replication prevents in your answer.)

4. In this article, the researchers provide results from inferential statistics on the relationship among variables. Thinking back to the section on drawing conclusions

from inferential statistics, what is one factor that you want to consider when interpreting correlational findings?

   5. From Question 2, we see that the researchers found results of statistical significance. However, do you think the results were of practical significance? Why or why not?

Answers

   1. In this situation, you would fail to reject the null hypothesis. This is because there were no differences in oxytocin levels based on demographic factors.

   2. For the relationship between oxytocin levels and bonding behaviors, the researchers would reject the null hypothesis. This is because the obtained p-value for each relationship was less than the conventional level of .05. This indicates that the results are so extreme they are unlikely due to chance.

   3. The researchers might want to replicate the findings in order to reduce the chance of making a decision error. If the results were consistent upon replication, the researchers could be confident that a Type I or Type II error was not committed.

   4. You would want to be sure to not infer cause and effect. Rather, you can only conclude that these variables are related.

   5. We believe that this study is of practical significance. In the discussion section of the manuscript, the authors argue several compelling reasons as to why the results help to advance our understanding of parent–infant bonding behaviors. We encourage you to read what they had to say!

Chapter Summary

   ◆ Upon the completion of a study, a researcher has one of two choices to make: rejecting the null hypothesis or failing to reject the null hypothesis (pp. 238–241).
      ◆ *Rejecting the null hypothesis* indicates that there is a statistically significant difference between the means of the groups in the study (pp. 238–240).
      ◆ *Failing to reject the null hypothesis* indicates that there is not a statistically significant difference between the means of the groups in the study and that the means are equal (pp. 238–240).
   ◆ The *level of significance* is indicated by the alpha level (α) (p. 240).
      ◆ Traditionally, psychologists accept an alpha level of .05 (p. 240).
      ◆ If the obtained p-value in a study is less than the conventional alpha level, we reject the null hypothesis (p. 240).
      ◆ If the obtained p-value in a study is more than the conventional alpha level, we fail to reject the null hypothesis (p. 240).
   ◆ When conducting research, there are four possible decision outcomes. The first two are to reject the null or to fail to reject the null hypothesis. The other two are types of errors (pp. 241–243):
      ◆ A *Type I Error* occurs when a researcher rejects the null when the null is in fact true (pp. 241–243).
      ◆ A *Type II Error* occurs when a researcher fails to reject the null even though the null hypothesis is false (pp. 242–243).

- When evaluating the results, researchers either use descriptive or inferential statistics (pp. 244–250).
- *Descriptive statistics* are used by researchers to describe data sets (pp. 244–246).
  - *Measures of central tendency* are numbers that represent the scores in the data set (p. 244).
    - The *mean* is the average of the scores in the data set (p. 244).
    - The *median* is the number in the middle of a data set (p. 244).
    - The *mode* is the most frequently occurring number in a data set (p. 244).
  - A *normal distribution* of scores occurs when most scores cluster around the middle, and few, but equal, numbers cluster on the extremes (pp. 244–245).
  - A *skewed distribution* is one in which the most frequently occurring scores are not in the middle (pp. 245–246).
- *Inferential statistics* are used so that inferences can be drawn about a population from the sample used (pp. 246–249).
  - There are three types of t-tests (p. 247).
    - The *one-sample t-test* is used to determine when a mean is significantly different from a constant (p. 247).
    - The *dependent t-test* is used to determine if the mean difference between pairs is significantly different from zero (p. 247).
    - The *independent t-test* evaluates whether or not means from two different groups are significantly different from one another (p. 247).
  - *Bonferroni correction* can be used when conducting multiple statistical tests. The correction is used to limit the possibility of making a Type I Error (p. 247).
  - *Analysis of Variance (ANOVA)* is used when you have an independent variable with three or more levels or when you have multiple independent variables (pp. 247–248).
- In the field of psychology, many times researchers achieve results which are statistically significant. However, researchers should also be aware of the *practical significance* their results carry. In other words, does a statistically significant result have a practical impact on society (p. 250)?

APA Learning Goals Linkage

- **Goal 2.** *Research Methods in Psychology*
  Students will understand and apply basic research methods in psychology, including research design, data analysis, and interpretation.

  Sections Covered: Are You Equipped?, Examining the Results—Rejecting the Null or Failing to Reject the Null Hypothesis, Type I and Type II Errors, Introduction to Interpreting Statistical Results, Drawing

(Continued)

(*Continued*)

Conclusions from Descriptive Statistics, Drawing Conclusions from Inferential Statistics, Statistical Significance versus Practical Significance

Explanation of the Goal: While reading this chapter, we have introduced many basic statistical results and discussed ways to interpret these results. Furthermore, we have demonstrated how to evaluate the appropriateness of conclusions derived from psychological research, as was evident in the Are You Equipped? section on gift giving with new acquaintances. Lastly, time was spent distinguishing between statistical significance and practical significance. This is especially important when interpreting results that might be statistically significant but of little practical importance (e.g., preference for class time).

- **Goal 3.** *Critical Thinking Skills in Psychology*
Students will respect and use critical and creative thinking, skeptical inquiry, and, when possible, the scientific approach to solve problems related to behavior and mental processes.

Sections Covered: Are You Equipped?, Examining the Results—Rejecting the Null or Failing to Reject the Null Hypothesis, Heinz Ketchup Example Revisited, Drawing Conclusions from Descriptive Statistics, Are You Equipped Now?

Explanation of the Goal: Throughout Chapter 14, we have worked on approaching problems effectively by generating multiple solutions. For example, we generated both null and research hypotheses in the You Try It! section on the Heinz Ketchup Example Revisited. We also used critical thinking skills when presenting hypothetical outcomes for a study. Specifically, we generated possible research outcomes when discussing types of errors. Likewise, we have worked on using scientific evidence to resolve conflicting claims. This was illustrated in the examples of gift-giving behaviors, gender differences in caffeine consumption, and mother's weight and child's fat mass.

- **Goal 4.** *Application of Psychology*
Students will understand and apply psychological principles to personal, social, and organizational issues.

Sections Covered: Heinz Ketchup Example Revisited, Type I and Type II Errors, Drawing Conclusions from Inferential Statistics, Are You Equipped Now?

Explanation of the Goal: As we concluded our discussion of hypothesis testing and introduced the topic of interpreting statistical results, many examples relating to Goal 4 were included. Specifically, this chapter looked at the impact of ketchup color on the everyday lives of

(*Continued*)

(Continued)

consumers, the decisions of juries to understand errors in hypothesis testing, and the relationship between mother's weight and child's fat mass in drawing conclusions about correlational findings. Additionally, the follow-up review actively engaged you to think about how applying psychological principles can facilitate your understanding of behaviors and thoughts at the biological level.

• **Goal 7. *Communication Skills***

Students will be able to communicate effectively in a variety of formats.

Sections Covered: Examining the Results—Rejecting the Null or Failing to Reject the Null Hypothesis, Type I and Type II Errors, Introduction to Interpreting Statistical Results, Drawing Conclusions from Descriptive Statistics, Drawing Conclusions from Inferential Statistics

Explanation of the Goal: For this goal, we have shown how to apply basic mathematical concepts and operations to support measurement strategies. This can first be seen in our discussion of descriptive statistics. Descriptive statistics are used to describe data sets. Measures of central tendency such as the mean, median, and mode are common ways to describe research findings. From this information, you can draw conclusions about the shape of the distribution. Second, inferential statistics can be used to draw inferences about a population from the sample used. T-tests and ANOVAs are examples of some basic inferential statistics presented in this chapter. Coverage of this information is needed so that you can accurately communicate your research findings to others and to allow you to effectively interpret and draw conclusions presented by other researchers.

CHAPTER

15

APA Style: Sixth Edition

Are You Equipped?

Two of our former undergraduate students provided us with the reference list below used for a brief report on sleep. The students purposefully made some APA-style mistakes. Can you spot them?

Buboltz, W. C., Loveland, J., Jenkins, S. M., Brown, F., Soper, B., Hodges, J., & (2006). College Student Sleep: Relationship to Health and Academic Performance. College students: Mental *health* and coping strategies. Landow, Mery V. (Ed.); pp. 1–39. Hauppauge, NY, US: Nova Science Publishers, 2006.

Harrison, Y., & Horne, J. (2000). The impact of sleep deprivation on decision making: A review. *Journal of Experimental Psychology: Applied, 6 (3)*, 236–249.

Horne, J.A., Anderson, N.R., & Wilkinson, R. T. (1983). Effects of sleep deprivation on signal detection measures of vigilance: implications for sleep function. *Journal of Sleep Research & Sleep Medicine, 6* (4), 347–358.

Kellah, E. (2006).The Relationship of University Students' sleep habits and academic motivation. *NASPA Journal, 43(3)*, 432–445.

Epstein, Lawrence, and Mardon, Steven. (2007). The Harvard Medical School Guide to a Good Night's Sleep. McGraw-Hill, New York, NY.

Schenck, Carlos, H. (208). Sleep: A Groundbreaking Guide to the Mysteries, the Problems, and the Solutions. Penguin Group New York, NY.

Amschler, D., & McKenzie, J. (2005). Elementary Students' Sleep Habits and Teacher Observations of Sleep-Related Problems. *Journal for School Health*, *75, Issue 2*, 50–56.

In this chapter, we are going to talk about the standard format for writing within the field of psychology known as APA style. If you were not able to spot all the mistakes in the example above, you will be able to do so after reading this chapter. (We would like to thank Sabrina and Jorge for purposely formatting a reference section with mistakes for this introduction!)

As you go through this chapter, we also want you to keep in mind how the material relates to the American Psychological Association's goals for psychology majors. Specifically, this chapter will address the following goals:

◆ **Goal 2. Research Methods in Psychology**
Students will understand and apply basic research methods in psychology, including research design, data analysis, and interpretation.

◆ **Goal 3. Critical Thinking Skills in Psychology**
Students will respect and use critical and creative thinking, skeptical inquiry, and, when possible, the scientific approach to solve problems related to behavior and mental processes.

◆ **Goal 5. Values in Psychology**
Students will be able to weigh evidence, tolerate ambiguity, act ethically, and reflect other values that are the underpinnings of psychology as a discipline.

◆ **Goal 6. Information and Technological Literacy**
Students will demonstrate information competence and the ability to use computers and other technology for many purposes.

◆ **Goal 7. Communication Skills**
Students will be able to communicate effectively in a variety of formats.

◆ **Goal 8. Sociocultural and International Awareness**
Students will recognize, understand, and respect the complexity of sociocultural and international diversity.

◆ **Goal 10. Career Planning and Development**
Students will emerge from the major with realistic ideas about how to implement their psychological knowledge, skills, and values in occupational pursuits in a variety of settings.

AN INTRODUCTION TO APA-STYLE WRITING

Writing within the field of psychology follows a standard form developed by the American Psychological Association (APA). APA created this format so that all authors could communicate their findings in the same manner. Think of how difficult it would be if each individual author in the field of psychology could decide the format of his or her manuscript! It can seem like a chore to learn the fine details of APA-style (now on the sixth edition). However, we encourage you to hang in there. Once you learn the general format, you will appreciate how it simplifies communication for the field. This chapter is divided into two sections. The first section will cover the basic parts of a manuscript and the formatting for each. The second section will be devoted to referencing the works of others in APA-style.

Most bodies of work in APA-style contain the following: a title page, an abstract, an introduction to the topic, a method section describing the research methods used, a results section containing the findings, a discussion of the work, and a reference list. In this chapter, we are going to discuss each of these sections briefly. For a detailed explanation, be sure to consult the *Publication Manual of the American Psychological Association*, *6th Edition* [American Psychological Association (APA), 2010]. For APA-style, the preferred typeface is Times New Roman and the font size is 12 point. The standard margins are 1 inch all around and double spacing should be used throughout.

The Title Page

The first page of a manuscript is the title page. You can see an example of a title page in the appendix. You will notice that the title page has a title, a running head, an author byline, institutional affiliation of the author(s), author note (if desired), and page numbers beginning with 1. Below is a summary of each part of the title page:

- In the header of the title page, you will find the running head and page numbers. The running head is contained in the header, aligned left, and appears on all pages of the manuscript. The running head is a shortened version of the title and should be no more than 50 characters. The page number appears in the header and is aligned right. The title page is page number 1.

- The title should provide readers with the main topic of the manuscript. It is recommended that titles contain meaningful terms, as it will be shortened for the running head, and be no more than 12 words. The title is centered in the upper half of the page in uppercase and lowercase letters.

- On the line immediately following the title, you center the name of the author(s). The preferred format is first name, middle initial(s), and last name.

- On the following line, you list the affiliation of the author(s). The affiliation is typically a college or university.

- An author note can also be included on the title page. An author note has many purposes but the main purposes are to provide readers with the contact information for one of the authors and provide acknowledgments.

Abstract

Although we are discussing the abstract early on in this chapter because it appears after the title page, your abstract should be the last part of the manuscript that you write. You should write the abstract last because it provides a summary or overview of the entire manuscript. Most people will read the abstract through an electronic database to decide if they want to read the entire manuscript. Therefore, your abstract should be well written and accurately convey the contents of the manuscript. A good abstract is written as a report, stating the facts. In other words, an evaluative tone is not used. If your abstract is for an experiment or study, it should summarize your research question, participants, methods, results, and conclusions. Abstracts range in length from 150 to 250 words, so it is important to concisely summarize your work.

You should begin the abstract on a new page (immediately following the title page). Abstracts will have a header. In the header, the running head is aligned left and page number 2 is aligned right. The title, **Abstract**, is centered on the top line and written in uppercase and lowercase letters using boldface type. The abstract is written as one paragraph, with no indentation.

Introduction

The purpose of the introduction in a manuscript is to introduce the topic and place the topic in the context of research within the field. In short, the introduction provides readers with background information on a topic that they may or may not know. Introductions typically follow an inverted triangle format. See Figure 15.1 for an illustration. Introductions follow the inverted triangle by starting off broad in scope and becoming narrower as they proceed.

FIGURE 15.1 The Inverted Triangle Represents the Way an Introduction should be Written.

Introductions start with broad knowledge on the topics of interests. After introducing the reader to the topics of interest, the introduction moves on to discuss previous literature in the area. At this stage of the introduction, the triangle (below) begins to narrow. The introduction is now more focused and provides a concise overview of previous work. There are different ways that you can summarize this previous work. For example, you could present the research chronologically, starting with the earliest publication date. However, the best way to structure this section is by topic. In other words, structure this part of the introduction so that conceptually similar works are presented together. This allows the reader to know what work has been conducted in a particular area as well as the findings. Next, you present the reader with the specific problems with previous research or explain why additional research is needed. This information provides a transition for the reader. The transition allows the reader to begin thinking about what research could be conducted next. Finally, you end the introduction with the purpose of your study, your hypotheses, and a brief overview of the methods. If you have done a good job on the introduction, the reader will understand why your study is needed and the reasoning behind your hypotheses. If your introduction lacks smooth transitions or fails to "set up" the purpose of your study, readers can feel confused or feel that the study does not significantly add to the body of knowledge on the topic. One strategy that we recommend is to read your introduction and stop at the section immediately before the purpose. At this point, ask yourself if your study is the next logical extension to the previous work and if findings from your study would add a needed piece of information to the puzzle.

TABLE 15.1   Writing Your Introduction.
Outline of Introduction
1. Introduction of Topic

2. Review of Previous Findings on Topic
    a. Chronological Order
    b. Topical Order

3. Explanation of Why Additional Research Is Needed
    a. Problems/Inconsistencies
    b. Gaps in the Literature
    c. Tensions

4. Current Study
    a. How It Solves or Addresses Issues Brought Up
        in #3
    b. Hypothesis(es)
    c. Overview of Methods

Introductions are placed on a new page, with a running head. Specifically, introductions are placed on page 3 of a manuscript (the title page is number 1 and the abstract is number 2). You begin the introduction with the title of the manuscript on the top line. The title should be centered and use uppercase and lowercase letters. The text of the introduction begins on the next line and new paragraphs are indented. The remaining sections of the manuscript (method, results, discussion) follow the introduction but do not require a page break. When writing the introduction, be sure to use either past tense (e.g., "Raacke found that . . .") or present perfect tense (e.g., "Previous researchers have found that . . ."). Transitional devices keep the flow of the introduction smooth. These transitions can link statements (then, since), show cause and effect (therefore), or serve as addition links (moreover).

Method

The purpose of the method section is to provide readers with information on how you conducted your study. In fact, enough detail should be provided so that a reader could replicate (reproduce) your study if he or she desired. Besides replication purposes, providing details allows the reader to identify strengths or weaknesses in your methodology. The method section has two subsections, which describe the participants and the materials/procedure used. The first subsection, participants, provides the reader with information on the sample of participants. This includes sex, age, race/ethnicity, the total number of participants, the total number of participants in each condition, and, if available, information on sexual orientation and socioeconomic status. This description of the sample is needed so the reader can draw generalizations about the population of interest. The second section, materials and procedures, provides the reader with specific information on the materials needed to carry out the experiment and step by step instructions for the procedure. Although you need to describe materials such as the survey given to participants or equipment used to collect data, information on the computer software to analyze the data is not needed. When describing the procedure, be sure to include:

- The experimental design used (e.g., identify variables and type of design).
- Information on how the participants were selected.
- Information on how the participants were assigned to conditions.
- A description of any controls features used such as counterbalancing.
- A paraphrased version of the instructions given to participants.
- A step-by-step description of what participants did.

The method section is written in past tense or present perfect tense as is the introduction. When writing the method section, use a personal pronoun over the third person. For example, "we had participants complete the three surveys" is preferred over "the authors had participants complete three surveys." The method section utilizes many of APA's stylistic rules. This is because the method section contains numbers and the identification of groups of people. In general, you should use numerals for numbers 10 or higher and write out (express in words) number under 10. Anytime a number begins a sentence, it is written out. APA provides guidelines for the most appropriate terminology when referring to groups of people. For example, terms such as *lesbian, gay men*, and *bisexual individuals* are preferred over the term *homosexual. Blacks* and *African Americans* are currently both approved terms. However, do not use hyphens for multiword names. Treat *black* and *white* as proper nouns and provide parallel labels (*Whites* and *Blacks*, not *Whites* and *African Americans*). Other acceptable terms include *American Indian, Native American, and Native North American.*

The word **Method** is centered on the page using boldface and written in uppercase and lowercase letters. The method section begins wherever the introduction ends. Thus, you do not begin the method sections on a new page. The subsections of the method section, participants and materials/procedures, are aligned left in boldface and written in uppercase and lowercase letters.

Results

The results section allows you to present the findings of your study to readers. You present these findings by providing information on the descriptive and inferential statistics that were utilized. The results section also includes references to tables and figures that aid readers in understanding the findings. However, the results section is not the appropriate section to evaluate your hypotheses. This is saved for the discussion section. The results section begins with the word **Results** in boldface centered on the page, written in uppercase and lowercase letters.

We realize that our discussion of the results section is very brief. However, depending on the instructor of your course, you may or may not cover statistics. If you do cover statistics and need to know how to reference specific procedures in APA-style, consult the *Publication Manual* (APA, 2010).

Discussion

After the results section, you will need to center the word **Discussion** in boldface using uppercase and lowercase letters. Do not begin a new page. When writing the discussion section, you are encouraged to use present tense. Every discussion section has standard components. First, you should briefly restate the purpose of your study. Even though this information is presented at the beginning of the manuscript, it is helpful to remind the reader. Second, you evaluate your hypotheses. In other words, discuss if your hypotheses were supported or not supported. If the hypotheses were not supported, provide some insights as to why this unexpected outcome may have occurred. Third, relate your findings to previous research in the field. This comparison usually involves work cited in the introduction section of your manuscript. However, it is acceptable to bring in new references that are relevant to your findings. A crucial component to the discussion section involves addressing potential limitations and shortcoming of your study. It may seem strange that you would want to draw the reader's attention to these issues. However, any skilled reader would pick up on the limitations that you mention and it is a good practice to acknowledge your own weaknesses. Remember that no study is ever perfect, so there will always be something for you to discuss. At the end of your discussion, present readers with information regarding why your findings are important to the field (practical significance) and provide suggestions for future research.

Tables and Figures

Tables and figures are often used to simplify results that would be difficult to present in the results sections. Keep in mind that tables and figures should not duplicate information already given in the manuscript. The results section should instruct the reader to look at the tables and/or figure and also draw the reader's attention to the important information.

YOU TRY IT!

Questions
1. Why is it beneficial for the field of psychology (and most social sciences) to have an agreed-upon formatting style?
2. What are the main parts of a manuscript?
3. Why/how do you use an inverted triangle within the introduction?
4. What are the two subsections of the method section?
5. What are some important factors that your discussion section should address?

Answers
1. First, it is beneficial for the field of psychology and other social sciences to have an agreed-upon formatting style because it brings simplicity to reading the works of others. Second, by using a standard style, readers know what to expect and where to look for information.

2. The main parts of a manuscript are as follows: title page, abstract, introduction, method, results, discussion, references, and tables/figures.

3. It is helpful to use an inverted triangle approach when writing an introduction because it allows the reader to see why the study was conducted. This approach starts off broad and introduces readers to the general topics. Next, the introduction
(Continued)

(Continued)

> begins to narrow in focus by presenting the reader with a summary of previous research in the area. Finally, the introduction specifies how the current study will contribute to the literature and the predicted hypotheses.
>
> 4. The two subsections of the method section are the participants and the materials/procedure.
>
> 5. Some important factors that your discussion section should address are evaluation of hypotheses, relation of results to previous research, limitations of current design, and future research ideas.

Section Summary

- There are eight main sections to an APA-style manuscript (pp. 258–264):
    - Title page
        - A title page includes a running head, page number, title, author name(s), and affiliations (p. 259).
    - Abstract
        - A 150–250-word summarization of your entire article in block format (pp. 259–260).
    - Introduction
        - The purpose of the introduction in a manuscript is to introduce the topic and place the topic in the context of research within the field (pp. 260–261).
        - An introduction follows an inverted triangle format by starting off broad in scope and becoming narrower (pp. 260–261).
    - Method
        - The purpose of the method section is to provide readers with information on how you conducted your study (pp. 261–262).
        - The method section includes information on the experimental design used, how the participants were selected, how the participants were assigned to conditions, a description of any controls features used such as counterbalancing, a paraphrased version of the instructions given to participants, and a step-by-step description of what participants did (pp. 261–262).
    - Results
        - The results section allows you to present the findings of your study to readers. You present these findings by providing information on the descriptive and inferential statistics that were utilized (p. 262).
    - Discussion
        - The discussion section is the part of your manuscript where you restate the purposes of your study, evaluate your hypotheses, relate the results to prior research, and discuss any limitations to your work (pp. 262–263).

- References
  - The reference section is a list of all the work cited in the manuscript (p. 258).
- Tables and figures
  - Tables and/or figures are located after the reference section and are a visual representation of results not reported in the manuscript (p. 263).

REFERENCES

APA-style has many details regarding how to reference the works of others. In the remainder of this chapter, we will discuss how to cite a reference within the body of a manuscript and in the reference list. When you are writing a paper in psychology, it is very important to reference the sources that contributed to your work. This practice is important because it gives credit to previous authors for their contributions. When writing an introduction for example, the bulk of the writing should be cited from sources. Only smaller portions of the introduction such as transitions and general statements of fact will not have references. This may sound strange. You might initially think that the bulk of your paper should be your own thoughts on an issue. However, the standard form in the field is to begin papers with a summary of what others have done on a given topic. Once you become accustomed to it, you will see how your own writing style comes through in the way in which you organize and talk about the work of others. Besides, discussing someone else's work or ideas without referencing it is considered plagiarism. Here are a few general guidelines about referencing within the text (i.e., within the body of the manuscript) and in a reference list (found at the end of a document):

- References cited in the text must appear in the reference list.
- References cited in the reference list must appear in the text.
- Only include sources that you actually used in the text in the reference section. This is different from bibliographies. Bibliographies can include suggestions for further reading on a topic.

Within-Text Citations

Nearly all of your references within the text will occur without quotes. The limited use of quotes is discussed in the next section. Most often you will be explaining in your own words the ideas, theories, and research findings of others. Even though you are communicating this information using your own words, it is still necessary to cite the original source. There are three standard ways for citing a reference within the text of a manuscript. First, you can provide the last name of the author as part of the text, with the date of publication in parenthesis. A second option would be to give the author's last name, followed by a comma, and date of publication in parentheses at the end of a sentence or paragraph. A final approach is to give the date and author's name as part of the text.

♦ *Example #1*
    Raacke (2009) found that college students . . .

♦ *Example #2*
    It was found that college students study best at night (Raacke, 2009).

♦ *Example #3*
    In 2009, Raacke found that college students . . .

The three examples above illustrate the appropriate form when there is only one author. When there are two authors, you would cite both authors on the first time the reference occurs and any subsequent references. Note that when both authors' last names are given in the text with the date in parentheses as in Example 1, the word "and" is inserted between the authors' last names. However, when the authors' last names and date of publication are given in parentheses as in Example 2, there is an ampersand (&) inserted between the authors' last names.

♦ *Example #1*
    Raacke and Bonds-Raacke (2009) found that college students . . .

♦ *Example #2*
    It was found that college students study best at night (Raacke & Bonds-Raacke, 2009).

♦ *Example #3*
    In 2009, Raacke and Bonds-Raacke found that college students . . .

When you have three to five authors, you should cite all the authors' last names and date of publication on the first citation of the reference. You would apply the same rules as above on using commas, the word "and," and the ampersand.

♦ *Example #1*
    Raacke, Bonds-Raacke, and King (2009) found that college students . . .

♦ *Example #2*
    It was found that college students study best at night (Raacke, Bonds-Raacke, & King, 2009).

♦ *Example #3*
    In 2009, Raacke, Bonds-Raacke, and King found that college students . . .

However, on subsequent references with three to five authors, only the first author's last name is given, followed by *et al.*

    ◆ *Example #1*
        Raacke et al. (2009) found that college students . . .

    ◆ *Example #2*
        It was found that college students study best at night (Raacke
        et al., 2009).

    ◆ *Example #3*
        In 2009, Raacke et al. found that college students . . .

When there are six or more authors, use the first author's last name followed by et al. for the first and all citations. These rules which apply to works by one to six or more authors will generally suffice. However, there are some special circumstances you might find helpful to know about. For example, it is not uncommon for one author to have multiple publications in the same year. To distinguish between the works, you follow the date of publication by the suffixes *a, b, c,* and so on. The suffixes appear in the reference list also (to be discussed in the next section). You assign the suffixes alphabetically by the first letter of the first word of the title. So, the letter *a* should be given to the reference with the first letter in the title that comes first in the alphabet.

    ◆ *Example #1*
        Bonds-Raacke and Raacke (2007a) found that using social net-
        working . . .

    ◆ *Example #2*
        Using social networking sites is related to self-esteem (Bonds-
        Raacke & Raacke, 2007b).

It is also common to cite two or more works within the same parentheses. When doing so, use semicolons to separate the references and list the works alphabetically by the first author's last name.

    ◆ *Example*
        Using social networking sites is related to self-esteem (Bonds-
        Raacke & Raacke, 2007; Burns, 2006; Thomas, 2009).

These two examples are not the only special circumstances that you may encounter when writing a manuscript. You might need to arrange multiple works by the same author with different publication years in parentheses or differentiate in the text authors with the same last name or surname. Therefore, be sure to consult the *Publication Manual* (APA, 2010) when needed.

You will need to use quotations if you decide to replicate work from another author word for word. Keep in mind that direct quoting should be kept to a minimum and should only be used when the original wording could not adequately be expressed in your own words. Be sure that your direct quotes are accurate in content, spelling, and grammar. If you are quoting a source and have fewer than 40 words included, the quotation is included as part of the text. Specifically, the material being quoted is surrounded with double quotation marks. The page number is given in the citation, in addition to author's last name, and date of publication.

> ◆ *Example #1*
>   Bonds-Raacke (2009) stated that "couples taking college courses together reported an increase in satisfaction with college life" (p. 25).
>
> ◆ *Example #2*
>   Results indicated that "couples taking college courses together reported an increase in satisfaction with college life" (Bonds-Raacke, 2009, p. 25).

Longer quotations, 40 or more words, are not included within the text. Rather, a block quotation format is used. This means that you indent the entire quote five spaces from the left and do not use quotation marks. The authors and publication date can either be provided at the end of the quote with the pages numbers (Option 1) or at the beginning (Option 2). Examples are provided below to illustrate each option.

> ◆ *Option 1*
>   The authors acknowledge the issue of the sample:
>
>   This study is not without limitations. To begin, the primary demographics of users were traditional age, first-year college students. It could certainly be the case that the identified dimensions for this sample would not be the same for users of friend networking sites with varying demographics. (Bonds-Raacke & Raacke, 2009, p. 25)
>
> ◆ *Option 2*
>   Bonds-Raacke and Raacke (2009) acknowledge the issue of the sample:
>
>   This study is not without limitations. To begin, the primary demographics of users were traditional age, first-year college students. It could certainly be the case that the identified dimensions for this sample would not be the same for users of friend networking sites with varying demographics. (p. 25)

Reference List

The reference list is found at the end of a manuscript and contains information on all of the sources cited within the text of the manuscript. The purpose of a reference list is to allow readers to locate the original work of the sources you cited.

The reference list should be double-spaced and follow the hanging indent format. Furthermore, the word **References** should be centered in boldface at the top of a new page. The reference list is organized alphabetically by the last names of the first authors. Here are some other general guidelines for alphabetizing the list:

- If two different authors have the same last name, you alphabetize by the initials of the first name.

> Locklear, A. B. (2010).
> Locklear, D. E. (2009).

- As in within-text citations, if the same first author is cited in more than one reference, the references are listed from earliest date of publication, and if the same first author has more than one reference with the same date of publication, suffixes following the date are assigned alphabetically by the first word in the title.

> Hunt, A. B. (1992). Factors that predict academic success.
> Hunt, A. B. (1994a). American Indian academic challenges.
> Hunt, A. B. (1994b). Success rates of college students.

- Remember to only use initials for the first and middle names, as these are never written out in the reference list.

> Bonds-Raacke, J. M. (CORRECT)
> Bonds-Raacke, Jennifer Marie (INCORRECT)

- Prefixes such as *Mc* should be listed alphabetically by the literal spelling.

> McIntry, J. D. (1989).
> Morgan, A. D. (1998).

- If an author has a work published alone and is also the first author of another work with coauthors, the one author published work is listed first (even if multiple author work was published earlier).

> Morgan, A. D. (1998).
> Morgan, A. D., Bonds-Raacke, J.M., & Raacke, J. D. (1997).

- References with the same first author but different second author should be alphabetized by the last name of the second author.

> Morgan, A. D., Bonds-Raacke, J.M., & Smith, J. D. (1997).
> Morgan, A. D., Raacke, J. D., & Thomas, R. P. (1997).

Typical Sources

The *Publication Manual* (APA, 2010) gives a thorough listing of types of sources and the appropriate way of listing them. However, the most commonly cited types of sources are periodicals (i.e., journals, newsletters, and magazines) and books. You can either read journal articles from the original journal or retrieve them through an electronic database, for example in a PDF format.

If you read a journal article from the original journal, the appropriate form is:

> Author, A. A. (xxxx). Title of journal article. *Title of Journal, volume number* (issue number), pp–pp.
>
> Raacke, J. D. (2010). College student perceptions of movies. *College Student Journal, 4* (2), 18–25.

In this example, we want to call your attention to the following elements:

- The first letter of the author's last name and the first and middle initials, are capitalized. The author's last name is followed by a comma with a period after each initial.

- The publication date is given in parentheses and followed by a period.

- For the periodical article title (i.e., title of manuscript), you capitalize only the first word of the title, any proper nouns, and any word appearing after a colon. The title is followed by a period.

- For the periodical title (i.e., title of journal), you capitalize important words in the name of the journal and italicize the name of the periodical.

- The periodical title is followed by a comma and then the volume number of the journal, which is also in italics. If available, the issue number can be added in parentheses but not in italics. The issue number is provided when a new issue of the journal begins with page one instead of continuing to number where the previous issue stopped. Please note that the issue number in the reference above was for example purposes only. Because, page numbers are not continuous from the previous issue for the *College Student Journal*, issue numbers are not included.

- Following either the volume, or the issue number if available, there is a comma.

- The reference ends with the inclusive page numbers of the article and a period.

Note that the same format is used with as many as seven authors. Commas are used to separate authors and to separate last names and initials. An ampersand is placed before the last author.

Raacke, J. D., Bonds-Raacke, J. B., & Davis. S. (2010). College student perceptions of movies. *College Student Journal, 4,* 18–25.

If you read a journal article obtained through an electronic source such as a
PDF form, the format is the same with the addition of a digital object identifier
(DOI) reference at the end. The DOI can be found on the first page of a journal
article. It is most frequently located by the copyright information. It is not
required that you include the retrieval date, unless you believe that the source of
the information may change.

Raacke, J. D., Bonds-Raacke, J. B., & Davis. S. (2010). College student perceptions of movies. *College Student Journal, 4,* 18–25. doi: 10.2000/456

Other frequently used sources are books and book chapters. If you are
citing an entire book, the author is listed, followed by the date of publication,
title of work, location of publisher, and publisher.

Author, X. X. (xxxx). *Title of book.* Location: Publisher.

Harris, R. J. (2009). *A look at media influences.* Manhattan, KS: Kansas State
Press.

In this example, we want to call your attention to the following elements:

- The first letter of the author's last name and the first and middle initials are
  capitalized. The author's last name is followed by a comma with a period
  after each initial.
- The publication date is given in parentheses and followed by a
  period.
- For the book title, capitalize only the first letter of the first word and
  any proper nouns. Place the title in italics and follow the title with a
  period.
- Next, provide the location of the publishers. For within the United States,
  provide the city and state using official U.S. state abbreviations. For outside
  the United States, provide the city and country. After the state or country,
  use a colon.
- Finally, give the name of the publisher. Words such as "Publishers" or
  "Company" do not need to be included.
- Close the element with a period.

If you are referencing a specific chapter within an edited book, use the following format:

> Author, A. B. (xxxx). Title of book chapter. In A. Editor and B. Editor (Eds.), *Title of book* (pp. XX–XX). Location: Publisher.
>
> Bonds-Raacke, J. M. (2006). Gender portrayals in Disney movies. In R. Harris and J. Shanteau (Eds.), *Media portrayals* (pp. 25–40). Manhattan, KS: Kansas State Press.

In this example, we want to call your attention to the following elements:

- The first letter of 3the author's last name and the first and middle initials are capitalized. The author's last name is followed by a comma with a period after each initial.
- The publication date is given in parentheses and followed by a period.
- For the chapter title, capitalize only the first letter of the first word and any proper nouns and follow the title with a period.
- Use the word "In" preceding the editors' names. When listing the editors' names, provide the initial for the first name, followed by a period, and provide the whole last name. Use (Ed.) or (Eds.) followed by a comma.
- Place the title of the book in italics, capitalizing the first letter of the first word and any proper nouns.
- In parentheses, use the abbreviation pp. and provide inclusive page numbers followed by a period. The pages numbers are not in italics.
- Next, provide the location of the publishers. For within the United States, provide the city and state using official U.S. state abbreviations. For outside the United States, provide the city and country. After the state or country, use a colon.
- Finally, give the name of the publisher. Words such as "Publishers" or "Company" do not need to be included.
- Close the element with a period.

Again, we have only provided you with a brief introduction on how to reference materials in the reference list. If you run across a situation that we have not addressed, be sure to look it up. With practice, using the *Publication Manual* (APA, 2010) becomes easy.

YOU TRY IT!

Questions

1. When citing a source within the body of a manuscript, you have three standard options to pick from. The first option is to provide the last name of the author in the text and the date of publication in parenthesis. What are the other two options?

2. When you have three authors, how is the reference cited the first time and on subsequent citations?

3. How do you decide when to use a direct quote within the text and when to use a block quotation format?

(Continued)

4. If an author has a work published alone and is also the first author of another work with coauthors, which work is listed first on the reference page?

5. When referencing a journal, what elements of the reference are in italics?

Answers

1. The other two options for referencing a citation are to (a) give the author's last name, followed by a comma, and date of publication in parenthesis at the end of a sentence and (b) provide both the author's name and date as part of the text.

2. When you have three authors, the last names of all three authors are listed on the first citation. However, on subsequent citations, only the last name of the first author followed by *et al.* is listed.

3. A direct quote is used when there are fewer than 40 words. However, when there are 40 or more words, a block quotation is used.

4. If an author has a work published alone and is also the first author of another work with coauthors, the one author work is listed first (no matter what the publication date).

5. When referencing a journal, the title of the journal and the volume number (not issue number) are in italics.

Section Summary

- Referencing the work or ideas of others is important (p. 265).
  - Within-text citations (pp. 265–268)
    - There are three standard ways for citing a source within the body of a manuscript (p. 266).
    - When you have a source with one or two authors, information on both authors is given at each citation. However, if there are three to five authors, information on all authors is only provided on the first citation. Finally, when there are six or more authors, information is only provided on the first author for all citations (pp. 266–269).
    - Direct quotations should be kept to a minimum and block quotes are used with longer quotes (p. 268).
  - Reference list (pp. 268–269)
    - Reference lists contain information to locate all sources cited in your manuscript (pp. 268–269).
    - Reference lists are organized alphabetically by the last name of the first author (p. 269).
  - Typical sources (pp. 269–272)
    - The most commonly cited sources are periodicals and books (pp. 269–270).
    - Each type of source is cited using a standard format (pp. 270–271).

Are You Equipped Now?

Now that we have covered some of the rules of writing in APA-style, it is time to practice! Go back to the Are You Equipped section at the beginning of this chapter. In that section, two of our students had prepared a reference list and your job was to look for the APA-mistakes. Try this exercise again.

To show you the APA-mistakes, we inserted comments below. We decided that inserting comments might be helpful to you. This is because with technological advances it is not uncommon for reviewers to provide feedback to authors in this manner. Thus, it is helpful to have experience with these tools. We also provided the corrected version so that you can see the final product.

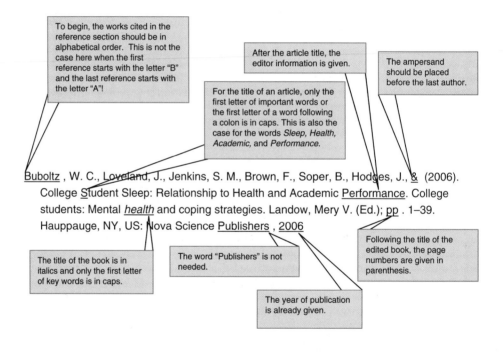

To begin, the works cited in the reference section should be in alphabetical order. This is not the case here when the first reference starts with the letter "B" and the last reference starts with the letter "A"!

After the article title, the editor information is given.

The ampersand should be placed before the last author.

For the title of an article, only the first letter of important words or the first letter of a word following a colon is in caps. This is also the case for the words *Sleep, Health, Academic,* and *Performance.*

Buboltz , W. C., Loveland, J., Jenkins, S. M., Brown, F., Soper, B., Hodges, J., & (2006). College Student Sleep: Relationship to Health and Academic Performance. College students: Mental *health* and coping strategies. Landow, Mery V. (Ed.); pp . 1–39. Hauppauge, NY, US: Nova Science Publishers , 2006

The title of the book is in italics and only the first letter of key words is in caps.

The word "Publishers" is not needed.

Following the title of the edited book, the page numbers are given in parenthesis.

The year of publication is already given.

Harrison, Y., & Horne, J. (2000). The impact of sleep deprivation on decision making: A review. *Journal of Experimental Psychology: Applied, 6 (3)*, 236–249.

The issue number should not be included because page numbers are continuous from previous issue.

There needs to be a space before the letter "A".

Horne, J.A ., Anderson, N.R., & Wilkinson, R. T. (1983). Effects of sleep deprivation on
  signal detection measures of vigilance: implications for sleep function. *Journal of Sleep
  Research & Sleep Medicine, 6* (4), 347–358.

The " I " in "implications" should be in caps because it follows a colon.

In the title of a journal article, only the first letter of important words is in caps. This is also the case for *University* and *Students*.

The issue number should not be included because page numbers are continuous from previous issue.

Kellah, E. (2006).The Relationship of University Students' sleep habits and academic
  motivation. *NASPA Journal, 43 (3),* 432–445.

The issue number should not be included because page numbers are continuous from previous issue.

In the title of a journal article, only the first letter of important words is in caps. This is also the case for the words *Good, Night's,* and *Sleep.*

First names are not used. Only the first letter of the first name is given.

Epstein, Lawrence , and Mardon, Steven. (2007). The Harvard Medical School Guide to a
  Good Night's Sleep. McGraw -Hill, New York, NY.

The location of the publication comes before the name of the publishers.

First names are not used.

The title of the book should be in italics.

Only the first letter of key words is in caps. This also is the case for the words *Guide, Mysteries, Problems,* and *Solutions.*

Schenck, Carlos , H. (208). Sleep : A Groundbreaking Guide to the Mysteries, the Problems,
  and the Solutions. Penguin Group New York, NY

There should be a colon before the location of the publishers and the location should come before the name of the publisher.

Only the first letter of
key words are in caps.

Amschler, D., & McKenzie, J. (2005). <u>Elementary</u> Students' Sleep Habits and Teacher
Observations of Sleep-Related Problems. *Journal for School Health*, *75*, <u>Issue</u> *2*, 50–56.

The issue number is given in parenthesis
following the volume number. The word
"issue" is not used. In addition, the issue
number should not be included because
page numbers are continuous from previous
issue.

Corrected Version:

Amschler, D., & McKenzie, J. (2005). Elementary students' sleep habits and teacher observations of sleep-related problems. *Journal for School Health*, *75*, 50–56.

Buboltz, W. C., Loveland, J., Jenkins, S. M., Brown, F., Soper, B., & Hodges, J. (2006). College student sleep: Relationship to health and academic performance. In M. V. Landow (Ed.), *College students: Mental health and coping strategies* (pp. 1–39). Hauppauge, NY: Nova Science.

Epstein, L., & Mardon, S. (2007). *The Harvard Medical School guide to a good night's sleep.* New York, NY: McGraw-Hill.

Harrison, Y., & Horne, J. (2000). The impact of sleep deprivation on decision making: A review. *Journal of Experimental Psychology: Applied*, *6*, 236–249.

Horne, J. A., Anderson, N. R., & Wilkinson, R. T. (1983). Effects of sleep deprivation on signal detection measures of vigilance: Implications for sleep function. *Journal of Sleep Research & Sleep Medicine*, *6*, 347–358.

Kellah, E. M. (2006). The relationship of university students' sleep habits and academic motivation. *NASPA Journal*, *43*, 432–445.

Schenck, C. H. (2008). *Sleep: A groundbreaking guide to the mysteries, the problems, and the solutions.* New York, NY: Penguin Group.

Chapter Summary

* There are eight main sections to an APA-style manuscript:
  * Title page (pp. 258–264)
    * A title page includes a running head and page number, title, author name(s), and affiliations (p. 259).
  * Abstract
    * A 150–250-word summarization of your entire article in block format (pp. 259–260).

- Introduction
    - The purpose of the introduction in a manuscript is to introduce the topic and place the topic in the context of research within the field (pp. 260–261).
    - An introduction follows an inverted triangle format by starting off broad in scope and becoming narrower (pp. 260–261).
- Method
    - The purpose of the method section is to provide readers with information on how you conducted your study (pp. 261–262).
    - The method section includes information on the experimental design used, how the participants were selected, how the participants were assigned to conditions, a description of any controls features used such as counterbalancing, a paraphrased version of the instructions given to participants, and a step-by-step description of what participants did (pp. 261–262).
- Results
    - The results section allows you to present the findings of your study to readers. You present these findings by providing information on the descriptive and inferential statistics that were utilized (p. 262).
- Discussion
    - The discussion section is the part of your manuscript where you restate the purposes of your study, evaluate your hypotheses, relate the results to prior research, and discuss any limitations to your work (pp. 262–263).
- References
    - The reference section is a list of all the work cited in the manuscript (p. 258).
- Tables and Figures
    - Tables and/or figures are located after the reference section and are a visual representation of results not reported in the manuscript (p. 263).
- Referencing the work or ideas of others is important (p. 265).
    - Within-text citations (pp. 265–268)
        - There are three standard ways for citing a source within the body of a manuscript (p. 266).
        - When you have a source with one or two authors, information on both authors is given at each citation. However, if there are three to five authors, information on all authors is only provided on the first citation. Finally, when there is six or more authors, information is only provided on the first author for all citations (pp. 266–269).
        - Direct quotations should be kept to a minimum and block quotes are used with longer quotes (p. 268).
    - Reference list (pp. 268–269)
        - Reference lists contain information to locate all sources cited in your manuscript (pp. 268–269).

> ◆ References lists are organized alphabetically by the last name of the first author (p. 269).
> ◆ Typical sources (pp. 269–272)
>> ◆ The most commonly cited sources are periodicals and books (pp. 269–270).
>> ◆ Each type of source is cited using a standard format (pp. 270–271).

APA Learning Goals Linkage

◆ **Goal 2. *Research Methods in Psychology***
Students will understand and apply basic research methods in psychology, including research design, data analysis, and interpretation.

Sections Covered: Introduction, Discussion

Explanation of the Goal: As we have shown, when writing an introduction it is important to keep this goal in mind. First, when summarizing research in the introduction section, you must carefully evaluate conclusions drawn from psychological research. These conclusions are used to guide and direct the current research and consequently need to be reported correctly. Second, we showed that in the discussion section of a paper, the conclusions drawn about the methodology and results are important. This is because the discussion section allows you to generalize research findings and mention possible limitations to the study.

◆ **Goal 3. *Critical Thinking Skills in Psychology***
Students will respect and use critical and creative thinking, skeptical inquiry, and, when possible, the scientific approach to solve problems related to behavior and mental processes.

Sections Covered: Introduction, Discussion, Review

Explanation of the Goal: There have been several instances in this chapter where you have engaged in critical thinking. For example, when writing an introduction to a paper, you must identify the components of arguments from various sources. As an author, you need to be able to evaluate the conclusions, assumptions, and gaps in the literature that are related to your chosen topic of research. Furthermore, the use of critical thinking is seen in the discussion of a paper. Specifically, you develop sound arguments based on reasoning and evidence from your methodology and results to make conclusions and inferences about your work.

◆ **Goal 5. *Values in Psychology***
Students will be able to weigh evidence, tolerate ambiguity, act ethically, and reflect other values that are the underpinnings of psychology as a discipline.

Sections Covered: Within-text Citations

(Continued)

(*Continued*)

Explanation of the Goal: The importance of this goal can be seen in our discussion of the use of quotes and perils of plagiarism. Specifically, we wanted you to recognize the necessity of ethical behavior in all aspects of science and practice of psychology and how this relates to writing in the field.

- **Goal 6. *Information and Technological Literacy***
  Students will demonstrate information competence and the ability to use computers and other technology for many purposes.

    Sections Covered: An Introduction to APA-Style Writing, Within-text Citations, Reference List

    Explanation of the Goal: Although the focus of this chapter has been on writing, information and technological literacy were also included. The impact of this goal is evident in the use of software to produce understandable reports, as well as the use of technology to locate appropriate psychological literature. Furthermore, the use of information and technology ethically and responsibly was discussed when looking at quoting, paraphrasing, and citing references correctly.

- **Goal 7. *Communication Skills***
  Students will be able to communicate effectively in a variety of formats.

    Sections Covered: Introduction, Methods, Results, Discussion, Tables and Figures

    Explanation of the Goal: Throughout this chapter we have worked on using APA-style effectively to communicate to an audience. In particular, we have demonstrated the need for professional writing conventions in the use of proper grammar, audience awareness, and formality in writing in APA-style. We have also stressed the importance of exhibiting quantitative literacy and the application of basic mathematical concepts when writing the results section of a manuscript. Lastly, we have stressed the importance of providing rationale for information displayed in tables and figures in a manuscript.

- **Goal 8. *Sociocultural and International Awareness***
  Students will recognize, understand, and respect the complexity of sociocultural and international diversity.

    Sections Covered: Methods

    Explanation of the Goal: As psychology majors, it is important that you recognize sociocultural and international diversity. This awareness is particularly important in the method section of a manuscript. When describing the participants in a study, it is necessary to interact effectively and sensitively with participants of diverse backgrounds, abilities, and cultural perspectives.

(*Continued*)

(Continued)

◆ **Goal 10.** *Career Planning and Development*

Students will emerge from the major with realistic ideas about how to implement their psychological knowledge, skills, and values in occupational pursuits in a variety of settings.

Sections Covered: An Introduction to APA-Style Writing

Explanation of the Goal: This chapter has directly related to this goal. We have demonstrated the importance of APA-style writing to the field of psychology. This understanding of how to communicate within psychology will be expected whether you choose to pursue a graduate-level degree or choose to immediately work in the field after receiving your undergraduate degree. By developing this skill, writing in APA-style, you will be making relevant strides to achieving any career goal related to the field of psychology.

APPENDIX

Sample APA-Style Manuscript

MySpace & Facebook:
Applying the Uses and Gratifications Theory
to Exploring Friend Networking Sites

John Raacke, Ph.D. and
Jennifer Bonds-Raacke, Ph.D.
University of North Carolina at Pembroke

282 Appendix

Abstract

The increased use of the internet as a new tool in
communication has changed the way people interact.
This fact is even more evident in the recent development and use of friend networking sites. However, no
research has evaluated these sites and their impact on
college students. Therefore, the present study was
conducted to evaluate: (a) why people use these friend
networking sites, (b) what are the characteristics
of the typical college user, and (c) what uses and
gratifications are met by using these sites. Results
indicated that the vast majority of college students
are using these friend networking sites for a significant portion of their day for reasons such as making
new friends and locating old friends. Additionally,
both men and women of traditional college age are
equally engaging in this form of online communication
with this result holding true for nearly all ethnic
groups. Finally, results showed that many uses and
gratifications are met by users (e.g., "keeping in
touch with friends"). Results are discussed in light
of the impact that friend networking sites have on
communication and social needs of college students.

Keywords: Facebook, social networking, uses
& gratifications

MySpace & Facebook:
Applying the Uses and Gratifications Theory to Exploring Friend Networking Sites

Although the internet originated in the US, its use has spread quickly throughout the world. In the mid-1990s, the vast majority (nearly 70%) of internet users resided in North America. However by 2005, that number has been estimated to drop to 30% (Lievrouw, 2000). During this time, the internet has grown in its use, the amount of information available, and its online communication capabilities (Harris, 2006). Of late, research has begun to focus on the way the internet is used with regards to relationship building. Research has shown that online communication fosters relationship building, improving communication between parties (Kiesler, 1997) and consistently documents both sex and generational differences in online communication. For example, women are more likely to engage in online communication to maintain personal connections with family, friends, and coworkers, whereas men use online communication for pursuing sexual interests and romance (Weiser, 2000). In terms of generational differences, young adults spend more time using online communication and are more comfortable doing so as compared to older generations (Howard, Rainie, & Jones, 2001; Thayer & Ray, 2006).

Recently, a new means of online communication has emerged with its own set of idiosyncrasies. This new communication style occurs through the use of social networking sites. Social networking sites are virtual places that cater to a specific population in which people of similar interest gather to communicate, share, and discuss ideas. One specific type of social networking site that has seen an increase in activity are friend networking sites, such as MySpace or Facebook (Thayer & Ray, 2006). MySpace and Facebook are two friend networking sites that have become extremely popular among high school and college students. It has been estimated that MySpace has over 20 million registered users, with a sign up rate of over 230,000 users per day (CNN, 2006) and Facebook has been estimated to have approximately 9.5 million users as of September 2006 (FOXNews, 2006). These networking sites have a number of features that allow individuals to communicate with others. For example, these sites allow users to post information about themselves, post pictures, leave messages for friends about upcoming events, and link (i.e., provide a hyperlink) their sites to friends' sites. Therefore, these sites allow for a varying amount of flexibility in communication style (Murphy, 2005).

Surprisingly, peer reviewed published research evaluating the impact of these friend networking sites on behavior is scarce at best. Only one study has evaluated the impact of friend networking sites on users (Valkenburg, Peter, & Schouten, 2006). This study assessed the impact of friend networking sites (i.e., MySpace and Facebook) on adolescent well being. Results showed the more an adolescent frequented friend networking sites, the greater the likelihood their social well being was impacted by information received from that site (by way of posted messages from other users). However, research is needed to

examine these friend networking sites for numerous
reasons. First, research needs to be conducted to
document the prevalence of these websites among
college students. Second, research is needed to
investigate the characteristics of the typical user
of friend networking sites (e.g., sex, age, ethnicity).
Finally, what are the personal and social needs
individuals are obtaining from using these friend
networking sites should be explored.

One way to explore the needs individuals are
meeting by using friend networking sites is to apply
the uses and gratification theory (previously applied
to using the internet in general) (Papacharissi &
Rubin, 2000). The uses and gratifications theory is
concerned with how individuals use the media (in this
case friend networking sites), and therefore it
emphasizes the importance of the individual. There
are criticisms of the uses and gratifications
theory (e.g., failure to integrate separate research
findings) (Anderson & Meyer, 1975; Blumler, 1979;
Carey & Krieling, 1974; Elliot, 1974; Swanson,
1977; Swanson, 1979). However, researchers from the
uses and gratifications camp have responded to
these criticisms by highlighting the recently
developed methodologically oriented line of
research that draws a distinction between concepts
that are antecedents to behavior (e.g., uses and
gratifications sought) and those which are
consequents of behavior (e.g., gratifications
obtained) (Rubin, 2002).

Therefore, the purpose of the present study was
three-fold. One, general information regarding the

prevalence of the use of friend networking sites among college students were obtained. For example, researchers evaluated how much time students spend on these sites and how much effort they put into their accounts. Two, information regarding characteristics about the users of these sites was also obtained (e.g., sex, age, and ethnicity). Finally, the researchers evaluated these friend networking sites using the uses and gratifications theory. Specifically, two of the current directions under this theory, i.e., effectiveness of different media (or content) to meet an individual's needs and the background of the individual (e.g., demographic variables), were evaluated for both uses and gratifications of having a friend networking account, as well as failed uses and gratifications for not having a friend networking account.

Method

Participants

A total of 116 students from a four-year, public East coast university were recruited to participate in this study on "Student Internet Usage" with no mention made of friend networking sites. Of the participants, 53 (45.7%) were men and 63 (54.3%) were women with a mean age of 19.7 years (SD = 3.7). In addition, of the participants, 55 (47.4%) were Caucasian, 25 (21.6%) were African American, 18 (15.5%) were Native American, 10 (8.6%) were Multi-racial, and 8 (6.9%) were of Hispanic origin.

Materials and Procedure

Upon arriving to the study, participants were given a two part packet to complete. The first page contained only one question, "Do you have a MySpace or Facebook account?" Students responded by checking "yes" or "no" to this question. Directions then instructed those participants who had checked "yes" to proceed to page two of the packet (Part I) and those who checked "no" to proceed to page five of the packet (Part II).

Part I of the packet, completed by students having either a MySpace or Facebook account, contained four sections. Section one asked participants general information about their accounts. For example, participants were asked about what type of accounts they had and how long they had these accounts. In section two, participants were asked to indicate what uses and gratifications they obtained from using these friend networking sites, such as "to keep in touch with current friends" and "to make new friends." In section three, participants were asked to predict why other students would not have a MySpace or Facebook account. Sample failed uses and gratifications were "they do not have any friends" and "they do not want to keep in touch." The final section of Part I collected demographic information, including sex, age, and ethnicity.

Part II of the packet, completed by students NOT having either a MySpace or Facebook account, also contained four sections. Section one asked participants general information about why they did not have a MySpace or Facebook account. For example, participants were asked if they had heard of these sites before and if these sites were popular among their friends. Section two had participants indicate failed uses and gratifications for not having a friend networking site. Failed uses and gratifications included: "I have not made many friends yet" and "I feel intimidated." In section three, participants predicted uses and gratifications for individuals having a friend networking account. Specifically, participants were asked to predict why other students would have a MySpace or Facebook account. Sample uses and gratifications were "to keep in touch with friends meet new people" and "to occupy time." The final section of Part II collected demographic information, including sex, age, and ethnicity.

Results

The results section contains two parts, with Part I describing the results pertaining to the participants who indicated that they currently had either a MySpace or Facebook account (which will be referred to as "users") and Part II describing the results pertaining to the participants who did not have an account at either site (which will be referred to as "non-users").

Users: General Information

Of participants surveyed, 101 or 87.1% (49 men and 52 women) indicated having either a MySpace or Facebook account. Of the participants who had accounts, 84 (83.2%) had MySpace accounts, 91 (90.1%)

had Facebook accounts, and 75 (74.3%) had accounts
at both sites. Over 70% of participants had their
accounts for 7 months - 24 months. On an average day,
users reported spending 1.46 hours on their accounts
and 1.10 hours on others' accounts. Users also
reported logging into their account an average of
4.19 times per day. A large percentage of users
(87.1%) made information about themselves (e.g., age,
sex, physical description) available on their website,
while only 51.5% of users set their websites to
private (requiring others to request permission to
view the contents). However, only 12.9% of users
posted their schedules on their accounts. When asked
to rate on a 7-point Likert-scale, with 1 indicating
"never" and 7 indicating "constantly" how often they
changed the appearance of their website and how often
they updated the websites, the means were 2.83 and
2.98 respectively. Participants were also asked how
many friends they had linked to the account. The mean
number of friends linked was 235.51 (the mode and
median were 200). On follow-up questions regarding
friends, 52.5% of participants knew all their friends
linked to their accounts and 79.2% of participants
had additional friends who did not have a MySpace or
Facebook account. In general, participants responded
feeling somewhat happy (mean of 4.81 on 7-point
Likert-scale, with 1 indicating "not at all happy"
and 7 indicating "very happy") and somewhat excited
(mean of 4.56 on a 7-point Likert-scale, with 1
indicating "not at all excited" and 7 indicating
"very excited") about receiving new messages on
their accounts.

Users: Uses and Gratifications

Very popular uses and gratification for having either account included: "to keep in touch with old friends" (96.0%), "to keep in touch with current friends" (91.1%), "to post look at pictures" (57.4%), "to make new friends" (56.4%), and "to locate old friends" (54.5%). Less commonly reported uses and gratifications included: "to learn about events" (33.7%), "to post social functions" (21.8%), "to feel connected" (19.8%), "to share information about yourself" (13.9), "for academic purposes" (10.9%), and "for dating purposes" (7.9%).

When asked to predict why other people did not have either accounts, very popular failed uses and gratification included: "they just have no desire to have an account" (70.3%), "they are too busy" (63.4%), "they think it is a waste of time" (60.4%), "they think it is stupid" (55.4%), "they have no internet access at home" (51.5%), and "they are not good at using technology" (34.7%). Less commonly reported failed uses and gratifications included: "they have not heard of these websites" (17.8%), "they do not want to keep in touch" (15.8%), "they are loners" (10.9%), "they do not want to conform" (7.9%), "they are not cool" (7.9%), "they do not have any friends" (7.9%), "they feel intimidated" (5.9%), and "they think others would not be interested in their accounts" (5.0%).

Users: Sex Differences

First, a MANOVA was conducted to determine the effect of sex of participant on the 7 interval

dependent variables related to general account
information. The 7 dependent variables were: hours
per day on your account, hours per day on others
account, number of times per day logging into your
account, days per week logging into account, changing
appearance of account, updating account, and number
of friends linked to account. Results indicated that
sex significantly affected the combined dependent
variables, Pillai's Trace = .27, F (7, 86) = 4.43,
p < .001, η^2 = .27, power = .99. Univariate ANOVAs
were conducted as follow-up tests. ANOVA results
indicated that: number of times per day logging into
your account significantly differed by sex [F (1, 92)
= 4.04, p < .05, η^2 = .04, power = .51] with men
logging into their accounts more frequently than
women (5.00 times per day versus 3.45); how often
they changed the appearance of the website significantly differed by sex [F (1, 92) = 9.29, p < .01,
η^2 = .09, power = .85] with women changing the
appearance more often than men (3.38 on a 7-point
Likert-scale versus 2.26); and number of friends
linked to account significantly differed by sex
[F (1, 92) = 5.18, p < .05, η^2 = .05, power = .62]
with men reporting more friends linked to account
than women (280.02 versus 193.28). Additionally,
with regard to general account information, a series
of a two-way contingency table analyses was conducted
to evaluate whether men or women were more likely to:
make personal information available, make schedules
available, set website to private, and know friends
linked to the account. For each analysis, the two
variables were sex of participant (i.e., men and

women) and level of agreement with the statement
(i.e., yes and no). Results indicated that
women (63.5%) were significantly more likely than
men (38.8%) to set their website to private,
χ^2 (1, N=101) = 6.16, p < .05.

Second, a series of a two-way contingency table
analyses was conducted to evaluate whether men or
women were more likely to engage in each of the uses
and gratifications for having an account. The 11
dependent variables were: to keep in touch with
current friends, to keep in touch with old friends,
to make new friends, to locate old friends, for dating
purposes, to feel connected, to learn about events, to
share information about yourself, to post / look at
pictures, for academic purposes, and to post social
functions. For each analysis, the two variables were
sex of participant (i.e., men and women) and level of
agreement with the statement (i.e., yes and no).
Results indicated that men (16.3%) were significantly
more like than women (0.0%) to use the friend
networking sites for dating purposes [χ^2 (1, N=101) =
9.22, p < .01] and men (44.9%) were significantly more
likely than women (23.1%) to use the friend networking
sites to learn about events [χ^2 (1, N=101) = 5.38,
p < .05].

Third, a series of a two-way contingency table
analyses was conducted to evaluate whether men or
women were more likely to select failed uses and
gratifications as reasons why others did not use
friend networking sites. The 14 dependent variables
were: they have not heard of these websites, they do
not have internet access at home, they are not good

at using technology, they are too busy, they do
not have any friends, they do not want to keep in
touch, they are "loners," they think it is stupid,
they are not cool, they feel intimated, they just
have no desire to have an account, they do not want
to conform, they think it is a waste of time, and
they think others would not be interested in their
accounts. For each analysis, the two variables were
sex of participant (i.e., men and women) and level
of agreement with the statement (i.e., yes and no).
Results indicated men (30.6%) were significantly
more likely than women (5.8%) to select that others
had not heard of these websites as a failed use and
gratification [χ^2 (1, N=101) = 10.63, p < .001];
women (75.0%) were significantly more likely than
men (51.0%) to select that others are too busy as
a failed use and gratification [χ^2 (1, N=101) = 6.25,
p < .05]; men (14.0%) were significantly more
likely than women (1.9%) to select that others
do not have any friends as a failed use and
gratification [χ^2 (1, N=101) = 5.29, p < .05]; men
(18.4%) were significantly more likely than women
(3.8%) to select that others are "loners" as a
failed use and gratification [χ^2 (1, N=101) = 5.48,
p < .05]; women (82.7%) were significantly more
likely than men (57.1%) to select that others
just have no desire to have an account as a failed
use and gratification [χ^2 (1, N=101) = 7.89,
p < .01].

Finally, a MANOVA was conducted to determine the
effect of sex on the 5 dependent variables related to
feelings upon receiving a new message. The 5 dependent

variables were: happy, excited, anxious, upset, and concern over terminated account. Results indicated that sex did not significantly affect the combined dependent variables.

Non-Users: General Information, Uses and Gratifications, and Sex Differences

Of the total participants surveyed, 15 or 12.9% (4 men and 11 women) indicated that they did not have either a MySpace or Facebook account. These non-users had by in large: not previously had accounts at either site (86.7%), had heard of MySpace (86.7%), and had heard of Facebook (60.0%). Although the non-users reported hearing other people frequently talk about these sites (mean of 5.20 on 7-point Likert-scale with 1 indicating "never" and 7 indicating "all the time") and that the sites were relatively popular among their friends (mean of 5.17 on 7-point Likert-scale with 1 indicating "not at all popular" and 7 indicating "very popular"), the non-users reported feeling no pressure to get an account (mean of 2.40 on 7-point Likert-scale with 1 indicating "not at all " and 7 indicating "very much") nor did they report feeling left out by not having an account (mean of 2.60 on 7-point Likert-scale with 1 indicating "not at all" and 7 indicating "very much"). Although 60% of non-users indicated that they had viewed someone else's account, only 33.3% of non-users reported that they had considered getting an account in the future.

When examining the failed uses and gratifications for not having an account, the two most popular

responses were "I just have no desire to have an
account" (73.3%) and "I am too busy" (46.7%). Less
frequently reported failed uses and gratifications
included: "I do not want other people to know about my
personal business" (26.7%), "I think it is a waste of
time" (20.0%), "I think it is unsafe" (13.3%), "I do
not have internet access at home" (13.3%), "I have
not heard of these websites" (6.7%), "I do not want to
keep in touch" (6.7%), and "I do not want to conform"
(6.7%). No participants reported not using the websites
because: "I am not good at technology," "I have not made
many friends yet," "I feel intimidated," "I think it is
stupid," and "I am a loner."

When asked to predict what uses and gratifications
users obtained from the websites, non-users most
frequently listed "to keep in touch with friends meet
new people" (93.3%). Other commonly reported uses and
gratifications included: "it is the thing to do"
(46.7%), "to be like others" (40.0%), "to share
information" (40.0%), "to occupy time" (40.0%), "to
look cool" (26.7%), "pressure from friends" (20.0%),
"to talk bad about other people" (13.3%), and "I do
not know not sure" (6.7%). Finally, MANOVA results
indicated that general information about non-users,
failed uses and gratifications, and predicted uses
and gratifications did not significantly differ by
sex of participant.

Non-Users versus Users

Results indicated two significant differences
between users and non-users in terms of demographics.
First, users (19.05 years) were significantly

chronologically younger than non-users (24.80 years), $t(114) = -6.60$, $p = .000$. In addition, a two-way contingency table analysis was conducted to evaluate whether different ethnic groups were more likely to use friend networking sites. For this analysis, the two variables were ethnicity of participant (i.e., Hispanic, Caucasian, African-American, Native American and Multi-racial) and whether or not the participant had an account (i.e., yes and no). Results indicated a difference did exist among the ethnic groups, χ^2 (4, N=116) = 19.63, $p < .001$. Additional inspection of the data indicated that Native Americans were less likely to be users than all other ethnic groups.

Discussion

A large percentage (87.1%) of participants indicated having a friend networking account. This is impressive especially considering that no mention was made of friend networking sites in the research project description made available to participants. It is possible that time of the year (spring semester) increased the number of participants having accounts and that the same study conducted with primarily freshman in the fall semester would have a lower percentage. Still, most participants indicated that they had their accounts for 7-24 months, extending back past the start of the fall semester. In addition, what is important to note is the number of college students using these sites and the amount of time per day students spend on these friend networking sites. Specifically, students spend almost three hours per

day on their accounts or someone else's account.
This number must also be considered in light of the
fact that students having both MySpace and Facebook
accounts were instructed to answer questions thinking
of the account they used most frequently. That means
that 74.3% of the participants devoted some additional
time per day, on top of the three hours, to their
other friend networking account. One reason why
participants might be spending so much time per day
on their accounts is the number of friends they have
linked to their account. If participants are to
interact with 200 plus friends per day, that requires
substantial time!

When examining the characteristics of users,
women and men were equally likely to have accounts
at a friend networking site. However, their uses and
gratifications for doing so varied in some specific
cases (see below). A difference was found between
users and non-users with users being significantly
younger than non-users, supporting findings of
previous research. This could be due to the fact
that younger users are more comfortable with on-line
communication in general. A difference was also
observed between users and non-users with regards
to ethnicity. Specifically, Native Americans
participants were significantly less likely to be
users than Hispanic, Caucasian, African-American,
and Multi-racial participants.

With so many college students using these friend
networking sites and spending a significant amount of
their time on them, users must be meeting personal and
social needs from these sites. For example, popular

uses and gratifications such as "to keep in touch with old friends," "to keep in touch with current friends," "to make new friends" indicate that users are meeting a "friend" need. Similarly, uses and gratifications such as "to learn about events," "to post social functions," and "to feel connected" indicate that users are meeting a need by using the site as a source of information. Currently, the authors are gathering more data and using factor analysis to investigate what, if any, underlying constructs explain these uses and gratifications.

Sex differences did occur when comparing uses and gratifications for users. However, sex differences were not found for the most popular uses and gratifications indicating that in general men and women meet the same needs by using the sites. A sex difference did occur with the number of friends linked to the account, with men having significantly more friends linked to their accounts than women. Developmental research notes similar findings with men reporting more friends than women throughout the lifespan (Fehr, 2000).

Limitations of the current exploratory study include the fact that primarily freshman college students were surveyed. Future research should investigate if the usage of such friend networking sites changes as students continue their degrees. A second limitation was the small number of non-users. To better understand why individuals do not use these sites, more data from non-users need to be collected. In addition to investigating the underlying structures for the uses and gratifications, future research should examine the personality characteristics of users and non-users. Finally, results indicated that Native American students were significantly less likely than all other ethnic groups to be users of friend networking sites. Again, this result should bring forth further investigation.

References

Anderson, J. A., & Meyer, T. P. (1975). Functionalism and the mass media. *Journal of Broadcasting, 19,* 11–22.

Blumler, J. G. (1979). The role of theory in uses and gratifications studies. *Communication Research, 6,* 9–36.

Carey, J. W., & Kreiling, A. L. (1974). Popular culture and uses and gratifications: Notes towards an accommodation. In Blumler, J. G., & Katz, E. (Eds.) *The uses of mass communications: Current perspectives on gratification research* (pp. 225–248). Beverly Hills, CA: Sage.

CNN (2006). *MySpace cowboys*. CNN.com. Retrieved August 2006, from http://money.cnn.com/magazines/fortune/fortune_archive/2006/09/04/8384727/index.htm.

Elliot, P. (1974). Uses and gratifications research: A critique and a sociological alternative. In Blumler, J. G., & Katz, E. (Eds.) *The uses of mass communications: Current perspectives on gratification research* (pp. 249–268). Beverly Hills, CA: Sage.

MYSPACE & FACEBOOK   20

Feher, B. (2000). The life cycle of friendship.
    In Hendrick, C. & Hendrick, S. (Eds.) *Close
    relationships: A sourcebook* (pp. 71-82). Thousand
    Oaks, CA: Sage.

FOXNews (2006). *Angry students lash out at
    Facebook.com privacy changes*. FOXNews.com. Retrieved
    September 2006, from http://72.14.209.104/search?
    q=cache:G27bD-yC8BUJ:www.foxnews.com/story/0,293

Harris, R. J. (2006). *A cognitive psychology of mass
    communication* (4th ed.). Mahwah, New Jersey: Lawrence
    Erlbaum Associates.

Howard, P., Rainie, L., & Jones, S. (2001). Days and
    nights on the Internet: The impact of diffusing
    technology. *American Behavioral Scientist, 45,*
    450-472.

Kiesler, S. (Ed.) (1997). *Culture of the Internet.*
    Mahwah, New Jersey: Lawrence Erlbaum Associates.

Lievrouw, L. A. (2000). Babel and beyond: Languages on
    the Internet. *ICA News, 28*(3), 6-9.

Murphy, D. (2005, July). A virtual student body:
    A behind the scenes look at the facebook.com, the
    college world's most popular online social network.
    PC Magazine, p. 82.

Papacharissi Z., & Rubin, A. (2000), Predictors of
    Internet use. *Journal of Broadcasting and Electronic
    Media, 44,* 175-196.

Rubin, A. M. (2002). The uses-and gratifications
    perspective of media effects. In Bryant, J., &
    Zillmann, D. (Eds.) *Media effects: Advances in
    theory and research* (2nd ed.) (pp. 525-548). Mahwah,
    New Jersey: Lawrence Erlbaum Associates.

Swanson, D. L. (1977). The uses and misuses of uses and gratifications. *Human Communication Research, 3,* 214-221.

Swanson, D. L. (1979). Political communication research and the uses and gratifications model: A critique. *Communication Research, 6,* 37-53.

Thayer, S. E. & Ray, S. (2006). Online communication preferences across age, gender, and duration of internet use. *CyberPsychology & Behavior, 9,* 432-440.

Valkenburg, P. M., Peter, J., & Schouten, A. (2006). Friend networking sites and their relationship to adolescents' well being and social self-esteem. *CyberPsychology & Behavior, 9,* 584-590.

Weiser, E. (2000). Gender differences in Internet use patterns and Internet application preferences: A two-sample comparison. *CyberPsychology & Behavior, 4,* 167-178.

REFERENCES

A

Aeschbach, D., Cutler, A. J., & Ronda, J. M. (2008). A role for non-rapid-eye-movement sleep homeostasis in perceptual learning. *Journal of Neuroscience, 28,* 2766–2772. doi:10.1523/JNEUROSCI.5548-07.2008

Amdur, R. (2003). *The institutional review board member handbook.* Boston, MA: Jones and Bartlett.

American Psychological Association. (2002). Ethical principles of psychologists and code of conduct. *American Psychologist, 57,* 1060–1073. doi: 1060-1073 10.1037/0003-066X .57.12.1060

Anderson, N. H. (1979). Algebraic rules in psychological measurement. *American Scientist, 67,* 555–563.

Aron, A., Aron, A., & Coups, E.N. (2009). *Statistics for psychology* (5th ed.). Upper Saddle River, NJ: Prentice Hall.

Asch, S. E. (1951). Effects of group pressure upon the modification and distortion of judgment. In H. Guetzkow (Ed.), *Groups, leadership and men.* Pittsburgh, PA: Carnegie Press.

Asch, S. E. (1955). Opinions and social pressure. *Scientific American, 193,* 31–35.

B

Bandura, A. (1965). Influence of models' reinforcement contingencies on the acquisition of imitative responses. *Journal of Personality and Social Psychology, 1,* 589–595.

Barlett, C. P., Harris, R. J., & Bruey, C. (2008). The effect of the amount of blood in a violent video game on aggression, hostility, and arousal. *Journal of Experimental Social Psychology, 44,* 539–546.

Barlett, C., Harris, R., Smith, S., & Bonds-Raacke, J. (2005). Action figures and men. *Sex Roles, 53,* 877–885.

Baum, C. (Producer), & Shyer, C. (Director). (1995). *Father of the bride II* [Motion Picture]. USA: Touchstone Pictures.

Biederman, I., Yue, X., & Davidoff, J. (2009). Representation of shape in individuals from a culture with minimal exposure to regular, simple artifacts: Sensitivity to nonaccidental versus metric properties. *Psychological Science, 20,* 1437–1442. doi: 10.1111/j.1467-9280.2009.02465.x

Bonds, J. M., & Nicks, S. D. (1999). Sex by age difference in couples applying for marriage. *Psychological Reports, 84,* 42–44.

Bonds-Raacke, J. M., Cady, E. T., Schlegel, R., Harris, R.J., & Firebaugh, L. (2007). Remembering gay/lesbian television and film characters: Can Ellen and Will improve heterosexuals' attitudes towards homosexuals? *Journal of Homosexuality, 53,* 19–34.

Bonds-Raacke, J. M., & Raacke, J. D. (2007). The relationship between physical attractiveness of professor and students' ratings of professor quality. *Journal of Psychiatry, Psychology, and Mental Health, 1,* 1–7.

Bravata, D. M., Smith-Spangler, C., Sundaram, V., Gienger, A. L., Lin, N., Lewis, R., . . . Sirard, J. R. (2007). Using pedometers to increase physical activity and improve health: Asystematic review. *Journal of the American Medical Association, 298,* 2296–2304. doi: 10.1186/1471-2458-9-309

Brescoll, V. L., & Uhlmann, E. L. (2008). Can an angry woman get ahead? Status conferral, gender, and expression of emotion in the workplace. *Psychological Science, 19,* 268–275.

Bushman, B. J., & Anderson, C. A. (2001). Media violence and the American public: Scientific facts versus media misinformation. *American Psychologist, 56,* 477–489. doi: 10.1037/0003-066X.56.6-7.477

C

Cameron, L., & Rutland, A. (2006). Extended contact through story reading in school: Reducing children's prejudice toward the disabled. *Journal of Social Issues, 62,* 469–488.

Campbell, D. T., & Stanley, J. C. (1969). *Experimental and quasi-experimental designs for reasearch.* Boston, MA: Houghton Mifflin.

Casby, A., & Moran, A. (1998). Exploring mental imagery in swimmers: A single-case study design. *Irish Journal of Psychology, 19,* 525–531.

Catz, S. L., Kalichman, S. C., Benotsch, E. G., Miller, J., & Suarez, T. (2001). Anticipated psychological impact of receiving medical feedback about HIV treatment outcomes. *AIDS Care, 13,* 631–635.

Christiansen, N. D., Kaplan, M. F., & Jones, C. (1999). Racism and the social judgment process: Individual differences in the use of stereotypes. *Social Behavior and Personality, 27,* 129–144.

Cohen, J. (1965). Some statistical issues in psychological research. In B. B. Wolman (Ed.), *Handbook of clinical psychology.* New York, NY: Academic Press.

Costello, E. J., Worthman, C., Erkanli, A., & Angold, A. (2007). Prediction from low birth weight to female adolescent depression. *Archives of General Psychiatry, 64,* 338–344.

Cowan, N. (2010). The magical mystery four: How is working memory capacity limited, and why? *Current Directions in Psychological Science, 19,* 51–57. doi: 10.1177/0963721409359277

Cox, D. S., Cox, A. D., Sturm, L., & Zimet, G. (2010). Behavioral interventions to increase HPV vaccination acceptability among mothers of young girls. *Health Psychology, 29,* 29–39.

Curtiss, S. (1977). *Genie: A psycholinguistic study of a modern-day "Wild Child."* New York, NY: Academic Press.

D

Darley, J. M., & Batson, C. D. (1973). "From Jerusalem to Jericho": A study of situational and dispositional variables in helping behavior. *Journal of Personality and Social Psychology, 27,* 100–108.

DeNoon, D. (2006, October 20). Study suggests possible link between TV viewing and autism in children. *FoxNews.com.* Retrieved from *http://www.foxnews.com*

Desrumaux, P., Bosscher, S. D., & Léoni, V. (2009). Effects of facial attractiveness, gender, and competence of applicants on job recruitment. *Swiss Journal of Psychology, 68,* 33–42.

Dommeyer, C. J. (2008). The effects of the researcher's physical attractiveness and gender on mail survey response. *Psychology & Marketing, 25,* 47–70. doi: 10.1002/mar.20198

Drews, F. A., Pasupathi, M., & Strayer, D. L. (2008). Passenger and cell phone conversations in simulated driving. *Journal of Experimental Psychology: Applied, 14,* 392–400. doi: 10.1037/a0013119

Dunn, E. W., Huntsinger, J., Lun, J., & Sinclair, S. (2008). The gift of similarity: How good and bad gifts influence relationships. *Social Cognition, 26,* 469–481.

Durán, R. J. (2009). Legitimated oppression: Inner-city Mexican American experiences with police gang enforcement. *Journal of Contemporary Ethnography, 38,* 143–168.

Dye, M. W. G., Green, C. S., & Bavelier, D. (2009). Increasing speed of processing with action video games. *Current Directions in Psychological Science, 18,* 321–326. doi: 10.1111/j.1467-8721.2009.01660.x

E

Ebbinghaus, H. (1885/1913). *Memory: A contribution to experimental psychology.* New York, NY: Teachers College, Columbia University.

Eissenberg, T., Panicker, S., Berenbaum, S., Epley, N., Fendrich, M., Kelso, R., Penner, L., & Simmerling, M. (2004). IRBs and psychological science: Ensuring a collaborative relationship. Available at *http://www.apa.org/research/responsible/irbs-psych-science.aspx*

F

Farrelly, P. (Producer), Farrelly, B. (Producer), Wessler, C. B. (Producer), Thomas, B. (Producer), Farrelly, P. (Director), & Farrelly, B. (Director). (2000). *Me, myself, & Irene* [Motion Picture]. USA: 20th Century Fox.

Farris, C., Treat, T. A., Viken, R. J., & McFall, R. M. (2008). Perceptual mechanisms that characterize gender differences in the decoding of women's sexual intent. *Psychological Science, 16*, 348–354.

Feldman, R., Weller, A., Zagoory-Sharon, O., & Levine, A. (2007). Evidence for a neuroendocrinological foundation of human affiliation plasma oxytocin levels across pregnancy and the postpartum period predict mother-infant bonding. *Psychological Science, 18*, 965–970.

G

Gazdzinski, S., Kornak, J., Weiner, M. W., Meyerhoff, D. J., & Nat, R. (2008). Body mass index and magnetic resonance markers of brain integrity in adults. *Annals of Neurology, 63*, 652–657. doi: 10.1002/ana.21377

Gentile, D. A. (2009). Pathological video game use among youth 8 to 18: A national study. *Psychological Science, 20*, 594–602. doi: 10.1111/j.1467-9280.2009.02340.x

Gerbner, G., & Gross, L. (1976). Living with television: The violence profile. *Journal of Communication, 26*, 172–199.

Graesser, C. C. (1991). A social averaging theorem for group decision making. In N. H. Anderson (Ed.). *Contribution to information integration theory, Vol. 2.* Hillsdale, NJ: Lawrence Erlbaum.

Grinter, R. E., & Palen, L. (2002). Instant messaging in teenage life. *Proceedings of the ACM conference on computer supported cooperative work* (pp. 21–30.) NY: ACM Press. Retrieved from *http://www.cc.gatech.edu/~beki/Publications.html*

H

Harris, R. J. (2004). *A cognitive psychology of mass communication* (4th ed.). Mahwah, NJ: Lawrence Erlbaum Associates.

HealthOrbit (2008, April 1). Longer work days leave Americans nodding off on the job. *HealthOrbit.com.* Retrieved from *http://www.healthorbit.com*

HealthOrbit (2008, April 9). Overweight kids have fewer cavities, new study shows. *HealthOrbit.com.* Retrieved from *http://www.healthorbit.com*

HealthOrbit (2008, April 17). Men more likely to have problems with memory and thinking skills. *HealthOrbit.com.* Retrieved from *http://www.healthorbit.com*

Hermand, D., Mullet, E., & Lavieville, S. (1997). Perception of the combined effects of smoking and alcohol on cancer risks in never smokers and heavy smokers. *Journal of Health Psychology, 2*, 481–491.

Howard, R. (Producer), Grazer, B. (Producer), & Howard, R. (Director). (2001). *A beautiful mind* [Motion Picture]. USA: Universal Studios.

J

Janiszewski, C., & Uy, D. (2008). Precision of the anchor influences the amount of adjustment. *Psychological Science, 19*, 121–127.

Johnson, P. M., & Kenny, P. J. (2010). Dopamine D2 receptors in addiction-like reward dysfunction and compulsive eating in obese rats. *Nature Neuroscience, 13*, 635–641. doi:10.1038/nn.2519

Jones, M. H., & Estell, D. B. (2007). Exploring the Mozart effect among high school students. *Psychology of Aesthetics, Creativity, and the Arts, 1*, 219–224.

K

Kellogg, W. N., & Kellogg, L. A. (1933). *The ape and the child: A study of environmental influence upon early behavior.* Oxford, England: Whittlesey House.

Kopycka-Kedzierawski, D. T., Auinger, P., Billings, R. J., & Weitzman, M. (2008). Caries status and overweight in 2 to 18 year old US children: Findings from national surveys. *Community Dentistry and Oral Epidemiology, 36*, 157–167. doi: 10.1111/j.1600-0528.2007.00384.x

Kuoch, H., & Mirenda, P. (2003). Social story interventions for young children with autism spectrum disorders. *Focus on Autism and Other Developmental Disabilities, 18*, 219–227.

L

Landis, C. (1924). Studies of emotional reactions. *Comparative Psychology, IV*, 447–509.

Larson, S. G. (2003). Misunderstanding margin of error. *The Harvard International Journal of Press/Politics, 8*, 66–80. doi: 10.1177/1081180X02238785

Lawlor, D. A., Timpson, N. J., Harbord, R. M., & Leary, S. (2008). Exploring the developmental overnutrition hypothesis using parental–offspring associations and FTO as an instrumental variable. *PLoS Medicine, 5*, 484–493.

Lewin, T. (2009, October 24). No Einstein in your crib? Get a refund. *The New York Times.* Retrieved from *http://www.nytimes.com*

Lilienfeld, S. O., Lynn, S. J., Ruscio, J., & Beyerstein, B. L. (2010). *50 great myths of popular psychology: Shattering widespread misconceptions about human behavior.* Malden, MA: Wiley-Blackwell.

Linnau, K. F., & Mann, F. A. (2003). Doll's head "Bezoar": Complete craniocervical dislocation causing bowel obstruction. *American Journal of Roentgenology, 180*, 986.

Loftus, E. F. (1997). Repressed memory accusations: Devastated families and devastated patients. *Applied Cognitive Psychology, 11*, 25–30.

Loftus, E. F., & Palmer, J. C. (1974). Reconstruction of automobile destruction: An example of the interaction between language and memory. *Journal of Verbal Learning and Verbal Behavior, 13,* 585–589.

M

McConnell, J. V., Cutler, R. L., & McNeil, E. B. (1958). Subliminal stimulation: An overview. *American Psychologist, 13,* 229–242.

Middlemist, R. D., Knowles, E. S., & Matter, C. F. (1976). Personal space invasions in the lavatory: Suggestive evidence for arousal. *Journal of Personality and Social Psychology, 33,* 541–546.

Milgram, S. (1963). Behavioral study of obedience. *Journal of Abnormal and Social Psychology, 67,* 371–378.

Miller, L. C., & Fishkin, S. A. (1997). On the dynamics of human bonding and reproductive success: Seeking windows on the adapted-for human-environmental interface. In J. Simpson & D. T. Kenrick (Eds.), *Evolutionary social psychology* (pp. 197–235). Hillsdale, NJ: Erlbaum.

O

O'Neil, J., Steele, G., Huisingh, C., & Smith, G.A. (2008). Escalator-related injuries among older adults in the United States, 1991–2005. *Accident Analysis & Prevention, 40,* 527–533.

Ong, A. D., & Weiss, D. J. (2000). The impact of anonymity on responses to "sensitive" questions. *Journal of Applied Social Psychology, 30,* 1691–1708.

P

Paquette, I., & Finlayson, S. R. (2007). Rural versus urban colorectal and lung cancer patients: Differences in stage at presentation. *Journal of the American College of Surgeons, 205,* 636–641. doi:10.1016/j.jamcollsurg.2007.06.196

Pavlov, I. (1928). *Lectures on conditioned reflexes.* New York, NY: International Publishers.

Piaget, J. (1954/1981). *Intelligence and affectivity: Their relationship during child development.* Palo Alto, CA: Annual Review, Inc.

Publication manual of the American Psychological Association (6th ed.). (2010). Washington DC: American Psychological Association.

R

Raacke, J. D., & Bonds-Raacke, J. M. (2008). MySpace and Facebook: Applying the uses and gratifications theory to exploring friend-networking sites. *CyberPsychology and Behavior, 11,* 169–174.

Reitman, I. (Producer & Director). (1984). *Ghostbusters* [Motion Picture]. USA: Sony Pictures Incorporated.

Rosenthal, R. (1994). Science and ethics in conducting, analyzing, and reporting psychological research. *Psychological Science, 5,* 127–134.

Rothbaum, B. O., Hodges, L. F., Anderson, P., Price, L., & Smith, S. (2002). 12-month follow-up of virtual reality and standard exposure therapies for the fear of flying. *Journal of Consulting and Clinical Psychology, 70,* 428–432.

Rulence-Pâques, P., Fruchart, E., Dru, V., & Mullet, E. (2005). Algebraic rules in sport decision-making. *Theory and Decision, 58,* 387–406.

S

Shadish, W. R., Cook, T. D., & Campbell, D. T. (2002). *Experimental and quasi-experimental designs for generalized causal inference.* Boston, MA: Houghton Mifflin.

Smith, A. P., Tyrrell, D. A. J., & Willman, J. S. (1987). Selective effects of minor illness of human performance. *British Journal of Psychology, 78,* 183–188.

Stroop, J. R. (1935). Studies of interference in serial verbal reactions. *Journal of Experimental Psychology, 18,* 643–662.

T

Tamir, M., Mitchell, C., & Gross, J. J. (2008). Hedonic and instrumental motives in anger regulation. *Psychological Science, 19,* 324–328.

Taveras, E. M., Rifas-Shiman, S. L., Oken, E., Gunderson, E. P., & Gillman, M.W. (2008). Short sleep duration in infancy and risk of childhood overweight. *Archives of Pediatric Adolescence Medicine, 162,* 305–311. doi: 10.1001/archpedi.162.4.305

The Women's Conference (2010). *We honor Dr. Jane Goodall.* Retrieved from *http://www.womensconference.org/dr-jane-goodall/*

Tversky, A., & Kahneman, D. (1974). Judgment under uncertainty: Heuristics and biases. *Science, 185,* 1124–1131.

Tversky, A., & Kahneman, D. (1981). The framing of decisions and the psychology of choice. *Science, 211,* 453–458.

V

Vivian, J. (2008). *The media of mass communication* (9th ed.) Boston, MA: Allyn & Bacon.

W

Watson, J. B. & Raynor, R. (1920). Conditioned emotional reactions. *Journal of Experimental Psychology, 3,* 1–14.

Weis, R., & Cerankosky, B. C. (2010). Effects of video-game ownership on young boys' academic and behavioral functioning: A randomized, controlled study. *Psychological Science, 21,* 463–470. doi: 10.1177/0956797610362670

Witt, C. M., Jena, S., Brinkhaus, B., Wegsheider, K. & Willich, S. N. (2006). Acupuncture in patients with osteoarthritis of the knee or hip: A randomized, controlled trial with an additional nonrandomized arm. *Arthritis & Rheumatism, 54,* 3458–3493. doi: 10.1002/art.22154

Worth Publishers (Producer). (2002). *The frontal lobes and behavior: The story of Phineas Gage* [DVD]. Available from Worth Publishers.

Worth Publishers (Producer). (2002). *Life without memory: The case of Clive Wearing* [DVD]. Available from Worth Publishers.

Z

Zarkadi, T., Wade, K. A., & Stewart, N. (2009). Creating fair lineups for suspects with distinctive features. *Psychological Science, 20,* 1448–1453. doi: 10.1111/j.1467-9280.2009.02463.x

GLOSSARY

AB design A methodology where measurements are taken before and after the administering of an independent variable.

ABA design A methodology where measurements are taken before and after the administering of an independent variable as well as after the removal of the independent variable.

APA American Psychological Association

APS Association for Psychological Science

Analysis of variance (ANOVA) Used when you have an independent variable with three or more levels or when you have multiple independent variables.

Applied research Research is conducted to solve a practical problem within a field of study.

Archival research A nonexperimental method where the researcher uses existing records and selects portions of the records to examine.

Attitudinal measure A measure assessing a person's attitudes to the topic.

Attrition Participants systematically drop out of an experiment or do not return to complete additional parts of a study, changing the experimental results.

Authority The appearance of expertise in a field of study.

Basic research Research is conducted to further the collective knowledge about a topic within a field of study.

Behavioral measure A measure to investigate a person's behaviors.

Between subjects design Participants will be exposed to only one level of the independent variable.

Between subjects factorial research design A research design in which all independent variables are between subjects.

Biased sample A sample in which not everyone in the population has an equal or known chance of being selected.

Bonferroni correction Can be used when conducting multiple statistical tests. The correction is used to limit the possibility of making a Type I Error.

Carryover effects These occur when the effects of prior treatment conditions influence subsequent treatment conditions.

Case study A research methodology that is an in-depth observation of an individual, animal, event, or treatment method.

Ceiling effect When scores fall primarily at the upper range of a response option.

Closed-ended questions Questions in which the answers must be selected from a predetermined list of responses.

Cluster sampling Involves identifying naturally occurring clusters of individuals from the population to select from to be included in the sample.

Cognitive measure A measure of one's mental ability or knowledge of a topic.

Confederate A participant in a study but is also part of the research team. The participation of confederates is meant to influence the other participants.

Construct validity The likelihood that the device or scale used to measure a variable actually is related to the topic or theory of interest.

Content analysis A research methodology where a researcher counts the number of times a particular piece of content occurs.

Control Direct manipulation of a desired variable or the management or removal of unwanted factors that can influence observations or experiments.

Control group The group that is not exposed to the independent variable.

Convenience sampling A procedure which involves using those participants who are readily available or will volunteer to participate.

Convergent validity States that your measure should converge or be similar to other measures of the same variable.

Correlational research methods Research methodologies that evaluate the relationship between variables.

Counterbalancing Involves making sure that all combinations of the order of presentation occur in a study.

Degree of response A measure of intensity of a response.

Demand characteristics The change in the dependent variable is due to the researcher somehow communicating to participants how they should act or behave.

Dependent t-test Used to determine if the mean difference between pairs is significantly different from zero.

Dependent variable The variable in a study that is observed or measured.

Describe The first goal of psychological research is to *describe* behavior or mental processes.

Descriptive statistics Used by researchers to describe data sets.

Diffusion of treatment Change in the dependent variable is due to participants in different groups communicating with each other.

Directional research hypothesis A hypothesis that predicts a specific direction that the results will occur.

Divergent validity or discriminant validity Argues that your measure should be dissimilar to measures of different variables.

Double blind study An experiment in which neither the participant nor the researcher knows which group the participant have been placed into.

Effect size The amount of overlap between populations.

Empirical Acquisition of knowledge via objective and systematic collection of data.

Ethnography Used to describe a culture in detail by recoding and transcribing events that are witnessed.

Everyday experiences Using experience from life to obtain a research idea.

Experimental group The group that is exposed to the independent variable in a study.

Experimental research A class of research methodologies that involve manipulation of a variable.

Explain The second goal of psychological research is to *explain* behavior or mental processes.

External validity The extent to which the obtained results in a study can be generalized to other settings.

Extraneous variable Variable that is not controlled for in the experiment that may have an effect on the dependent variable.

Factorial research design A research design that uses more than one independent variable.

Failing to reject the null hypothesis Indicates that there is not a statistically significant difference between the means of the groups in the study and that the means are equal.

Fatigue Occurs when participants become tired during an experiment.

Floor effect When scores fall primarily at the lower range of a response option.

Frequency of responding A sum of the number of times a person/group responds to a question.

Functional problems Using real-world problems as a source for a research idea.

History An event beyond the researcher's control that can explain the change in the dependent variable.

Hypothesis A statement about the relationship between variables.

Independent t-test Evaluates whether or not two means are significantly different from one another.

Independent variable The variable in a study that is being manipulated.

Inferential statistics Used so that inferences can be drawn about a population from the sample used.

Influence The fourth goal of psychological research is to *influence* behavior or mental processes.

Instrumentation Change in the dependent variable is due to how the dependent variable was measured.

Interaction Occurs when the effect of one independent variable depends on another independent variable.

Internal consistency A reliability assessment similar to a split-half method. However, the splitting occurs more than once and an average of the correlations is taken.

Internal validity Confidence in saying the observed change in the dependent variable is due to the independent variable and not due to any outside influences.

Internet A worldwide, publicly accessible network containing vast amounts of information.

Interrater or interobserver reliability A reliability assessment used when a research design calls for observations of an event. Two or more observers compare results from their observations. The higher the observer consensus, the higher the reliability.

Interval scale Classification of data on a scale that assumes equal distance between numbers.

Intuition Understanding through the use of common sense based on observation.

Large number of records Occurs when a researcher uses terms in a search engine that are too broad.

Level of significance The probability of obtaining data assuming the null hypothesis is true. This is indicated by the alpha level (α).

Levels of the independent variable The number of conditions for a specific independent variable.

Main effect Determining if an independent variable has had an effect on the dependent variables while ignoring or collapsing across the other independent variables in the factorial research design.

Matched subjects design A methodology where participants are matched on a particular characteristic before being assigned to the different levels of the independent variable.

Maturation The change in the dependent variable is due to internal changes within the participants over time.

Mean The average of the scores in the data set.

Measures of central tendency Numbers that represent the scores in the data set.

Median The number in the middle of a data set.

Mixed subjects factorial research design A research design in which not all of the independent variables are one type (i.e., one independent variable is between and the other within subjects).

Mode The most frequently occurring number in a data set.

Multiple baseline designs A methodology where researchers have a small number of participants receive the independent variable at varying times.

Multiple dependent variables Most studies have more than one dependent variable. Having multiple dependent variables increases the amount of information collected.

Naturalistic observation A research methodology where a researcher observes people or animals in their natural setting.

Negative correlation Two or more variables vary in opposite directions.

Nominal scale Classification of data into one of two or more categories.

Nondirectional research hypothesis A hypothesis that does not make a prediction about the direction that the results will occur in.

Nonexperimental research A class of research methodologies that involve the study of how variables are related.

Nonprobability sampling procedures A procedure where not all individuals within the population of interest have an equal likelihood or known probability of being selected.

Normal distribution of scores Occurs when most scores cluster around the middle, and few, but equal, numbers cluster on the extremes.

Nuisance variable A variable that is not controlled for in the experiment that influences all participants in the same manner.

Null hypothesis Hypothesis that states there is *no* difference between scores on the dependent variables.

One-sample t-test Used to determine when a mean is significantly different from a constant.

Open-ended questions Questions in which a response is elicited and there is not a predetermined list of responses.

Operational definition Defines how a concept or idea will be measured.

Order effects Effects of a study are due to the participants experiencing the same order of presentation of the levels of the independent variable.

Ordinal scale Classification of data into an order or rank of magnitude.

Parallel-forms method A reliability assessment in which a measure is divided in half and given to two groups of people. The reliability is high if each measure given is highly correlated.

Percent correct Average of correct responses to overall responses represented as a percentage.

Physiological measure Measures that are biological in nature (i.e., heart rate, pulse, blood pressure, etc.).

Placebo An inert substance that has no effect.

Placebo control group Exposed to an inert substance or object that is similar to the independent variable but has no effect.

Placebo effect Change in the dependent variable is due to the participant believing a change will occur.

Population The entire group of individuals in which you are interested in studying.

Positive correlation Two or more variables vary in the same direction.

Power The probability of rejecting the null hypothesis when it is indeed false.

Practice effects Participants improve performance due to subsequent experiences on the same task.

Predict The third goal of psychological research is to *predict* behavior or mental processes.

Prior research Using what others have done as a starting point to obtain a research idea.

Probability sampling procedures A procedure where individuals from the population have a known probability (or chance) of being selected for a study.

Pseudoscience Any theory, method, or belief that appears to be based in science but is not.

PsycARTICLES® A full-text electronic psychological database by APA.

PsycINFO® Largest electronic psychological abstract database by APA.

Qualitative Research methodologies where researchers seek subjectivity through in-depth collection of information and emerging hypotheses.

Quantitative Research methodologies that seek objectivity through testable hypotheses and carefully designed studies.

Quota sampling In quota sampling, a convenience sample is selected that is comprised of subgroups similar in number to the population.

Random assignment A procedure in which a selected participant has an equal probability of being placed into each group of a study.

Ratio scale Classification of data on a scale that assumes equal distance and a true zero value.

Regression to the mean The change in the dependent variable is due to extreme scores moving toward the mean on later measures.

Rejecting the null hypothesis Indicates that there is a statistically significant difference between the means of the groups in the study.

Reliability The consistency of your measure to produce similar results on different occasions.

Replication A research experiment or study that is reproduced using the exact methodology and procedure.

Research hypothesis Hypothesis that there *is* a difference between scores on the dependent variables.

Research matrix A visual representation of a research design.

Research question States a research idea in a clearly defined manner that is testable.

Research topic A broad concept or idea.

Sample Smaller group of individuals that is representative of the larger population.

Sample size The number of individuals needed or that are selected for a study.

Sampling with replacement Individuals are selected one at a time with each individual being replaced before the next is sampled. Here, each selection has exactly the same probability of being selected.

Sampling without replacement Individuals are selected and are not replaced before the next is sampled. Here, the probability of being selected changes with each removal.

Science The accumulation of knowledge via systematic observation or experimentation using the scientific method.

Selection Change in the dependent variable is due to how participants were selected for the experiment or how they were assigned to groups.

Self-correcting A system of challenges by which scientific claims can be verified.

Simple probability sampling All individuals in a population have a equal probability of being selected.

Single blind study A study in which the participant has no knowledge of which experimental group he or she may be participating within—only the researcher knows.

Single case design A design that focuses on a single participant, single group of participants, or a small group of participants.

Skewed distribution A skewed distribution is one in which the most frequently occurring scores are not in the middle.

Small number of (or no) records Occurs when a researcher uses terms in a search engine that are too specific.

Snowballing sampling A procedure where a sample is acquired by a referral process among similar individuals.

Split-half method A reliability assessment in which a measure is split in half and the two halves are compared. If the correlation is high, the measure is said to have high reliability.

Statistical variance The degree of spread among data when surrounding the mean.

Stratified probability sampling A probability sampling technique where a researcher begins by identifying subgroups (or strata) and then randomly samples from each subgroup.

Subject variable A characteristic or attribute of a participant that can impact a study.

Survey research A research methodology where one designs a questionnaire to obtain information regarding behaviors, attitudes, or opinions.

Systematic probability sampling Random sampling in which a systematic approach is used.

Tenacity The persistence to maintain over time.

Testing Change in the dependent variable is due to the participants becoming more familiar with the test or testing procedures.

Test–retest Reliability A reliability assessment where your measure is tested on two different occasions for consistency.

Theory An overarching principle that explains separate research findings in an area.

Treatment conditions Refers to levels or number of groups in the independent variable.

Type I Error Occurs when a researcher rejects the null when the null is in fact true.

Type II Error Occurs when a researcher fails to reject the null even though the null hypothesis is false.

Using synonyms When conducting searches, you may need to think of a synonym for your research topic.

Validity The accuracy of a measure to evaluate what it is supposed to measure.

Variable An event or characteristic that has at least two possible values.

Within subjects designs Design in which participants are exposed to all levels of the independent variable.

Within subjects factorial research design A research design in which all independent variables are within subjects.

INDEX

CREDITS

Image Credits

Page 103   View of PsycINFO Search Engine: © EBSCO Publishing, Inc. All rights reserved.

Page 104   Search Window Results for Overlapping Topics: © EBSCO Publishing, Inc. All rights reserved.

Page 104   Search Window Results When Further Narrowing Topic: © EBSCO Publishing, Inc. All rights reserved.

Text Credits

All   APA Guidelines for the Undergraduate Psychology Major. Washington, D.C. Retrieved from www.apa.org/ed/precollege/about/psymajor-guidelines.pdf

Page 22   Biederman, I., Yue, X., & Davidoff, J. (2009). Representation of shape in individuals from a culture with minimal exposure to regular, simple artifacts: Sensitivity to nonaccidental versus metric properties. *Psychological Science, 20*, 1437–1442. Psychological science by Biederman, I., Yue, X., & Davidoff, J. Copyright 2009 by SAGE PUBLICATIONS INC. JOURNALS. Reproduced with permission of SAGE PUBLICATIONS INC. JOURNALS in the format Textbook via Copyright Clearance Center.

Page 22   Cowan, N. (2010). The magical mystery four: How is working memory capacity limited, and why? *Current Directions in Psychological Science, 19*, 51–57. Current directions in psychological science: a journal of the American Psychological Society by Cowan, N. Copyright 2010 by SAGE PUBLICATIONS INC. JOURNALS. Reproduced with permission of SAGE PUBLICATIONS INC. JOURNALS in the format Textbook via Copyright Clearance Center.

Page 23   Dye, M. W. G., Green, C. S., & Bavelier, D. (2009). Increasing speed of processing with action video games. *Current Directions in Psychological Science, 18*, 321–326. Current directions in psychological science: a journal of the American Psychological Society by Dye, M. W. G., Green, C. S., & Bavelier, D. Copyright 2009 by SAGE PUBLICATIONS INC. JOURNALS. Reproduced with permission of SAGE PUBLICATIONS INC. JOURNALS in the format Textbook via Copyright Clearance Center.

Page 23   Weis, R., & Cerankosky, B. C. (2010). Effects of video-game ownership on young boys' academic and behavioral functioning: A randomized, controlled study. *Psychological Science, 21,* 463–470. Psychological science by Weis, R., & Cerankosky, B. C. Copyright 2010 by SAGE PUBLICATIONS INC. JOURNALS. Reproduced with permission of SAGE PUBLICATIONS INC. JOURNALS in the format Textbook via Copyright Clearance Center.

Page 24   Zarkadi, T., Wade, K. A., & Stewart, N. (2009). Creating fair lineups for suspects with distinctive features. *Psychological Science, 20,* 1448–1453. Psychological science by Zarkadi, T., Wade, K. A., & Stewart, N. Copyright 2009 by SAGE PUBLICATIONS INC. JOURNALS. Reproduced with permission of SAGE PUBLICATIONS INC. JOURNALS in the format Textbook via Copyright Clearance Center.

Page 40   Sample consent form: Lyndon, A. E., & Dutton, L. B. (February, 2010). *Predicting unwanted pursuit perpetration among college students.* Paper presented at the National Summit on Interpersonal Violence and Abuse Across the Lifespan: Forging a Shared Agenda, Dallas, TX.

Page 46   American Psychological Association. (2002). Ethical principles of psychologists and code of conduct. *American Psychologist, 57,* 1060–1073. doi: 1060–1073 10.1037//0003-066X .57.12.1060.

Page 148   Cohen, J. (1988). *Statistical Power Analysis for the Behavioral Sciences,* (2nd ed.) Lawrence Erlbaum: Hillsdale, NJ. Statistical power analysis for the behavioral sciences by Cohen, J. Copyright 1988 by TAYLOR & FRANCIS GROUP LLC - BOOKS. Reproduced with permission of TAYLOR & FRANCIS GROUP LLC - BOOKS in the format Textbook via Copyright Clearance Center.

Appendix   John Raacke, Jennifer Bonds-Raacke. MySpace & Facebook: Applying the Uses and Gratifications Theory to Exploring Fiends Networking Sites. *CyberPsychology & Behavior.* April 2008, 11(2): 169–174. doi:10.1089/cpb.2007.0056. Published in Volume: 11 Issue 2: April 18, 2008.